Greek Philosophical Terms:

A Historical Lexicon

GREEK PHILOSOPHICAL TERMS

A Historical Lexicon

F. E. PETERS

New York: NEW YORK UNIVERSITY PRESS

Preface

The glory and the bane of Greek philosophy is its lack of a past. Drawing on nothing more than common speech and the elastic potential of the Greek language the Hellenic philosophers not only formulated a problematic within which all subsequent thinkers cast their own reflections, but devised as well a sophisticated and complex terminology as a vehicle for their thoughts. Both the terms and the concepts they employed have since been overgrown with a millennium and a half of connotation that not even the most determined can completely strip away. The contemporary philosopher or theologian may attempt to rethink the concept, but he is betrayed in the utterance. For what the thinker has striven to clear away the reader or listener supplies anew. "Soul" and "God" carry their history heavily with them.

By a not too peculiar irony we read *their* philosophical future back into our Greek past in a variety of ways. One has experience of a Whiteheadean and Nietzschean Plato, a Thomistic and Hegelian Aristotle, and even an Existential Diogenes. As in much else, the Greeks invented this particular historical fallacy. It is clear that the Stoics read themselves back into Heraclitus; and the Neoplatonists, Plotinus into Plato.

It is an obvious necessity to make some sort of attempt at coming to the Greeks on their own terms. This can, I think, best be accomplished not by the usual chronological and historical approach that, for all its divisions into "schools" and "successions," obscures rather than illuminates the evolutions we might otherwise discern in ancient philosophy, but rather from the direction of the problematic as revealed by a consecutive treatment of some of the basic concepts. This can be done in a number of ways and on different scales, but the method and scale adopted in this work is the one most conformable to the needs of what may be termed an "intermediate student" of the subject, not the beginner who is making his first acquaintance with Greek philosophy and who would be better served by a history of ancient philosophy and, perhaps, a dictionary of basic terms, nor, on the other hand, the professional scholar who would require a treatment both more massive and more nuanced.

v

Since such a "student" may be presumed to have some familiarity with the material it has been judged safe to substitute, in a fairly thorough way, a terminology transliterated directly from the Greek for their English equivalents in a modest effort at lightening the historical baggage. Jargon can be more easily cured than preconceptions, and it is this hope that prompts the frequency of *stoicheion* for element and *physis* for nature. There is, moreover, a complete English-Greek cross-index at the end.

The following treatment, then, singles out a few of the trees from the forest that threatens to overwhelm all of us at times, and attempts to trace their progress from acorn to fully grown oak. It also essays, if the metaphor may be indulged a bit longer, to display some of the interlocking root structure. Each entry is thoroughly cross-referenced, and if these references are pursued there will emerge a fairly complete philosophical context for each term. Every entry will supply some information, but meaning must be sought in the larger complexes. Finally, each entry is designed to be read with the texts of the philosophers themselves, and there are full textual citations at every step of the way. These are the final elements in the construction of a fruitful context where the prior history of the concept will illuminate a philosophical text, while the text will embellish the understanding of the term.

Both originals and translations of Plato and Aristotle are easily at hand. For the earlier and later philosophers the following will cover all but very few of the citations made in the text:

Pre-Socratics
H. Diels, *Die Fragmente der Vorsokratiker*, 5th–7th eds., edited by W. Kranz, 3 vols., Berlin, 1934–1954. (Abbrev. Diels in text.)

K. Freeman, *Ancilla to the Presocratic Philosophers*, Oxford, 1948; a translation of the fragments in Diels.

G. S. Kirk and J. E. Raven, *The Presocratic Philosophers*, Cambridge, 1957; texts and translations of some of the pre-Socratic fragments.

Post-Aristotelians
J. von Arnim, *Stoicorum Veterum Fragmenta*, 4 vols., Leipzig, 1903–1924. (Abbrev. *SVF* in text.)

C. J. De Vogel, *Greek Philosophy: A Collection of Texts*, vol. III, Leiden, 1964. An excellent selection of texts, without translations, from post-Aristotelian philosophy.

The following authors are also frequently cited:

Aetius, *Placita*, edited by H. Diels in *Doxographi Graeci*, Berlin, 1879. (Abbrev. Aetius in text.)

Diogenes Laertius, *Lives of the Eminent Philosophers*, ed. and trans. R. D. Hicks, Loeb Classical Library, London, 1925. (Abbrev. D.L. in text.)

Philo, *Works*, ed. and trans. F. H. Colson *et al.*, 10 vols., Loeb Classical Library, London, 1929 to date.

Plotinus, *Enneads*, ed. E. Bréhier, 6 vols., Paris, 1924–1938; trans. S. MacKenna, 2nd ed., London, 1956.

Plutarch, *Moralia*, ed. and trans. F. C. Babbitt *et al.*, Loeb Classical Library, London, 1927 to date.

Proclus, *Elements of Theology*, ed. and trans. E. R. Dodds, 2nd ed., Oxford, 1963.

Sextus Empiricus, *Adversus Mathematicos*, ed. and trans. R. G. Bury, Loeb Classical Library, 3 vols., London, 1935–1953.

I would like to express my gratitude to the Arts and Science Research Fund of New York University for a subvention toward the preparation of the manuscript of this work, and particularly to the two selfless workers who turned the inscrutable text into clean copy, Eileen Markson and Kristin Helmers.

Language and Philosophy

Philosophers have been uneasy about language almost from the beginning. The sculptor may curse his stone or the painter his oils, but neither contemplates suing for divorce. The philosopher, on the other hand, lives constantly in the shadow of infidelity, now suspecting metaphor, now tautology, or occasionally succumbing to the ultimate despair, the fear that he is dealing with *nomina tantum*. The Greeks' bouts with these maladies were occasional and mild; they were spared, moreover, the final indignity of desertion to mathematics, though the flirtation was long and serious. They trusted in names and their self-assurance was such that they could even afford to be playful about them. And when they came to devising names for the strange new things that they themselves had wrought, they approached the task with both confidence and inventiveness.

Prephilosophical language had been shaped by popular usage and the more transcendent intuitions of religion and mythology. The former was, of course, marked by its predilection for things; but there was, in addition, an accumulating store of more or less abstract terms flowing from the moral sensibilities of the epic tradition. *Dike, time, arete*, though calculable in purely material terms, were already at hand as abstracts and the first generation of philosophers, who still subscribed to most of the poetic conventions, drew heavily upon this epic vocabulary. But for the rest, there were things: gold, chariots, the soul (*psyche*), spears, and the spirit (*thymos*), all material objects and all capable of fairly precise localization.

But there was another factor at work as well. The search for understanding no more began with Thales than logic with Aristotle. All primitive men try to come to terms with the more numinous aspects of their environment through the media of ritual and myth, and the Hellenic version of the latter was a particularly rich and imaginative attempt at organizing and explaining higher levels of reality in some coherent fashion. Myth is, among other things, explanation and, whatever dimensions its moralizing content might assume, the didactic element is never completely absent.

Myth was the immediate forerunner of philosophy and provided it not only with certain embryonic conceptualizations, but with insights into the working of the world as well. Myth already presupposes a world order, what the philosophers would call a *kosmos*, but bases it chiefly upon the genealogical relationships between the gods whose family structure, derived from human paradigms, both preserved and explained the order of terrestial reality. It also embodied the notion of what was later to be called causality, though in its mythological form it might be better termed the principle of responsibility, since both it and the patterns of order are founded on the characteristic mythological principle of anthropomorphism. The divine (*theion*) had been personalized by myth into a god (*theos*) and could thus be linked and systematized and held *responsible* for phaenomena.

The earliest philosophers, for all their revolutionary achievements, were indebted to the mythological world view. Eventually the anthropomorphic bases upon which it had been constructed came under attack, but the effects were not at first critical since the pervasive hylozoism of those early thinkers enabled them to explain action and reaction in terms of the life and movement naturally inherent in material things. Once Parmenides had denied the hylozoistic premiss, however, the mythological personalized god reappeared, not, to be sure, in his grosser Homeric shapes, but as an artist who molds or a thinker who moves, both unmistakably personalized but deprived of physical aspect and will.

Thus, at the end of the philosophically abhorred infinite regress there was preserved what can be fairly identified as the god of the mythologers. What the philosophers had, in effect, done was to lay exclusive claim to the entire intermediary area of secondary causality. Myth was banished from these regions and causality replaced responsibility. But before this could be done or, rather, in the course of doing it, a new form of discourse had to be shaped and a new language to express it. If Thales did, indeed, say that water was the *arche* of all things (Aristotle, *Meta.* 983b), the wonder of it all is not so much the substitution of water for Zeus (the mythologers had already personified Oceanus to serve the same genetic end), as the intrusion of *arche* for the mythologer's *pater*. Thales (or perhaps Anaximander) was in search of a starting point other than the common mythological one of father and chose a term, *arche*, already in fairly common use, to express the new concept. The older senses of *arche* continued to be employed, but a radical new dimension had been added to the language.

What did the philosophers do to language? At first they did nothing since they did not know, fortunately perhaps, that they were philosophers and so continued to use words in their common acceptance, which, as a matter of fact, tended to be in rather concrete, individualized senses: the hot and the good were both some *thing*. The great terminological changes introduced by the philosophers—and an inspection of usage suggests that they took place only gradually—were tied to the "discoveries" of incorporeality and universal predication or, to put it more baldly, the realization that there were things and things. The dimensions of this new order of reality, which was not tied to objects in the ordinary sense and which could be generalized, were only gradually understood, and the stubborn "thisness" of language, consecrated by an epic tradition that revelled in the physical, never completely disappeared. Its most obvious aftereffects are probably to be seen in the persistent Greek habit of philosophizing through metaphor. Just as the geometer might offer a proof "by construction," so the philosopher was perfectly content to substitute analogy for analysis.

Language began to change. Prephilosophical staples like *eros* and *chronos* (both of which myth had already appropriated for its own purposes), *eidos*, *physis*, and the already mentioned *arche* developed new connotations, while other old words like *hyle* and *stoicheion* were expropriated for radical new purposes. The concrete yielded to the abstract, as *poion*, "just such a thing," gives way to *poiotes*, "quality" (in *Theaet.* 182a Plato apologizes for the awkward new term). Indeed, this progresses to the point where only names (Callias, Socrates) will serve to denote the individual, or to such Aristotelian peculiarities as "this something or other here" or the untranslatable *to ti en einai*. The combinatory powers of the language are tapped to describe the new complexities (*hypostasis*, *hypokeimenon*, *symbebekos*, *entelecheia*), and there appears a veritable treasure trove of abstract terms to identify newly isolated processes (*apodeixis*, *synagoge*, *phronesis*, *genesis*, *kinesis*, *aisthesis*, *noesis*).

All these refinements and new formations led, in time, to a sophisticated technical vocabulary that bore little resemblance to common usage. Literary considerations also came into play. A Stoic pamphlet addressed to a popular audience will obviously make more concessions to the general than a commentary by Simplicius, but the impression of popularity in the former work may be heightened by the passage of technical terms into common parlance. Plato went to some pains to vary his terminology in what seems to be a deliberate attempt to resist the congealing of technical terms, and the implication of the Socratic-centered Platonic dialogue is still that two reasonably educated citizens can sit down and discuss these matters. Whether this is the truth of the matter or mere literary rhetoric we cannot tell. But no such premiss is visible in Aristotle who insists on a standardized technical usage. With Aristotle the professionalism implicit in the founding of the Academy comes of age in language.

Philosophical language did become technical even though standardization was, and remains, an unfulfilled dream. Since the ancient philosophical tradition was strongly oriented to schools there was a certain degree of consistency within, say, the Platonic or Peripatetic school. But even here the pervasive post-Aristotelian thrust toward syncretism tended to muddy the conceptual waters: Plotinus' use of *eidos* will owe something to Plato, Aristotle, and the Stoics without, at the same time, specifying either the debt or its extent.

Whether this terminological virtuosity was for good or for ill may be debated. But it is clear that in manufacturing a new currency for a new way of seeing reality the Greeks were borne by the counters themselves into a world far removed from this material one. Most of the philosophers were at one in agreeing that this world of concrete, discrete beings is an exceedingly disorderly place and that "there is no science of the individual." Such was not true, however, of the newly isolated universal terms that, like the gods of the now disreputable mythology, could be manipulated and, once endowed with an order of reality, could be constructed into a world of order and stability. The Platonic *eidos* and the Aristotelian *kategoria* are, each in its own way, the Greeks' ultimate tribute to language, and the Proclean *kosmos noetos* undoubtedly its most baroque monument: a universe in which every concept is matched with its appropriate universal term and the whole arranged in a hierarchical order of mathematical precision and exceeding beauty.

Contents

Greek Philosophical Terms

a

adiáphoron: *without difference, morally indifferent or neutral state*

1. Since the end of man is, according to the oldest Stoic formulae, to live harmoniously with nature (see *nomos* 2), the good will consist in those things which are helpful or have some value toward this kind of life, while evil will reside in those things which make no such contribution (D.L. VII, 94, 105). Between these two absolutely helpful and harmful classes of acts (justice, prudence, moderation, etc. on the one hand, cowardice, injustice, immoderation on the other) there exists another group of things like life, health, and pleasure that are characterized as morally indifferent (*adiaphora*) in that they have no immediate connection with the end of man (D.L. VII, 101–103). They do, however, contribute to or impede that end indirectly and hence are further divided (D.L. VII, 105–106) into preferable acts (*proegmena*), acts to be avoided (*apoproegmena*), and absolutely indifferent acts, the first category constituting the "duties" (*officia*) of the Roman ethicians and defined as those acts for whose performances some reasonable defense (*eulogos, probabilis*) can be given (Cicero, *De fin.* III, 17, 58).

2. These latter distinctions provoked considerable controversy in both the Stoa and the Academy. There was no question that one had a moral obligation to choose the good; what was at stake was the moral implications of dividing the *adiaphora* into justifiable and nonjustifiable acts. There were those moral rigorists like Aristo of Chios and the Sceptic Pyrrho who denied that any moral value at all could be attached to these reasonably defensible and so "befitting" (*kathekonta*) activities (Cicero, *De fin.* IV, 25, 68). Further, the Sceptics' attacks on epistemological certitude had its inevitable effects in the moral sphere and we find the two eminences of the New or Sceptical Academy, Arcesilas and Carneades, advancing a theory that once certitude has been undermined the moral act can only be that for which some reasonable defense can be made, the former approaching the now central *kathekonta* by applying an intellectual criterion (rationally probable, *eulogon;* Sextus Empiricus, *Adv. Math.* VII, 158), Carneades by putting forth an experimental one (the practically probable, *pithanon; idem, Pyrrh.* I, 227–229).

3. That these attitudes, coupled, in the case of Carneades, with a trenchant criticism of Stoic epistemology, had an effect on the thinking of the Stoa in ethics is clear from its own focusing on the correct choice of the *kathekonta* as the central problem of the moral life (Stobaeus, *Ecl.* II, 76) and its retreat from Zeno's earlier insistence that virtue alone (in this context, life according to nature) suffices for man's happiness and its admission of the need for satisfactions flowing from a correct choice of the *kathekonta* (D.L. VII, 128).

aēr: air

1. For Anaximenes the *apeiron* of Anaximander and the *arche* of all things was air (Aristotle, *Meta.* 984a; Simplicius, *In Phys.* 24, 26), probably because of its connection with breath and life (cf. *pneuma*). It was, as were most of the pre-Socratic *archai*, divine (*theion*), Cicero, *De nat. deor.* I, 10, 26. The later popularizer of *aer* was Diogenes of Apollonia who made it the substance of both soul (*psyche*) and mind (*nous*), frs. 4, 5, an affinity parodied by Aristophanes, *Clouds*, 227 ff.; what is striking in Diogenes' conception is, of course, the association of a purposeful activity with his *aer-nous* (see *telos*).

2. The connection *aer-pneuma-psyche-zoe-theion* remained a constant one. The air-like nature of the soul is raised in *Phaedo* 69e–70a; Cebes fears it, but from another point it suggested a sort of impersonal immortality: the body might perish, but the *psyche* would be reabsorbed into the purest part of the *aer*, i.e., *aither* (q.v.), as yet undistinguished as a fifth element (see Euripides, *Helen* 1014–1016; *Suppliants* 533–534). Since the heavenly bodies (*ouranioi*) dwell in the *aither* another possibility was that the soul might be absorbed into the stars (see Aristophanes, *Peace* 832). This belief was incorporated into later Pythagoreanism, but with the reservation of *aither* to the supralunary world; it was the *aer* between the moon and the earth that was filled with *daimones* and heroes, D.L. VIII, 32; compare Philo, *De gigant.* 2 and 3 where the *daimones* are now angels, and the consequent identification in *De somn.* I, 134–135 of the *aer* and Jacob's Ladder (*Genesis* 28, 12–13); see *kenon*.

agathón: something good, the good, an ultimate principle, summum bonum

1. Plato, perhaps displaying his Socratic heritage, gives one of the ethical *eide* a central position in his hierarchy: in the *Republic* (see 504e–509e) the form of the Good stands at the center of the Platonic state, and it is the chief duty of the philosopher to contemplate it, *ibid.* 540a (for the problems arising from its transcendence at this stage, see *hyperousia*). It is, moreover, the term of the process of dialectic (*dialektike*, q.v.). Plato's turning toward the conditions of the *kosmos*

aisthetos in the later dialogues is reflected in his general reflections on the Good in the *Philebus;* the contrasting claims of pleasure (*hedone*) and wisdom (*phronesis*) to be the highest good are being examined, and the conclusion turns to an examination of the "mixed life" (see *hedone* and the mixed result of the operation of *nous* and *ananke* in the *Timaeus*), which is found to combine both pleasure and wisdom (59c–64a). What is notable here is not only the blending of the *eide* in this life, but the presence of measure and proportion (64a–66a) and, more importantly for Plato's growing theism, the advancing emergence of a transcendent, intelligent cause of good in the universe (see *ibid.* 26e–31b and *theos, nous*).

2. Aristotle is critical of Plato's theory of the Good (see *Eth. Nich.* I, 1096a–1097), but what he understands by that is clearly the *eidos-agathon* theory of the *Republic* (see *ibid.* 1095a and *Eth. Eud.* I, 1217b). Yet he accepts (*Eth. Nich.* I, 1094a) a Platonic definition of good as "that at which all things aim"; for Aristotle, this is happiness (*eudaimonia*) (*ibid.* I, 1097a–b), defined as activity (*praxis*) in accordance with virtue (*arete*), *ibid.* I, 1100b; and the highest virtue is *theoria*, i.e., contemplation for its own sake, *ibid.* x, 1177a–b (for the highest type of *theoria* and hence the Cosmic Good, cf. *telos*). The Epicureans return to the position rejected by Socrates (*Gorg.* 495c–499b), Plato (*Phil.* 55b–c), and Aristotle (*Eth. Nich.* VII, 1153b–1154a), namely that pleasure (*hedone*) is the highest good (D.L. x, 129). In the Stoa the good was identified with the profitable (D.L. VII, 9 and 101–103).

3. Plotinus' "theology" of the Good is to be found in *Enn.* VI, 15–42, including (25) a description of the hierarchy of goods leading up to the Ultimate Principle; the One (*hen*), which he identifies with the Good, is the final unification of the Socratic and Parmenidean strains in the Platonic tradition.

agénētos: ungenerated, uncreated (universe)

In *De coelo* I, 279b Aristotle says that all his predecessors agreed that the *kosmos* had a beginning. Xenophanes is, perhaps, to be excluded from them, on the basis of an interpretative reading of frs. 14 and 26, and surely the entire Eleatic school stemming from Parmenides, with its banishment of *genesis* from the realm of Being (see *on*), is also to be excepted, as Aristotle specifically does in *Meta.* 986b. In *Tim.* 28b Plato clearly says that the *kosmos* is subject to *genesis*. Aristotle, who earlier in his career had supported the same position (*De phil.*, fr. 18), takes this to mean that it had a beginning in time and criticizes it severely (*De coelo* I, 279b). But there was another interpretation of the passage, as Aristotle himself (*loc. cit.*) is aware, put forth by Xenocrates (see Plutarch, *De an. proc.* 1013a), and adopted by most later Platonists, that *genesis* here means "in a perpetual state of change" (see *on*). The same interpretation, adapted to his emanationist theories, can be seen in Plotinus (see *Enn.* II, 9, 2). Aristotle is emphatic in his belief that the universe is both ungenerated (*agenetos*) and incorruptible (*aphthartos*). This becomes the basic position, but Philo, by reason of the account in *Genesis*, must, of course, stand outside it (see *De opif.* 2, 7–9).

ágnōstos: unknown, unknowable

1. Because of the transcendence of God certain problems arise in the possibility of his being an object of knowledge. A simple agnosticism is held by Protagoras (Diels, fr. 80B4) where the question is separated into knowledge of whether the gods exist, and what their nature is; the *agnosia* problem treats more properly of the latter (on the question of their existence, cf. *theos*).

2. Because of the importance of transcendence in the Platonic tradition, the question of the knowability of God was central there; the Platonic proof text on the difficulty of knowing God was *Tim.* 28c, supported by the pessimistic remarks in *Parm.* 141e–142a, *Symp.* 211a, and especially, *Ep.* VII, 341b–d. As is indicated in the texts cited, the problem is the transcendence of the supreme principle, the "Good beyond Being" of *Rep.* VI, 509b (see *hyperousia*). But if the essence of God could not be apprehended directly, the same and similar texts of Plato suggest alternative ways of knowing God, ways highly developed in later Platonism (e.g. Albinus, *Epit.* x and Maximus of Tyre, VII and XVIII; compare Proclus, *Elem. theol.*, prop. 123). The major ones are:

   a) by inductive return to the source (*epagoge*, the medieval *via eminentiae*); see *Symp.* 209e–211c and compare Plotinus, *Enn.* I, 6.

   b) by analogy (*analogia*); see *Rep.* VI, 508a–c and compare Plotinus, *Enn.* VI, 7, 36; because Proclus denied any participation (*methexis*) between the One and the rest of reality (*Elem. theol.*, prop. 23), he is barred from the *via analogiae.*

   c) by "removal," negation (*aphairesis*; the *via negativa*); see the first "hypothesis" of the *Parmenides*, which later Platonists took in a very unhypothetical sense; compare Plotinus, *Enn.* VI, 7, 32.

   d) by mystical union (*ekstasis*); cf. *Symp.* 210e–211a, *Ep.* VII, 340c–d; compare *Enn.* VI, 9, 9–11 and, for Plotinus' personal experience, Porphyry, *Vita Plot.* 23; see *hen*.

ágrapha dógmata: unwritten doctrines

One of the common methods used to obliterate the difference between what Aristotle says about Plato's *eide* and the preserved account in the dialogues is to presume that Aristotle, as a member of the Academy, had access to unpublished material (had not Plato said in *Ep.* VII, 341c that he would never publish anything on the ultimate principles?). There are only two possible references to such material in Aristotle; in *De an.* I, 404b he refers to something called "On Philosophy," possibly a reference to his own dialogue by that name, though later commentators took it as a reference to a Platonic lecture (cf. Simplicius, *In De an.* 28, 7–9), and in *Phys.* IV, 209b where he refers to Plato's "unwritten doctrines" (*agrapha dogmata*). What were these *agrapha dogmata?* The one identifiable possibility is a single lecture "On the Good" that Plato gave to a disenchanted public who came to hear about happiness, but were treated to mathematics, geometry, and astronomy instead (Aristoxenus, *Harmonics* II, 30–31); it was attended by Aristotle and other members of the Academy, who took notes that they later published (Simplicius, *In Phys.* 151, 453); cf. *arithmos.*

For a related problem as it concerns Aristotle, cf. *exoterikoi.*

ágraphos nómos: *unwritten law*
See *nomos.*

aïdios: *everlasting, perduration in time (aidios kata chronon)*
Although the distinction in terminology is not always maintained by the philosophers, the concepts of "everlasting perduration *in* time" (*aidios*) is separate and different from "eternal" (*aionios*), i.e., not belonging to the order of time (*chronos*), but to the order of eternity (*aion*, q.v., and Plotinus, *Enn.* III, 7, 3); "eternal" is used loosely to describe both concepts, e.g. the "eternity of the *kosmos*"; but *aidios* is really a question of the occurrence or the possibility of occurrence of corruption (*phthora*), and so the concept will be discussed under *aphthartos;* see also *aion, chronos.*

aiốn: *life-span, eternity*
1. In its earliest and nonphilosophical use, *aion* means a life-span; its conceptual introduction into philosophy may be seen in Parmenides, fr. 8, line 5, where the denial of becoming (*genesis*) in true being (see *on*) leads to its corollary, the denial of the temporal distinctions "past" and "future" and the affirmation of total present simultaneity. Melissus interprets this as *apeiron*, without limit, going on forever (frs. 2, 3, 4, 7), a notion later distinguished as *aidios* (q.v.), perduration in time, and the same type of interpretation may be seen in Aristotle, *De coelo* I, 279a where *aion* embraces "all time even to infinity [*apeiron*]."

2. The fundamental distinction between time (*chronos*) and *aion* that is implied in Parmenides is made fully explicit in Plato, *Tim.* 37d where time is created to serve as an image (*eikon*) of the state of the

eide, from which Plato, like Parmenides, has banished all *genesis*, or as Plotinus puts it (*Enn.* III, 7, 4), *aion* is the "manner of existence" of Being. But Plato's admission, through the intermediary of the soul, of both *nous* and *kinesis* into the intelligible world creates a problem unknown to the static universe of Parmenides. The solution is to be found in Aristotle's discussion of the First Mover whose "span of existence" (*aion*) is unending (*aidios*), *Meta.* 1072b; the reason for this is the peculiar type of activity involved in a *noesis* thinking itself, what Aristotle calls "the activity of immobility" (*energeia akinesias*) in *Eth. Nich.* 1154b. This is the foundation of the treatment of eternity in both Plotinus, *Enn.* III, 7, 4 and Proclus, *Elem. theol.*, prop. 52; in the following proposition Proclus hypostatizes *aion* as a separate substance, probably as a result of a similar practice in later Greek religious thought. See *chronos*.

aísthēsis: *perception, sensation*

1. Perception is a complex of problems rather than a single question. It enters philosophy modestly enough as an attempt on the part of the early *physikoi* to explain the physiological processes involved in perceiving an object. A variety of solutions were worked out, mostly in terms of the contact, mixture, or penetration of the bodies involved. There were, of course, certain anomalies as, for example, the case of vision where contact was apparently absent, but the first major crisis did not occur until grades of knowledge were distinguished and sense perception was separated from another more reliable type of perception that had little or nothing to do with sensible realities or sensible processes. *Aisthesis* found itself involved in the epistemological doubts raised by Heraclitus and Parmenides and debarred from any genuine access to truth (see *aletheia, doxa, episteme*).

2. Other changes were afoot as well. The particle or somatic theory upon which the *physikoi's* theory of perception was based began to be replaced by theories on change that took as their point of departure a new dynamic view of the "powers" of things (see *dynamis, genesis*). Aristotle, who was a dynamist, incorporated the analyses worked out for change in sensible beings into his metaphysic and for the first time *aisthesis* became a philosophical question as well as a physiological one.

3. A third major change was precipitated by the growing belief in the incorporeal nature of the soul (*psyche*, q.v.), the principle of life in beings and the source of their sensitive activities. What then was the general relationship between the immaterial soul and the material body, and the specific one between that part or faculty of the soul known as *aisthesis* and that part of the body which it employed, its *organon?* What had once been a simple contact between bodies was

now extended to a chain of causality that began with a perceived body and its qualities, and passed, via a medium (this in the still perplexing question of vision), a sense organ, and a sense faculty to the soul, becoming, at least for those who held the immateriality of the soul, noncorporeal at some point in the process.

4. Finally, beginning with Parmenides' attack on *aisthesis* and his exaltation of *episteme* as the only genuine source of truth, it was no longer possible to treat thought (*noesis, phronesis*) as merely a quantitatively different form of *aisthesis*, but as different in kind, and increasing attention was paid to both the faculty and the process of this higher type of perception (see *nous, noesis*).

5. These, then, are some of the complexities of the problematic of *aisthesis*. The chief ancient authority on the subject, Theophrastus, whose treatise *On the Senses* is the major source of what we know of the ancient theories, prefers to approach the question from a physical point of view. The opening paragraph of his work distinguishes two types of explanation of how *aisthesis* occurs. One school bases it on the similarity (*homoion*, q.v.), the other on the opposition (*enantion*) of the knower and the thing known. The first group includes — on the testimony of Theophrastus — Parmenides, Empedocles, and Plato; the latter, Anaxagoras and Heraclitus.

6. The reference to Parmenides is, of course, to the second part of his poem, "The Way of Seeming" (see *on, episteme*). We know that Parmenides had scant epistemological respect for *aisthesis* (cf. fr. 7), and it is not at all clear that the theories put forth in the "Way of Seeming" are indeed his. But what emerges from Theophrastus' summary (*De sens.* 3–4) is that "Parmenides" held that sensation and thinking (*phronesis*) were identical (whatever else he may have believed, it is certain that the genuine Parmenides never held *that*), and that knowledge arises from the presence of identical opposites (*enantia*) in the subject and object of knowledge, so that, for instance, even a corpse, being cold, can perceive cold.

7. Whosesoever theory this actually is, it had a marked effect on Empedocles, who had a fairly elaborate theory of sensation and who, unlike Parmenides, took the senses seriously (fr. 3, lines 9–13). For Empedocles material things are constituted by mixtures of the four basic elements (*stoicheia*, q.v.) "running through each other" (fr. 21, lines 13–14). Each object gives off a constant stream of effluences (*aporrhoai*, fr. 89) that enter the congruent passages (*poroi*) in the appropriate senses and sensation ensues (Theophrastus, *De sens.* 7; Aristotle, *De gen. et corr.* II, 324b). But it is not merely a question of symmetry between the effluence and the pore; what is also required is that like comes in contact with like on the level of substance: we see earth with earth, fire with fire (Aristotle, *Meta.* 1000b).

8. When it comes to a question of thought (*phronesis*), Empedocles seems to be moving toward a distinction between it and sensation, but still on the quantitative level. For him, as for the Atomists, it
is a special type of sensation that occurs in the blood (hence the heart
as the seat of thought) since the blood appears to Empedocles to be the
most perfect blend of the *stoicheia* (fr. 105; Theophrastus, *De sens.* 9).

9. The Atomists, who had reduced all things to the atoms
(*atoma*) and the void (*kenon*), appropriately reduced all sensation to
contact (Aristotle, *De sens.* 442a), and explained its operation in terms
clearly derived from Empedocles. Here too bodies give off effluences,
now called *eidola* (q.v.; cf. Alexander of Aphrodisias, *De sens.* 56, 12),
that are similar in shape to the thing whence they are emitted. These
enter the sentient, or rather, penetrate between the *atoma* of the sentient, and sensation results (Aetius IV, 8, 10).

10. This may have been Leucippus' theory; but as far as the
troublesome question of sight is concerned, Democritus seems to have
added certain refinements, again suggested by Empedocles. The visual
image (*emphasis*) occurs not in the eye of the beholder, but is due to a
contact in the air between the object and the beholder. When once
formed the *emphasis* travels back along the air and, being moist, is
admitted by the moist éye of the beholder (Theophrastus, *De sens.* 50;
compare Empedocles in Aristotle, *De sens.* 437b–438a). This explanation is interesting not only insofar as it turns attention to air as a
medium of perception, but also in indicating, by the reference to the
moisture of the *emphasis* and the eye, that Democritus has likewise
founded the possibility of sensation, as distinct from the mere mechanics, on the principle of "like knows like."

11. Theophrastus (*ibid.* 49) remarks that the Atomists explain
sensation in terms of change (*alloiosis*). This can hardly be qualitative
change as understood in the Aristotelian sense since the Atomists are
on record as having reduced all the *pathe* of a thing to quantity (see
pathos); it must refer rather to the motion of the impinging *atoma*
disturbing the position of the atoms in the percipient (compare Lucretius III, 246–257). All sensations can be explained in terms of the
various shapes and movements of the *atoma* in contact with the percipient (Theophrastus, *De sens.* 66); what we experience as sweetness
and heat and color are no more than subjective impressions (fr. 9; cf.
nomos, pathos).

12. Empedocles and the Atomists, then, are firmly within what
Theophrastus calls the "like-knows-like" tradition. Here too belongs
Diogenes of Apollonia for whom the *arche* of all things was *aer* (q.v.),
which does equal service as the principle of all cognition (Theophrastus, *De sens.* 39). Knowledge occurs when air outside the organism is
mixed with that which is within, both the purity of the entering air and

the diffusion of the resultant mixture determining the type of cognition. Thus *phronesis* is the result when both the inhaled air is purer and the mixture of blood and air is spread throughout the body (*ibid.* 44; cf. the satiric remarks in Aristophanes, *Clouds* 227–233).

13. At the head of the opposite tradition stands Alcmaeon of Crotona, an early disciple of Pythagoreanism whose opinions we know only in a summary unaccompanied by much evidence or detail (Theophrastus, *De sens.* 25–26). He maintained that the like is known by the unlike, that the brain is the seat of the *psyche* (see *kardia*), and, more importantly, that there is a difference between *aisthesis* and *phronesis*. It is this distinction that sets man apart from all the other animals and thereby grounds an intellectualist ethic, as well as being at the root of the quest for the higher, immaterial faculty of the soul, the *logistikon* of Plato and the *dianoetike* of Aristotle (see *psyche*), and the progenitor of the exalted role of *nous* (q.v.) in the subsequent history of Greek philosophy. But we only know that Alcmaeon made this distinction; we do not know on what grounds, though it is almost certainly tied to the well-known Pythagorean belief in an immortal soul (see *psyche, athanatos, palingenesia*).

14. "Like knows unlike" appears again with Anaxagoras, and here it is based on the empirical evidence that sensations, especially tactile sensations, rest on contrast, e.g. we feel the cold because of the heat within us (Theophrastus, *De sens.* 27), a theory that is in perfect accord with Anaxagoras' doctrine of "a portion of everything in everything" (see *stoicheion*). Further, every sensation, since it is a change, is accompanied by pain (*ponos;* compare *hedone*).

15. In the *Theaetetus* (155d–157d) Plato presents a theory of sensation that is ostensibly attributed to Protagoras or some such variety of a Heraclitan relativist. But since it is not refuted in the sequel and coheres with other passages in the dialogues, it is not unlikely that it represents Plato's own views on sensation as well. It hinges on the point, frequently made by Heraclitus, that among the *aistheta* the only reality is change, or, to put it in the language of a more sophisticated generation, the *aistheta* are not really substances but qualities (see *pathos;* Plato makes the same point in *Tim.* 49b–50, and compare *stoicheion*); they are powers (*dynameis*) with the capacity of either affecting (*poiein*) other things or being affected (*paschein*) by them (*Theaet.* 156a). It may likewise be true, as earlier thinkers had maintained, that the *kosmos* is nothing else but *kinesis* (*loc. cit.*), but here too further refinements are possible. Even at this stage (see *Theaet.* 181c) Plato is capable of dividing the generic *kinesis* (q.v.) into alteration (*alloiosis*) and locomotion.

16. It is within this context that the Platonic theory of sensation unfolds. It finds its most generic statement in *Phil.* 33d–34a and *Tim.*

64a–d. The *dynamis* of the agent acts upon the body of the patient. If the affected part is an immobile one in which earth predominates (e.g. bone, hair) the affection is not spread; pain or pleasure might result, but not sensation. But if it is mobile, like one of the sense organs, the affection spreads until it reaches the consciousness (*phronimon*) and sensation results (compare *Tim.* 43c, and see *psyche* 17).

17. Both these passages would seem to suggest that perception is a pure possibility in the percipient; but when Plato turns to a discussion of sight he reaches back to Empedocles and Democritus for the theory that makes the image (*emphasis*) a cooperative production of both the object and the subject. Both are essentially qualities in a state of change (*alloiosis*), but once brought within range of each other, and with the aid of the light of the sun (*Tim.* 45b), the *dynamis* of whiteness in the object and the quality of light in the eye initiate locomotion and this "gives birth" to color, which causes the eye to be seeing and the object to become a colored thing (*Theaet.* 156c–e). These qualitative changes, when reported to the soul, result in sensation (*Tim.* 45c–d, 81c–d). The *Theaetetus* passage goes on (157a) to draw the Heraclitan moral: if the subject and object are not within range of each other we have no very certain idea of what the *dynamis* in the object is really like (for Plotinus' changes, see *sympatheia*).

18. Plato appears, however, to be speaking out of both sides of his mouth. His theory, as thus described, is strongly dynamistic in its linking of the *pathe* with the powers and in suggesting that the *dynamis* is a real quality inherent in the perceived object (cf. Theophrastus, *De sens.* 60). But he has also, in his other account of postcosmic *genesis* (q.v.), reduced all bodies to the geometrical solids and so, in the last resort, his account of the sensible *pathe* in *Tim.* 61d ff. smacks of a variety of Atomism with its reduction of quality to quantity in the order of shape (*schema*), position (*thesis*), and movement (*kinesis*), in this instance, of course, locomotion.

19. Aristotle rejects both the Atomistic and Heraclitan taint visible in Plato's theory of *aisthesis*. Put in its most general terms, *aisthesis* is the reception of a sensible *eidos* without its matter. Aristotle can, like all his predecessors, explain sensation in physical terms, and he does so subsequently by applying the physical doctrine of the "mean." But first he locates the entire problem of cognition within the cadres already enunciated in the *Physics* and the *Metaphysics*: act (*energeia*) and potency (*dynamis*). To perceive something means two things: to be able to perceive something whether one is perceiving it or not, and actually to perceive. Thus, any sensible faculty of the soul, though it may be the *eidos* or *ousia* of the organ in which it operates (just as the *psyche* as a whole is the *ousia* of the entire body; *De an.* II, 412), it is, nevertheless, a capacity (*dynamis*) with respect to the perceptible object: it is potentially (*dynamei*) what the object is ac-

tually (*entelecheia; ibid.* 11, 418a). This coheres with what was said of the relationship of *energeia/dynamis* in the central passage on the subject in the *Metaphysics: energeia* is prior to *dynamis* (the object must be red before the eye "becomes red"; see *De an.* 11, 425b) and the *energeia* ends as an actuality in the thing moved (vision is in the eye; *ibid.* 111, 426a); see *energeia* and *Meta.* 1050a.

20. Sensation may be described, then, as an alteration (*alloiosis*) in that it represents the passage from potency to actuality of one of the sense faculties. In this way too Aristotle can resolve the problem of "like knows like." Anaxagoras was correct in suggesting that "like knows unlike" since otherwise change could not take place; but this is only the way in which the process begins; when it ends the subject has become like the object known (*De an.* 11, 417a–418a).

21. The explanation becomes somewhat clearer when Aristotle turns to describing the sensation process in purely physical terms. Physical bodies have perceptible qualities that differentiate them; these are the "opposites" (*enantia*, q.v.), hot-cold, moist-dry, etc. The perceiving subject too, being corporeal, possesses them. But if it is to perceive them in another, the appropriate organ (*organon*) must be in a state of balance with regard to these extremes. Aristotle sees the capacity to perceive as a kind of mean or proportional state (*mesotes, logos*) between these extreme opposites so that it is "actually neither, but potentially both" (*ibid.* 11, 423b–424a).

For Aristotle's distinction between sensation and thought, see *noesis;* on the question of a medium (*metaxu*) for sensation, see *sympatheia.*

22. Aristotle goes to some pains to distinguish mere contact from the sensation of touch. Plants are alive and thus have a nutritive soul (*threptike psyche*); i.e., they are affected by things; they absorb the form *as well as* the matter of the things other than themselves. But they do not perceive, as animals do: the function of the *aisthetike psyche*, the distinctive *ousia* of animals, is to receive the form of sensible things *without* the matter (*ibid.* 111, 424a–b) and so be subject to the consequent *pathe* of appetite (*orexis*), pleasure (*hedone*), and pain (*ibid.* 11, 414b). This distinction disappears in Epicurus; an *eidos* without *hyle* was and remains unthinkable in the Atomist tradition. Sensation is again reduced to contact, and the different sensations explained in terms of the shape, arrangement, and motion of the *atoma* (see Lucretius 11, 381–477, especially 434–435). Where the contact is not immediate, as in vision, the theory of effluences is once again invoked: bodies give off outlines of themselves in the form of *eidola* (q.v.; the *simulacra* of Lucretius 1v, 49–50 ff.) that, if the eye be turned toward them, impress their pattern on the eye and set in train sensation (D.L. x, 46–50).

23. But some of the old Democritean positions now seem unten-

able. Epicurus still holds to the essential corporeality of the soul (cf. D.L. x, 63), but its relationship to the body has been redefined (see the remarks of Lucretius III, 370 ff.), and a new ingredient added, the mysterious "nameless element" (see *psyche* 27 for both developments). It is the organic grouping (see *holon*) of the latter's atoms that transmits sensation, which is the motion of the *atoma*, to the other constituents of the soul, thence to the rest of the body (Lucretius III, 242–251, 271–272), a process that is possible only because the soul atoms are contained within the sheath (*stegazon*) of the body (D.L. x, 64; see *genesis*).

24. From the time of Aristotle a new affirmative note appears in the epistemology of *aisthesis*. For Aristotle himself the senses are incapable of error with regard to their proper objects (*De an.* III, 428b), but in Epicurus it becomes, in one form or other, the only criterion of truth (Sextus Empiricus, *Adv. Math.* VIII, 9; D.L. x, 31; Lucretius IV, 479; see *energeia, prolepsis*). Among the Stoics the same assent to the truth of the senses is found (*SVF* II, 78). This assertion of physiological accuracy is, however, of little significance since for them, as for Aristotle, truth in its primary sense is a noetic function. It is only when the impressions (*typoseis*) on the sense organs are carried, via the *pneuma* (q.v.; see *psyche*), to the rational faculty (*hegemonikon*, q.v.) and there assented to (see *katalepsis*) that primary truth is possible; see *phantasia, noesis* 16.

25. The operation of *aisthesis* is just part of the larger Stoic problem of the materiality of the *pathe* (q.v.). Zeno's use of the expression "impression [*typosis*] on the *hegemonikon*" (*SVF* I, 58; Aristotle had used the same expression: *De mem.* 450a) provoked a reaction on the part of Chrysippus who attempted to palliate the materiality of the image by substituting expressions like "alteration [*heteroiosis*] in the *hegemonikon*" (Sextus Empiricus, *Adv. Math.* VII, 233, 237) or by reducing all the *pathe* to judgments (*kriseis; SVF* III, 461; see *noesis* 17).

26. Plotinus' account of sensation begins with the acceptance of the Aristotelian premiss that the soul is an *eidos* of the body (*Enn.* I, 1, 4; but see *hyle* 11). The composite, i.e., the animal, senses because of the presence of the soul (1, 1, 7), but the soul itself is impassible (*apathes*): its faculties are like reflections of itself that enable the things that possess them to act (1, 1, 8).

27. The soul in and of itself is capable only of intellectual activity. How, then, is the contact with the sensible (*aistheton*) achieved? This is the function of the corporeal organs of the body (IV, 5, 1) that are capable of serving as intermediaries. The *organon* is the material thing that is affected (*pathein*), and the *pathos* of the organ represents a proportional mean (*meson kata logon*) between the sensible object and the noetic subject (IV, 4, 23; the language smacks of Aristotle but

the concept clearly owes something, as does indeed the Aristotelian mean itself, to the Platonic notion of limit; cf. *peras*). In this way the *pathe*, which are corporeal in the organ (and this is a type of *aisthesis*), are noetic when they are received by the soul (and this is true *aisthesis;* I, 1, 7). The function of the organ, then, is to convert the impressions (*typoseis*) on the senses into activations (*energeiai*) of the soul so that the impassibility of the soul may be maintained against the Stoics (compare III, 6, 1). The process of judging these intelligible forms transmitted from the sense is discursive reasoning (*dianoia;* I, 1, 9); see *noesis* 19–20.

For the extension of the similarity principle beyond the bounds of *aisthesis*, see *sympatheia*.

aísthēsis koinē: *common sense, sensus communis*
In Aristotelian psychology the "common sense" is a faculty of the *psyche* that has as its function 1) the perception of the "common sensibles" that are the object of no single sense: movement and rest, number (*arithmos*), shape, size (*De an.* 418a, 425b), 2) the perception of things incidentally sensible (*loc. cit.*), 3) the distinction between senses (*ibid.* 431a–b), and 4) the perception that we perceive (*ibid.* 425b).

aisthētón: *capable of being perceived by the senses; the object of the senses, the sensible (opposite of noeton)*
The sensibles (*aistheta*) are frequently contrasted to the Platonic forms (*eide;* see *Phaedo* 78d–79a, *Tim.* 28a–c), and as such can lead only to opinion rather than to true knowledge (see *doxa, episteme*). But they are not the lowest objects on the epistemological scale; they are only reflections of the true reality of the *eide*, but beneath them are the "images of images," shadows, reflections, etc. (*Rep.* 509d–510a; cf. *eikon, mimesis*). Plato's growing interest in the world of the *aistheta* in the later dialogues is reflected in their being granted a quasi-being (*Soph.* 204b), and in his devotion of a large part of the *Timaeus* to a description of their creation and operation. For Aristotle the sensible singular object is the only true reality (see *tode ti, on, ousia*); some are appropriate to individual senses, others are common, *De an.* II, 418a (see *aisthesis koine*). For the materialists of the Atomist tradition all of truth and all of reality is in the *aistheta*, so Epicurus in Sextus Empiricus, *Adv. Math.* VIII, 9; see *aisthesis, eidolon*.

aithēr: *ether*
An etymology (fanciful) is given in Plato, *Crat.* 410b. It is the purest form of *aer* (*Phaedo* 109a–110b, *Tim.* 58d). For Aristotle it constitutes a fifth element (*quinta essentia*), moving naturally in eter-

nal circular motion, the stuff of the heavens (*De coelo* I, 268b–270b). The "fifth element" soon makes its appearance in the Academy as well, in Philip of Opus' *Epinomis* 984b where it has the added virtue of corresponding to the fifth "Platonic body" (see *stoicheion*). The presence of *aither*, with its "natural" (*physei*) circular movement (*De coelo* I, 269b) also leads to Aristotle's dropping the theory of heavenly bodies possessed by souls; see *ouranioi*. Cicero (citing Aristotle?) suggests that *nous* is also composed of *aither* (*Acad. post.* I, 7, 26); see *zoon, stoicheion, kosmos, aphthartos;* for the material element involved, see *hyle.*

aítion (or aitía): *culpability, responsibility, cause*

1. Since metaphysics is defined as a study of ultimate causes, Aristotle begins his work on the subject by a detailed review of his predecessors' search for causes (*Meta.* 983a–993a; recapitulated 988a–b). Plato has no formal treatment of causality as such, though there is a criticism of the pre-Socratic search for a moving cause in *Phaedo* 95d–99d, *Timaeus* 46c–47e, and *Laws* 892c, where the earlier physicists are blamed for mistaking accessories (*synaitia*), which operate from necessity (*ananke*) and without intelligent design (*techne*), for the only genuine cause of motion, the *psyche* (compare Aristotle *De an.* 414a and *symbebekos*). But in *Phil.* 26d–27c he reduces reality to a formal (see *peras*), an efficient (see *demiourgos*), and a "material" (see *apeiron*) element.

2. Aristotle's own doctrine of four causes—formal (*eidos*), material (*hyle;* see also *hypokeimenon*), efficient (*kinoun*), and final (*telos*)—is to be found in *Phys.* II, 194b–195a and *Meta.* 1013a–1014a. One peculiar development of the doctrine is the identification of the material cause with the premisses of a syllogism that necessarily "cause" the conclusion (cf. *Anal. post.* II, 94a, *Phys.* II, 195a). There is another, more ethically oriented division of the types of causalities in *Eth. Nich.* 1112a. Later philosophers made some additions to the Aristotelian analysis: Philo's *logos* is the instrumental cause of creation (*De cher.* 35, 126–127), and Seneca (*Ep.* 65, 8) has a list of five.

For unintended causes, see *tyche.*

alétheia: *truth*

The presence and even the possibility of truth is closely related to the Greek distinction between *doxa* and *episteme* (qq.v.) and their proper objects. Thus there is really no critical problem until Parmenides distinguishes being from nonbeing, associates the latter with sense perception, asserts that there is no truth in the phenomenal world of *doxa* (Diels, frs. 28B1, B11, B30), and contrasts the latter with the "Way of Truth" (*ibid.* 28B4). As a corollary of this and of the realization of the arbitrary nature of laws and customs (see *nomos*), Protagoras propounded his theory of the relativity of truth, described in Plato, *Theaet.* 151e–152e, 161e–167a. Aristotle's theory of truth and falsity rests on the assumption that truth is not in things (*Meta.* 1027b–1028a), nor in our knowledge of simple substances (where only knowledge or ignorance is possible), but in the judgment, i.e. the joining together of concepts which do not correspond to the reality (*Meta.* 1051b, *De an.* III, 430a; see *doxa*). For Epicurus all our sense perceptions are true and thus *aisthesis*, sensation, is the ultimate criterion of truth (Sextus Empiricus, *Adv. Math.* VIII, 9; Lucretius, *De rerum nat.* IV, 469–479; see *prolepsis*). The Stoic criteria are described in D.L. VII, 54.

The possibility of error and falsity is discussed under *doxa* and *noesis*.

álgos: pain
See *hedone*.

allēgoría: *allegorical interpretation, exegesis*
See *mythos, theos*.

alloíōsis: change, qualitative change, alteration
See *pathos, metabole, aisthesis*.

analogía: proportion, analogy
See *agnostos, dike, thesis, onoma*.

anámnēsis: *remembrance, recollection*
Plato's acceptance of the Pythagorean theory of rebirth (see *palingenesia, psyche*) provided the opportunity for solving a serious epistemological problem, i.e., how does one know the unchanging realities already formulated by Socrates as ethical definitions and en route to becoming the Platonic *eide*, particularly if sense knowledge (see *doxa*) is so clearly untrustworthy? There will be later solutions, like *eros* and *dialektike*, but in the first instance it is *anamnesis* that guarantees this knowledge. In *Meno* 80e–86c Socrates had illustrated the possibility of eliciting, by means of diagrams (these will reappear in *Rep.* 510d; see *dianoia, mathematika*) and proper questioning, knowledge of objects incapable of being perceived by the senses; in *Phaedo* 72e–77a it is offered as a proof of the preexistence of the soul and connected with the doctrine of *eide*. We have knowledge of the *eide* that we cannot have acquired through the senses, therefore it must have been acquired in a prenatal state during which we were in contact

with the forms. The theory appears once again in a mythical and religious context in *Phaedrus* 249b–c, and at least by implication in the vision granted the souls before their birth in *Tim.* 41e–42b (compare the vision in *Phaedrus* 247c–248b, and the difficulty in recalling it, *ibid.* 249e–250d); see *eidos.*

anánkē: *necessity*

1. The pre-Socratic use of *ananke* is not uniform; in Parmenides (Diels, fr. 28A37), it governs all things in an almost providential manner, in a not very different fashion from its personification in the "Myth of Er" in Plato's *Rep.* 614c–621d, and the Orphic figure in Empedocles (Diels, fr. 115). But with the Atomists (see D.L. ix, 45; Diels, fr. 67b2) we enter the area of the mechanical necessity of purely physical causes operating without purpose (*telos*).

2. For Socrates and Plato true causality always operates with purpose, while the operations of the physical elements are merely conditions or "accessory causes" (*synaitia*) (see *Phaedo* 99b, *Timaeus* 46c). Yet *ananke* too has its role in the formation of the *kosmos;* reason (*nous = Demiourgos*) overcomes physical necessity (*Timaeus* 47e–48a). Necessity, the quasi-cause, is only worth studying for its relationship with *nous*, the divine (*theion*) cause.

3. In Aristotle *ananke* has varied meanings (see *Meta.* 1015a–c), but as in Plato the physical necessity in matter must submit, not so much to *nous* as to the purpose (*telos*) in his new understanding of *physis* (*Phys.* ii, 200a). The role of *ananke* in syllogistic reasoning should also be noted: the conclusion of a valid syllogism flows necessarily from the premisses (*Anal. pr.* i, 24b).

For necessity in a providential sense, see *heimarmene, pronoia.*

anaplērōsis: filling up
See *hedone.*

apátheia: *unaffected, without* pathe (q.v.)

1. The Aristotelian concept of virtue, founded, as it is, upon the doctrine of the mean (*meson*, q.v.), has no place for the state of *apatheia*. It does, however, have a significance in his psychology: it is the apparent *apatheia* of *nous* that suggests that this faculty, unlike the *psyche*, is incorporeal and immortal, since the *pathe* are always associated with matter (*De an.* 403a, 408b).

2. The situation with Epicurus is somewhat more complex. Since both pleasure and pain are *pathe* (D.L. x, 34), there can be no question of *apatheia* being a virtue in this hedonistic philosophy. But the highest type of pleasure is, for Epicurus, precisely static (see

hedone), and this state of equilibrium or freedom from disturbance (*ataraxia*) has at least a superficial resemblance to *apatheia*.

3. The radical point of difference between Epicurus and the Stoics in this regard is the latter's insistence that *all* the *pathe* are irrational movements against nature, at least as defined by Zeno (*SVF* I, 205, 206; see *horme*). This created difficulties for Chrysippus who failed to see how irrational affects could occur in the rational faculty (*hegemonikon;* see *SVF* III, 459, 461). But though the intricacies of this were debated, the Stoa was at one in agreeing that the *pathe* were both violent and unnatural and hence should be extirpated (see Seneca, *De ira* I, 8, 2–3; *SVF* I, 207, III, 389). Thus it would seem that the Stoic is concerned with eradicating the *pathe*, the Peripatetic with moderating them, and the Epicurean with discriminating between the good and evil among them (see Seneca, *Ep.* 116, 1), attitudes reminiscent of the different approaches to *katharsis* (q.v.) as harmonization and purgation.

4. The practice, if not the enunciation of *apatheia* had its origins in the Cynic and related movements immediately preceding Zeno, and was frequently accompanied with the charge that its practitioners were merely indulging in insensitivity (Seneca, *Ep.* 1, 9, 1). The Stoics were at some pains to distinguish their version of *apatheia* from insensitivity or from mere stupidity (D.L. VIII, 117; Seneca, *Ep.* 1, 9, 3). Indeed, it is likely that it was exactly this type of criticism that resulted in the later Stoa's not altogether consistent distinction between good (*eupatheiai*) and evil *pathe* (D.L. VII, 116).

ápeiron: *unlimited, indefinite*

1. The *arche* (q.v.) of all things was, according to Anaximander, the *apeiron*, the unlimited. The term is capable of various constructions depending on how one understands the limit (*peras*, q.v.) that is being denied in the compound word. Aristotle includes in his *Physics* a lengthy discussion of the various meanings of the word (202b–208a), some of which, e.g. spatial infinity, may be rejected as being anachronistic to Anaximander's thinking. What *is* involved in his idea of *apeiron* is perduration in time (see Diels, fr. B3 and *aidios, aphthartos*), an infinite supply of basic substance "so generation [*genesis*] and destruction [*phthora*] not fail" (Aristotle, *Phys.* III, 203b), and, finally, indetermination, i.e., without internal limits within which the simple physical bodies, air and water, were not as yet distinguished (Diels, fr. *cit.;* Aristotle, *Phys.* I, 187a). It is also possible that Anaximander visualized this huge mass of material that surrounds our *kosmos* (Aristotle, *ibid.* 203b) as a sphere, and so without limit, i.e., beginning or end, in that sense as well.

2. The subsequent history of the concept as understood by Anaxi-mander lies in the direction of an interest in the exact nature of what is outside the furthermost sphere of *ouranos* (q.v.), which marks the limit of our universe (see *kenon*). With the Pythagoreans new consid-erations lead into other aspects of *apeiron;* Limited and Unlimited stand at the head of the Pythagorean Table of Opposites cited in Aristotle, *Meta.* 986a. This is no longer the *apeiron* of Anaximander, but either the spatial limit (or its absence) inherent in the Pythago-reans' geometrical approach to number and bodies (see *arithmos*), or else a musical concept where limit (*peras*) is thought of as the imposi-tion of some finite measure (in terms of music, *harmonia;* in terms of mathematics, proportion or *logos*) upon a continuum infinite at either end. This type of dual infinity is the reason, Aristotle conjectures in *Phys.* III, 206b, why *apeiron* passed into the notion of "indefinite dyad" (see *dyas*). The latter of the two points of view is probably the one that lies behind Plato's employment of *peras* and *apeiron* as principles of being in *Phil.* 23c–25b (the earlier use, *ibid.* 15d–17a, seems to refer to a mere indefinite multiplicity of particulars).

3. The prominence of *apeiron* in the *Philebus* guaranteed its continued use as a metaphysical principle in the subsequent Platonic tradition, but with somewhat different emphases. For Plato *peras* and *apeiron* appear as co-principles in much the same way the *chora* of the *Timaeus* exists side by side with the *eide*. Indeed, Aristotle saw both the *apeiron* and *chora* as the Platonic equivalents of *his* co-principle of being, *hyle* (see *dyas* and *Phys.* IV, 209b). Plotinus accepted the identification of *apeiron* as a material principle, but his more rigorous monism led him to subordinate it to the One as a kind of evolutional "moment" when, as "Otherness," it issues from the One and is without definition (*aoristos*) until it turns and contemplates the One (*Enn.* II, 4, 5; see *hyle* and compare Proclus' triad of "moments" in *Elem. theol.*, prop. 35: immanence, procession [*proödos*, q.v.], and reversion [*epis-trophe*, q.v.]); see *trias* 3.

4. Another factor in the continued interest in *apeiron* as an onto-logical principle was its inclusion, through its identification with the material principle, in the problematic of evil; see *kakon*.

apha*í*resis: *taking away, abstraction*

1. For Aristotle the chief objects of abstraction are the "mathe-maticals" (*mathematika*, q.v.; *Anal. post.* I, 81b, *Meta.* 1061a–b), and the process is described in *De an.* III, 431b as "thinking [*noesis*] of things that are embodied in matter as if they were not." The objects of the science of Physics are separate substances in an ontological sense (see *choriston*), but since they embody *physis* and are subject to change they are not conceptually separable from matter (*Meta.*

1025b), a mistake the Platonists make (*Phys.* II, 194a), while the objects of Mathematics are not separate substances in the ontological sense, but can be separated from matter conceptually; see *mathematika, hyle.*

2. The fact of the basic unknowability of matter and the consequent necessity of grasping it by analogy (*Meta.* 1036a, *Phys.* I, 191a; Plato had the same difficulty: see the "bastard reasoning" of *Tim.* 52b) leads Aristotle to a somewhat more detailed exposure of how the *aphairesis* process works. Primary here is his distinction between sensible and intelligible matter (*aisthete* and *noete hyle;* see *Meta.* 1036a, 1045a. Plotinus uses the same terms but in a different sense; see *hyle*). The latter is the kind of matter that the mind grasps in the abstractive process when it contemplates sensible things (*aistheta*) but not *qua* sensible, i.e., as mathematical bodies composed of form and spatial extension (*megethos;* see *mathematika* and compare *Meta.* 1059b, 1077b), or by analogy, the potential principle in definition, i.e., the *genos* with respect to the difference (*Meta.* 1045a; see *diaphora*).

For *aphairesis* as the theological *via negativa*, see *agnostos.*

áphthartos: *indestructible; for the indestructibility of the soul, cf athanatos*

1. In Aristotle's discussion of the possible meanings of the term (*De coelo* I, 280b) he accepts as the primary connotation "that which exists and which cannot be destroyed, i.e., it will or might cease to exist"; and while he finds agreement among his predecessors that the world is a product of *genesis* (see *agenetos*), there are those willing to admit its destruction (*ibid.* I, 279b). Among these latter there are some who posit a single destruction and others who maintain that the destruction of the *kosmos* is recurrent. Aristotle does not specify who the first group are, but Simplicius, in commenting this passage, identifies them as the Atomists, and the identification seems likely (see Diels, frs. 67A1, 68A40; compare Epicurus in D.L. x, 73 and Lucretius, *De rerum nat.* v, 235 ff.). Among the proponents of cyclic destruction Aristotle names Empedocles, whose theory of the mixing of the four elements through Love and Strife is indeed cyclic (fr. 17, lines 1–13), and Heraclitus. The position of Heraclitus is much more obscure; fr. 30 denies any dissolution of the *kosmos* and Plato specifically distinguishes between the position of Empedocles and Heraclitus on the question of the destruction of the *kosmos* (*Soph.* 242d). There are, on the other hand, passages in later authors suggesting that Heraclitus held a doctrine of periodic conflagration (cf. *ekpyrosis*). At first sight Philo too seems to maintain the destructibility of the *kosmos* (*De opif.* 7); but his actual view is based on a distinction found in Plato; in *Tim.* 41a–b, when talking of the heavenly gods (*ouranioi*), Plato says that

the union of their bodies and souls could be dissolved but they *will not
be* because they are the handiwork of the *Demiourgos*. Philo similarly
feels that the *kosmos*, though naturally destructible, will not be destroyed because of a providential divine sustenance (*De Decalogo* 58).

2. A similar argument appears in Plotinus *Enn.* II, 1, 3–4, where
it is the Soul that holds the *kosmos* together eternally; but here the
relationship is not the volitional, providential one found in Philo, rather
it is founded on the mimetic element in the Platonic tradition, e.g. time
is an *eikon* of eternity (*aion*) and this world is a reflection of the
intelligible universe (*kosmos noetos*); further, creation in the sense of
"procession" (see *proödos*) and "return" (see *epistrophe*) are both
perdurative in nature.

apódeixis: *pointing out, demonstration, proof*
In technical Aristotelian methodology *apodeixis* is a syllogistic
demonstration that, if the premisses be true and primary, will lead to
episteme (Aristotle, *Anal. post.* I, 71b–72a). Individuals are not subject to definition and hence undemonstrable (Aristotle, *Meta.* 1039b);
see *dialektike, katholou.*

aporía: *with no way out, difficulty, question, problem*
1. *Aporia* and its cognate verb forms are closely related to dialectic (*dialektike*, q.v.) and hence to the Socratic custom of interlocutory
discourse. According to Aristotle's analysis (*Meta.* 982b), philosophy
begins with a sense of wonder (*thauma;* Aristotle makes the point here
that philosophy and mythology share wonder as a common point of
departure) growing from an initial difficulty (*aporia*), a difficulty
experienced because of conflicting arguments (see *Top.* VI, 145b).
Both the *aporia* and its attendant wonder can be paralleled in Socrates'
frequent protestations of his own ignorance (e.g. *Meno*, 80d, *Soph.*
244a), and in the *nolle contendere* brought on by his own deliberate
interrogation (*elenchos*) (see *Theaet.* 210b–c and *katharsis*).
2. But this initial state of ignorance, compared by Aristotle to a
man in chains (*Meta.* 995a32), yields to a further sense where *aporia,*
or, more specifically, *diaporia*, an exploration of various routes, as-
sumes the features of a dialectical process (*Meta.* 995a–b; see *dialektike*), and where the investigation of the opinions (*endoxa*, q.v.) of
one's philosophical predecessors is a necessary preliminary to arriving
at a proof (*De an.* I, 403; *Eth. Nich.* VII, 1145b). Thus, the *aporiai* are
posed, previous opinions on these problems are canvassed, and a solution (*euporia, lysis*, the latter literally a "loosing," maintaining the
metaphor of the chaining in *Meta.* 995a32) is worked out. The solution
may take a variety of forms, e.g., validating the *endoxa* (*Eth. Nich.*

VII, 1145b), positing a hypothesis (*De coelo* II, 291b–292a), or even (*Eth. Eud.* VII, 1235b, 1246a) allowing the existence of a reasonable (*eulogon*) contradiction. But whatever the solution, the posing of the problem and the working from problem to solution, which is the heart of the philosophical method, is a difficult and onerous task (*Meta.* 996a).

aponía: *painlessness*
See *hedone.*

aporrhoaí: *effluences*
See *aisthesis.*

archē: *beginning, starting point, principle, ultimate underlying substance* (Urstoff), *ultimate undemonstrable principle*

1. The search for the basic "stuff" out of which all things are made is the earliest one in Greek philosophy and is attended by the related question of what is the process whereby the secondary things came out of the primary one or ones. Or, to put it in strictly Aristotelian terminology: what is the *arche* (or *archai*) and what is the *genesis* of the *syntheta?*

2. The pre-Socratic search for an *arche* in the sense of a material cause (Aristotle had located the investigation within his own categories of causality; see *endoxon* for the method involved) is described by Aristotle in *Meta.* 983–985b, and the word *arche* may have first been used in this technical sense by Anaximander (Diels 12A9). The first candidates for the basic ingredient of things were individual natural substances, e.g. water or moisture (Thales; see *Meta.* 983b) and air (see *aer*), but with Anaximander's suggestion that the *arche* was something indeterminate (*apeiron*, q.v.) an immense abstractive step away from the purely sensory had been taken. It opened the possibility that the *arche* was something more basic than what could be perceived by the senses, even though the *apeiron* was, at this stage, unmistakably material. Thus Anaximander opened the line of enquiry that led to the single spherical One of Parmenides (see *on, hen*) with its related distinction between true knowledge (*episteme*, q.v.) and opinion (*doxa*, q.v.), and to the plural geometrical and mathematical *archai* of the Pythagoreans (see *arithmos, monas*) and the *atoma* (q.v.) of Leucippus and Democritus.

3. What might be termed the sensualist tradition continued to seek the ultimate irreducible entities in sensibly perceived bodies until Empedocles standardized them at four, the *stoicheia* (q.v.) of earth,

air, fire, and water, but there is scarcely anyone except Empedocles himself who accepts these as true *archai;* rather they are stages between the still more remote *archai* and the higher complexities of composite bodies (*syntheta*).

4. The search for *archai* then takes a new tack. Both Parmenides and Empedocles had been emphatic in their denial of change, the former by attributing it to an illusion of the senses, the latter by maintaining the eternity of the *stoicheia*. But it was a stricture that was soon violated; Anaxagoras and the Atomists, each in their own way, reassert *genesis* and so, too, the possibility that the Empedoclean *stoicheia* change into each other.

5. A new analysis of *genesis* by Plato and Aristotle rejects the old notions of change as mixture or conglomeration or association, and concentrates instead—the lead had been given by Anaxagoras (see frs. 4, 12)—on the old notion of contrary "powers" (see *dynamis, enantion, pathos*). This is well within the sensualist tradition since these powers can be sensibly distinguished (reduced by Aristotle, *De gen. et corr.* II, 329b, to the sense of touch, *haphe*); but there is a nod as well in the direction of the *apeiron* with the isolation of the other great *arche* of change, the undefined, imperceptible substratum (see *hypokeimenon, hypodoche, hyle*).

6. This, then, is the eventual solution (among the "geneticists"; the Atomist and Pythagorean versions continue to flourish) of the problem of the *archai* of physical bodies: opposed powers, some of which can act (see *poiein*) while others can be acted upon (see *paschein*), a material substratum in which change occurs, and, eventually, an initiator of change (see *nous, kinoun*).

7. A related problem is that posed by the resolution of proof (*apodeixis*) back to its ultimate *archai*, the first premisses of knowledge or the ultimate principles upon which a syllogism rests. For the Platonists for whom true knowledge is essentially innate, based as it is on a prenatal exposure to the *eide* (see *anamnesis, palingenesia*), the question is of little moment, except, perhaps, in the later theory of dialectic where the entire *anamnesis* approach to knowledge tends to recede into the background (see *dialektike*). As for the sensualist who founds all knowledge on sense perception, he is forced, for the validation of the premisses of noetic knowledge, either to identify *aisthesis* and *noesis* (so the Atomists, though Epicurus hedges a bit with his notion of "self-evidence"; see *enargeia*), or to link the two, as Aristotle did, with the concept of intuition (see *epagoge, nous*).

For another orientation to the question of the *archai* of physical bodies, see *syntheton;* for the process whereby the *archai* become more complex entities, see *genesis;* for the existence of two ethically opposed *archai*, see *kakon*.

areté: excellence, virtue

1. The concept of virtue had a long evolutionary history in Greek culture before its incorporation into the problematic of philosophy. The pre-Socratics, whose chief concern was with a corporeal *physis* (q.v.) were not much interested in speculations about *arete;* there are some random thoughts on the subject, as in Heraclitus' designation of prudence as the highest virtue (Diels, fr. 12) and Democritus' insistence on the interior character of *arete* (Diels, frs. 62, 96, 244, 264), but there is no true philosophical attention to *arete* until the generation of Socrates.

2. Socrates' own identification of virtue and knowledge was a commonplace for his successors (Aristotle, *Eth. Eud.* I, 1216b, *Eth. Nich.* VII, 1145b), and the "Socratic dialogues" of Plato are directed toward a search for the definitions of various virtues, e.g. *Laches* 190c–199e; and it is probably a hypostatization of these definitions that culminates in the Platonic theory of forms (see *eidos*). For Plato there is an *eidos* of *arete* (*Meno* 72c) and of the various species of *aretai* (*Parm.* 130b); in *Rep.* 442b–d he describes the four "cardinal virtues" desirable in the ideal state, a discussion that has as its correlatives the classes of men in the state and the divisions of the soul (see *psyche, sophrosyne*).

3. For Aristotle virtue is a mean (*meson*, q.v.), and he distinguishes between moral and intellectual virtues (*Eth. Nich.* II, 1103a–b). The Socratic intellectualist approach to virtue is still visible in Aristotle, but it is tempered by a recognition of the volitional elements as well (see *proairesis*). For the Stoic the essence of virtue was "living harmoniously with nature" (see *nomos*).

For other aspects of morality, see *praxis, phronesis, adiaphoron, dike,* and, for its ontological correlatives, *agathon, kakon.*

arithmós: number (see also arithmos eidetikos and arithmos mathematikos)

1. The Pythagorean consideration of number is obscured by an initial major difficulty: the general inability of the pre-Socratics to distinguish between the concrete and abstract, and the consequent lack of distinction between arithmetic and geometry. The original Pythagorean insight was probably the reduction of the basic intervals of music to mathematical ratios (see *harmonia*), which they extended to the principle that things are, in effect, numbers (Aristotle, *Meta.* 1090a). And these "things" include, to the confusion of Aristotle, not only sensible material things, but abstractions like justice, marriage, opportunity, etc. (*Meta.* 985b, 990a, 1078b), and qualities like white, sweet, and hot (*ibid.* 1092b). Again, for Aristotle mathematical number was

abstract (see *mathematika*), and he could distinguish between sensible solids and geometrical bodies (*ibid.* 997b). But for the Pythagoreans *arithmos* was corporeal and had magnitude (*ibid.* 1080b, 1083b; see *megethos, asymmetron*), a not unlikely possibility considering the Pythagorean habit of constructing solids out of the spatial arrangement of those points (Aristotle, *Phys.* III, 203a; Sextus Empiricus, *Adv. Math.* x, 280; a method of generating solids later replaced by the "fluxion" method of moving a point into a line, Aristotle, *De an.* 409a; Sextus Empiricus, *op. cit.* x, 281). But while it is probable that the early Pythagoreans *thought* of numbers as corporeal, it is unlikely that they *said* that they were at a time before the concrete and abstract were distinguished. The first man to have *said* they were corporeal was Ecphantus (Aetius I, 3, 19) who posited a type of number-atomism.

2. Since the common Greek view was that number was a "plurality of units" (*plethos monadon;* see *Meta.* 1053a and *monas*), the question arose as to the generation of the unit itself; its constituative elements are described as "the odd and the even" and "the limited and the unlimited," the latter serving a similar role in Plato as the principles of numbers and *eide* (see *dyas, peras*).

3. The most perplexing aspect of ancient number theory is Aristotle's repeated assertions that Plato taught that the *eide* were numbers (e.g. *Meta.* 987b), a position that must be distinguished from 1) the existence of the *eide* of numbers (see *arithmos eidetikos*) and 2) the existence of the "mathematicals" as an intermediate grade of being (see *mathematika, metaxu*). But nowhere in the dialogues does Plato seem to identify the *eide* with number. To meet this difficulty some have postulated a theory of later "esoteric" Platonism known to Aristotle (but see *agrapha dogmata*), while others have attempted to see the emergence of the *eide-arithmos* theory described in such passages as *Phil.* 25a–e, the reduction of physical bodies back to geometrical shapes in *Tim.* 53c–56c (see *stoicheion*), and the increasing stress on a hierarchy among the Forms (see *Soph.* 254d and *genos, hyperousia*), which, according to Theophrastus, *Meta.* 6b, would suggest the descending series: *archai* (i.e., *monas/dyas* or *peras/apeiron*, qq.v.), *arithmoi, eide, aistheta*. Still others say that Aristotle either deliberately or unknowingly confused the position of Plato with those of Speusippus and Xenocrates (see *mathematika*).

4. For Aristotle number is only mathematical number, the product of abstraction (see *mathematika, aphairesis*), perceived not by a single sense but by the "common sense" (*De an.* III, 425a–b; see *aisthesis koine*). The rebirth of Pythagoreanism in the early centuries of the Christian era assured the continued survival of the *eidos-arithmos* theory (see D.L. VIII, 25; Porphyry, *Vita Pyth.* 48–51), so

that, for Plotinus, number has a transcendent position among the intelligibles (*Enn.* VI, 6, 8–9).

arithmós eidētikós: *ideal number*

That there are *eide* of numbers in Plato just as there are of other entities is a matter of no dispute (cf. *Phaedo* 101b–c), and Aristotle is correct in saying that they are singular (*Meta.* 987b) and "incomparable" (*ibid.* 1080a), i.e., incapable of being added, subtracted, etc., from each other. Plato also asserted, on the testimony of Aristotle, *Phys.* III, 206b and *Meta.* 1073a, that the ideal numbers went only to ten.

For the identification of *eidos* and *arithmos*, see *arithmos*.

arithmós mathēmatikós: *mathematical number; the abstract numbers that are the object of mathematics*

See *mathematika, metaxu, aphairesis.*

asýmmetron: *incommensurable (scil. megethos, magnitude)*

1. The discovery that the diagonal of a square could not be described in terms of a proportion (*logos*) with the length of its side probably followed upon the working out of the Pythagorean theorem. In antiquity it was attributed to the Pythagorean Hippasus who was drowned for his revelation of the irrationality (*a-logos*) of the diagonal of the square (Iamblichus, *Vita Pyth.* 247; the proof of incommensurability is given by Aristotle in *Anal. pr.* 41a). Proofs for the incommensurability of $\sqrt{3}$, $\sqrt{5}$, etc. followed quickly (see Plato, *Theaet.* 147d–148b).

2. Philosophically these discoveries raised serious questions as to the nature of number (*arithmos*, q.v.) and the relationship between arithmetic and geometry. Incommensurability began and, for the most part, remained a geometrical problem; these were, after all, incommensurable magnitudes (see Euclid, *Elem.* X, *passim*). Where the difficulty arose, and Hippasus' fate bears testimony to its gravity, was in the Pythagorean insistence on a correspondence between numbers and things. Numbers for the Greeks were the integers and there were no integers to express the new incommensurable magnitudes. One reaction, witnessed by Aristotle, was to distinguish between number and bodies and thus cut geometry loose from arithmetic (see *megethos*). The other, which had some support in the Academy (see *Epinomis* 990c–991b), was to attempt to incorporate $\sqrt{2}$ into the family of the *arithmoi.*

ataraxía: *without disturbance, equilibrium, tranquillity of the soul*

See *hedone.*

athánatos: *immortal, the incorruptibility of the psyche; for the incorruptibility of natural bodies, see aphthartos*

1. The belief in the immortality of the soul begins with its association with *aer*, the vital element in life (see Anaximenes, Diels, fr. 13B2), and the vitalistic assumption that what is alive is divine (Cicero, *De nat. deor.* I, 10, 26; see *theion*) and so immortal. Hence there is no pre-Socratic attempt to demonstrate that the soul as such is immortal; it is part of something else that is immortal. The problem of psychic, individual immortality arises with the new shamanistic, religious view of the *psyche* (q.v.) as the real person, locked in the soul as in a prison; but here too it is rather religious exposition than philosophical argumentation, a preference best seen in Plato's four great eschatological myths: *Phaedo* 107c–114c; *Gorgias* 523a ff.; *Republic* 614b–621d; *Phaedrus* 246a–249d. But Plato also has what he calls "proof" (*apodeixis;* see *Phaedrus* 245c). The proof from *anamnesis* (q.v.) reaches back into religious Pythagoreanism (*Phaedo* 72e–77a), while that from the kinship to the *eide* (*ibid.* 78b–80c) is purely Platonic.

2. These are unitary proofs pertaining to the soul as a whole, but the distinction of the mortal and immortal parts of the soul in the *Timaeus* (see *psyche*) introduces a new direction; not even in his earliest writings does Aristotle maintain the immortality of the entire *psyche;* it is only *nous* that can make that claim (*Eudemus*, fr. 61; *De an.* I, 408b, III, 430a). The materialist is normally led to deny the immortality of the soul; so the Atomists (see Lucretius, *De rerum nat.* III, 830–1094), and so, in the first instance, the Stoics (*SVF* I, 146, II, 809; D.L. VII, 157), though later, with Poseidonius (Cicero, *Tusc.* I, 18–19; compare *De republica* VI, 26–28), they affirmed a kind of astral immortality (see *aer*). For Plotinus there is never a question of the soul's immortality; what is discussed is the individuality of the immortal soul after its separation from the body (*Enn.* IV, 3, 5).

átomon: *"uncut," indivisible material, particle, atom*

1. Parmenides' criticism of Milesian vitalism and its unexplained *genesis* and *kinesis* bore its fruit in the views of Empedocles and Anaxagoras, who reduced all *genesis* to one or other type of mixture of indestructible matter (see Empedocles, Diels 31A28, 30; Anaxagoras, fr. 12) and who posited a source of motion that was different from the thing moved (see *kinoun*). But both Empedocles and Anaxagoras had

posited a plurality of types of basic substance and so had failed to meet the Parmenidean hypothesis that true being is one (see *on* and Melissus, fr. 8). Out of this complex of problems and partial solutions grew the Atomist position: the existence of both being and nonbeing (i.e., the void; see *kenon*), being in the form of an infinite number of indestructible indivisible particles substantially identical and differing only in shape and size, by the aggregation (*synkrisis*) of which sensible things come into existence (Diels, frs. 67A14, 68A37; Aristotle, *Meta.* 985b; see *genesis*).

2. The atoms have eternal motion (Aristotle, *De coelo* III, 300b; see *kinesis*) and the most mobile are the spherical soul or fire atoms (*idem, De an.* I, 405a); all sensation is reduced to contact (*idem, De sensu* 442a); all other sensible qualities are merely convention (*nomos;* Democritus, fr. 9; see *pathos*). The later variations by Epicurus and Lucretius may be found in D.L. x, 35–39 and *De rerum nat.* I, 265–328, 483–634; II, *passim.*

For the Pythagorean version of number-atomism, see *arithmos, monas, megethos;* for the *atomon eidos* as the *infima species* in division, see *diairesis, diaphora, eidos;* for the kinetics of Atomism, see *kinesis;* for the formation of compound bodies, see *genesis;* on the general question of indivisible magnitudes, see *megethos.*

autárkeia: *self-sufficiency*
Self-sufficiency is a characteristic of happiness (*eudaimonia*) as a goal of human life (Aristotle, *Eth. Nich.* I, 1097b), and thus of the contemplative life, which is the highest good for man (*ibid.* x, 1177a). Thereafter *autarkeia* as a quality of virtue becomes a commonplace in both the Stoa (D.L. VII, 127) and the later Platonic tradition (Plotinus, *Enn.* I, 4, 4).

autómaton: *spontaneity*
See *tyche.*

b

boúlēsis: *wish*
See *proairesis; kinoun* 9.

boúleusis: *deliberation*
See *proairesis.*

c

chốra: land, area, space

See *hyle, hypodoche, topos.*

chōristón: *separate, hence* 1) *separate substance*
            2) *conceptually separate* (*see aphairesis*)
Separateness is a characteristic of substance (*ousia*) that, unlike
the other *kategoriai*, is capable of separate existence; all the other
modifications of being exist *in* something (*Meta.* 1028a–b, 1029a28,
1039a32). One of the most frequent Aristotelian charges against Plato
is that he gave the *eide*, which Aristotle understands in the sense of a
universal (*katholou*), a separate substantial existence, i.e., he hypostatized them (see *Meta.* 1086a, 1087a).
On the separability of the agent intellect, see *nous, ousia.*

chrónos: time
1. Time as a personification, *Chronos*, appears in the quasi-
mythical cosmogonies before assuming a place in the philosophical
cosmologies. *Chronos* for *Kronos*, the father of Zeus, was a fairly
common substitution (see Plutarch, *De Iside* 32), and the first to have
done so may have been the sixth-century protophilosopher Pherecydes
(D.L. I, 119). Whoever its originator, a powerful Time is a staple in
the poets (cf. Pindar, *Ol.* II, 17 and fr. 145), and particularly in the

tragedians (*Oed. Col.* 607–623 is only one of a great many examples from Sophocles, who was especially fond of the figure) where Time is a figure of might who not only stands at or near the head of the genealogical process, as in the cosmogonies, but rules and governs the *kosmos.*

2. The thought of one poet on time bears particular note since it is remarkably similar to what an almost contemporary philosopher was saying on the same subject. Solon, in fr. 12, line 3, uses the expression "in the court [*dike*] of *Chronos,*" and an almost identical figure occurs in the preserved fragment of Anaximander where the elements "make reparation [*dike*] to each other for their injustices according to the assessment [*taxis*] of *Chronos.*"

3. The figurative language disappeared as philosophical speculation drew apart from its mythological origins, so that, for instance, when even the poet-philosopher Empedocles is speaking in a context akin to that of Anaximander, *chronos* appears with considerably less suggestion of personification (fr. 30). Where both Anaximander and Empedocles would agree, however, is in placing time outside the *kosmos,* which is, in turn, somehow regulated by time.

4. A change begins to appear with the Pythagoreans for whom the *kosmos* was both a living, breathing creature (*zoön,* q.v.) and the principle of Limit (*peras*). Outside the *kosmos* are only various manifestations of the Unlimited (*apeiron*), which the *kosmos* "inhales" and upon which it imposes Limit (cf. Aristotle, *Phys.* 203a, 213b; Aetius II, 9, 1). Among these *apeira* is, we are told (Aristotle, fr. 201), time. It is likely that the inhaling process involved limiting the raw, perdurative aspect of time (perduration is an early feature of the *apeiron,* q.v.) by its reduction to number (*arithmos*), an association that continued through all subsequent discussion of time.

5. This Pythagorean insight, despite the fact that it is glimpsed only fitfully through Aristotelian asides, was of great importance. It distinguished an unlimited, extracosmic time from a numerable, cosmic time and, in effect, moved the latter into the context of quantity. Plato continued along the same path but added considerable new dimensions to both Pythagorean notions of time. He took over the concept of *aion* (q.v.), which had occurred in pre-Socratic thought as a designation of the life-span of the universe, and applied it to extracosmic time, not now seen as an undefined Pythagorean *apeiron,* that probably included some kind of unregulated motion, but as the motionless mode of the *eide* (*Tim.* 37d). Cosmic time, on the other hand, is identified with the periodic revolution of the heavenly sphere (*Tim.* 39c; Aristotle, *Phys.* 218a–b and Simplicius, *ad loc.*). *Chronos* for Plato is, in short, "an everlasting likeness [*eikon*], moving according to number, of eternity [*aion*] that rests in the one" (*Tim.* 37d). Thus the stability and unity

of *aion* are contrasted with the movement and plurality, or better, the numerability of *chronos*, and the whole incorporated into his theory of *mimesis* (q.v.).

6. For both Plato and Aristotle time and motion are closely associated in a kind of reciprocal relationship. Plato, as we have seen, identified the two, and though Aristotle is critical of that identification (*Phys.* 218b), he does assert their close relationship (*ibid.* 220b). He likewise agrees with Plato that the best unit for measurement is regular, circular motion because it is primary and best known (*ibid.* 223b), but he does not specify, as does Plato, that this is the diurnal movement of the heavens, a position also criticized by Plotinus (*Enn.* III, 7, 9). But where the two men most clearly part company is in the absence in Aristotle of the contrast between time and eternity and all the demiurgic apparatus of the *mimesis* theory.

7. Its existence as an *eikon* allows Plato to assign, at least by implication, an ontological status to time. It even has a purpose in the scheme of things, to enable men to count (*Tim.* 39b). But Aristotle, for whom time is "the calculation [or numbering, *arithmos*] of motion according to prior and posterior" (*Phys.* 219b), is not convinced. Time is not synonymous with movement but must be calculated *from* movement. And calculation demands a calculator: hence, if a mind did not exist, neither would time (*ibid.* 223a). It is the recognition of sequence (prior and posterior) that makes men aware of time (*ibid.* 219a).

8. The Epicurean contribution to a philosophy of time consisted chiefly in an attempt to define its mode of existence. Time is not a *prolepsis* (q.v.), a universal grasp built up over a series of experiences, but rather an immediate perception (D.L. x, 72). It seems to be a quality associated with the actions and movements of things, in short, "an accident of an accident" (Sextus Empiricus, *Adv. Math.* x, 219; compare Lucretius I, 459–461). Such distinctions tend to be blurred in Stoicism, which assumed all such entities, including time (*SVF* II, 1142), under the general rubric of "bodies." But in general the Stoa stayed well within the Platonic and Aristotelian guidelines (without, of course, the Platonic furbelows of *aion* and *eikon*), substituting the more corporeal "interval" for *arithmos*, but preserving the link with motion (*SVF* II, 509, 510).

9. Plotinus devotes considerable attention to the problem of time, considering it, as did Plato, closely bound to the question of eternity. Any attempts to separate the questions, as Aristotle did, are doomed to failure (*Enn.* III, 7, 7–10). Plotinus is impatient with philosophical treatments of time in terms of number or measure of motion (see *Enn.* III, 7, 8), even with Plato's identification of time and the movement of the heavens. Instead he casts the problem of both *aion* and *chronos* in terms of life, the former representing the life of the intelligibles (III, 7,

2). Time, on the other hand, is a kind of degeneration of this total self-presence due to the soul's inability to accept this *tota simulteitas* (compare the similar degeneration of *theoria* into *praxis* in the soul: see *physis*); time, then, is the life of the soul progressing from state to state (III, 7, 11).

d

daímōn or daimónion: *supernatural presence or entity, somewhere between a god (theos) and a hero*

1. The belief in supernatural spirits somewhat less anthropomorphized than the Olympians is a very early feature of Greek popular religion; one such *daimon* is attached to a person at birth and determines, for good or evil, his fate (compare the Greek word for happiness, *eudaimonia*, having a good *daimon*). Heraclitus protested against this belief (fr. 119; see *ethos*), but not with any great effect. In the shamanistic view of the *psyche* (q.v.), *daimon* is another name for the soul (Empedocles, fr. 115), probably reflecting its divine origins and extraordinary powers. Socrates is at least partially in the archaic religious tradition when he speaks of his "divine something" (*daimonion ti*) that warns him to avoid certain actions (*Apol.* 31d; its operation is considerably wider in Xenophon's account in *Mem.* I, 1, 4); notable is Socrates' constant use of the impersonal form of the word or synonym "divine sign" (see *Phaedrus* 242b), perhaps the rationalist's slight correction of what was a popular contemporary belief in divination, divine dream messages, prophecies, etc., a belief that Socrates shared (*Apol.* 21b, 33c, *Crito* 44a, *Phaedo*, 60e; see *mantike*). It is probably a mistake to think that either Socrates or his contemporaries distinguished altogether too carefully between the *daimonion* and the *theion* (q.v.), since the Socratic defense against atheism in *Apol.* 27d rests on an argument that to believe in *daimones* is to believe in gods.

2. The idea of the *daimon* as a kind of "guardian angel" is still visible in Plato (*Rep.* 620d), though there is an attempt to escape the fatalism implied in the popular belief by having the individual souls choose their own *daimon* (*Rep.* 617e). Whether this individual *daimon* is within us or not was much debated in later philosophy. At one point (*Tim.* 90a) Plato himself identifies it with the soul, and a reflection of

this can be seen, for example, in Marcus Aurelius II, 17, III, 16 (see *noesis* 17).

3. But another notion, that of the *daimon* as an intermediary figure between the Olympians and mortals, is also present in Plato, e.g. the "daemonic" Eros in *Symp.* 202d–203a, and the regulations in *Laws* 714a–b. This position had a great vogue among the later transcendentalists of both the Neopythagorean and Platonic variety; the true gods (see *ouranioi*) dwelled in the *aither* (q.v.) while the lesser *daimones* inhabited the lower *aer* and exercised a direct providence (see *pronoia*) over the affairs of men (D.L. VIII, 32).

4. Plutarch has a highly developed demonology (*De def. orac.* 414f–417b), and with his typical religious conservatism he traces the cult of these intermediaries back to oriental and primitive Greek sources (e.g. Hesiod, *Erga* 159–160; compare Plato, *Rep.* 468e–469b), and to Empedocles (*ibid.* 419a; his account of the origin of the *daimones* is in *De genio Socr.* 591c–f). One source overlooked by Plutarch is contact with the Semitic tradition, a connection explicit in Philo who had earlier identified the *daimones* of Greek philosophy with the angels of the Jewish (Iranian?) tradition (*De somn.* 141–142, *De gigant.* 6–9).

dēmiourgós: *maker, craftsman*

1. Plato's description of the maker of the lower gods, the soul of the universe, and the immortal part of the human soul is in *Timaeus* 29d–30c; he uses the preexistent *eide* as his model, *ibid.* 30c–31a (see *mimesis*). The *demiourgos* is probably to be identified with the intelligent, efficient cause posited by Plato in *Phil.* 27b (compare *Soph.* 265c). But he is not omnipotent: he makes the *kosmos* as good "as possible" (*Timaeus* 30b) and must cope with the countereffects of "necessity" (*ananke*), *ibid.* 47e–48a.

2. The *demiourgos* continues to play an important role in later Platonism: what is chiefly notable is that, with the transcendence of the supreme divine principle, the demiurgic function is performed by a secondary emanation, by the *Logos* in Philo (*De cher.* 35, 136–137, *De spec. leg.* I, 81) and *Nous* in Numenius (see Eusebius, *Praep. Evang.* XI, 17–18) and Plotinus (*Enn.* II, 3, 18). The ethical dualism of the Gnostics appears in their making the *demiourgos* create the world without a knowledge of the *eide* (see Iranaeus, *Adv. haer.* I, 5, 3); see *mimesis, techne.*

diaíresis: *separation, division, distinction*

1. Division, a procedure that did not interest Socrates since the thrust of his enquiry was *toward* a single *eidos* (see *epagoge*), becomes an important feature in the later dialogues where Plato turns his atten-

tion to the question of the relationship between *eide*. Expressed in terms of Aristotelian logic *diairesis* is part of the progress from genus to species; but as is clear from a key passage in the *Parmenides*, where he first puts the question (129d–e), Plato did not see it as a conceptual exercise. The dialectical search of which *diairesis* is part has as its object the explication of the ontological realities that are grasped by our reflection (*logismos*).

2. The pursuit of the interrelated *eide* begins with an attempt at comprehending a generic form (*Phaedrus* 265d); this is "collection" (*synagoge*, q.v.). It is followed by *diairesis*, a separation off of the various *eide* found in the generic *eidos*, down to the *infima species* (*Soph.* 253d–e). Plato is sparing of details in both the theory and practice of *synagoge*, and, while the *Sophist* and *Politicus* are filled with examples of *diairesis*, there is relatively little instruction on its methodology. We are told, however, that the division is to take place "according to the natural joints" (*Phaedrus* 265e). What these are becomes clearer from the *Politicus:* they are the differences (*diaphorai*, q.v.) that separate one species from another in the generic form (*Pol.* 262a–263b, 285b).

3. The method of division raises certain serious questions, so serious, indeed, that they might very well shake confidence in the existence of the *eide* (see *Phil.* 15a–b). Describing the relationship of sensibles to the *eide* in terms of participation (*methexis*) suggests the subordination of things to the *eide*, a subordination at the heart of the Platonic metaphysic. And though Plato avoids the term *methexis*, preferring the expression "combination" or "communion" (*koinonia;* earlier, in *Phaedo* 100d, Plato had apparently contemplated using *koinonia* to describe the relationship of sensibles to the *eide*) when describing the interrelationship of the *eide* (see *Soph.* 251d, e), the difficulty persistently refuses to disappear. Does not the arrangement of the specific *eide* under the generic *eidos* suggest the very same principle of subordination among the *eide* themselves? Do the species constitute the genus or are they derived from it? Plato clearly did not see the *eide* in this way (see *Soph.* 251a–259d), as Aristotle himself is willing to admit (see *Meta.* 1031a), but it may have been at least one of the reasons why Speusippus, who practices *diairesis*, but in a radical form (see Aristotle, *Anal. post.* ii, 97a and *diaphora*), denied the existence of the *eide*.

4. Aristotle, however, is convinced of the incompatibility of the subsistent, indivisible *eide* and the process of *diairesis* (*Meta.* 1039a–b). His own theory of division is set forth in *Anal. post.* ii, 96b–97b: one must divide the genus by differences (*diaphorai*, q.v.) that pertain to the essence, must proceed in the correct order, and, finally, be all-inclusive.

With Epictetus *diairesis* reappears in a moral context; see *proairesis*.

dialektikḗ: *dialectic*

1. On the testimony of Aristotle dialectic was an invention of Zeno the Eleatic (D.L. IX, 25), probably to serve as a support for the hypothetical antinomies of Parmenides (Plato, *Parm.* 128c). But what was a species of verbal polemic (what Plato would call "eristic" or disputation; see *Soph.* 224e–226a, *Rep.* 499a, *Phaedrus* 261c) for the Eleatics was transformed by Plato into a high philosophical method. The connecting link was undoubtedly the Socratic technique of question and answer in his search for ethical definitions (see Plato, *Phaedo* 75d, 78d; Xenophon, *Mem.* I, 1, 16; and *elenchos*), a technique that Plato explicitly describes as dialectical (*Crat.* 390c). With the hypostatization of the Socratic definitions into the Platonic *eide* (perhaps reflected in the transition from *Phaedo* 99d–100a to *ibid.* 101d; see *eidos*) the role of dialectic becomes central and is the crown of the ideal curriculum described in the *Republic*: after ten years devoted to mathematics the philosopher-to-be will devote the years between thirty and thirty-five to the study of dialectic (*Rep.* 531d–534e, 537b–539e).

2. What is dialectic? The question is not an easy one since Plato, as usual, thought about it in a variety of ways. There is the view of the *Phaedo* and the *Republic*, which envisions dialectic as a progressively more synoptic ascent, via a series of "positions" (*hypotheseis*, q.v.; the theory of Forms is one such in *Phaedo* 100b), until an ultimate is reached (*Phaedo* 101d, *Rep.* 511e·). In the *Republic*, where the context of the discussion is confessedly moral, this "unhypothetized principle" is identified with the good-in-itself (*auto to agathon; Rep.* 532a–b) that subsumes within itself all the lower hypotheses (*ibid.* 533c–d).

3. If the dialectic of the *Phaedo* and the *Republic* may be described as "synoptic" (*Rep.* 537c), that which emerges from the *Phaedrus* onwards is decidedly "diacritic" (see *Soph.* 226c, 253d). It is introduced in *Phaedrus* 265c–266b (compare *Soph.* 253d–e) and consists of two different procedures, "collection" (*synagoge*, q.v.) and "division" (*diairesis*, q.v.), the latter process in particular being amply illustrated in subsequent dialogues like the *Sophist*, *Politicus*, and *Philebus*. The earlier dialectic appeared similar to the operations of *eros* (q.v.), but here we are transported into an almost Aristotelian world of classification through division: ascent has been replaced by descent. While it is manifest that we are here still dealing with ontological realities, it is likewise clear that a crucial step has been taken along the road to a conceptual logic. The term of the *diairesis* is that *eidos* which stands immediately above the sensible particulars (*Soph.* 229d), and, while this is "really real" (*ontos on*) in the Platonic

scheme of things, it is significant that the same process, *diairesis*, ends, in Aristotle, in the *atomon eidos*, the *infima species* in a logical descent (*De an.* II, 414b); see *diairesis*.

4. Aristotle abandons the central ontological role given to dialectic in Plato's *Republic;* he is concerned, instead, with the operations of the mind that culminate in demonstration (*apodeixis*). Dialectic is not strict demonstration (*Anal. pr.* I, 24a–b; *Top.* I, 100a–b) in that it does not begin from premises that are true and primary, but from opinions (*endoxa*) that are accepted by the majority or the wise. The irony of this distinction is, of course, that Aristotle's own procedure is most frequently what he has described as "dialectical" (see *endoxon*). But as a theoretician Aristotle has little love of dialectic (cf. *De an.* I, 403a; *Top.* 105b), and suggests in *Meta.* 987b that it, or rather the confusion between thought and reality, may have been Plato's undoing.

5. For the Stoics dialectic is reduced to logic, i.e., a study of the forms of internal and external discourse (D.L. VII, 43; cf. *logos, onoma*), while in the same breath they extend its preserves to embrace ethics and even physics (*ibid.* VII, 46, 83). The result is that logic is no longer an instrument (*organon*) of philosophy as understood by the Peripatetic school (the collection of the logical treatises into an *Organon* is post-Aristotelian, though Aristotle certainly foresaw the propaedeutic role of the *Analytics;* cf. *Meta.* 1005b).

6. The rehabilitation of dialectic in its Platonic sense was undertaken by Plotinus (*Enn.* I, 3). It is once again, as in the *Republic*, a cognitive approach to the intelligibles (see *noesis*), but with distinctly Stoic overtones: dialectic is an education for virtue and so includes both actions and objects as well as the *noeta*.

diánoia: understanding

On the Platonic line *dianoia* is a type of cognition between *doxa* and *noesis* (*Rep.* 510d–511a; for the special objects of *dianoia* on the Platonic line, see *mathematika*). In Aristotle it is used as a more general term for intellectual activity. Where it is opposed to *nous* (= intuitive knowledge) it means discursive, syllogistic reasoning (Aristotle, *Anal. post.* II, 100b), and (*ibid.* I, 89b) it is subdivided into the following species: *episteme*, knowledge pursued for its own sake (see also *theoria*), *techne* (knowledge applied to production), and *phronesis* (knowledge applied to conduct). In Stoicism it is identical with the *hegemonikon* (*SVF* II, 459).

For its location in the general context of intellection, see *noesis*.

diaphorá: difference, specific difference

1. The presence of *diaphorai* is explicit in the Platonic dialectical process of division (*diairesis*, q.v.) where the "generic form" is di-

vided according to kinds (*Soph.* 253d–e), or, as he puts it in *Phaedrus* 265e, "at the natural joints." What these "natural joints" are is described more fully in *Pol.* 262a–263b, 285b. The genus must be divided only where it separates into two specific Forms. To divide a genus into parts will not do since a part (*meros*) and a specific Form (*eidos*) are not the same thing (*ibid.* 262b). The *diaphorai*, therefore, must distinguish species.

2. This makes sense in a system of concepts, but creates great difficulties if the *eide* are autonomous, indivisible substances, as Plato undoubtedly saw them; there is no place in the Platonic theory for either "generic" or "specific" Forms (see *diairesis*). Plato's successor Speusippus, who denied the *eide*, used an exhaustive method of *diairesis*, attempting to include all the *diaphorai*, presumably since, with the disappearance of the hypostatized *eide*, it was the *diaphorai* that gave the new conceptual *eidos* its content (see Aristotle, *Anal. post.* II, 97a).

3. In Aristotle the process of *diairesis* proceeds by dividing the genus by means of specifically distinct *diaphorai* down to the *infima species* where the activity will terminate in definition (*horismos;* see the definition of *horismos* in *Top.* I, 103b). In *Top.* VI,.143a–145b there are elaborate rules for the choice of *diaphorai* in *diairesis*.

4. As for the ontological aspects of the problem, in the *Metaphysics* Aristotle moves the discussion into the categories of matter and form. Genus stands to *diaphora* as sensible matter to form, and so may be characterized as "intelligible matter" (*hyle noete;* the characterization is not particularly felicitous since he uses the expression in another sense as well; see *hyle, aphairesis*), while all the *diaphorai* are resumed in the final one, that of the *atomon eidos* or *infima species*, and serves as its essence (*ousia*) (*Meta.* 1038a, 1045a).

diáthesis: *disposition*
See *hexis.*

díkē: *compensation, legal proceedings, justice*
1. As is the case with most Greek ethical terms, *dike* had a fairly complex history before its incorporation into the problematic of philosophy. From the time of Homer *dike* had bound into it the transgression of certain limits, probably those dictated, in the first instance, by the class structure of society, and the payment of a compensation for this transgression. With the decline of an aristocratic class consciousness *dike* began to be seen as something pervasive in the society, applicable to all citizens alike, and guaranteed by Zeus himself. The limits within which the new *dike* was operative were now defined by written law

(*nomos*, q.v.), and a new.abstract term *dikaiosyne*, "righteousness," "justice," came into use to describe the moral quality of the man who observed the limits of the law and was thus "just" (*dikaios*).

2. The first usage of *dike* in a philosophical context occurs in the only extant fragment of Anaximander (Diels 12B1) where the elements (*stoicheia*), which are naturally opposed forces (see *enantia*), are required to make reparation (*dike*) to each other for their mutual transgression in the process of *genesis-phthora*. The limits that are violated here are not those of a human society but the order implicit in the world seen as a *kosmos* (q.v.), this in an era before the operation of the physical world was made discontinuous with that of human life. One notes a correction in Heraclitus (fr. 80): the strife between the elements is not, as Anaximander would have it, a species of injustice that demands compensation, but the normal order of things, the tension of opposites that is the reality of existence.

3. Although the fragments of Democritus betray a certain interest in ethical behavior in general and justice in particular (see frs. 45, 174), this is the ethical concern of a philosopher rather than an attempt to construct a philosophical ethic. The impetus for just such an attempt lay in the Sophists' attacks on the bases of conduct on the grounds that they were tied to a relative, arbitrary law (see *nomos*). Thus was the notion of *dike* drawn into the controversy surrounding *nomos* vs. *physis*, and issues in a series of Sophistic positions that described justice as consisting solely in obedience to the arbitrary laws of the state, laws that were, in turn, the instruments whereby the powerful in the society sought to preserve their position: thus Archelaus (Diels 60A1), Antiphon (Diels 87B44), and the attitudes embraced by Callicles in Plato's *Gorgias* (e.g. 483a–484a) and Thrasymachus in Book I of the *Republic* (e.g. 338c).

4. The Socratic reply to these positions may, of course, be viewed merely as a refinement of his general thrust of the virtues (specifically including *dikaiosyne;* see Aristotle, *Eth. Eud.* I, 1216b) into the realm of permanent, cognitionally grasped definitions (see *arete*); but there is besides the impassioned defense of justice and law as an inviolable social contract in the *Crito*. Plato's own answer to Socrates' antagonists is to be found in *Republic* II–X, and is embodied in an investigation of justice as it exists on the larger scale of the *polis* (*Rep.* 369a), whence it emerges as a kind of cooperative disposition to do one's own work (see 433e, 443b).

5. This does not respond to Callicles' contention that the unjust always seem to have a better time of it; the wicked do, indeed, prosper. Plato has no great assurances to give about the fate of the just in this life—though he is sure the gods will not neglect them (*Rep.* 613a–b;

compare *Laws* x, 899c–900b) –but it is in the future life that justice receives its ultimate reward, as depicted in glowing terms in the "Myth of Er" in *Republic* x.

6. Aristotle's major treatment of justice occurs in *Eth. Nich.* v where it is divided into a) "distributive," i.e., dealing with the division of goods, honors, etc. among those who participate in a political system, and b) "corrective," i.e., regulatory of the inequities in either transactions or crimes (1130b–1131a). In both instances justice is a kind of proportion (*analogia*), and thus it too can be assimilated to the doctrine of the "mean" (see *meson*). Aristotle is firm in his rejection of the Sophists' contention that what is just is merely a matter of convention: there are at least some activities that are just by nature (1134b). Finally (1137a–b) he introduces the notion of the equitable or the decent (*epieikeia*) that tempers the legal demands of justice, "what the lawgiver would have said if he were there" (compare Plato, *Polit.* 294a–295e).

7. For the Stoics *dikaiosyne* is one of the four cardinal virtues (*SVF* i, 190), defined by Chrysippus as "the science of distributing what is proper to each" (*SVF* iii, 262), and based on nature, not convention (D.L. vii, 128). Carneades the Sceptic returned, however, to the Sophists' contention that law is a convention set up by men on strictly utilitarian grounds, a position that he can illustrate by the conflicting counsels of prudence and justice (Cicero, *De republica* iii, 11, 18–19; Lactantius, *Instit.* v, 16, 3–6). See *arete, nomos*.

dóxa: 1] opinion, 2] judgment

1. Opinion: the distinction between true knowledge (*episteme*, q.v.) and an inferior grade of cognition goes back as far as Xenophanes (fr. 34), but the classic pre-Socratic exposition of it is to be found in Parmenides' poem (fr. 8, lines 50–61) where sensation (*aisthesis*) is relegated to the position of "seeming" or "opinion" (*doxa*). The distinction is based on the ontological status of the object of sense perception (*aistheta*) that, because of their exclusion from the realm of true being (*on*), cannot be the objects of true knowledge.

2. The distinction is incorporated, on the same grounds, into Platonic epistemology, though by now the position had been buttressed by the insistent Sophist attacks on *aisthesis* as relative (see Plato, *Theaet.* 166d–167a, citing Protagoras). In *Rep.* 476e–480a Plato sets Parmenides' distinction as a series of epistemological and ontological correlatives: true knowledge is of true reality, i.e., the *eide*, while ignorance is of the completely nonreal. Between the two there is an intermediate stage: a quasi-knowledge of quasi-being. This intermediate faculty (*dynamis*) is doxa and its objects are sensible things (*aistheta*) and the commonly held opinions of mankind. The results

are later schematized in the Diagram of the Line (*Rep.* 509d–511e) where the realm of *doxa* is further refined by being divided into belief (*pistis*, q.v.) whose objects are the sensibles, and "knowledge of appearances" (*eikasia*, q.v.), a category of cognition introduced by Plato's view of the nature of productive activity (see *techne, mimesis*).

3. The dichotomy between *episteme* and *doxa* remains fundamental to Plato, even though he betrays a growing interest in the sensible world (see *aistheton, episteme.*)

4. Judgment: Plato's view of *doxa*, founded as it is on the separation of the *eide* from sensible things, finds no support in the Aristotelian view of reality, but there is another context within which the problematic of *doxa* may be treated. The question of truth and error arises particularly in the realm of judgment, a problem that also has its origins in the Parmenidean premises about being (*on*, q.v.): since only being can be thought or named, how is it possible to make a false judgment, that is, a definition about nonbeing (fr. 3; fr. 8, line 34)? In *Soph.* 263d–264b Plato shows that, just as there is false assertion or discourse (*logos*), so too there is false judgment (*doxa*) that is the externalization of this discourse. The possibilities of false judgment are discussed in *Theaet.* 187c–200d, but since the true position waits upon the solution of the problem of nonbeing (*me on;* see *on, heteron*), the final analysis is not put forth until *Soph.* 263b–d: error (*pseudos*) is a judgment (*doxa*) that does not correspond to reality, either to the "reality" of the sensible situation, or to the true reality of the *eidos* in which the sensible participates.

5. Aristotle's treatment of *episteme* and *doxa* moves into another area. Knowledge is either immediate (see *nous*) or discursive (*dianoia*, q.v.). The latter may be described as *episteme* if it proceeds from premises that are necessary, *doxa* if the premises are contingent (*Anal. post.* 1, 88b–89b), i.e., if they could be otherwise, and indeed Aristotle defines *doxa* as "that which could be otherwise" in *Meta.* 1039b.

6. When discussing the types of syllogisms in *Top.* 1, 100a–b Aristotle approaches the contingency of *doxa* from a somewhat different angle. A demonstrative syllogism (*apodeixis*, q.v.) rests upon premises that are true and primary. It thus differs from a dialectical syllogism (*dialektike*, q.v.) whose premises are based on *endoxa*, which are now defined as opinions that are accepted by the majority or the wise. For the implications of this for Aristotle's method, see *endoxon*.

7. The Epicurean view of *doxa* shares both Platonic and Aristotelian traits. It is opinion, a certain spontaneous movement in us that is akin to but distinct from sensation (*aisthesis*, q.v.). For Epicurus all

aisthesis is true but not necessarily self-evident (*enargeia*, q.v.), and so *doxa* is capable of extending beyond the evidence of the senses, as, for example, in assigning by its judgment sense data to the wrong *prolepsis* (q.v.), and thus is the source of error and falsity (D.L. x, 50–51).

dýás: dyad, pair

According to one account of Pythagoreanism preserved in a late author (D.L. viii, 25), the Dyad was derived from the Monad (*monas*); but on the basis of the "Table of Contraries" in *Meta.* 986a, the *Monas* and *Dyas* would seem to rank as co-principles, and if the *Monas* is associated with the Good (*agathon*) (Aetius 1, 7, 18; see *Eth. Nich.* 1096b), so the *Dyas* is ranked with *kakon* (*ibid.* 1106b, 29). Aristotle makes various attempts to identify a material principle in Plato (see *hyle*): in *Meta.* 987b and 988a it is the *dyas*, and finally, in 1081a and 1099b, the indefinite dyad (*aoristos dyas*). Plato may himself have used the expression, but not in the dialogues; perhaps in his lecture "On the Good" (see Alexander of Aphrodisias, *In Meta.* 55; Simplicius, *In Phys.* 453–455; and *agrapha dogmata*). From *Phil.* 23c–26d we know that Plato used the *apeiron* as an *arche*, and Aristotle conjectures in *Phys.* iii, 206b that the reason why the "indeterminate" is twofold is that it is a spectrum unlimited in either direction. Plato's own successor, Speusippus, identified it with plurality (Aristotle, *Meta.* 1087b); see *arithmos*.

dýnamis: *active and passive capacity, hence* 1] *power and* 2] *potentiality*

1. The "powers" make their first appearance with Anaximander, not, as later, as qualities of things, but as the things themselves; opposites (see *enantia*) that are separated off from the *apeiron: the* hot and *the* cold (Diels, fr. 12A10) and have almost the status of elements. With Anaximenes (Diels, frs. 13A5, A7, B1) the distinction between substances (earth, fire, water) and their qualities ("powers"), hot and cold has begun. Empedocles' theory of elements (see *stoicheion*) shifted attention to the substances away from the dynamic qualities, but with Anaxagoras the primary role is once again given to the opposed powers (frs. 8, 12, 15, 16). The Atomists stand in another tradition: the Pythagorean number theory had, in effect, reduced qualitative differences to quantitative ones (see *arithmos*), and Democritus follows them in reducing the perceptible qualities to contact (*haphe*) with geometrical shapes (Diels, fr. A135; cf. *pathos*); they are no longer dynamic but merely conventional (*nomos*), *ibid.* B9.

2. Plato is aware of the *dynameis* both as a medical term (*Phaedrus* 370c–d, and see *eidos*) and in their relationship with the elements (*Tim.* 33a), and these powers, also called *pathe*, exist in the Receptacle

(*hypodechomene*) before *Nous* begins its work. But once the primary bodies have been formed, these powers disappear and the sensible qualities are reduced, in true Atomist fashion, to the geometrical shapes of the elementary particles (*ibid.* 61c–68d; see *genesis*).

3. In Aristotle the powers (generally called *poion* or *pathos*) once again are central. Empedocles' *stoicheia* were irreducible, and Plato's reducible back to the geometric figures (*Tim.* 53c–56c); to both of these Aristotle opposed his own theory of the composition of the *stoicheia* from 1) underlying matter and 2) the presence of one of each set of the powers: hot-cold, dry-moist (*De gen. et corr.* 329a–330a). Thus change or reduction of one element into another consists of the passage of one opposite to another in the substratum (see *hypokeimenon, genesis*).

4. All of these usages pertain to *dynamis* as a "power," but in the *Metaphysics* Aristotle develops another sense of *dynamis*, i.e., potentiality, and he distinguishes the two in *Meta.* 1045b–1046a; potentiality cannot be defined, but only illustrated (*ibid.* 1048a–b), e.g. the waker is potentially the sleeper; the passage from potency to actuality (*energeia*) is either through art or by an innate principle (*ibid.* 1049a); *energeia* is logically and ontologically prior to *dynamis* (*ibid.* 1049b–1050a), hence the necessity of a first mover (see *kinoun*) always in a state of *energeia* (*ibid.* 1050b).

5. The Stoic doctrine of the "powers" pushed Aristotle's theory of the elements one step further; each *stoicheion* had *one* power instead of one each of the opposed sets: fire had heat, air had cold (these were the active [*poiein*] qualities); earth had the dry and water the moist (passive [*paschein*] qualities; see *SVF* II, 580), and the stress on fire in the system (see *pyr*) is clearly a function of its being the most active power. Indeed, the Stoics reduced all of reality to two basic *archai:* the active (*poioun*) and the passive (*paschein*, q.v.; cf. D.L. VII, 134).

6. We see, then, that for the Milesians and their successors *dynamis* was an active force in things, first thought of as a separate natural entity but then refined, from Plato on, into the notion of an active quality (*poiotes*, q.v.). In post-Aristotelian philosophy, however, the name is frequently applied to the great number of intermediary movers or intelligences associated with the plants of the *aither* or the *daimones* who inhabit the air (see *nous* 17), and identified by Philo as angels (cf. *De gigant.* 6–9).

7. But there were other factors at work in the Philonian notion of *dynamis.* In Scripture God is said to have "powers," translated by the Septuagint as *dynameis*, and these Philo identifies with the Platonic *ideai* (*De spec. leg.* 45–48; for the distinction between *eidos* and *idea*, see *noeton* 2). Thus they assume the role of the transcendent *noeta* in the mind of God and, as the immanent *eide*, become a creative force in

the universe. In Philo it is the latter that give order to the universe while they, in turn, are controlled by the transcendent God (*De fuga* 101). The same treatment can be seen in Plotinus. The *noeta* that exist in a unified form in the cosmic *nous* (see *noeton* 5) are described as a universal *dynamis* with boundless capacity (*Enn.* v, 8, 9). But each of these is potentially (and in the sequel will be actually) a separate *eidos* and so an individual *dynamis* (v, 9, 6) that will later be operative in both the noetic and sensible world (IV, 4, 36).

8. But the noetic and sensible world descends, according to the Neoplatonic vision of the universe, in a uniform causal series from a single source (see *proödos*) and is linked together by a cosmic *sympatheia* (q.v.). A corollary of this, and a characteristically symmetrical touch, is that all the entities in the series, *noeta* and *aistheta*, are also subject to the thrust of return (*epistrophe*, q.v.) to their source. *Epistrophe* was hardly a novel concept. It is implicit in the Pythagorean view of the soul as a divine part that tries to restore its true harmony (*harmonia*, q.v.). It may be seen, as well, in the related Platonic notions of *katharsis, eros, dialektike* (qq.v), and the call to "assimilation to God" (see *homoiosis*). But here as elsewhere, including Plotinus, the return, in whatever form, is a function of the conscious soul and particularly its intellectual faculty. After Plotinus, however, it is extended to the entire range of creation (see Proclus, *Elem. theol.*, prop. 39).

9. There were, to be sure, some precedents for this. Plato had allowed to plants a certain choice of the good life (*Phil.* 22b); Aristotle's *physis* (q.v.) works toward a *telos*, and he had spoken, moreover, of *genesis* in the sensible world as an imitation of the activity of the divine *nous* (see *Meta.* 1050b and *kinoun* 9). But these were not the immediate progenitors of Proclus' symmetrical *epistrophe;* they are rather to be sought in the later development of the notion of *dynamis.* The Stoics had already developed a theory of *logoi spermatikoi* (q.v.) that, somewhat like the Aristotelian *physis,* governed the growth and development of things. But here the stress is on the rational (*logos*) element; from the time of Poseidonius this yields to the more dynamic concept of a vital force (*zotike dynamis;* see *sympatheia* 3) in all beings that are linked together by the affinities of *sympatheia.* This was systematized into a vast body of knowledge, the study of the innate affinities and antipathies of natural objects. This is the "physics" of late antiquity, associated with the name of Bolus of Mendes.

10. These sympathetic *dynameis* are not, at this point, magical, but they soon become so under other influences. The religious view of late antiquity, perhaps influenced by the earlier demands that the gods act in such a way that they preserve their transcendent immobility (see

nous 2), was that the gods no longer worked in person but through their *dynameis* in things. These *dynameis* could be and were personified; Philo's usage has already been noted (6 *supra*) and the philosophers found it a convenient way to reconcile the multiple gods of mythology with their own henotheism (see the fragments of Porphyry's *On the Images of the Gods;* Macrobius, *Saturnalia* I, 17–23; Proclus, *Theol. Plat.* v–vi; it also gave them ample scope to display their by then highly developed powers of etymologizing: see *onoma* 7). It is this religious point of view that is given its classic theoretical justification in props. 144–145 of Proclus' *Elem. theol.* where he affirms that the distinctive characteristic of the divine powers (*theiai dynameis*) radiates downward in the casual sequence and is found on all levels of reality.

11. This view of the *dynameis* in things goes far beyond the Bolean physics that attempted to discover and use, largely for therapeutic purposes, the occult sympathy between natural objects; here we have the theoretical ground for the magical art of *theourgia* (see *mantike* 4–5) that seeks to manipulate the gods through their occult "tokens" (*symbola*) in natural objects and that, since Iamblichus, was a standard part of the Neoplatonic repertory (see *De myst.* v, 23; Proclus, *In Tim.* I, 139, 210).

For related questions in the history of *dynamis*, see *genesis, pathos, poiein, stoicheion;* for its Aristotelian correlative, *energeia.*

e

échein: 1] *to have,* 2] *to be in a certain state;* see hexis
"Possession" is one of Aristotle's *kategoriai.* It appears as such in *Cat.* 1b–2a, but is omitted in other listings, e.g. *Anal. post.* I, 83b. "To be in a certain state" (*pos echein*) is one of four Stoic categories (*SVF* II, 369); it is discussed by Plotinus (*Enn.* VI, 1, 25), who also uses this Stoic term in discussing *psyche* (*Enn.* IV, 7, 4) and *hyle* (*ibid.* II, 4, 1).

eídōlon: image
In the Atomists' theory of visual perception (*aisthesis,* q.v.) images of the same shape as the body are given off by the perceived object and enter the pores of the viewer (Alexander of Aphrodisias, *De sensu* 56, 12; Plutarch, *Symp.* VIII, 735a). In Epicureanism these enter

into the senses of men during sleep as well, and are thought by men to be gods (Sextus Empiricus, *Adv. Math.* IX, 19; so too in Cicero, *De nat. deor.* I, 19, 49; for an ethical correlative, see *hedone*). Plato uses "image" in the *Sophist*, and further divides it into "likeness" (*eikon*) and "semblance" (*phantasma*), *ibid.* 236a–b; it is like the real, but has existence *secundum quid*, *ibid.* 239c–240b (see the description of *eikon* in *Tim.* 52c). In Plotinus *eidolon* is generally used in the sense of *eikon;* see *Enn.* V, 2, 1 and III, 9, 3 where *hyle* is an *eidolon* of the soul, and II, 4, 5 where sensible matter is an *eidolon* of intelligible matter (see *hyle*).

eídos: *appearance, constitutive nature, form, type,*
    species, idea

1. *Eidos* was a well-established and fairly sophisticated term long before its canonization by Plato. Its first meaning, and the usage is current in Homer, is "what one sees," "appearance," "shape," normally of the body, and pre-Socratic philosophy continued to use it in this sense (see Empedocles, frs. 98, 115 and Democritus, cited in Plutarch, *Adv. Col.* 1110). By the time of Herodotus *eidos*, and its cognate *idea* that had come into use, had been broadened and abstracted into "characteristic property" (I, 203) or "type" (I, 94). Thucydides' use is similar (see III, 81), and in one instance (II, 50) he speaks of "the *eidos* of the disease," an expression that leads into the development of the term in contemporary medical circles. Here *eidos/idea* had apparently been isolated as a technical term, frequently linked to the notion of power (*dynamis*, q.v.), and meaning something approximately like "constitutive nature" (see Hippocrates, *V.M.* 15, 19; *Nat. hom.* 2, 5; *De arte* 2).

2. Whatever the exact interpretation of the latter texts, it does seem clear that there was an approach to the form of things that was not necessarily tied to its outward appearance (though its connection with *dynamis* suggests that its identification rested upon an awareness of its visible effects), but rather to some kind of inner intelligibility (*De arte* 2 significantly connects *eidos* with the imposition of names; see *onoma*).

3. Was there a parallel development among the philosophers? Both Plato and Aristotle seem to suggest that there was. Plato, in a rare glance at the history of philosophy (see *endoxon*), says that discussions on the nature of reality have polarized into factions, which he calls the Giants and the Gods. The first are materialists (*Soph.* 246a–248a; compare the somewhat different but parallel attitudes in *Phaedo* 96a–d and *Laws* x, 889a–890a) and Plato is probably referring to the Atomist tradition. The Gods, on the other hand, are described as "friends of the *eide*" (*ibid.* 248a–249d) and they hold a theory of

suprasensible reality that is indistinguishable from Plato's. They are not the Eleatics since they believe in a plurality of such entities (see *on*).

4. Their identity has been sought in a passage in Aristotle where we are told (*Meta.* 987a–b) that Plato followed the Pythagoreans in many respects, attributing to Plato only verbal differences from the Pythagoreans and some refinements introduced under the influence of the Heraclitan Cratylus and of Socrates himself.

5. Were the Pythagoreans the originators of the *eide* theory? There have been those who thought so, arguing, *inter alia*, from the strongly Pythagorean environment of the *Phaedo* where the theory is propounded by Plato for the first time. But there is little to support this from the strictly Pythagorean evidence and the statement is an isolated one in Aristotle, added, perhaps, when he came to the conclusion that Plato had identified the *eide* with number (*arithmos*, q.v.).

6. The origin of the theory must be sought closer to home. Socrates had been interested in defining ethical qualities (see *Meta.* 987b), probably as a reaction against Sophist relativism (see *nomos*), and there is reason to believe that the Platonic *eide* were hypostatized versions of just such definitions (*logoi;* see *Phaedo* 99e, *Meta.* 987b, and compare the connection with predication, *infra*). Indeed, in the "Socratic dialogues" one can see Socrates himself moving in just such a direction (see *Lysis* 219d, *Euthyphro* 5d, 6d; the *Euthyphro* passages actually use *eidos*, but the meaning is still close to "appearance"; in *Meno* 72c–e the usage has already become more abstract). But, on the testimony of Aristotle, Socrates "did not separate the universal definition" (*Meta.* 1078b), i.e., it had no transcendent, subsistent (*choriston*, q.v.) existence.

7. For Plato the *eide* did exist separately (see *Tim.* 52a–c) and the reasons may be sought in epistemological considerations as well as the ethical ones that troubled Socrates and that were almost certainly operative upon Plato as well. We have already noted the suggested influence of Heraclitus on Plato (see *Meta.* 987a, 1078b) to the effect that, given the changing, fluctuating nature of sensible phenomena (see *rhoe*), true knowledge (*episteme*) is impossible, impossible, that is, unless there is a stable, eternal reality beyond the merely sensible. The *eide* are that suprasensible reality and so the cause of *episteme* and the condition of all philosophical discourse (*Phaedo* 65d–e, *Parm.* 135b–c, *Rep.* 508c ff.). For the further epistemological corollaries, see *doxa*, *episteme*, *noesis*.

8. Though the *eide* are the centerpiece of Platonic metaphysics, nowhere does Plato undertake a proof for their existence; they first appear as a hypothesis (see *Phaedo* 100b–101d) and remain so, even though subjected to a scathing criticism (*Parm.* 130a–134e). They are

known, in a variety of methods, by the faculty of reason (*nous; Rep.* 532a–b, *Tim.* 51d). One such early method is that of recollection (*anamnesis*, q.v.), where the individual soul recalls the *eide* with which it was in contact before birth (*Meno* 80d–85b, *Phaedo* 72c–77d; see *palingenesia*). Without the attendant religious connotations is the purely philosophical method of *dialektike* (q.v.; see *Rep.* 531d–535a; for its difference from mathematical reasoning, *ibid.* 510b–511a; from eristic, *Phil.* 15d–16a). As it is first described the method has to do with the progress from a hypothesis back to an unhypothetized *arche* (*Phaedo* 100a, 101d; *Rep.* 511b), but in the later dialogues *dialektike* appears as a fully articulated methodology comprising "collection" (*synagoge*, q.v.) followed by a "division" (*diairesis*, q.v.) that moves, via the *diaphorai*, from a more comprehensive Form down to the *atomon eidos*. Finally, one may approach the *eide* through *eros* (q.v.), the desiderative parallel to the earlier form of dialectic (see *epistrophe*).

9. The relationship between the indivisible, eternal *eide* and transient, sensible phenomena (*aistheta*) is described in a number of different ways. The *eide* are the cause (*aitia*) of the *aistheta* (*Phaedo* 100b–101c), and the latter are said to participate (*methexis*, q.v.) in the *eide*. In an elaborate metaphor, pervasive in Plato, the *aistheton* is said to be a copy (*eikon*, q.v.) of its eternal model (*paradeigma*), the *eidos*. This act of artistic creation (*mimesis*, q.v.) is the work of a supreme craftsman (*demiourgos*, q.v.).

10. There is little question of the transcendence of the *eide* (cf. *Tim.* 51b–52d), but Plato's use of *methexis* suggests a degree of immanence as well (*Phaedo* 103b–104a, *Tim.* 50c; and see *genesis*), and this is the point of much of the criticism in the *Parmenides* (see 130a–132b) and in extended passages in the *Metaphysics*. Where, then, is one to locate the *eide*? Here analogy comes into play. Just as the *aistheta* are contained in some sort of organic unity that is the *kosmos*, so the *eide* exist in some "intelligible place" (*topos noetos*, *Rep.* 508c, 517b; the expression *kosmos noetos*, q.v., does not occur until later Platonism) located "beyond the heavens" (*Phaedrus* 247c). The image becomes sharper in *Tim.* 30c–d where the *eide* are organized within the "intelligible living being" (*zoön noeton*). See also *ekei*.

11. At first glance there appears to be a Platonic *eidos* for each class of things. Thus there are ethical *eide* (*Parm.* 130b, *Phaedrus* 250d), mathematical *eide* (*Phaedo* 101b–c; see *arithmos eidetikos*), *eide* of natural objects (*Tim.* 51b, *Soph.* 266b; compare *Meta.* 1070a), even trivial ones (*Parm.* 130c). What is perhaps more surprising is to find *eide* for artificial objects (*Rep.* 596a–597d, *Soph.* 265b, *Ep.* VII, 343d; compare *Meta.* 991b), relations (*Phaedo* 74a–77a, *Rep.* 479b, *Parm.* 133c), and negatives (*Rep.* 476a, *Theaet.* 186a, *Soph.* 257e). Behind all of this stands the presumption of *methexis:* since the sensi-

bles participate in the *eide* they must be named univocally (*homonymos*) with them (*Parm.* 133d, *Soph.* 234b; see D.L. III, 13), and so the modes of predication may be taken as criteria for the existence of the various *eide* (*Rep.* 596a). Are, then, the *eide* merely ideas or concepts? The question is actually raised in the dialogues, only to be denied (see *Parm.* 132b–c, 134b).

12. At various points in the dialogues Plato seems to grant a preeminence to one or other of the *eide*. Thus, both the Good (*Rep.* 504e–509c) and the Beautiful (*Symp.* 210a–212b) are thrown into relief, to say nothing of the notorious hypotheses of the One in the *Parmenides* (137c–142; see *hen, hyperousia*). But the problem of the interrelationship, or, as Plato calls it, "combination" or "communion" (*koinonia*), and, by implication, of the subordination of the *eide* is not taken up formally until the *Sophist*. It is agreed, again on the basis of predication, that some *eide* will blend with others and some will not, and that it is the task of dialectic to discern the various groupings, particularly through the diacritic method known as *diairesis* (q.v.; *Soph.* 253b–e).

13. To illustrate the process Plato chooses (*ibid.* 254b–255e) five *eide*–Existence (*on*, q.v.), the Same, the Different (*heteron*, q.v.), Motion (*kinesis*, q.v.), and Rest, which he calls (254d) "greatest kinds" (*megista gene*). Both words in this expression are open to differing interpretations. A reading of *megista* as a true superlative, "*the* greatest," and of *gene* as "genera" or "classes" leads to the discovery of Platonic *summa genera*, the equivalent of Aristotle's *kategoriai*. The passage was so read by Plotinus (see *Enn.* VI, 1–3) who speaks of the *gene* of being. But there is grave doubt as to whether *gene* should be read as *genera* in the Aristotelian sense; Plato's own usage is frequently to employ *genos* as a synonym for *eidos*, and so the expression in question may mean nothing more than "some very important *eide*."

For some other aspects of the Platonic *eidos*, see *arithmos, mathematika, metaxu, monas, dyas*.

14. In his *Metaphysics* Aristotle subjects the *eidos*-theory to a lengthy critical analysis (see 987a–988a, 990a–993a, 1078b–1080a; compare the contemporary Aristotelian dialogue, *De phil.* frs. 8, 9). Assessments of the validity of this critique hinge on two essential and obscure points: the distinction between Plato and his successors on the subject of the *mathematika* (q.v.), and the existence and Aristotle's use of sources unavailable to us (see *agrapha dogmata*).

15. The chief difference between the Platonic and Aristotelian view of the *eide* is that for the latter the *eidos* is not (except in the cases of the first mover and/or movers, and that of the *nous* "that comes from outside"; see *kinoun, nous*) a separate subsistent (*choriston*,

q.v.), but a prinicple of complete substances. It is the formal cause of things (*Phys.* II, 194b), a correlative of matter in composite beings (*ibid.* I, 190b), and the intelligible essence (*ousia*) of an existent (*Meta.* 1013a, *De gen. et corr.* II, 335b; see *ousia*). In knowing things we know their *eidos* (*Meta.* 1010a), i.e., the appropriate faculty (*nous* or *aisthesis*) becomes the thing it knows by reason of the *eidos* of the known object entering the soul (*De an.* III, 431b–432a). *Eidos* is, in brief, an actualization (*energeia, entelecheia*, qq.v.; *Meta.* 1050b, *De an.* II, 412a).

16. As in Plato, Aristotle's *eidos*, considered from a logical point of view, has an intimate connection with predication. The conceptual *eidos* is the universal of predication and the subject of definition (*Meta.* 1036a, 1084b). But they differ from the Platonic version of the *eide* not only by reason of the fact that they are not hypostatized into substances, but also because they are "classified," i.e., they range up from the *atomon eidos*, which cannot be broken down into narrower species but only into individuals (and this "division" of the *infima species* is a function of its connection with matter not by reason of the presence of a *diaphora* [q.v.]; see *hyle*), through ever wider *eide*, called *gene*, up to the *summa genera*, the *kategoriai* (q.v.); on the *eidos* as universal, see *katholou*.

17. The *eide* continued to be important in later philosophy. The Aristotelian *eide* that are immanent in matter and direct the entire teleological structure of the individual existents were incorporated into Stoicism as the *logoi spermatikoi* (q.v.). The Platonic transcendental version of the *eide* seems to have given way under the Aristotelian critique, but they reappear in the Platonic tradition with Antiochus of Ascalon (Cicero, *Acad. post.* 8, 30–33). But it was a perilous time for orthodoxy and very quickly the *eide* are being construed as the thoughts of God (Philo, *De opif.* 4, 17–20; Albinus, *Epit.* 9, 1–2). Even though Plato had denied a purely noetic status to his *eide* (see *supra* 11), the notion may have found some support in the Academy (see Aristotle, *De an.* III, 429a). But it was doubtless Aristotle's designation of God as *nous* (q.v.) that was the mediating factor here, encouraged, to be sure, by the entire Platonic *mimesis* metaphor with its very strong suggestion that what Aristotle called a formal cause exists first as a *paradeigma* in the mind of the craftsman before becoming immanent in things. Thus by positing the *eide* as the thoughts of God, a position that continues down through Plotinus (see *Enn.* V, 1, 4) into Christianity, and at the same time keeping the Aristotelian *eide* as immanent formal causes with an orientation toward matter (see Philo, *De opif.* 44, 129–130), an at least partial solution to the dilemma of immanence vs. transcendence was reached. But the problem continued as a serious one in Platonism, discussed at length by both Plotinus (*Enn.* VI, 4) and Proclus (*Elem. theol.*, prop. 23); see *noeton* 2.

For the epistemological difficulties arising from transcendence, see *agnostos;* for the hierarchization of the *eide* in later Platonism, *hypostasis;* for the *eide* of individuals, *hyle;* for the location of the *eide* in both their transcendent and immanent manifestations, *nous; noeton.*

eikón: *image, reflection*
Eikasia, the state of perceiving mere images and reflections, is the lowest segment of the Platonic Line (*Rep.* 509e). The *eikon* has a qualified type of existence (*Tim.* 52c) and a not very complimentary role in Plato's theory of art (*Rep.* 598e–599a; see *techne, mimesis*). The visible universe is the *eikon* of the intelligible one that embraces the *eide* (*Tim.* 30a–d; see *kosmos noetos*), and time is an image of eternity (see *chronos*). In Plotinus soul is an image of *nous* (*Enn.* v, 1, 3), the created world is an image of its Father (*Enn.* v, 8, 12), and matter (*hyle*) an image of being (*on*) (*Enn.* i, 8, 3), etc.; see *kosmos, mimesis, doxa.*

ekeí: *there, yonder*
The next life, so Plato, *Phaedo* 61e, 64a1; the intelligible world, the *kosmos noetos,* Plotinus, *Enn.* ii, 9, 4; ii, 4, 5.

éklampsis: *shining forth emanation, radiation*
In Plotinus the metaphorical explanation of the creation process (see *Enn.* v, 1, 6; iv, 3, 9, etc.) that flows from the One without diminution. It is a more specific metaphorical expression for the concept that finds its most general statement in procession (*proödos*, q.v.).

ekpýrōsis: *conflagration*
According to late authorities Heraclitus held a theory of periodic destruction of the world by fire (D.L. ix, 8). It was part of early Stoic doctrine (*SVF* i, 98), but was dropped by Panaetius (Philo, *De aet.* 76), who maintained the eternity of the *kosmos;* see *aphthartos, genesis.*

ékstasis: *standing out from, ecstasy, mystical union*
See *agnostos.*

élenchos: *scrutiny, refutation, interrogation*
See *aporia, katharsis, epagoge.*

enantía: *opposites*
1. The doctrine of the original existence of opposed natural substances first appears in Anaximander (Aristotle, *Phys.* 187a). Four are later isolated by Heraclitus (fr. 126), and posited as the four irreducible elements by Empedocles (fr. 17; see *stoicheion*). Opposition, as a

general force, plays a considerable role in both Pythagoras and Heraclitus. There is a list of ten sets of Pythagorean opposites in *Meta.* 986a that Aristotle identified with the elements (*stoicheia*). In Heraclitus the function of the opposites is both more explicit and more obscure: there is an essential unity (*logos*) of opposites, a unity that is not obvious, but that maintains the unity-plurality in the opposites (cf. frs. 1, 10, 54, 60, 88). Parmenides' theory of sensation is based on the excess of one of a set of opposites (Diels, fr. 28A46).

2. In the early *Phaedo* (70e) the passage from one opposite to another is the coping stone of Plato's theory of *genesis*, as it is to be for Aristotle (*Phys.* 188a–189b; see *genesis*). That these are qualities (*poiotetes*) and not substances (Forms) even for Plato is clear from *Phaedo* 102b–103b. Aristotle reduces the basic *enantia* involved in *genesis* among the elements to hot and cold, dry and moist (*De gen. et corr.* II, 329b–330a); see *poion, dynamis, genesis, logos, dike*.

enárgeia: *clarity, self-evidence*

Epicurean sensualism reduced all knowledge and all truth back to sensation (*aisthesis*) since what are described as the three criteria of truth, *aisthesis, prolepsis*, and *pathos*, are either one form or other of sensation itself (see *pathos*) or the result of repeated sensations (see *prolepsis*). Thus Epicurus finds himself in much the same position as Aristotle when the latter comes to speak of the primary premisses (*archai*) of a syllogism. Since there is nothing more basic than the *archai* of a syllogism, how is their validity to be established without recourse to circular argument? And just as Aristotle resorts to an intuitive grasp of the *archai* (see *epagoge, nous*), so Epicurus has *aisthesis* serve as the guarantor of its own validity, and this by reason of its clear and self-evident nature (*enargeia;* see D.L. x, 38, 48, 52; Sextus Empiricus, *Adv. Math.* VII, 216), a quality that is also present in *prolepsis* (D.L. x, 33).

For the extension of judgment beyond the clear evidence of the senses and the consequent possibility of error, see *doxa*.

éndoxon: *opinion, general opinion*

1. In the *Anal. post.* Aristotle sets forth in some detail a method of scientific procedure that he designates "demonstration" (*apodeixis*) and that can be described as the progress, via the syllogistic route, from known premisses to new, true, and valid conclusions. As theory it is admirable, but as method it is given the lie in most of the Aristotelian *corpus*, where the actual procedure followed is more often aporematic (see *aporia* and the schematic passage in *Meta.* 995a–b).

2. This latter course, which sees philosophy as starting from problems that demand solution, is thoroughly Socratic, as is the conse-

quent soliciting of opinions that are then dialectically worked toward a solution. What the historical Socrates did in conversation and Plato refined into the literary form of dialogue, Aristotle analyzed into method: "A syllogism is demonstrative [*apodeixis*] when it proceeds from premisses that are true and primary . . . ; it is dialectical when it reasons from *endoxa* . . . *Endoxa* are propositions that seem true to all or to the majority or to the wise" (*Top.* I, 100a–b).

3. It is this procedure, termed dialectical (*dialektike*, q.v.), that is frequently invoked by Aristotle in the course of his philosophizing, stripped, to be sure, of its ideal syllogistic rigors.

4. The definition of *endoxa* in the above cited text suggests that opinions have both a quantitative and qualitative basis. The first seems Socratic, i.e., canvassing what may be termed the "common-sense" view, and this approach is followed at various points in the ethical treatises (see *Eth. Nich.* VII, 1145b), as well as at the very opening of the *Metaphysics* (982a). In this latter text Aristotle is seeking the nature of *sophia* and the procedure he adopts is to start from commonly held views of what a wise man is. And he can take this tack because of a presumption that is left unspoken in Plato: the unitive and progressive nature of philosophy where the truth is not the preserve of any one man but the result of a continuous and cumulative investigation (*Meta.* 993a–b).

5. But the definition of *endoxa* in the *Topics* opens the possibility of an appeal to qualitative opinion, to the "professional" rather than the "common-sense" view, to "what seems true to the *sophoi*." Thus begins the history of philosophy, cast not in the role of an independent *historical* discipline, but as part of the method of *philosophy*, the major premiss, so to speak, in a dialectical syllogism. In Aristotle considerations of the opinions of his philosophical predecessors are always woven into his own investigations. The first to effect a physical separation of the historical material was Aristotle's own student Theophrastus whose *Opinions of the Natural Philosophers* was a free-standing work and the ancestor of all the succeeding doxographical collections (see Theophrastus' parallel detachment of the character sketches from their ethical context in his *Characters*).

6. The historical approach to philosophy is not completely unknown to Plato; he gives at least one review of the course of pre-Socratic speculation (*Soph.* 242b–249d; see *eidos*), and some of the central dialogues engage in dialectical discourse not with some representative of the *communis opinio*, but with dramatic recreations of an earlier generation of philosopher-sophists (e.g. Parmenides, Protagoras, Gorgias). The difference in Aristotle's attitude is expressed in the previously cited text of the *Metaphysics* (993a–b): philosophy is cumulative, evolutionary, progressive. Plato's delineations may be historical

but there is no evidence of a concept of philosophy as part of man's *social* history; indeed, the implications of the *anamnesis* (q.v.) theory is that each man must emerge from the Cave; mankind makes no progress in this regard.

7. Aristotle's historical perspectives appear early; the fragments (e.g. 3, 6, 7) of Book I of the early dialogue *On Philosophy* show Aristotle pursuing the evolution of *sophia* in a context even wider than that of the *Metaphysics*. Here he has before him a historical panorama that embraces not only the Greek sages of the past but a wider purview that takes into account not only the religio-mythical quest for truth (see *mythos, aporia*), but the wisdom of the East as well; in short, a tradition that begins with the Egyptians, passes through Zoroaster, and climaxes in Plato.

8. The fragmentary nature of the dialogue does not permit much speculation on the methods employed there, but there is abundant evidence for Aristotle's use of his predecessors in the preserved treatises. Book I of the *Metaphysics* includes a survey (983b–988a) of previous opinions on causality; *Physics* I has a similar review (184b–189b) on the *archai*. The *De anima* presents a history of the speculations on the nature of the soul (403b–411b), and *De gen. et corr.* on the nature of *genesis* (314a–317a). Each of these passages has its own proper thrust. At times, as in the *Metaphysics* passage, the *endoxa* provide a confirmation to Aristotle's own theorizing; or, again, as in the *De anima*, they set out and limit the terms of the problem, the solution of which will begin afresh in Book II (see 403b). But in every case the positions of other philosophers are presented from a problematic rather than from a historical point of view and, in addition, are subjected to a critique in greater or lesser detail, again from the problematic point of view. Thus the review in *Meta.* I, chaps. 3–6 is followed, in chaps. 8–10, by a criticism of previous speculation.

9. Aristotle's presentation and criticism of the work of his predecessors, and particularly of Plato, has been much criticized (see *agrapha dogmata*). The problem seems to arise from the fact that while Aristotle had a point of view that enabled him, or even demanded of him, that he incorporate the earlier history of the quest for *sophia* into his own investigations, it was this strictly procedural approach, which saw history only as *aporia* (q.v.) or *lysis*, that prevented him from doing strict justice to the historical reality of his predecessors' work.

10. In the period following Theophrastus two further developments become visible. First, the collection of *endoxa* that in Aristotle serves to delineate the evolutionary nature of philosophical enquiry is turned to new purposes. The marked strain of scepticism that powerfully shaped the problems and methods of post-Aristotelian thought down to the beginnings of the Christian era found a new use for the

doxographical technique, employing it now, in a manner quite the opposite of the Aristotelian usage, to reinforce, on historical grounds, a position of methodical doubt. How can it be, they ask, that we have any guarantee of certitude when the great philosophers of the past were in such contradiction on the basic questions of philosophy? Chapter and verse are cited and the cumulative effect is to persuade the reader that the only reasonable course is a sceptical suspension of judgment (*epoche;* see Cicero, *Acad. pr.* 48, 148 and Sextus Empiricus, *Pyrrh.* I, 36–38). Such is, for instance, the transparent purpose of the doxography in Cicero, *Acad. pr.* 36, 116–47, 146, borrowed, no doubt, from some former teacher in the sceptical New Academy.

11. The New Academy also plays a part in the historiography of the period. The polemic of the age of Cicero is dominated by a struggle over the orthodoxy of the various schools. Philosophy had already passed into its "classical" stage and the battle for a protective place under the mantles of the past masters was at its height, a battle in which one of the favored techniques was the writing—and rewriting—of the history of philosophy. Again the chief witness are the pages of the *Academica* of Cicero. Two views emerge, the Sceptic and the Stoic. The first sees the pre-Socratics as a series of proto-Sceptics, the movement coming to a climax in the *aporia* (q.v.) of Socrates. Plato's dogmatism is more apparent than real and the New Academy from Arcesilas to Carneades is in the mainstream of Socratism, as were the Cyrenaics (*Acad. post.* 12, 44–46; 23, 72–74, 76). The Stoic view of history, derived from the Academic Antiochus by Cicero but probably attributable to the Stoic Panaetius, tends to disregard the pre-Socratics and begin the modern philosophical tradition with Socrates whose alleged scepticism was, in any event, nothing more than irony. It then proceeds to syncretize the Old Academy and Peripatos into a single system differing in name but essentially in agreement (*Acad. post.* 4, 15–18). The system of Zeno derives from that source and is nothing more than a correction of Platonism (*ibid.* 9, 25; 12, 43), while the Arcesilan New Academy is really an aberration (*Acad. pr.* 6, 16). It is in this fashion that Middle Stoicism can locate itself in the Platonic tradition (with visible philosophical effects in Poseidonius; see *noesis* 17 and *psyche* 29) and Antiochus effect his "restoration" of the Old Academy by championing Stoic doctrines (see Cicero's apt characterization in *Acad. pr.* 43, 132).

enérgeia: *functioning, activity, act, actualization*
1. The technical use of *energeia* is an Aristotelian innovation and a correlative of his concept of *dynamis* (q.v.) as capacity. The analysis of *genesis* (q.v.) in the *Physics* pursues the approach already set out by Plato in his account of precosmic *genesis* in the *Timaeus*, i.e., the passage of opposed powers or qualities in a substratum, with

the additional Aristotelian refinement of privation (*steresis*) that answers Parmenides' objections on the subject of nonbeing. But at the end of this treatment Aristotle refers to another line of approach, which he will develop more fully elsewhere, viz., an analysis based on *dynamis* and *energeia* (*Phys.* I, 191b).

2. This analysis, explained in the *Metaphysics*, presents methodological difficulties since neither *dynamis* nor *energeia* is susceptible of definition in the ordinary sense, but can only be illustrated by example and analogy (*Meta.* 1048a). But it is, nonetheless, of prime importance in that it transcends the mere kinetics of the *Physics:* we are now in the heart of an analysis of being (*ibid.* 1045b–1046a), an analysis that will enable Aristotle to deal with the transcendent, imperishable entities of the superlunary world and the Prime Mover.

3. The relationship between *kinesis* and *energeia* is first explored. We are told that it is movement that first suggests the notion of *energeia* (*ibid.* 1047a), but that there remains a difference in that *kinesis* is essentially incomplete (*ateles*), i.e., it is a process toward some yet unachieved goal (note that the *kinesis* of the elements ceases when they have reached their "natural place"; see *stoicheion*), while *energeia* is complete; it is not process but activity (*ibid.* 1048b).

4. Equally illuminating is Aristotle's derivation of *energeia* from function (*ergon*, q.v.). Function is that which a thing is naturally suited to do, i.e., the making or doing for which it has a capacity (*dynamis*). Thus we have the notion of *en-ergeia*, the state of being at work, functioning (*ibid.* 1050a). Quickly Aristotle binds in the related notion of end (*telos*). Since function is the end, *energeia* is obviously related to *entelecheia* (q.v.), being in a state of completion. In this way *energeia* is described and delimited: it is the functioning of a capacity, its fulfillment and actualization, normally accompanied with pleasure (for the ethical implications of this, see *hedone*), and prior to potency in definition, time, and substance (*ibid.* 1049b–1050a).

5. The priority of *energeia* in substance introduces important new considerations. *Dynamis* is the capacity of a thing to be other than it is; it does not exist necessarily. This may refer to either its *ousia* or the various *dynameis* toward changes of quantity, quality, or place. Thus the eternal movement of the heavenly bodies, being eternal, is pure *energeia;* it cannot be otherwise even though they may have *dynameis* for accidental change of place (*ibid.* 1050b; the eternal cyclic genesis of the elements is a *mimesis* of this; see *genesis*).

6. At the end of this dialectical process stands the ultimate *energeia* that in the last resort stands behind and actualizes every *dynamis* in the universe, the Prime Mover (see *kinoun*) whose absolutely pure *energeia* is *noesis:* "Life is the *energeia* of *nous;* he is that *energeia*" (*ibid.* 1072b).

énnoia: *concept*
According to Stoic epistemology (*SVF* II, 83) man is born with
his reason like a "papyrus role ready for writing" (the first appearance
of the *tabula rasa* image). Through sensation various images (*phantasia*) are presented to the reason for its "apprehension" (*katalepsis*). If
these are apprehended and held, they become, in effect, concepts (*ennoiai*) of the mind. Of these some occur naturally, i.e., without formal
instruction, and are termed "preconceptions" (*prolepsis*, q.v.); others
develop through formal education. The *ennoiai* are mere concepts; they
have no extramental or concrete reality (*SVF* I, 65; D.L. VII, 61), but
they do serve as an important criterion of truth, or rather one class of
them, the "common concepts" (*koinai ennoiai, notiones communes*),
which are identical with the naturally acquired, though not innate,
prolepseis (*SVF* II, 473). They embrace a certain knowledge of the
first principles of morality (*SVF* III, 619, 218), of God (*ibid.* II, 1009),
and of the afterlife (Cicero, *Tusc.* I, 13, 30–I, 14, 31).
For the connection between the concept and its name, see *onoma*.
On the possibility that the Platonic Form may be only a concept
(*noema*), see *eidos, noeton;* for its role in Stoicism, *noesis* 16.

entelécheia: *state of completion or perfection, actuality*
1. Although Aristotle normally uses *entelecheia*, which is probably his own coinage, as a synonym for *energeia* (q.v.), there is a
passage (*Meta.* 1050a) that at least suggests that the two terms,
though closely connected, are not perfectly identical. They are related
through the notion of *ergon* (q.v.): *ergon* is the function of a capacity
(*dynamis*) and so its completion and fulfillment (*telos*, q.v.). Thus the
state of functioning (*energeia*) "tends toward" the state of completion
(*en-telecheia*), especially since Aristotle has already pointed out (*ibid.*
1048b) that *energeia* differs from *kinesis* in that the latter is incomplete
(*ateles*), while the former is not.
2. The most curious use of *entelecheia* in Aristotle is probably its
substitution for *eidos* in the definition of *soul*, which thus becomes (*De
an.* II, 412a): "the first *entelecheia* of a natural body that potentially
has life."

enthousiasmós: *divine indwelling, possession*
See *mantike.*

epagōgé: *leading in, leading on, induction (Socratic,*
Aristotelian; for Platonic "induction," see
synagoge)
1. Aristotle, in a passage where he is describing the origin of the
theory of Forms, remarks that Socrates was the first to employ "induc-

tive arguments" (*epaktikoi logoi; Meta.* 1078b). But to understand *epaktikoi* in the sense of an Aristotelian "induction" (*epagoge*) is probably misleading since neither Socrates' methodology nor Plato's terminology point to a strictly Aristotelian usage. The developed Aristotelian *epagoge* is defined, in its most general terms, as "the leading on from particulars to the universal [*katholou*] and from the known to the unknown" (*Top.* VIII, 156a).

2. Plato uses *epagein* once in a sense akin to this (*Pol.* 278a), but his more common usage is in the sense of "cite" or "adduce" (see *Rep.* 364c, *Laws* 823a). In the dialogues most closely associated with the historical Socrates there is frequent reliance on individual instances, but they are cited either for purposes of refutation or correction (see *Rep.* 331e–336a) or to establish analogies (see Xenophon, *Mem.* III, 3, 9), in both instances a kind of testing device that is part of the Socratic method of *elenchos* (see *aporia, katharsis*), and that, by skillful use, might eventually reach definition, or, again, merely end in *aporia* (see *Theaet.* 210b–d).

3. The most fundamental import of *epagoge* in Aristotle is its role as the foundation stone of all scientific knowledge (*episteme*). It is through an induction of individual sense experiences (*aistheseis*) that we gain our knowledge of both the universal concept (*katholou*, q.v.) and the universal proposition (*arche*, q.v.), and it is these latter that serve as the undemonstrable premisses of all demonstration (*Anal. post.* II, 99b–100b; see *Meta.* 980a–981a). This *epagoge* is not a discursive process and, unlike complete induction, it cannot be reduced to a type of syllogism; rather it is an intuitive grasp of the mind, which Aristotle terms *nous* and which is as trustworthy as demonstration itself.

4. The point of Aristotelian *epagoge* is that the universal resides within the material confines of the individual sense data (*Phys.* I, 184a), and it is by repeated exposures to this sense experience that the mind comes to grasp the higher intelligibility of the universal (*Anal. post.* I, 87b–88a). But because of its intimate connection with sensation, induction remains both more convincing and more popular in its appeal (*Top.* I, 105a; compare *gnorimon*).

5. There is, finally, still another type of induction that Aristotle treats at some length, perfect induction or the canvassing of *all* the instances of a general proposition (*Anal. pr.* II, 68b). But here he is dealing with the reduction of induction to syllogistic form, something he can achieve only by means of a perfect induction.

epieíkeia: *equity*
See *dike*.

epistémē: 1] (*true and scientific*) *knowledge* (*opposed to doxa*) ; 2] *an organized body of knowledge, a science;* 3] *theoretical knowledge* (*opposed to praktike and poietike*)

1. The materialism of the pre-Socratics did not permit them to distinguish between types of knowledge; even Heraclitus, who insisted that his *logos* (q.v.) that is hidden, could be grasped only by the intelligence, was, when he came to explain *nous* (q.v.), a thorough-going materialist: knowledge was sensation of the like-knows-like type (see *homoios*). Heraclitus certainly held to the permanent order of the universe, surrounded as it was by an obvious process of change, but the succeeding philosophers preferred to emphasize the element of change ("all is in flux"; see *rhoe*), and the consequent worthlessness of sense knowledge (see Plato, *Crat.* 402a; Aristotle, *Phys.* VIII, 253b). A proponent of this denigration of *aisthesis* was Cratylus (see Aristotle, *Meta.* 1010a) who was a formative influence on the young Plato (*idem* 987a).

2. Sensualist perception theories were discredited, and when Socrates describes just such a process in *Phaedo* 96b, he is not happy with it; but it does suggest that the distinction between *doxa* and *episteme* was pre-Socratic. In the *Phaedo* context the differentiation does not appear to be any more than a distinction between levels of conviction; but the true father of the radical distinction that appears from Plato onward is the one pre-Socratic unconcerned with "saving the phenomena," Parmenides, whose poem sets over against the world of perception and opinion the realm of pure being and pure thought (*noema*, fr. 8, lines 34–36, 50–51). This is also the realm of Plato's *eide* (q.v.), immutable, everlasting, the ground of true knowledge (*episteme*). *Eidos* and *episteme* are locked together from their first implicit appearance in the *Meno* (as a corollary of *anamnesis*, q.v.), through a similar argument in *Phaedo* 75b–76 that strongly insists that true knowledge (*episteme*) of the Forms cannot come through the senses and so we must be born with it. The broadest statement of the collocation *episteme/eide* vs. *doxa/aistheta* is given in *Rep.* 476a–480a, and illustrated in the following Diagram of the Line (509d–511e) and the Allegory of the Cave (514a–521b). Sensation (*aisthesis*) reasserts its claim to be true knowledge in *Theaet.* 186d; this is rejected as well as the alternative "true judgment accompanied by an account" (*logos*, q.v.), *ibid.* 187b, but this too is refined and criticized (*ibid.* 201c–210d). The answer unfolds in the sequel, the *Sophist:* the only true knowledge is a knowledge of the *eide* and its method is dialectic (*dialektike*, q.v.). Even as late as the *Timaeus* the distinction between *episteme* and *doxa* and their differing objects is stressed (29b–d).

3. Plato's transcendent *eide* are replaced by Aristotle's immanent variety (see *eidos*), and the change is accompanied by a shift in the object of *episteme*. For Aristotle true scientific knowledge is a knowledge of causes (*aitia*), which are necessarily true (*Anal. post.* I, 76b), while opinion (*doxa*) is about the contingent (*symbebekos, ibid.* I, 88b). *Episteme* is demonstrative, syllogistic knowledge (see *apodeixis, ibid.* I, 71b), and sense knowledge is a necessary condition for it (*ibid.* I, 81a–b; see *epagoge*). This is all in a logical context; the causes mentioned above are the premisses of a syllogism and the causes of the conclusion. Aristotle takes up *episteme* from an ontological viewpoint in the opening of the *Metaphysics;* here too *episteme* is a knowledge of causes, but these *aitia* are causes of being, and the knowledge of the ultimate causes is the highest type of *episteme*, wisdom (*sophia*, q.v.); for *episteme* as a mental activity, see *noesis*.

4. In *Meta.* 1025b–1026a Aristotle gives his breakdown of *episteme* in the sense of an organized body of rational knowledge with its own proper object; the alignment is as follows:

Episteme

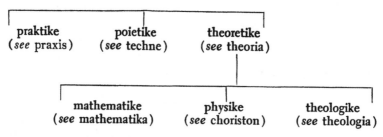

praktike (*see* praxis)   poietike (*see* techne)   theoretike (*see* theoria)

mathematike (*see* mathematika)   physike (*see* choriston)   theologike (*see* theologia)

For another, later division, see *philosophia;* for the Platonic "division of the sciences," see *techne*.

5. Aristotle frequently uses *episteme* alone for *episteme theoretike* in contrast with practical or productive "science," e.g. *Eth. Nich.* VI, 1139b; see *praxis, techne*.

epistrophé: *return*

The "return" of the Platonic tradition is distinct from, but connected with, the epistemological problem of knowing God (for the connection, see Proclus, *Elem. theol.*, prop. 39). It differs in that it is a function of desire (*orexis*). Its ontological ground is the identification of the transcendent One with the Good (Plato, *Rep.* 509b, *Phil.* 20d; Plotinus, *Enn.* v, 5, 13; Proclus, *Elem. theol.*, prop. 8) that is necessarily an object of desire, and the identity of the efficient and final cause, the effect, in Middle Platonism, of combining Plato's *demiourgos* with

Aristotle's *nous*. The dialectic of the *epistrophe* is the reverse of that of procession (*proödos*), and is worked out in Proclus, *Elem. theol.*, props. 31–39.

epithymía: *desire*

The desiderative (*epithymetikon*) is one of the three parts of the soul in Plato's *Republic* IV, 434d–441c (a distinction that Aristotle finds unsatisfactory [*De an.* 432a–b], but that is maintained by Plotinus, *Enn.* I, 1, 5 and 6). It is perishable and, according to *Timaeus* 70d–e, is located below the midriff. Aristotle makes *epithymia* but one of the three operations of the desiderative faculty (see *orexis*) of the sense-endowed soul (*De an.* 414b). The object of *epithymia* is the pleasant (*ibid.*). Epicurus divides desires into the natural and necessary, natural but not necessary, and neither (D.L. x, 127; Cicero, *Tusc.* v, 33, 93). For the Stoics *epithymia* is one of four chief affections (with pain, pleasure, and fear) (*SVF* I, 211); and just as fear is a flight from anticipated evil, desire is an appetite for an anticipated good (*SVF* III, 391); see also *hedone*.

érgon: *work, deed, product, function*

1. *Ergon*, the common Greek word for something done or made, is used by the philosophers in a twofold sense: either as the activity of a thing or as the product of that activity. Aristotle frequently marks the distinction (e.g. *Eth. Nich.* I, 1094a) and it leads him to the further point, a capital one in his ethical speculations, that some activities have as their end (*telos*) a product (not necessarily an "object"; a frequent Aristotelian example is that health is the *ergon* of medicine), while others have as their *telos* the activity itself (see *Eth. Eud.* 1219a). This is, in general, Aristotle's distinction between the activity known as *poiesis* and that called *praxis* (q.v.; see *episteme, techne*).

2. This distinction between *poiesis* and *praxis*, production and action, is an ethically oriented one, but it has metaphysical implications that go far deeper. These are set out in *Meta.* 1050a where Aristotle refines the concept of *ergon* into that of "being at work" (*en-ergeia*). This latter state is the end (*telos*) of being (at this point *energeia* is related to *en-telecheia*, "being at completion"), whether the activity issues in an external *ergon* or not. The only difference is that in *poiesis* the *energeia* is in the thing made, while *praxis* is the energizing of the doer. Thus movement exists in the thing moved, but sight is an *energeia* in the seer and life an *energeia* in the soul (compare the definition of soul under *psyche*).

3. This identification of *telos/ergon/energeia* (and, as the same passage continues, with *eidos* and *ousia*) leads to another important meaning of *ergon* as the function or proper activity of a thing. Prelimi-

nary here is the use of *ergon*, activity, as opposed to the things that happen to a subject (*pathemata;* see *De an.* I, 403a and *pathos, paschein*). Both of them, the *erga* and the *pathemata*, are important from a methodological point of view since they, together with the *dynamis* (q.v.), define the field of study of the *physikos* or natural philosopher (*De an.* I, 403b, *De coelo* III, 307b; compare *aphairesis*). Thence the usage shades off to proper activity or function both in a physical (see *De gen. anim.* 731a) and an ethical sense (*Eth. Nich.* I, 1097b), and even in more general expressions, like "the proper function of philosophy" (*Phys.* II, 194b) and "the function of dialectic" (*Soph. El.* 83a–b).

4. *Ergon* as function plays its role in Aristotle's ethic, just as it had for Plato before him. Both men are concerned to set up a norm of behavior, and both resort to phenomenological standards, attempting to connect excellence (*arete,* q.v.) with function (*ergon*). Plato defines this latter as "that which the thing in question does alone or best" (*Rep.* 353a) and has excellence consist in the specific power that allows that function to operate well. Aristotle's approach is somewhat different. For him *arete* is a certain high level of performance with regard to the function, a high level that is guaranteed by not taking any man as the norm but rather keying function on the performance of the "serious man" (*spoudaios; Eth. Nich.* I, 1098a).

5. What, then, is the *ergon* of man? For Plato it is the activities that only man can perform: management, rule, deliberation; and the *arete* peculiar to man that allows him to perform them well is *dike* (q.v.). For Aristotle the *ergon* of man is an "*energeia* of the soul according to *logos*," and, since the good of a thing is described in terms of its function, the good of man is this activity on a level of excellence (*Eth. Nich.* 1098a).

érōs: *desire, love*

1. Eros is one of the many personifications that appear in the prephilosophical cosmogonies. But unlike most of the others that represent states, e.g. Night, Chaos, Earth, Heaven (see the remarks of Aristotle in *Meta.* 1071b), Eros is a force. In the Orphic cosmogonies he unites all and from these unions is born the race of the immortal gods (see Aristophanes, *Birds* 700–702); in Hesiod he is among the first to emerge from Chaos and draws all else together (*Theog.* 116–120); according to Pherecydes (as reported by Proclus, *In Tim.* II, 54), when Zeus wishes to create (*demiourgein*) he changes into Eros. Eros, then, is a motive force on a sexual model used to explain the "marriage" and "birth" of the mythological elements, a species of "First Mover" in the ancient cosmogonies, and was recognized as such

by Aristotle (*Meta.* 984b). And even as the mythological trappings began to fall away in the speculations of the *physikoi* Eros, the mover, or now, more frequently, Aphrodite, continued to play a role in conjoining the opposite powers (see *enantion, dynamis*). Such is, for example, the case in Empedocles where it is Love (*philia*) and Aphrodite that unite the elements (fr. 17, lines 20–26; Diels 31A28; Aristotle, *Meta.* 985a, 1075b, sees moral forces at work as well). In Parmenides she is the *daimon* (q.v.) "who guides all" (fr. 12, line 3), an image that persists in Greek literature (see Euripides, *Hipp.* 447–450, 1278–1281) and is still visible in Lucretius' opening invocation of Venus "who alone governs the nature of things" (1, 21).

2. All of these instances of the employment of love have to do with the raising of a human emotion to the level of a cosmological force, an operation that is particularly clear to Empedocles (fr. 17, lines 22–24). And in one of the most extended treatments of *eros* by a philosopher, the *Symposium* of Plato, the same approach is still in evidence. The speech of Eryximachus (185e–188e) shows the extent of this principle of "attraction" in nature, and this and similar notions, familiar to both the mythologers and the *physikoi*, fill most of the other discourses. The speech of Socrates, however, strikes out in a new direction where human love is used as an important moral and epistemological concept.

3. Socrates as "the lover" (*erotikos*) was a commonplace at Athens. He appears as such in Xenophon (*Mem.* II, 6, 28; *Symp.* IV, 27) and the notion is frequently combined with the familiar irony: I know nothing, save about *eros* (see *Theag.* 128b, *Lys.* 204b, and compare Alcibiades' remark in *Symp.* 216d). That there were physically erotic traits in Socrates' relationships with the young men of Athens can scarcely be doubted; but his *eros* had another side as well, as Alcibiades, who had tried to seduce him (*Symp.* 217a–219d), discovered; Socrates could distinguish between passion and its object.

4. The philosophical question of love, here called *philia*, friendship, is first raised in the *Lysis* where Socrates, in searching for a definition of this attraction between men, suggests that perhaps it is analogous to the attraction of like to like (*homoios*, q.v.) that had already been enunciated by the poets and the *physikoi* (*Lys.* 214a–c; for the prime importance of this principle in perception theories, see *aisthesis, passim*). This is rejected, as is its converse, that unlike is attracted to unlike (216b). He settles, finally and without a great deal of conviction, on a principle that went back to medical theory and had important applications in contemporary theories of pleasure (see *hedone*): desire (*epithymia*), and its consequent, love, is directed toward the filling of a lack (*endeia*) and its object, therefore, is something that

is appropriate (*oikeion;* compare the later development of this in Stoicism under *oikeiosis*), i.e., something that is neither identical nor completely dissimilar and yet deficient in our constitution.

5. The theme is resumed in the *Symposium:* love is a desire directed toward the beautiful (*kallos*) and necessarily involves the notion of a want or lack (*endeia;* 200e–201b). Socrates then begins to cite the doctrine learned from a wise prophetess, Diotima. Eros, now reinvested with the trappings of myth, is a great *daimon* (q.v.), one of the intermediaries (*metaxu*) between the divine and the mortal (202e). Then, suddenly, the Socratic irony is explained: Eros is also midway between wisdom (*sophia*) and ignorance in that the man who has no sense of his own deficiency will have no love of wisdom (*philosophia;* 204a). Love is defined as the desire that the good be one's own forever (206a), the quest of a mortal nature to be immortal (207d) that it accomplishes by begetting (*genesis;* compare Aristotle's somewhat similar use of *genesis* under *kinoun* 9).

6. At *Symp.* 209e Diotima pauses (a break seen by some as the dividing line between Socratic and Platonic *eros*) and then launches into a final treatment of the true *eros.* Concourse with beautiful bodies begets beautiful discourses (*logoi*). The lover weans himself away from a single body and becomes a lover of all beautiful bodies (in *Charm.* 154b Socrates had confessed that all youths seemed beautiful to him), thence to beautiful souls, laws and observances, and knowledge (*episteme*), always freeing himself of bondage to the particular, until "suddenly" there is revealed to him the vision of Beauty itself (211b; the suddenness of the vision is stressed again in *Ep.* VII, 341). This is immortality.

7. What has been revealed is, of course, the transcendent *eide.* Socrates has much more to say on the purely psychological side of love in his first speech in the *Phaedrus* (237b–241d; defined, 238b–c, as an irrational desire toward the enjoyment of beauty). But he later recants and promises a palinode (243b–c), and it is here that *eros* and *philosophia* are rejoined. The irrationality of love is really a type of divine madness (*theia mania,* 245b–c; so too is *mantike,* q.v., which explains the presence of Diotima in the *Symposium*), and it is present in the soul as a reflex of the remembrance (*anamnesis,* q.v.) that the soul has of the *eide* that were revealed to her before her "loss of wings" (248c; see *kathodos*). It is the soul of the philosopher that first regains these wings by the exercise of her recollection of the *eide* and by governing her life accordingly (249c–d); the philosopher is stimulated to this by the vision of earthly beauty. It is beauty that particularly stirs our recollection because it operates through the sharpest of our senses, sight (249d–250d).

8. Platonic *eros* is a twofold activity: it is a communication with

and a movement toward the transcendent world of the *eide*, and at the same time it is the pouring out into the soul of the beloved, whose (male) beauty is an image of God, those "streams from Zeus" that enter his own soul (252c–253a). The beloved does not disappear into a mist of sublimation but remains a necessary partner in the quest for the *eide* (compare *Ep.* VII, 341c–d). What is sublimated in these relationships that are archetypally represented by Socrates and his young disciples is the purely sexual activity. Plato is aware that restraint here is difficult and not always successful, but he is not inclined to judge too harshly (255b–256e).

9. After Plato *eros* and its connected notions disappear from the exalted positions given them in these dialogues and take up a more modest stand in ethics under the rubric of friendship (Aristotle devotes Book VIII of the *Eth. Nich.* to *philia;* its wider aspects, *humanitas* and *philanthropia*, were much in vogue in Stoicism: Cicero, *De off.* I, 50–51 and see *oikeiosis*) or that of passionate love. Epicurus, and, indeed, most of the philosophers, were opposed to this latter on the grounds that it destroyed the *ataraxia* (q.v.) of the serious thinker (see D.L. x, 118), but the violent diatribe directed against *cupido* by Lucretius (IV, 1058–1287) suggests a personal rather than a philosophical *aporia*.

10. As might be expected the Platonic *eros* reappears in Plotinus, prefaced, in *Enn.* I, 6, by an aesthetic of sensible things. Plato had attempted something similar in the *Hippias Major* where beauty is defined first in terms of the useful and then of the pleasurable (295c, 298a; compare the parallel argument in *Gorg.* 474d). Plotinus goes another way; beauty (*kallos*) is not, as it was for the Stoics (see Cicero, *Tusc.* IV, 33), a question of measure (*metron*) or the symmetry of parts since this would be to suggest that beauty is confined to composites and cannot explain the beauty of a single star in the heaven at night. Plotinus' own explanation (I, 6, 2–3) is a curious blend of the Platonic transcendent Form that is shared (*koinonia, methexis*) by the object and the immanent Aristotelian *eidos* or Stoic *logos*. But the true essence of beauty is simplicity, a simplicity that is found preeminently in the One (VI, 7, 32). From these sensible beauties one passes, in approved Platonic fashion, to practices and sciences, thence by a purification (*katharsis*, q.v.) of the soul to the contemplation of the highest beauty that is the Good (I, 6, 6). To accomplish this the soul must put off the garments acquired by it during its descent (*kathodos*, q.v. and compare *ochema*). We see the Beautiful with an interior vision by becoming assimilated to it (I, 6, 9).

11. All of this is markedly Platonic in image and language. But there has been an equally notable shift in emphasis. Philosophy as a communal project between lovers is no longer in evidence in Plotinus for whom the return to the One is a "flight of the alone to the Alone"

(VI, 9, 11). The method of Plotinus is no longer dialogue, with its diastolic implications, but introspection, and his goal is an *unio mystica* (see *hen* 13). In Plato the veneration of Aphrodite Pandemus is one stage, and perhaps a stage that is never transcended, toward the worship of Aphrodite Urania. In Plotinus, who was "ashamed of being in a body" (Porphyry, *Vita Plot.* 1), the two goddesses are at odds. Earthly love is compared by him to the rape of a virgin on the way to her Father (VI, 9, 9).

éthos: *character, habitual way of life*
Heraclitus: "A man's *ethos* is his *daimon*," Diels, fr. 119. In Plato it is a result of habit (*Laws* 792e), and moral rather than intellectual (*dianoia*) in Aristotle (*Eth. Nich.* 1139a). Types of *ethos* at various ages in life are described by Aristotle, *Rhet.* II, chaps. 12–14. In Stoicism *ethos* is the source of behavior, *SVF* I, 203.

étymon: *true, true sense of a word, etymology*
See *onoma*.

eudaimonía: *happiness*
It does not, according to Democritus, consist in external goods (Diels, frs. B170, 171, 40). The just man is happy, so Plato, *Rep.* 353b–354a, and the best life is the happiest (*idem, Laws* 664c). Happiness is the ultimate practical good for men (Aristotle, *Eth. Nich.* I, 1097a–b), defined, *ibid.* I, 1098a, 1100b. It consists in intellectual contemplation, *ibid.* 1177a–1178a. In Stoicism happiness results from the harmonious life (D.L. VII, 8; see *nomos*), yet it is not an end (*telos*), but a concomitant state (Seneca, *De vita beata* 8 and 13; Plotinus, *Enn.* I, 4, 4; I, 4, 14); see *theoria*.

eupátheia: *good or innocent emotion, affect*
See *apatheia*.

exōterikoí lógoi: *external discourses, popular works*
1. One of the literary problems attendant upon the study of Plato's philosophy is the possibility that at least part of his thinking may not have been committed to writing, i.e., to expression in dialogue form (see *agrapha dogmata*). In the case of Aristotle we know for a certainty that the extant treatises do not represent his entire literary output. There were known in antiquity a series of dialogues published by Aristotle while still a member of the Academy, and the preserved fragments of which indicate a considerably more Platonic outlook on various problems, most notoriously his theory of the soul, than that which emerges from a reading of the treatises.

2. Modern scholarship locates the dialogues within the problem of Aristotle's philosophical evolution, but an ancient literary tradition, beginning with Cicero (*De fin.* v, 12; compare Aulus Gellius, *Noctes Att.* xx, 5, 1) read the differences between the dialogues and the treatises not as a function of an intellectual evolution, but rather as the difference between two distinct, albeit contemporary, types of literary composition: external discourses (*exoterikoi logoi*), i.e., quasi-popular works designed for a wide audience, and lectures (*akroatikoi logoi*) delivered in the Lyceum to more technically trained groups of students.

3. *Exoterikoi logoi* are, indeed, cited in the preserved treatises, and while some of the references conveniently fit what we know of a given dialogue (e.g. the reference in *Eth. Nich.* I, 1102a *could* fit the *Protrepticus*), there are other instances (e.g. *Phys.* 217b and *Pol.* 1323a when compared with *Eth. Nich.* I, 1098b) where it cannot be so, and the meaning here of *exoterikoi logoi* is more akin to "arguments current outside the Peripatetic School."

g

génesis: birth, coming-into-being, becoming (as opposed to being), process, passage to a contrary, substantial change

1. Even in its earliest attested usage (*Il.* xiv, 201, 246) *genesis* is something more than a biological process and the two meanings of "birth" and "beginning in being" are intertwined in the pre-Socratic texts. The presence of the word in the extant fragment of Anaximander has been attributed by most to the language of the Peripatetic epitomizer of the text (Theophrastus via Simplicius, *Phys.* 24, 17), but both the expression and the notion are unmistakable in Xenophanes (frs. 29, 30) and Heraclitus (frs. 3, 36) in speaking of the "birth" and "death" of physical bodies.

2. The pre-Socratics were immensely interested in change. Having decided upon one or a number of elemental principles (see *arche*), either natural bodies, like water or air, or substantivized versions of what were thought of as "powers" but were later to be considered as qualities (see *dynamis, pathos, poion*), e.g. the hot, the dry, etc., they discussed the mechanics of how one could become the other. This is

what Aristotle was later to call "absolute becoming" (*genesis haple*), change in the category of substance as opposed to the various changes (*metabolai*, q.v.) in the categories of accident (*De gen. et corr.* 1, 319b–320a). Thus in Anaximenes, who posited *aer* (q.v.) as his *arche*, simple bodies come into being from the condensation and rarefaction of *aer* (Simplicius, *Phys.* 24, 26), while for Anaximander, whose *arche* is an indefinite substance (*apeiron*, q.v.), the *genesis* of perceptibles involves some sort of separation process (Aristotle, *Phys.* 1, 187a).

3. In all of these thinkers, for whom life and movement are inherent in things, there is an insistence on change—Heraclitus is only the loudest voice in a chorus—and on the clearly perceptible fact that one body becomes another. The most eloquent proof of this is the fact that to deny change Parmenides had to deny perception.

4. But Parmenides did not hesitate to do either, and henceforward *genesis*, which had been a given of sense, becomes a problem. Parmenides explicitly denies the possibility of *any* type of change since coming-to-be in any of its modes implies the logically indefensible proposition of passing from nonbeing to being, and nothing can come from nonbeing (fr. 8, lines 19–21; compare lines 38–41 that would seem to imply the pre-Parmenidean technical use of *genesis;* see *on*).

5. Thus the Parmenidean "Way of Truth"; his successors, however, seem to have taken their cue from the "Way of Seeming." By abandoning the strict monism of Parmenides and resorting to the older doctrine of "opposites" (*enantia*, q.v.), both Empedocles and Anaxagoras were able to restore at least a secondary *genesis* in terms of the interplay of these opposite qualities or elements (*stoicheia*, q.v.). Simple coming-into-being (i.e., from nonbeing) is still unthinkable, but by resorting to various degrees of mixture (*krasis*) and association (*synkrisis*) composite bodies could come into being (Empedocles, fr. 9; Anaxagoras, fr. 17; see Aristotle's résumé in *Phys.* 1, 187a; see *stoicheion*).

6. The case of Anaxagoras is quite complex. First he is concerned to observe the Parmenidean prohibition against absolute *genesis*. Nothing can proceed from nothing and so everything that seems to become something else must have been that something else to begin with, or, as Anaxagoras himself put it, "all things have a portion of everything" (fr. 12; in fr. 11 he excludes *nous* that is external to the system; for the reasons, see *kinesis, kinoun*); and so it follows (fr. 17) that there is no such thing as *genesis* or *phthora* but only aggregation (*synkrisis*) and separation (*apokrisis*), i.e., by the arrangement of preexistent matter. *Genesis*, understood as Anaxagoras understood it, begins, then, from a primordial mixture (*meigma*), the ingredients of which are imperceptible (save perhaps air and fire, which have already begun to predominate in this nonhomogeneous mass) and are infinite

in number (fr. 1). In it were the various Milesian *dynameis* (q.v.), like the hot and the cold, the moist and the dry, etc., as well as the Empedoclean *stoicheia* and natural composite bodies, and what Anaxagoras calls "seeds" (*spermata*) (fr. 4).

7. These latter are the true *stoicheia* of Anaxagoras (Aristotle, *De coelo* III, 302a; see *stoicheion*) and, like the original *meigma* itself, they contain portions of everything. The original mixture was without movement, firmly clasped in a Parmenidean death grip. As in Empedocles, *kinesis* comes from the outside, supplied by *nous* that causes the mixture to rotate. The speed of the rotation effects the separation (*apokrisis*) of the "seeds" (fr. 12) that are qualitatively different (see fr. 4 and *pathos*). By aggregation (*synkrisis*) these are formed into compound bodies wherein predominate one or other of the types of "seed" (see fr. 12 and Aristotle, *Phys.* I, 187a).

8. The Atomists, by eliminating the *dynameis*, considerably simplified the operation (though they had marked difficulties in "saving the phenomena"; see *pathos, stoicheion*). The *atoma* are brought into collision by their eternal motion (see *kinesis*) and it is by this contact (*haphe*) that the higher composite bodies are formed. Some *atoma* bounce back into the void; others, because they are "hooked" or angled, catch together and, as further collisions result, perceptible bodies are built up (Simplicius, *De coelo* 295, 11). This is the Atomists' version of the composition of bodies by association (*synkrisis*) and it reappears, in more sophisticated form, in Epicureanism (D.L. x, 43; Lucretius II, 85–111). Here there is an attempt to explain the three states of matter in terms of density expressed in the distance between the atoms in the "association," with the added refinement that certain bodies (e.g. liquids) result from the containment of one type of atom within a sheath (*stegazon*) composed of another type, an explanation that also applies to the enclosing of the soul within the body (D.L. x, 65, 66; see *holon* 9).

9. That *genesis* had become the central question of post-Parmenidean philosophy is clear from Socrates' remarks in *Phaedo* 96a, a question that, as the same passage indicates, was being pursued in terms of a search for causes (*aitia*, q.v.) and had intrigued the young Socrates. For Plato himself *genesis* is a somewhat secondary problem in the light of his distinction between the *eide*, the realm of true being (*ontos on*), and this sensible world that is characterized by becoming (*Tim.* 27d–28a). Thus being is the only subject for true knowledge (*episteme*), while *genesis* can afford nothing better than opinion (*doxa*), the "likely account" of the *Timaeus*.

10. But having thus paid his debt to Parmenides, Plato does, on occasion, turn his attention to *genesis*: once in the context of attempting to elucidate his theory of participation (*methexis*) in the *Phaedo*, and,

again, in his account of the *kosmos aisthetos* in the *Timaeus*. The first, in *Phaedo* 102b–105b, which is enormously interesting as being the forerunner of Aristotle's own theory of *genesis*, rests on a premiss that is not generally emphasized by Plato, i.e., the immanence, in some form or other, of the *eide* (see *eidos*); the passage is replete with expressions like "the smallness in us." There is, moreover, the insistence that the immanent *eide* are not themselves subject to *genesis*. *Genesis* has to do with things and is nothing more than the replacement, in a subject (*Phaedo* 103e), of one form by its opposite (*enantion*, q.v.).

11. The same point of view appears in considerably more detail when Plato comes to speak of the Receptacle (*hypodoche*) in the *Timaeus* (49a ff.) and that is described as the "Nurse of Becoming." Plato begins by pointing out that the four Empedoclean "roots" are not irreducible elements; since they are constantly changing they are really qualities (*ibid.* 49d), even though, on the noetic level, there are *eide* of these four principal bodies. Thus he rejects all the post-Parmenidean theories of mixing and association, based as they are on the irreducibility of the *stoicheia*. The permanent thing in the process is the Receptacle, the quasi-being in which *genesis* takes place (*ibid.* 49e). The Platonic analysis of *genesis* yields, then, the eternal transcendent Forms, immanent mimetic versions of them that pass in and out of the Receptacle (*ibid.* 50c; Plato, *loc. cit.*, promises to describe the difficult relationship between the immanent qualities and the transcendent *eide*, a promise apparently unfulfilled), and, finally, the Receptacle itself that, like the Aristotelian *hypokeimenon* (q.v.), has no characteristics of its own (*ibid.* 51a–b).

12. All of this is, however, precosmic *genesis*, the situation "before the *ouranos* came into being" (*ibid.* 52d). The qualities, together with their associated "powers" (*dynameis*, q.v.; see *pathos, paschein*), drift about the Receptacle in chaotic fashion (*ibid.* 52d–53a). But then *nous* begins its operation and puts order into the chaos by constructing the primary qualities of earth, air, fire, and water into the four primary bodies of the sensible world (*ibid.* 53c) by identifying each of the "elements" with one of the primary geometrical solids capable of being inscribed in a sphere (see *stoicheion*). This looks like a Pythagorean version of Atomism. Aristotle has detected the atomistic parallels (*De gen. et corr.* I, 325b; see *aisthesis*), but the Pythagoreanism is equally clear when we see that the geometrical solids are, in turn, reducible to planes, with the distinct suggestion that the reduction process leads back to lines, points (*Tim.* 53d; see *Laws* x, 894a), and even beyond into the shadowy realms of the Pythagorean *archai* (see *arche, arithmos*, and the related references).

13. Aristotle has little patience with Pythagorean *archai* whether

in their *Timaeus* geometrical form or in their more arithmetical varieties, and he criticizes Plato's version (*De gen. et corr.* I, 315a–316b); but he was obviously more taken by Plato's precosmic *genesis* and his own analysis reflects it. It is Aristotle's contention that Parmenides' theses on nonbeing had frightened his successors off the subject of true *genesis* and into reducing all becoming to either qualitative change (*alloiosis*, q.v.) or merely shifting around the ingredients (*Phys.* I, 187a; *De gen. et corr.* I, 1–2). His own approach is strongly to reaffirm the role of the *stoicheia* as the ultimate irreducible *bodies* out of which all things are made and to insist, on the evidence of the senses, that the *stoicheia* do change into one another in a never-ending cycle (*De gen. et corr.* II, 331a, 337a; see *energeia*). There is, in short, *genesis*. The Parmenidean knot is cut by an explanation of the peculiar nature of the nonbeing involved in *genesis;* it is not absolute nonbeing but a relative type that Aristotle identifies as "privation" (*steresis*, q.v.). This provides the final piece in the puzzle of becoming. *Genesis* is possible because the *stoicheia* have their own *archai*, viz., a material, undefined substratum (*hypokeimenon*, q.v.) common to them all, sets of immanent, perceptible qualities, and the *steresis* of the opposed (*enantion*) qualities. *Genesis* is thus defined as "passage to the *enantion*" (*Phys.* I, 190a–192a; *De gen. et corr.* 324a, 328b–331a).

14. Aristotle disallows the post-Parmenidean association (*synkrisis*) as genuine *genesis* (*De gen. et corr.* I, 317a) and, though *mixis* is allowed to play a role, it is not in *genesis*, in one *stoicheion* becoming another, but in the forming of the next generation of bodies, the *syntheta* or composite bodies (*ibid.* II, 334b–335a).

15. *Genesis*, then, is affirmed and defined and set over against the various other changes (*metabolai*) that occur in substances-in-being: locomotion, alteration, growth. But among all these types of change *kinesis* (more properly, *phora*, q.v.) takes precedence, even to *genesis* (*Phys.* VIII, 260b–261a; compare Plato's grouping in *Laws* X, 894b–c and see *kinesis*), so there must be a continuous *kinesis* to ensure the everlasting cycle of *genesis:* this is the movement of the sun around the elliptic (*De gen. et corr.* II, 336a–b; compare *Rep.* 509b; the sun is, of course, a moved mover; the argument will eventually lead to the primary cause, the unmoved mover; see *kinoun, nous*). *Genesis* is, in turn, keyed on sets of opposed qualities that are active (*poiein*) and passive (*paschein*, q.v.).

16. Epicurus, as the faithful offspring of the Atomists, has no genuine *genesis* (see *kinesis*), but the Stoics appear to follow closer to the Aristotelian pattern. They extend, it is true, action and passion, which in Aristotle are characteristics of the qualities inherent in the *stoicheia*, deeper into the nature of things by associating the former with *logos* (q.v.) and the latter with *hyle* (q.v.), the two Stoic co-principles

of reality (*SVF*, I, 84, 493), but they continue in a somewhat more traditional fashion by affirming the four basic physical bodies or *stoicheia*, two of which are active (air and fire), and two passive (earth and water) (*SVF* II, 418).

17. But there have been alterations as well. Fire is now the hot (see D.L. VII, 136), not, as in Aristotle, a set of qualities, viz., hot and dry (*De gen. et corr.* II, 331a). Further, since the Stoics have given a primacy to fire (see *pyr*), this is the first element and, in a sense, a kind of *Urstoff;* the others are derived from it by a process not unlike the condensation/rarefaction of Anaximenes (D.L. VII, 142) and return to it at the periodic conflagration (*ekpyrosis*, q.v.).

18. Other difficulties arise. Despite the Aristotelian trappings, the Stoics are compelled, by their reduction of everything, including perceptible qualities, to body (see *poion*), to explain change in a fashion not radically different from the Atomists. They eschewed atomic "hooks," however, and turned to a theory of the interpenetrability of bodies that rests on the distinction of various types of mixtures, and particularly the varieties called *mixis* (for dry bodies) and *krasis* (for wet) where the two ingredients of the mixture totally interpenetrate each other without, at the same time, losing their own proper characteristics, a theory used to explain the relationship of soul and body as well (*SVF* II, 467, 471), and strongly attacked by both the later Peripatetics and Plotinus (see *Enn.* II, 7, 1 and *SVF* II, 473).

For the complementary notion of passing-out-of-being, see *phthora;* for *genesis* as process and its bearing on ethical theory, *hedone.*

génos: kind, genus

Genos is generally used in Plato as a synonym for *eidos*, e.g. *Soph.* 253b, and elsewhere as "type," approaching the Aristotelian *genos*, e.g. *Theaet.* 228e and *Soph.* 253d, where dialectic has to do with dividing the forms according to "kind" (*genos*); compare the "collection" (*synagoge*) into one generic "form," *Phaedrus* 265d, but this is still probably ontological rather than predicational. Aristotelian *genos*: Aristotle, *Top.* 102a–b, 120b–128b. For Aristotle the *kategoriai* are the *gene* of being (*De an.* II, 412a), the *summa genera* that cannot be subsumed into anything more general (see *Anal. post.* II, 100b, *Meta.* 1014b). In *Soph.* 254d Plato discussed "the most important *gene*" (Existence [*ousia*], motion, rest, sameness, difference; see *eidos, psyche tou pantos*), and Plotinus, in *Enn.* VI, 1–3, has apparently combined these *gene* with the Aristotelian modes of predication (*kategoriai*) and produced the *gene* of being; see *eidos, diaphora, katholou.*

gnōrimon: *knowable, intelligible*

1. Though the notion that the knowability of things is relative has its Platonic precedents, it is fundamental to Aristotelian epistemology, particularly as it applies to the objects of metaphysics. The distinction is set forth clearly in *Anal. post.* I, 71b–72a: things are knowable (*gnorimon*) in two different senses; what is innately (*physei*) more knowable is not necessarily better known to us (*pros hemas*). The practical application of this principle is twofold. In metaphysics one should begin with the things more intelligible to us and our way of knowing, and proceed to what is intrinsically more intelligible (*Meta.* 1029b); in ethics men should be educated to see that what is intrinsically good is also a good for them (*Eth. Nich.* v, 1129b; the ethical parallel is cited in *Meta., loc. cit.*).

2. The root of this principle is to be sought within the more general cadres of Aristotle's theory of knowledge, since the difference in the grades of intelligibility is not due to some defect in the object but rather in our way of knowing (*Meta.* 993b). The foundation of all our cognition is sense perception (*aisthesis*, q.v.), and even syllogistic demonstration (*apodeixis*) rests upon some form of induction (*epagoge*, q.v.), i.e., to a process that begins with the perception of particulars (*Anal. post.* II, 100b). Scientific knowledge (*episteme*) has to do with the universal (*katholou*), and even though sense perceptions immediately grasp a kind of "concrete universal" (see *Phys.* I, 184a), this is not the universal of science that is apprehended only by reason (*logos*).

3. The role of philosophy, then, is to proceed from what is intelligible to us, i.e., the glimmer of intelligibility that one has through immediately perceived sensibles (*aistheta*), to what is intelligible of itself (*physei*).

4. The Platonic antecedents of all this are clear. The language of *Meta.* 1029b cited above is reminiscent of Plato's distinction between the really existent (*ontos on*) intelligibles and the quasi-real (*pos on*) status of the sensible world, and Aristotle's description of the defects of our sense knowledge (*Meta.* 993b) echoes the imagery of the Allegory of the Cave in *Rep.* 516a. For both philosophers true intelligibility is a function of immateriality (see *Meta.* 1078a), and while they would agree that the highest type of knowledge is the study of the intelligible-in-itself (see *episteme, dialektike, theologia*), where they differ is in their attitudes toward a study of the sensibles. The Platonic curriculum in *Republic* x is structured to lead away from the sensible to the intelligible; the immanence of the Aristotelian *eidos* (q.v.) guarantees the value of a study of the *aistheta* (compare the parallel difference between the Platonic [*synagoge*] and the Aristotelian [*epagoge*] induc-

tion), whether in a historical sense as the investigation of the opinions of others (see *aporia, endoxon*), or as the extraction of the dimly and discursively apprehended intelligible from the immediately perceived sensible.

gnósis: 1) *knowledge;* 2) *Gnosticism*
1) The common Greek general term for knowledge. Typical of this ordinary usage is Aristotle, *Anal. post.* II, 99b–100b, where *gnosis* and its equivalents embrace sense perception (*aisthesis*), memory, experience, and scientific knowledge (*episteme*). For the special problems involved in the knowledge of God, see *agnostos;* 2) at some time before the Christian era the term began to take on another meaning; perhaps transitional in this process is the use of "true *gnosis*" as a synonym for Christian doctrine, Irenaeus, *Adv. haer.* IV, 33, 8. Its final technical meaning is a superior, secret knowledge that guarantees salvation to the "spirituals" (*pneumatikoi*), Irenaeus, *Adv. haer.* I, 6, 2.

h

haphḗ: *contact, touch, sense of touch*
See *genesis, arche, dynamis, aisthesis.*

harmonía: *blending of opposites, harmony*
1. The discovery, generally credited to Pythagoras, of the reduction of musical intervals to mathematical ratios had an extraordinary effect on the development of Greek philosophy: first it suggested that number was the constituative principle of all things (see *arithmos*); it was used to explain mixtures (see *holon*); it likewise spawned the theory of the *psyche* as a harmony of opposites, described by Plato, *Phaedo* 85a–86d (refuted by Socrates, 91c–95e), and Aristotle, *De an.* I, 407b–408a (see *psyche*). But the language of both the Platonic and Aristotelian accounts suggests that *harmonia* is not so much a mathematical-musical concept, but owes more to medical theory (Alcmaeon? see Aetius V, 30, 1). Any attempt to found a theory of the soul on the harmony of physical opposites is, of course, going to lead to a denial of the soul's immortality; it is certain that Pythagoras held the immortality of the soul (see *psyche, palingenesia*), and so his theory of harmony

was much more likely to have been mathematical rather than physical.

2. Another line of the *harmonia* theory leads to the extension of the ratio concept to either the sound or the distances of the planets and the development of the doctrine of the "harmony of the spheres" incorporated by Plato into his "Myth of Er" (*Rep.* 617b), and described by Aristotle, *De coelo* 11, 290b–291a and Cicero, *Somn. Scip.* 5. The ethical implications may be seen in the notions of *katharsis* and *sophrosyne* (qq.v.), in Plato's description of the "mixed life" in *Phil.* 64a–66a (see *agathon*), in Aristotle's doctrine of the "mean" (see *meson*), and in ancient theories on the nature of physical pleasure (see *hedone*); for Heraclitus' theory of "harmony," see *logos*. Pythagorean "harmonics" is a feature of the education of the philosopher in Plato, *Rep.* VII, 530c–531c, where it is transitional to the study of *dialektike* (compare *Timaeus* 47c–d and see *psyche tou pantos*).

For the Stoic ethical formula "harmoniously with nature," see *nomos*.

hēdonê: *pleasure*

1. The first discussions on the possibility of pleasure being the end of man probably took place in the heightened ethical – and subjectivist – climate of the generation of Socrates and the Sophists. But the direct evidence is faulty and one must generally resort to reconstructions out of the Platonic dialogues. For example, in the *Gorgias* (491e–492c) Socrates debates the question with an otherwise obscure Sophist named Callicles who upholds the hedonistic position. He does it in terms of a psychophysiological theory of sense pleasure that was apparently in vogue in the fifth century and beyond, that of depletion (*kenosis*) and refilling (*anaplerosis*). According to a medical theory put forth by Alcmaeon of Crotona health consisted in a state of balance (*isonomia*) of the elements in the body (see Aetius v, 30, 1). This theory had wide philosophical implications (see *harmonia, agathon, meson*), and particularly in its adaptation, perhaps by Empedocles (see Diels 31A95), to explain the origin and nature of pleasure. According to this view a depletion (*kenosis*) of one of the vital elements of the body leads to an imbalance, and the resultant painful sense of want (*endeia*) creates desire (*epithymia, orexis*, qq.v.), or the thrust toward a complementary "filling up" (*anaplerosis*). It is this latter redressing of the natural *isonomia* of the body that is responsible for pleasure.

2. Socrates uses this theory in the *Gorgias* to refute the radical hedonist Callicles, by pointing out that on these grounds the hedonist will be ever unsatiated. The same theory appears again in *Tim.* 64e–65b (on the Atomist antecedents of this passage, see *pathos*), *Rep.* 585a, and *Phil.* 31b–32b, but in these two latter passages at least it is

overlaid with a growing awareness of the psychic as opposed to the purely somatic nature of pleasure, and the identification of the body as an instrument of pleasure (see *Rep.* 584c, *Phil.* 41c), a distinction that allowed Aristotle eventually to deny the applicability of the *kenosis-anaplerosis* theory (*Eth. Nich.* 1173b). What led to this was undoubtedly the recognition of the obvious existence of a pleasure attendant upon intellectual activities (*Rep.* 585b–c, *Phil.* 51e–52a; in both these passages Plato makes some attempt at adapting the *kenosis* theory to this new type of pleasure, but without a great deal of success), as well as the more subtle psychological analysis of the role of memory in the pleasure of anticipation (*Phil.* 32b–36c; this analysis leads, 38a–40e, to a further discussion of the possibility of false pleasures due to our habits of "painted fantasies" [*phantasmata ezographemena*]).

3. Having expanded the horizons of pleasure (true/false, mixed/unmixed, psychic/somatic) Plato attempts to integrate it into the good life in the *Philebus*. The purely hedonistic position is rejected, as it was in the *Gorgias*, as well as a kind of radical antihedonism (*Phil.* 44a) that denied the existence of pleasure. Plato's own view is a moderate one, that the good life is the "mixed life," i.e., a life containing both the pleasurable and the intellectual (*phronesis*, q.v.; *Phil.* 20a–b, 59c–61c).

4. This position that attempts to reconcile the conflicting claims of hedonism and Socratic intellectualism may look to disagreements within the Academy itself. We are aware, from Aristotle, that Speusippus had denied that pleasure was in any sense a good (see *Eth. Nich.* VII, 1152b, 1153b), a stand apparently referred to in *Phil.* 53c–55d. Speusippus reasoned that a) pleasure is a process (*genesis*) and process is a means and not an end, and b) on the theory of the mean (*meson*, q.v.) both pleasure and pain are extremes and hence cannot be a good. In the *Philebus* passage Plato concurs in the first argument, at least insofar as it pertains to physical pleasure, but would not admit that it speaks to the higher, unmixed pleasures described in *Phil.* 51a–52b. As for Speusippus' second argument, that the good resides in the mean or neutral state between pleasure and pain, Plato is aware of the state (*Phil.* 42c–44a) but does not see it as a good; he is unwilling to banish pleasure from the good life.

5. Nor will he accept the empirical hedonism of another contemporary Academician, Eudoxus, who held that pleasure was the only good for man since all creatures pursue it (*Eth. Nich.* x, 1172b). This is not exactly the hedonistic view put forth by Philebus who had suggested (*Phil.* 60a–b) that all men *ought* to pursue pleasure since it is the highest good, and though the presence of pleasure in the Platonic good life in the *Philebus* and the associated admission that *phronesis* is

not an entirely sufficient end to man (*Phil.* 27b) may be a concession to the force of Eudoxus' point, the line against hedonism is firmly held.

6. Eudoxus is chosen by Aristotle as the exemplar of the hedonistic school, probably because of the latter's long association with the Academy. But an even more prominent proponent of the position, one of Plato's own contemporaries, was Aristippus, the founder of the Cyrenaic group, whose hedonism was at least as thoroughgoing, if better known to us, as Eudoxus'. Pleasure is the end of all activity and the object of all choice, as proven by our instinctive, untutored choice of pleasure. Thus all pleasure is good, and physical pleasures better than those of the soul (D.L. II, 87–88). And further, since happiness, i.e., pleasure calculated over a lifetime, is a kind of delusion since only the present is real, each moment's pleasure is to be sought for itself (Aelian, *Var. hist.* XIV, 6).

7. Aristotle, true to his historical method (see *endoxon*), reviews both the hedonist (*Eth. Nich.* x, 1172a–1174a) and antihedonist (*ibid.* VII, 1152b–1154b) positions. He is satisfied with neither, nor, indeed, with Plato's retorts to them. He denies that pleasure is a process (*ibid.* x, 1173a–b), but would prefer to call it an activity (*energeia*) or, more fully (*ibid.* VII, 1153a), "the unimpeded activity of a characteristic state [*hexis*] in accordance with nature." In accordance with this definition the entire moral status of the *hedonai* are worked out in terms of the *energeiai* with which each is properly associated. First, pleasure is a whole, complete in each moment of time, much like the act of seeing (*ibid.* x, 1174b). Pleasure is something that is superimposed upon and completes an activity when the latter is unobstructed, e.g. by a defect in the subject or object of that activity (*ibid.* x, 1174b). Eudoxus was almost correct: all men do seem to desire pleasure, but it is because all men desire to live and pleasure completes the basic activity of living; it is life that is desirable, not the pleasure (*ibid.* x, 1175a). In short, it is activities that are good or evil, not their superimposed pleasures (*ibid.* x, 1175b).

8. From these varying points of view evolves the hedonism of Epicurus. Like Eudoxus he is a hedonist on empirical grounds: pleasure *is* the good sought by men (D.L. x, 128). But the proof is the more sophisticated one of Aristippus that points to instinctive, unlearned behavior (D.L. x, 137; see Sextus Empiricus, *Adv. Math.* XI, 96). Here there is a correlation with his atomically based theory of sensation (*aisthesis*, q.v.): just as sensation is the criterion of truth, so the movements or experiences (*pathe*) of pleasure and pain, which are conceived of as types of atomic dislocation (see Lucretius II, 963–966), serve as criteria of good and evil since pleasure is what is natural, and so good, while pain is alien to nature, and so evil (D.L. x, 34).

9. Epicurus accepts the *kenosis-endeia-epithymia-anaplerosis* analysis of pleasure and pain (D.L. x, 144; compare Lucretius iv, 858–876) and insists on the primacy of physical pleasures, particularly those of the stomach (Athenaeus xii, 546). He also accepts the corollary that pleasure, being physical, must be measured by quantity (*poson*) not quality (*poion;* cf. Eusebius, *Praep. Evang.* xiv, 21, 3). But by subjecting the process to an even closer analysis Epicurus detects another, purer type of pleasure than the corrective "filling up" of a bodily want that is, after all, subtly mixed with pain (see Socrates' perceptive remark in *Phaedo* 60b). This purer pleasure is not, then, the kinetic pleasure of *anaplerosis*, but the static (*katastematike*) pleasure of equilibrium, the absence of pain (*algos*) from the body (*aponia*) and the absence of disturbance from the soul (*ataraxia*) (D.L. x, 131). This position may owe more than a little to Speusippus' neutral state (see Clement Alex., *Strom.* ii, 22, 133), but what is clear is that Epicurus was moving away from the more mechanical explanation of Aristippus who held only kinetic pleasure (D.L. x, 136) and downgraded the psychic side of pleasure. Epicurus, on the other hand, since he strongly maintained the experiential reality of past and future, a position that magnifies mental pleasures (and pains), shifts the focus of emphasis from "the pleasant moment" to "the happy life" (D.L. x, 137, 133). Thus it is the activity of the mind that holds the keys, viz., memory and imagination, to pleasure over the long run, the happy life, and that controls and tempers Epicurean hedonism.

hēgemonikón: *directive faculty of the soul*
In Stoicism the *hegemonikon* governs the other psychic faculties and is seated in the heart (*SVF* i, 143; ii, 836; ii, 879). According to Chrysippus, all psychic states (including virtues, vices, and *pathe*) are changes in the rational faculty (*hegemonikon; SVF* iii, 459; Sextus Empiricus, *Adv. Math.* vii, 233). It is a *tabula rasa* at birth (*SVF* ii, 83), an internal, independent principle (Marcus Aurelius, vii, 16; vi, 8); see *nous, psyche, aisthesis, kardia.*

heimarménē: *an allotted (portion), fate*
The Stoics identified fate with *logos* and *pronoia* and Zeus (*SVF* ii, 913, 937). The growing transcendence of God in later Greek philosophy (see *hyperousia*) leads to the reseparation of *theos* and *heimarmene,* Philo, *De migr. Abr.* 179–181; ps-Plutarch, *De fato* 572f–573b; see *pronoia.*

hen: *one, the One*
1. The pre-Socratic search for an *arche* for all things normally ended in a single principle, the reduction of the variety of existents

back to a single stuff, with no emphasis, however, on the uniqueness of the principle. The first dualists were apparently the Pythagoreans, "apparently" because the judgment rests on the exegesis of a difficult text in Aristotle, in addition to the fact that at some later date the Pythagoreans became monists and, as is usually the case with Pythagorean sources, the discrimination between early and late is not a simple matter.

2. In *Meta.* 986a Aristotle says that the Pythagoreans made the ultimate *stoicheia* limit (*peras*) and the unlimited (*apeiron*); they are the elements of odd and even, and these latter produce the one (*hen*), whence proceeds the whole series of *arithmoi*. This would seem to draw the distinction between pairs of opposed *stoicheia* (limit-unlimited, odd-even) and their product, *hen*, which is the *arche* or starting point of number. But a few lines later in the same passage Aristotle goes on to say that some Pythagoreans line up their *stoicheia* in two parallel columns, the left containing limit, odd, one, etc., and in the right, the unlimited, even, plurality. If we take into account what seems to be a later development in the school (see 10 *infra*), we thus have three very different points of view on the one: the one as posterior to the *stoicheia*, the one as a *stoicheion*, and the one prior to all else.

3. These speculations are based on physical and mathematical considerations (moral implications are not, of course, absent in these Pythagorean views; also in the left column in *Meta.* 986a is "the good"; see *Eth. Nich.* 1096b), but the next appearance of the one is in a context dominated by logic (compare Aristotle's remark in *De gen. et corr.* I, 325a). This is the "Way of Truth" of Parmenides where he seeks to illustrate that if being (*on*) is, then it is one in the sense of being both unique (*monogenes;* fr. 8, lines 11–13) and indivisible (*adiaireton; ibid.* lines 22–25).

4. To support the contentions of Parmenides, Zeno had constructed a number of dialectical antinomies. These take the form of positing a hypothesis, in this case that there are a plurality of beings, and showing that the conclusions that flow from it are just as absurd as the ones raised against Parmenides' One Being (*Parm.* 128a–e). Plato constructs just such a set of hypotheses and places them in the mouth of Parmenides himself in the dialogue of the same name. The subject is the one (*to hen*). The passages that follow (*Parm.* 137c ff.) involve a number of obscurities, not the least of which is whether the one under discussion is the One Being of Parmenides or Plato's transcendent Oneness itself (the Greek expression is ambiguous and in 135e Parmenides suggests that he would like to extend the dialectic of Zeno to the *eide;* but compare 137b). Again, is this Zenonian eristic or Platonic *dialektike* (it is called *gymnasia* at 135c–e)?

5. Whatever modern scholarship says on the subject, and it

tends to see the latter half of the dialogue as logical considerations about One Being, the judgment of the latter Platonic tradition is clear. The hypotheses of the *Parmenides* became for it a sacred text on the One as a transcendent *hypostasis*. It is cited more often than any other work except the *Timaeus* in the *Enneads*, and Proclus wrote a full-scale commentary on it.

6. Did Plato have a special doctrine of the One? As far as the unity of the individual *eide* is concerned, Plato maintains throughout that they are indivisible (*Phaedo* 78d, *Rep.* 476a), and he goes so far as to call them henads or monads (*Phil.* 15a–b, 16d–e). But we are considerably less informed on the *eidos* of one or Oneness itself. Plato does address himself to the one (*hen*) and the many (*plethos*) as a dialectical problem in *Phil.* 13e–18d. He mentions as already solved the question on many-in-one on the level of organic unities like man (14d–e; see *holon*), but there remains the perplexing question of the monadic *eidos* and its distribution through the plurality of material things (15b–c; the question is posed as if it is going to be solved, but it is not; see *methexis, mimesis*) and the related problem of the interrelationship (*koinonia*) of the *eide*. To solve this he resorts to the Pythagorean (or, as he calls it, Promethean; 16c) solution of converting *hen* and *plethos* with *peras* and *apeiron*, which are, in turn, integrated into his own procedures of collection (*synagoge*) and division (*diairesis,* q.v.). These latter are, in effect, a dialectical movement from many to one, and vice versa, but the one to which *synagoge* attains is in no wise a transcendent One but rather a generic *eidos* of the type described in *Soph.* 253d–e as "one *eidos* extending through many *eide* that lie apart."

7. The *Sophist* also raises the question of the One itself, i.e., the *eidos* of *hen*, against Parmenides (245a–b), not now of the Platonic dialogue, but the philosopher of the "Way of Truth." If the spherical One Being is such as Parmenides describes it in fr. 8, lines 42 ff., then it is a whole made up of parts and so must differ from the One itself, which is perfectly simple. But the text has no sequel short of informing us that there is an *eidos* of one. When, later in the same dialogue (254d ff.), Plato comes to discuss the "greatest kinds" of *eide*, the One is nowhere in evidence and Plotinus must devote a somewhat longish explanation of why its omission is appropriate (*Enn.* VI, 2, 9–12).

8. The importance of one in Plato is, then, except for the curious business of the *Parmenides*, of no more special importance than the other *eide* and perhaps less than the *megista gene* of the *Sophist*. What is more striking, however, is the position it seems to assume in the nearly contemporary Academy. Aristotle's own treatment of one is to class it among the "transcendentals": oneness, like being, is predicated analogously through all the *kategoriai* (*Meta.* 1003a–b, 1053b).

But as for unit-one, this can be nothing else but the *arche* of a mathematical series (*ibid.* 1016b), and so he is convinced that Plato must have held that One was a separate substance (*ibid.* 996a; refuted, 1001a–b) and the *arche* of all the *eide* since One and Being are the *summa genera* of which all the *eide* are species (*ibid.* 996a, 998b). The origins of this belief are somewhat difficult to understand, but they are obviously connected with his oft-repeated allegation that Plato identified the *eide* with numbers (see *arithmos* 3). A further remark carries us in the same direction. Aristotle also states that Plato identified the One with the Good (*ibid.* 1091a–b), and we know that this is based on more than a reading of the famous passage on the transcendent Good in *Rep.* 509b since we are informed from another source (Aristoxenus, *Elem. harm.* II, p. 30) that Plato made this identification in his lecture "On the Good" (see *agrapha dogmata*) that also had to do with mathematics.

9. Aristotle goes on to say that Speusippus, Plato's successor, avoided the difficulty because, even though he made the One an *arche*, he did not identify it with the Good (*ibid.* 1091b) but made this latter the result of an evolutionary process (*ibid.* 1072b–1073a). Speusippus' views on the *archai* themselves are likewise reported. He substituted for the Platonic *eide* the *mathematika* (q.v.; *Meta.* 1028b), deriving the numbers, in prescribed Pythagorean fashion, from One and Plurality (*ibid.* 1085b, 1087b). The One of Speusippus is not, then, an ultimate principle in a monist system, but one of two co-principles of number. Xenocrates belongs to the same tradition; he made the *eide* numbers (1028b, 1069a, etc.) and derived them from the Monad and the Dyad, based on an exegesis of *Timaeus* 35a (Plutarch, *De procr. an.* 1012d). He goes on to identify the One with the Father and Zeus, the First God, *nous*, while the Dyad may be called Mother of the Gods and the World Soul (Aetius I, 7, 30).

10. In all these theories of *archai* it is notable that the one remains as a stable factor; it is its correlative that shifts nuances: the *apeiron* of the Pythagoreans, the polarized Infinite Dyad of Plato (*aoristos dyas; Meta.* 987b; see *Phys.* 206b; the *dyas* does not appear in the terminology of *Phil.* 24a–25b but what is described is dual in nature) and Xenocrates, and the pluralistic *plethos* of Speusippus and the Pythagoreans. A considerably different view appears in the Pythagorean revival of the first century where writers like Eudorus (in Simplicius, *Phys.* 181) and Alexander Polyhistor (D.L. VIII, 25) describe a Pythagoreanism that held that the Infinite Dyad itself derived from the *monas*.

11. The affinities between Pythagoras and the Academy were soon exploited by both sides. Aristotle himself had already linked the two (see *mimesis* and compare the frequent juxtaposition of Speusip-

pus and Pythagoras in the *Metaphysics*). The derivation of the transcendent Platonic principles of the later dialogues in terms of Pythagorean number theory is particularly marked, and one such account by a later Pythagorean, Moderatus of Gades, has been preserved by Simplicius (*Phys.* 230–231). Present in it are all the later Neoplatonic hypostases: the first One, beyond Being; the second One, which is really real, intelligible, the *eide;* and the third One, which participates (*methexis*) in the first One and the *eide.* The stress on the One in Moderatus' tract is revelatory of its Pythagorean point of view. A similar account of the three hypostases by the Academic Albinus shows its orientation toward the *Philebus* and *Timaeus* by describing all three of the hypostases as *nous* (*Epit.* x, 1–2). But there is something of Aristotle here as well: the first *nous*, besides being the *demiourgos* (*ibid.* xii, 1) and the Father and cause of all goodness and truth, thinks itself (*ibid.* x, 3). But it was the One that eventually triumphed over *nous.* The second-century Pythagorean Numenius, whom Plotinus studied, had already reduced *nous* and the demiurgic function to the second place (see *nous* 18) and his "First God" is absolutely one and indivisible (Eusebius, *Praep. Evang.* xi, p. 537).

12. This is, in essence, the One, the first hypostasis of Plotinus, that is beyond Being and completely without qualification (*Enn.* vi, 9, 3). Oneness is not predicated of it (vi, 9, 5); indeed, nothing is *in* it: it *is* what it is, i.e., it is its own activity and essence (vi, 8, 12–13). Two corrections are in order, however. It is *not* a numerical unit (*monas;* vi, 9, 5), nor is it the Aristotelian thought about thought (vi, 7, 37; see *noesis* 18).

13. The transcendence of the One, affirmed with increasing emphasis in the later philosophical tradition, leads to a crisis in cognition (see *agnostos*). Plotinus confronts the problem of this transcendent first principle that is beyond Being, apprehension, and description by an application of the theory of *mimesis* and a remarkable resort to introspection. The question of *mimesis* may be approached from two directions. One, properly Aristotelian, is that of the unity of the person (see *Meta.* 1003b). From it one progresses, through ever higher grades of unity, to the absolute simplicity that is the One (vi, 9, 1–2). From a more Platonic point of view, intellection is a kind of movement, rotary in the heavens but deranged in us because of the contradictory motions coming from the body (*Tim.* 37a–b; *Laws* x, 897d; see *noesis* 11). For Plotinus the One is the immobile center of all these motions, and in a metaphor of dancers around a choirmaster he explains our irregular motions (e.g. sensation, discursive reasoning) by our turning away from the director toward the spectators (vi, 9, 8; on the "attention" principle see *noesis* 21, *nous* 18, and the extraordinary remarks in i, 4, 10). In both cases, then, the true unity is to be sought within

ourselves. The One is known not by reasoning, which is necessarily an exercise in plurality, but by the presence (*parousia*) in us of unity (VI, 9, 4). The grasp of the One is accomplished by interior reflection, the "flight of the alone to the Alone" (VI, 9, 11), which seeks to render the soul completely simple (VI, 9, 7). In the intelligible world this mystical union with the One is a permanent experience, the true heavenly Aphrodite; but here it is only occasional, and we experience rather the vulgar courtesan Aphrodite (VI, 9, 9; on Plotinus' own occasional mystical unification with the One, see Porphyry, *Vita Plot.* XXIII).

14. Just as Plotinus proceeds, in *Enn.* VI, 9, 1–2, from relative unity to absolute oneness, so Proclus derives the absolute One from the presence of ones that participate (*methexis*) in Oneness (*Elem. theol.*, props. 1–6; for the method, cf. *trias*). There is, as in Aristotle, a transcendent final cause (prop. 8), as well as a transcendent efficient cause (prop. 11); these are identical with each other and are the One (props. 12–13).

For the other Neoplatonic hypostases, see *nous, psyche tou pantos, psyche;* for the manner of progression, *proödos, trias*.

henás: *Henad*

Although the term is used in Plato, *Phil.* 15a and by Neopythagoreans to describe the *eide* (so Plotinus, *Enn.* VI, 6, 9), it is best known as a feature of Proclus' Neoplatonism where the Henads are plural unfoldings of the unity of the One, transcendent sources of individuality; see Proclus, *Elem. theol.*, props. 113–165. They are identified with the traditional gods.

héteron: *the other, otherness*

In Plato the Other is one of the major forms that pervades all the other forms, *Soph.* 255c–e. Some apparent nonbeing is merely the "other," *ibid.* 259a (see *on*). *Heteron* is a principle in the construction of World Soul, *Tim.*, 35a. In Plotinus it is the principle, inherent in *nous*, of the plurality of the *eide* (*Enn.* VI, 2, 22; IV, 3, 5); it produces matter, (*ibid.* II, 4, 5); see *prós ti, noesis*.

héxis: *state, characteristic, habit*

For Aristotle there are three states in the soul: emotions (*pathe*), capacities (*dynameis*), characteristics (*hexeis*) (*Eth. Nich.* 1105b). *Hexis* is defined (*ibid.*) as our condition vis-à-vis the *pathe*. *Arete* is a *hexis* (*ibid.* 1106a); only the beginnings of our habits are under voluntary control (*ibid.* 1114b). The Stoics disagreed with Aristotle and considered *arete* a *diathesis* rather than a *hexis* (*SVF* I, 202; II, 393). A peculiarly Stoic development of the term is the grouping of *hexis* with the four binding powers of things: *hexis, physis, psyche, nous*, and is translated, when used in this sense by Seneca (*Nat. Quaes.* II, 2) as *unitas* (see the peculiarly similar use of *hexis* in Plato cited under *phthora*). Among these *hexis* is the *unitas* of inorganic matter (see Sextus Empiricus, *Adv. Math.* IX, 81–85; Philo, *Leg. all.* II, 22, *Quod Deus* 35; *SVF* II, 457–460, 714–716). *Hexis* is defined, in the category of quality (*poion*), and distinguished from the more transient state, disposition (*diathesis*), *Cat.* 8b–9a.

hólon: *whole, organism, universe*

1. A critical moment in discussions of change occurs when Aristotle rejects, at a single stroke, the earlier theories that absolute *genesis* (q.v.) could take place by association (*synkrisis*) or disassociation (*diakrisis*) of particles and asserts that it comes about when this whole (*holon*) changes into that (*De gen. et corr.* I, 317a).

2. The question of wholeness had been raised previously. In the *Parmenides* wholeness is denied of the One because it connotes the presence of parts and, consequently, that the One is in some sense a plurality (137c–d); the unity (*hen*) of the One must be something quite distinct from "wholeness" (see *Soph.* 244d–245e).

3. The problem in Parmenides is a logical and conceptual one having to do with the notion of divisibility; with Empedocles the physical issue arises. It is Empedocles' desire to keep Parmenides' unity and at the same time posit a plurality of elements (*stoicheia*, q.v.) that adds this new dimension. *Genesis* is cyclic for Empedocles: the four "roots" are eternal but they are in a constant process of transformation (fr. 17, lines 1–13), passing, in the process, in and out of a sphere in which they are perfectly blended (frs. 27, 28). It is this sphere, obviously a compromised descendent of Parmenides' One Being, that first suggests that the elements can be submerged in some sort of a unified whole where their individual characteristics are lost, at least to sight. How this is accomplished he does not say, except to remark that the sphere is covered with a *harmonia*. The term (q.v.), a mathematical one, had a great vogue in Pythagorean circles, and the suspicion of just such an influence on Empedocles is strengthened when, later in the cosmic cycle, the four elements begin to combine into compound bodies (frs. 96, 98). Here we are told that flesh and blood and bones are formed of fixed numerical proportions of the elements that are all linked together by the "divine bonds of *harmonia*."

4. This is the first attempt at explaining organic compounds in terms of the numerical proportion (*logos*) of their ingredients. The same mathematical approach is visible in Anaxagoras, who held that bodies, even though they were composed of "seeds" that contain a portion of everything in them, have their identity from the quantitative

predominance of one or other of the types of seed within them (frs. 6, 12; see Aristotle, *Phys.* I, 187a).

5. Neither Plato nor Aristotle was much taken by this method, though it apparently could be applied to colors (see *Tim.* 68b, with a slight sceptical note; *De sensu* 440b). Plato preferred the more geometrical approach of composing compound bodies out of differently shaped particles (see *genesis, stoicheion;* he does, however, resort to numerical proportion for the composition of the marrow in *Tim.* 73c), while Aristotle felt that none of these pre-Socratic mixture techniques really explained the presence of a new "whole" since the original ingredients in no way lost their individual entities but merely became imperceptible to sense; the true *holon* should be homogeneous (*homoiomeres*) throughout (*De gen. et corr.* I, 327b–328a; on the *logos* of the mixture, see *Meta.* 993a, *De gen. anim.* I, 642a).

6. The influence of the *physikoi* is much less in evidence in Plato's more philosophical approach to the question in *Theaet.* 203e ff. where Socrates proposes, as an alternative in a dilemma, that the whole (*holon*) is something more than the total (*pan*) of its parts. The suggestion is not, however, pursued here, nor in his account of *genesis.* But in other places Plato is well aware that in a whole as opposed to a sum a crucial factor is the positioning (*thesis*) of the parts and that in the true *holon* the parts have a fixed spatial relationship to each other and to the whole. He applies this to the arrangement of parts in a tragedy (*Phaedrus* 268d) and, in the *Laws*, to the parts of the *kosmos.* The latter is a particularly interesting example since it stresses the teleological function of the parts with respect to the whole (x, 903c, 904b). Position (*thesis*) had, of course, been important among the pre-Socratics (see *aisthesis, genesis*), and it is not unlikely that its occurrence in Plato had Pythagorean origins (see *Parm.* 145a–c, Aristotle, *De coelo* 268a, and compare *Poet.* 1450b).

7. Aristotle's approach to wholeness is twofold. A whole is, by way of preliminary, something that has several parts (*mere, moria; Meta.* 1023a) that are potentially (*dynamei*) present in the whole (*Phys.* VII, 250a; *De gen. et corr.* II, 334b). The notion is not necessarily limited to physical bodies: Aristotle discusses the *mere* of tragedy (*Poet.* 1450a, 1459b), the *mere* of the soul (*De an.* III, 442a–b; see *psyche*), and *eidos* as a part of the *genos* (*Meta.* 1023b). But if it is true, as has been noted (*De gen. et corr.* I, 317a), that *genesis* is of a whole from a whole, what is it that differentiates this *holon* from a mere aggregate of particles and makes it something over and above a total (*Meta.* 1045a)? The total (*pan*) is something that has merely a positioning of parts (*ibid.* 1024a); a whole has an internal cause (*aition*) of unity that is its *eidos* or *ousia* (qq.v.; *ibid.* 1041b).

8. But the *eidos* is also the *energeia* (q.v.) and the *entelecheia* (q.v.) of a being, and so by the juxtaposition of these notions the Aristotelian concept of *holon* broadens out to include both function (*ergon*, q.v.) and finality (*telos*, q.v.). The *eidos* of living beings and the unitive cause of all their functions is the *psyche*. In this fashion parts (*mere*) are transformed, by the notion of function, into organs (*organa*). An organ is the part of a living creature that is directed toward an end or purpose that is an activity (*praxis; De part. anim.* 645b); nature (*physis*), the internal principle of growth in these beings, has made the organs to perform certain functions (*ibid.* 694b), and a body so constituted is an organism (see *ibid.* 642a, and compare the definition of soul in *De an.* II, 412a as the *entelecheia* of an organic body). The *organon*, then, is the physical part of a living being matched to each of the latter's potencies (*dynameis*) to enable them to function (*De gen. an.* I, 716a; IV, 765b).

9. A somewhat similar idea appears in Epicurus' notion of the *systema*. Democritus had reduced all the *pathe* of things to those directly associated with extended bodies *qua* extended, and relegated all the rest (e.g. color, sound) to a subjective impression of the senses (fr. 9; see *aisthesis, pathos*). But for his latter-day followers there were certain *pathe* that, though not present in the individual *atomon*, were present in an aggregate of them. In this sense the whole (*systema, athroisma*, or, as Lucretius calls it, *concilium*) is more than the sum of its parts (see D.L. x, 69). What is the difference here? First, there is the question of the position (*thesis*) of the *atoma* relative to each other, thus forming a pattern that is the superadded factor that allows the *atoma* to be colorless but their aggregate to be colored (Lucretius II, 757–771; see Plutarch, *Adv. Col.* 1110c). But in addition to this formation of a spatial pattern in the aggregate, the atoms also have their own individual movement, and it happens that when they are formed into *concilia* their movements harmonize and other aggregate *pathe* come into existence (*ibid.* II, 109–111). In this way it is in the *concilium* of the soul-atoms, contained within the sheath of the body, that the motion which is sensation occurs (D.L. x, 64; see *aisthesis*). For the various types of Epicurean *concilia*, see *genesis*.

10. The Stoic emphasis on the world as an entity under the unitive and providential direction of *logos* (q.v.) led to a fairly consistent use of "universe" (*holon*) as a synonym for *kosmos* and is particularly evident in Marcus Aurelius' description of men as the organs (as opposed to mere parts) of the universe (*holon; Med.* VII, 13). The Neoplatonists reverted instead to the *Parmenides* and *Theaetetus* texts, Proclus devoting props. 66–69 of the *Elem. theol.* to a consideration of wholeness, both as an unparticipated *eidos* (*holotes pro meron*) and as

participated in by various wholes-with-parts (*holotes ek meron*) that have wholeness as one of their *pathe.*

On the question of the unity of the soul, see *psyche.*

hómoios: *like, similar*

1. One of the most common Greek theories of knowledge was based on the dictum "like is known by like." Two aspects can be detected: 1) the knower cannot know an object without some sort of identity of elements between them, and 2) in knowing something we also, at the same time, become more like it. The first aspect is seen at its baldest in Empedocles' fr. 109: "we see earth with earth, water with water," explained (Diels 31A86) by the fact that things give off effluences and knowledge results when these fit into the corresponding passages in the senses; compare the similar theory in Democritus (Diels 68A135; see *aisthesis*). There is a more sophisticated version in Plato's *Tim.* 45b–46a where vision is explained by the going out of a beam of fiery light that coalesces, "like to like," with the similarly constituted rays of the sun; the intrusion of an object into this homogeneous beam causes sensation. Aristotle, who criticizes both versions of the theory (*De an.* I, 404b; *De sensu,* 437a–b), solves the problem by his theory of *dynamis:* the knower is the object potentially (*ibid.* 438b). The second aspect, the knower becomes the known, reflects the fully developed Aristotelian doctrine of knowledge (see *noesis*), and, in an ethical direction, those of *homoiosis, katharsis, harmonia;* see also *ouranos.*

2. For the use of medical homoeopathism by the philosophers, see *katharsis;* the perception theory is located in its larger context under *aisthesis;* for similarity in the procession-reversion diastole of Neoplatonism, see *proödos;* for its role in the action and passion on a cosmic scale, *sympatheia.*

homoíōsis: *assimilation (to God)*

Originally a Pythagorean idea (see Iamblichus, *Vita Pyth.* 137), assimilation to God was later adopted by Socrates and Plato as descriptive of the end of philosophy (Stobaeus, *Ecl.* II, 7, p. 49 and *Theaet.* 176a). The notion was also current among the Peripatetics; see Cicero, *De fin.* v, 4, 11; Julian, *Orat.* VI, 185a; and the famous call to make ourselves immortal in *Eth. Nich.* 1177b. It is central in Plotinus, *Enn.* I, 6, 6. For its philosophical origins, see *psyche, homoios, harmonia.*

hormê: *impulse, appetite*

Aristotle uses *horme* as a somewhat negligent synonym for *orexis* (q.v.), but with the Stoics it becomes the standard technical term for appetite. It is defined (*SVF* II, 458) as "the first movement [*kinesis*] of the soul" toward (or away) from something. The primary *horme* of all animals is self-preservation (*oikeiosis*, q.v.). The *hormai* present no problem on the animal level, but in dealing with man, whose character- istic note is rationality (*hegemonikon*, q.v.), the presence of *hormai* that are contrary to reason creates a difficulty. The violent or "exces- sive" impulses are the *pathe* (D.L. VII, 110; for the Platonic anteced- ents of this view, see *pathos*) and their exact nature *vis-à-vis* the rational faculty was debated (see *pathos*, *apatheia*). But the later doctrine of the school tended to allow for both the animal and rational nature of man and thus classify the *hormai* under the irrational part (see Cicero, *De off.* I, 28, 101; I, 36, 132); see *noesis* 17.

hóros or horismós: boundary, definition

The Socratic contribution to philosophy was induction (*epagoge*, q.v.) and definition, and these in the context of ethics (Aristotle, *Meta.* 1078b). True definition was impossible according to the Cynics (Aris- totle, *Meta.* 1043b; Plato, *Theaet.* 201c). Definitions are the starting point of demonstration (Aristotle, *Anal. post.* II, 90b). There is a distinction between nominal and causal definitions (*ibid.* 93b–94a). The parts of the definition are enumerated in *Top.* I, 103b. There is no definition of matter, only of *eidos* (Aristotle, *Meta.* 1035b–1036a), nor of individual sensible substances (*Meta.* 1039b). Properly, definitions are only of species, and of everything else in a secondary sense (*ibid.* 1030a). The Sceptics refused to define anything (D.L. IX, 106); see *diaphora, idion, ousia.*

hýlē: material, matter

1. *Hyle*, a purely Aristotelian term, does not have its origins in a directly perceived reality—as is true in the case of extension or magnitude (*megethos*, q.v.)—but emerges from an analysis of change (*Phys.* I, 190b–191a); it is not known directly but by analogy (*analogia, ibid.* 191a8). The difficulty in grasping the nature of matter is that it seems to be outside the range of knowledge (*Meta.* 1036a): when one has stripped away (*aphairesis*, q.v.) all the qualities of an existent, there seems to be nothing left. Nor does matter fit into any of the *kategoriai* (q.v.), since they are predicated of it, while it is predi- cated of nothing; it is not even a negation (*Meta.* 1029a). It is, in short, potency (*dynamis*), just as form is act (*De an.* II, 412a).

2. Once the peculiar nature of *hyle* has been delimited it can take its place among the four causes of things (*Phys.* II, 194b; see *aition*), where, like the *eidos*, it is an immanent (*enhyparchon*) cause (*Meta.* 1070b). It serves another function as well: it is the principle of individuation. Since the *eidos* is indivisible (*atomon*) it can merely

serve to constitute a being within a given genus or species; the individuals within the *infima species* are numerically distinct by reason of their matter (*Meta.* 1034a, 1035b; the individuation of pure forms, e.g. God, intelligences, is not treated; see *kinoun* 12 and compare *diaphora* 4).

3. *Hyle*, then, is the primary substratum of change (*hypokeimenon*, q.v.; *Phys.* I, 192a), the "thing" that receives the new *eidos* (*Meta.* 1038b; for the Platonic antecedents, see *genesis*). But to call it a "thing" is misleading. *Hyle* is like a substance (*tode ti;* see *Phys.* I, 190b, 192a), but it is not such because it lacks the two chief characteristics of substance: it is neither a separate existent (*choriston*, q.v.) nor an individual (*Meta.* 1029a).

4. Just as there are various types of change (see *metabole*), so too there must be various types of matter that serve as the substrata for these changes (see *Meta.* 1042b). Most notable of these is the matter associated with a change of place (*hyle topike;* see *phora*) that implies none of the others, or, to put it in another way, is not necessarily accompanied with "genetic and destructible matter" (*hyle gennete kai phtharte*), and so is not subject to *genesis* and *phthora* (q.v.; *Meta.* 1042b, 1044b, 1050b, 1069b). Thus is established the possibility of the indestructibility of the heavenly bodies whose only change is that of local motion (see *aither, ouranioi*). For the distinction of the matters involved in substantial (*genesis*) and qualitative (*alloiosis*) change, see *stoicheion*.

5. For Aristotle the composition of an individual, a Socrates or a Callias, is an extremely complex procedure that may be conceived as the imposition of a succession of increasingly specific *eide*. Each of these forms is imposed on a progressively more informed matter, and so there are distinctions in *hyle* ranging from a first matter (*prote hyle, materia prima*), the substratum of the form of the primary bodies or *stoicheia* (q.v.), earth, air, fire, and water, through a series of more highly informed matters down to "ultimate matter" (*eschate* or *teleutaia hyle*), the matter of this individual existent (*De part. anim.* II, 646a; see *Meta.* 1049a).

6. Aristotle was not unaware that Platonism (and its more remote ancestor Pythagoreanism) had been moving in a similar direction (*Phys.* I, 192a). But they either followed Parmenides and labeled the material concept as pure nonbeing (*me on;* see *on*), which it clearly was not since it both preceded and survived *genesis* (indeed, matter is eternal), or else they identified it with "the great and the small" (*Meta.* 987b; see *dyas*), which is, in Aristotle's mind, a rank confusion between a genuinely nondetermined principle and a privation. It was this inability to distinguish between *hyle* and *steresis* that prevented the Platonists from arriving at a valid concept of matter. Closer to

Aristotle's own thinking was the Platonic Receptacle (*hypodoche*) of *Timaeus* 49a that is (*ibid.* 51a) invisible and characterless, and that, like the Aristotelian *hyle*, is indestructible and known only indirectly by a kind of "bastard reasoning" (*ibid.* 52a–b). There are, of course, differences. What begins as a "receptacle" or "matrix" (see *Phys.* I, 192a) is surely different from substratum, but even further removed from the Aristotelian *hyle* is its final description as "area" or "space" (*chora; Tim.* 52a), a figure that, on the testimony of Plotinus (*Enn.* II, 4, 11), prompted some later commentators to suggest that it involved the notion of volume.

7. In Stoicism, where all is material, the Aristotelian distinction between matter and form is nonetheless preserved in the distinction between an active (*poiein*) and passive (*paschein*) principle (D.L. VII, 134). Both are material but the first is eternal, "first matter," which is identified with *logos* (*SVF* I, 87). The basic difference between Aristotle and the Stoics is, however, in the realm of magnitude. The Aristotelian analysis of change had led to the concept of matter as a substratum, as pure potentiality (*dynamis;* see *Meta.* 1039b, *De an.* 412a, 414a), akin to substance, while magnitude (*megethos*, q.v.) is an accident, i.e., a form, in the category of quantity (*poson*). Hence Aristotle, and Plotinus after him (see *Enn.* II, 4, 8–12), affirm the incorporeality of magnitude, while the Stoic analysis, based on action and passion, leads to the opposite conclusion (D.L. VII, 56; Cicero, *Acad. post.* I, 11, 39).

8. Plotinus' views on matter, found primarily in *Enn.* II, 4, are a reaction to both Aristotle and the Stoics and are based upon his reading of the Platonic proof-texts on *apeiron* in the *Philebus* (15d–17a, 23c–25b). Like Aristotle, Plotinus admits the existence of an intelligible matter (*hyle noete*). But whereas the intelligible matter of Aristotle was a purely conceptual entity involved in the process of abstraction (*aphairesis*, q.v.), the Plotinian version has a definite ontological status: it is the intelligible counterpart (the argument presumes the existence of a *kosmos noetos* [q.v.] in parallel with our *kosmos aisthetos*) of sensible matter, and its existence is proved by the divisibility of the genera of the *eide*, as is indicated in the *Philebus* (*Enn.* II, 4, 4). Corporeal matter, then, is an image (*eidolon*) of intelligible matter.

9. Plotinus also opposes Aristotle on the relationship between matter and privation (*steresis*). Aristotle had chided the Platonists on not distinguishing between them (*Phys.* I, 192a), but Plotinus reaffirms (II, 4, 14–15) the identification: matter is privation; it is, moreover, the Platonic indefinite or unlimited (*apeiron*, q.v.; see also *dyas*, which is described as indefinite, *aoristos*). But unlike the Platonic *chora* (extended corrections of the *chora* image in III, 6, 12–19),

Plotinian matter is derived from the One (II, 4, 5; V, 1, 5; see Proclus, *Elem. theol.*, props. 57–59).

10. Finally, Plotinus confronts Aristotle on the question of individuation. In *Meta.* 990b Aristotle had maintained that the logic of the Platonists' arguments would require them to posit an *eidos* of every individual thing. Aristotle escapes this necessity, as we have seen, by making *hyle* the cause of individual differences. But Plotinus (*Enn.* V, 7) admits the existence of *eide* of individuals to this same end.

For the equation of matter and evil, see *kakon;* for the pre-Socratic "materialists," *eidos.*

hyperousía: *beyond being, transcendence (divine): on the question of the transcendence of the Forms, see eidos*

1. The notion of transcendence begins properly with Parmenides' positing of an existent, and then proceeding to deprive it of all characteristics save oneness (fr. 8, lines 1–50). Plato explores the dialectical possibilities of this in the *Parmenides*, and especially in the first "hypothesis" (see 141d–142a) where he demonstrates that this One cannot even be said to "be." This may be dialectic, but on other grounds Plato is convinced of the transcendence of his supreme principle: in *Rep.* 509b the Good is beyond being, and compare the various texts cited under *agnostos.*

2. Stoic materialism had radically reduced divine transcendence (*SVF* I, 87 and see *pyr*), but in the first century of the Christian era divine transcendence once again comes to the foreground due to a revival of Pythagoreanism and Platonism (see *eidos*), coupled with the introduction of the Semitic tradition of transcendence, visible in Philo, *De opif.* 2, 7–9 and in *Leg. all.* III, 61, where the *Logos* is transcendent as well. The doctrine becomes a staple in Middle Platonism (see Albinus, *Epit.* X, 1–4), where it is closely connected with attempts to devise an **episte**mological approach to God (see *agnostos*). Divine transcendence finds its most famous exponent in Plotinus and his doctrine of the One (*hen*), *Enn.* VI, 9, 3, and 5, followed by Proclus, *Elem. theol.*, prop. 20; see also *hypostasis, theos.*

hypodochē or **hypodechoménē:** *receptacle*

According to Plato it is in this receptacle that *genesis* takes place, although the receptacle itself is always the same, *Tim.* 50b–51b. It is also called *chora* (area), *ibid.* 52a, and granted a quasi-existence (*pos on*), *ibid.* 52c (for the ontological aspects of this, see *on* and *genesis*). Aristotle identifies Plato's "receptacle" with matter (*hyle*), *Phys.* IV, 209b. For Plotinus the "receptacle" is "second" or sensible matter,

Enn. II, 4, 6; II, 4, 11; see *topos* and compare *hypokeimenon, hyle, genesis.*

hypokeímenon: *substratum*

Aristotle's analysis of *genesis* in the *Physics*, based, apparently, on a Platonic prototype (see *genesis*), leads him to the isolation of three principles (*archai*) involved in all changes from one thing into another: the immanent form (*eidos*, q.v.), the privation (*steresis*, q.v.) of the form of the thing it is going to become, and, finally, the substratum (*hypokeimenon*) that persists through the change and in which the *genesis* takes place (*Phys.* I, 190a–b). Its name is dictated by its function; thus from a predicational point of view the substratum is that of which other things are predicated and which is not predicated of anything else (*Meta.* 1028b–1029a). But the passages in the *Physics* are considering *hypokeimenon* in the context of material change, and so it is not merely a logical concept but, together with *eidos*, a genuine co-principle of being (*Phys.* I, 190b), what is, from a slightly different point of view, matter (*hyle*) and, like matter, is known not directly but analogically (*ibid.* 191a). Both the logical and ontological aspects of *hypokeimenon* persist in later thinkers: it is the first of the four Stoic *kategoriai* (q.v.), *SVF* II, 369, and identified with matter in Plotinus, *Enn.* II, 4, 6; see *hyle, hypodoche, symbebekos.*

hypólēpsis: *judgment*
See *doxa, noesis.*

hypónoia: *underlying sense, hidden meaning*
See *mythos.*

hypóstasis: *standing under, hence, substance; real being,*
frequently in opposition to appearances

In Plato's system all the *eide* are *hypostases* in that they are really real (*ontos on*), but the notion of *hypostasis* does not formally appear until later Platonism began to arrange the most important *eide* in an ontologically descending hierarchy, perhaps on the analogy of number (see *monas*), since it early appears in a Neopythagorean numerical interpretation of Plato (Moderatus in Simplicius, *Phys.* 230–231). It is clearly a product of syncretism, a blending of the Parmenidean One (see *hen*), Aristotle's Intelligence (see *nous*) combined with Plato's *Demiourgos*, and Plato's World Soul (see *psyche tou pantos*). These three supreme *archai* of being are already in evidence in Albinus (*Epit.* x) and Numenius (in Eusebius, *Praep. Evang.* XI, 17), but their integration into a complex metaphysical and ethical world view is the work of Plotinus: One, *Nous, Psyche* (the latter subdivided, see *physis*), see the summary passages in *Enn.* II, 9, 1; V, 2, 1; VI, 7, 42 and Proclus' dialectic derivation in *Elem. theol.*, prop. 20.

For the individual *hypostases*, see *hen, nous, psyche tou pantos;* for their progression, *proödos, trias.*

hypóthesis: *suggestive, posited starting point, hypothesis*

The tentative definition suggested by Socrates' interlocutors, Xenophon, *Mem.* IV, 6, which Socrates himself explains more fully in *Phaedo* 100a–e where it serves as a kind of criterion against which to measure the congruence of "deductions"; the theory of forms is just such a hypothesis here. Again (*ibid.* 101d) the pushing *back* of the hypothesis to something more basic is described, back to what in *Rep.* 511b is called the "unhypothetized principle" (see *Parm.* 135e). In Aristotle the "primary" (*ex arches*) hypotheses are the undemonstrable first principles: axioms and postulates (*Anal. pr.* I, 24a, 72a; see *noesis, nous, epagoge*).

i

ídion: *property*

In terms of Aristotelian logic a property is not something that reveals the essence of a thing, like "animal" (the *genos*), but that belongs to an essence and to that essence alone, e.g. "grammar-learning" as applied to a man. Unlike an accident (see *symbebekos*), it cannot belong to anything else, i.e., every man is a grammar-learner and vice versa, *Top.* I, 102a. Together with *genos, diaphora,* and *symbebekos,* it constitutes the four "predicables" treated *ibid.* I, 101b–104a. Their relationship with the ten *kategoriai* or "predicaments" is dealt with *ibid.* I, 103b; see *symbebekos.*

isomoiría: *equal share, balance, equilibrium*
See *meson.*

isonomía: *equal share, balance, equilibrium*
See *hedone.*

k

kakón: *evil*

1. Before Socrates made ethics a subject of philosophical discourse considerations of good and evil had been the preserve of the poets and the lawgivers. But the increasing awareness of moral relativism and the Sophists' assertion of the purely arbitrary character of law (*nomos*, q.v.) led Socrates to seek for absolute standards of moral conduct.

2. But the Socratic emphasis is on virtue (*arete*) and good (*agathon*). Indeed, from his intellectualistic point of view there would seem to be no such thing as evil, since no one errs willingly, but through ignorance (Aristotle, *Eth. Nich.* VII, 1145b). Plato continued in this tradition with his lengthy discussions of the possibility of false judgment (see *doxa*).

3. But there were new considerations as well. Plato is more aware of the volitional element and admits that the soul can cause both good and evil (*Laws* 896d; compare *Theaet.* 176a and see *psyche*), and the hypostatization process that led him to convert Socratic definitions into ontological realities suggests, in one place at least, the existence of an *eidos* of evil (*Rep.* 476e). This is perhaps consonant with, or at least explicable, in the context of the ethical origins of the theory of *eide*, but the assertion, in *Laws* 896e, that there is an evil as well as a good World Soul (*psyche tou pantos*, q.v.) is to move ethical dualism, pervasive in the early Plato on the level of body and soul, onto the cosmic stage, perhaps the result of increased contacts with the Iranian tradition.

4. Aristotle rejects both the *eidos* of evil and the evil World Soul in *Meta.* 1051a. The characteristic Aristotelian doctrine associates moral evil with excess as a correlative of his theory of the "mean" (see *meson*). In *Eth. Nich.* 1106b Aristotle quotes with approval the related Pythagorean judgment that evil is to be identified with the indeterminate (*apeiron;* compare the Pythagorean "Table of Opposites" in *Meta.* 986a, and see *kinoun* 2).

5. In post-Aristotelian philosophy the implications of both the Platonic and Aristotelian positions were explored. The Epicureans, with their thoroughgoing sensualism, stand somewhat apart: all evil can be equated with pain (*algos, ponos*) either of the body or the mind

(D.L. x, 128; see *hedone*), and its existence poses no theological problems since the gods do not concern themselves with the world (D.L. x, 123–124). But for the Stoics and their doctrine of providence (*pronoia*, q.v.) evil is more of a problem: how to explain the presence of evil in a universe governed by an all-good God? One suggestion (its history was venerable) was that evil is God's instrument for educating and chastising men (Plutarch, *De Stoic. repugn.* 1040c; Seneca, *De prov., passim*). The other relied on the organic nature of the universe as a whole: "all things work unto good" (Plutarch, *op. cit.*, 1050e; Seneca, *Ep.* 74, 20). But there is another possibility, the one broached by Plato in the *Laws* and that openly admits the existence of a radical, subsistent principle of evil, whether theistic as in the *Laws* and Iranian Zoroastrianism (so Plutarch, *De Iside* 46, 48), or metaphysical, e.g. matter.

6. Both the Pythagoreans and Plato had, as noted above, admitted the indeterminate (*apeiron*) as a co-principle of being, and the former at least had identified it with evil. Aristotle had equated it with his material principle (*hyle*) but had failed to draw the conclusion that matter and evil are to some extent synonymous. There are, to be sure, some hints of this in both Plato (*Pol.* 273b; *Tim.* 68e) and Aristotle (*De gen. anim.* IV, 770b: matter resists form), but the exploration of the ethical qualities of matter remained for later philosophers.

7. Stoic (and Epicurean) monism tended to obscure rather than illuminate the problematic of matter but there were other forces at work. There was, for one, the Neopythagorean interest in the *Timaeus* that served to reenforce the equation of Plato's *chora* with Aristotle's *hyle* (so Moderatus cited in Simplicius, *In Phys*, pp. 230–231). Again, and more importantly, there was the growth of the oriental tradition of ethical dualism whose most important witness is Plutarch's *De Iside*, and which found its natural philosophical ally in Aristotle's *eidos/hyle* dichotomy. By the time of Numenius, evil (*kakon*, *malum*) is firmly identified with matter (*hyle*, *silva*) and the position was held by a variety of Gnostic sects (see *Corpus Hermeticum* I, 1, 4–5).

8. Plotinus, who opposed the Gnostic view of the universe and, indeed, any type of dualism, was, nonetheless, affected by the identification of matter and evil. His solution to the problem of evil unfolds within strictly controlled limits. First, it is not a question of dualism: matter is generated from the One under the guise of "Otherness" (*Enn.* II, 4, 5). This refers first and foremost to intelligible matter (*hyle noete;* see *hyle;* Proclus doubts whether this should be called matter at all: *Theol. Plat.* III, 9) that is always defined and hence the possibility of evil in the *kosmos noetos* is ruled out (*Enn.* I, 8, 2). On the question of sensible matter (*hyle aisthete*) Plotinus, while admit-

ting that it is the cause of evil (1, 8, 4), is at some pains to point out that it is *not* a substance but a privation (*steresis*), the absence of any good (1, 8, 11).

9. Proclus opposes this on a number of counts: he fails to see how a privation, which is essentially a negation, can be the cause of anything (*De mal. subst.*, p. 240) and so prefers to revert to the Platonic (and more voluntaristic) position that the soul is the cause of evil or, to put it another way, that the evil in the *kosmos* is moral and not metaphysical (*op. cit.*, p. 233).

On "original sin" as a source of evil, see *kathodos*.

kállos: beauty
See *eros*.

kardía: *heart*
1. Behind the long-standing debate on the seat of the soul that was conducted in philosophical circles there stands a prephilosophical physiology that had, in effect, decided the question and that, supported by the massive authority of Homer, tended to dominate even the accumulating medical evidence to the contrary. The Homeric hero both feels (*Il.* IX, 186; XIII, 493; etc.) and thinks (*Il.* IX, 600; XXII, 296) with the *phrenes* or midriff, whence the later *phronesis*, thought or wisdom.

2. A great number of thinkers went along the same path, encouraged no doubt by medical theories of vital heat carried through the system by the blood. The thermal theory of thought finds its chief propagator in Heraclitus who identified the soul with fire (fr. 36) and connected it with consciousness (Diels 22A16). In Empedocles the blood appears as a factor linked with perception, and the seat of perception is located in the heart (fr. 105). Perhaps Democritus too is to be placed here, though the evidence is contradictory (rational faculty in the breast in Aetius IV, 4, 6; in the brain, *ibid.* IV, 5, 1), and it was not, in any event, their vital heat that suggested the comparison of soul and fire atoms to Democritus, but rather the latter's shape and mobility (Aristotle, *De an.* I, 405a). Aristotle calls the heart the *arche* of life, movement, and sensation (*De part. anim.* 666a–b), and though the Epicureans dispersed the soul all over the body (see *psyche*), the rational faculty (Lucretius: *animus*) was in the breast (Lucretius III, 141–142), as it was for the Stoics (*SVF* II, 879).

3. The other school of thought, which located the seat of perception in the brain (*enkephalos*), had its origin in Pythagorean medical circles, specifically with Alcmaeon of Crotona (Theophrastus, *De sens.* 26; see also *aisthesis*) who maintained that there were passages (*poroi*) connecting the senses to the brain, a position he was said to have

arrived at by actual dissections on the optic nerve (Diels 24A11) and that reappears among the philosophers with Diogenes of Apollonia. Here the physiological reasoning is crossed with more philosophical considerations, i.e., that air (*aer*, q.v.) is the divine *arche* of all things, and the source of life, soul, and intelligence (frs. 4, 5). How perception occurs we are told by Theophrastus (*De sens.* 39–44). Man inhales air that travels, via the various senses, to the brain. If the air is pure and dry, thought (*phronesis*) takes place (see *aisthesis* and compare the similar Hippocratic text in Diels 64C3).

4. Socrates had heard of the brain theory as a young man and was interested in it (*Phaedo* 96b). He must have passed his interest on to Plato who, in the *Timaeus*, locates the rational part (*logistikon*) of the human soul in the head (44d) and makes the brain the source of the reproductive powers (73c–d; see *psyche*).

5. But even though the question continued to be debated (see *SVF* II, 885; Cicero, *Tusc.* I, 9, 19), it was the view of Aristotle that prevailed. Aristotle knew, to be sure, the medical assertions of the connection of the senses with the brain, but he was not convinced by the evidence (*Hist. anim.* 514a). What he finds more persuasive is that there is no sensation in the brain itself (*De part. anim.* 656a).

6. Plotinus, however, following the Platonic tradition, continues to locate the *arche* of sensation in the brain, or as he carefully puts it, "the point of departure [*arche*] of the operation [*energeia*] of the faculty [*dynamis*], since it is the *arche* of the *kinesis* of the instrument [*organon*]" (*Enn.* IV, 3, 23).

katálēpsis: *grasping, apprehension*
The act of grasping an impression (*phantasia*): the act is a primary one in Stoic epistemology, and described by Cicero, *Acad. post.* I, 11, 40–42; apprehension is the criterion of truth for the Stoics, Sextus Empiricus, *Adv. Math.* VII, 152; the volitional element is underlined, *ibid.* VIII, 397; see *phantasia, prolepsis, ennoia, noesis*.

katēgoríai: *accusations, predications, categories,*
praedicamenta, summa genera (scil. *entis*)
The ten (in some lists only eight) most general ways in which a subject may be described; a logical structuring that corresponds to the real existence of things: the *eide* of being in *Meta.* 1003b21 or, again, the *summa genera* of being (see *genos*). The most complete list is given in *Cat.* 1b–2a: substance (*ousia*), quantity (*poson*), quality (*poion*), relation (*pros ti*), place (*pou*), time (*pote*), position (*keisthai*), state (*echein*), action (*poien*), affection (*paschein*); for their relationship with the four predicables, see *Top.* 103a–b and *idion*. Aristotle's *kategoriai* are criticized by Plotinus in *Enn.* VI, 1, 1–24. The

Stoics reduced the categories to four: subject (*hypokeimenon*), quality, state, relation, *SVF* II, 369; they are discussed by Plotinus, *Enn.* VI, 1, 25–30.

kathársis: *purgation, purification*

1. *Katharsis*, a word with both religious and medical implications, seems to fluctuate between affirmative and negative functions at the hands of the philosophers. Among the Pythagoreans *katharsis* had, as might be expected, strong religious connotations. *Katharsis* is a purification of the soul, effected, we are told (Iamblichus, *Vita Pyth.* 110), through *mousike* (q.v.), i.e., by rendering it harmonious; indeed, this is philosophy (*ibid.* 137). This Pythagorean identification of *katharsis* and *philosophia* is found in Plato (see *Phaedo* 67a–d), and the analogy with music runs through the dialogues. In *Phaedo* 61a Socrates equates philosophy and music, and in the *Republic* (431e, 432a, 433d) music is the foundation of the master virtue *sophrosyne* (q.v.). We are further told, in *Tim.* 90d, that the care of the soul consists in bringing its modulations into harmony with the cosmic order (see *ouranos*).

2. But when Socrates informs us, in *Soph.* 226a ff., that his art is "cathartic," we have passed over to other grounds where the function of *katharsis* is described as "the removal of evil from the soul" (*ibid.* 227d), just as the medical art does for the body. Here the problem is not seen as a kind of imbalance (see *hedone*) that can be set aright by harmonization, but as the presence of something essentially alien to the system. Medical men are familiar with this type of purgation (*Crat.* 405a), and it may be extended, by analogy, to a misuse by tyrants practiced upon the state (*Rep.* 567c). Socrates effects his *katharsis* of the soul by the best possible purgative, interrogation (*elenchos*) that cleanses the soul of false opinions (*Soph.* 230d).

3. Aristotle applies the theory to music (*Pol.* 1341b–1342a): some music is educational, presumably the "harmonizing" type of the Pythagorean tradition; but there is also "cathartic" music in the medical, purgative sense. This latter type has its effect by the homoeopathic principle of inducing exactly the same effect that one seeks to cure. Plato knows of this practice (see *Rep.* 560d, *Laws* 790c–791b), and as is clear from these passages in Plato and Aristotle, both men were aware that the homoeopathic principle enunciated by physicians had already been extended to the cure of certain psychic states, most particularly religious possession or *enthousiasmos* (see *mantike*). Aristotle took the further step and incorporated it into his theory of art, with the well-known result of tragedy's being defined in terms of effecting a homoeopathic *katharsis*/purgation of the *pathe* of pity and fear (*Poet.* 1449b).

4. Plotinus discusses the relationship of *katharsis* and *arete* in *Enn.* I, 2, 4; with Plato he makes *katharsis* a necessary condition to assimilation to God (*ibid.* I, 6, 6; see *homoiosis*).

káthodos: *descent, fall (of the soul)*

1. The origins of the figure of the fall or banishment of the soul from its natural, immortal abode are religious, as appears from its first occurrence among the philosophers in Empedocles' *Purifications* (fr. 115; it may have been held in some form by Heraclitus as well; see frs. 62, 68; Plato, *Gorg.* 492e–493b; Plotinus, *Enn.* IV, 8, 1) where the banishment is the result of a primal crime (bloodshed or flesh-eating; frs. 136, 137, 139) committed by one of the *daimones* (q.v.) whose natural lot was immortality. Because of this crime it is subjected, for the period of a "great year" (30,000 seasons in Empedocles, fr. 115, line 6; the figure varies elsewhere), to successive reincarnations in this world of change.

2. This account is closely tied to the Pythagorean view of the immortal soul (see *psyche*) and the attendant doctrine of *palingenesia* (q.v.). This type of belief is common in Plato and expressed in a series of great myths (see *athanatos*). Plato knows Empedocles' version (and, apparently, the related myth of the devouring of Dionysus by the Titans, the creation of man from the ashes of the latter, and the consequent "Titanic nature" of mortals whose Dionysiac spark is thus embedded in a Titanic element that is the direct result of an "original sin"; see *Laws* 701c) and employs it, with characteristic Platonic changes, in *Phaedrus* 248c–249d. The soul loses its wings and falls into the sensible world. But whereas the emphasis in Empedocles is on the immortal soul's coming into the cyclic *kosmos*, the fall consequent upon sin (its nature is not specified) is used by Plato to explain the presence of the soul in the body and is integrated, via the link between recollection (*anamnesis*, q.v.) and the *eide*, into Plato's epistemological and metaphysical doctrines.

3. The question of the descent of the soul, its manner and its purpose, continued to exercise the thinkers of the Platonic tradition, and the best testimonial to their interest is undoubtedly the essay devoted to the question by Plotinus (*Enn.* IV, 8) and the passages of Iamblichus' *De anima* preserved in Stobaeus. A great variety of views are recorded, and the mechanics and landscape of the trip through the spheres, compounded of Plato's remarks (the prenatal vision of the spheres given the soul in *Phaedrus* 274c–248c and *Rep.* 616d–617d, and the suggestion, in *Rep.* 614d, that the descent, at least for some, is through the heavens) and a great deal of astronomical lore, are lovingly detailed. Typical is Porphyry's allegorical interpretation of the "Cave of the Nymphs" in *Od.* XIII, 102–112 (with some of the details bor-

rowed from Numenius; cf. *De antro nymph.* 21, 28)); Odysseus' travels become, in this symbol-enamored age, the archetypal enactment of the soul's wanderings: *ibid.* 34–35 and Macrobius' account of the *descensus animae* in his commentary on the *Somnium Scipionis* (1, 11, 11–12, 18); atypical is Plotinus' internalization of the phenomenon (*Enn.* IV, 8, 1).

4. Why this occurred at all is considerably more perplexing. The *Phaedrus* announces it as an "ordinance of Necessity," but proceeds to link it with a mischance (*syntychia*) of the soul (248c). The *Timaeus* shows a different point of view. The *kosmos* must contain all the beings of the *kosmos noetos* (q.v.), otherwise it will be incomplete; for this reason mortal creatures are brought into creation (41b–d). Plotinus subscribes to this view that the engagement of the soul in a mortal body is the fulfillment of a divine purpose and dictated by the very nature of the soul (*Enn.* IV, 8, 7). The same view is taken by Proclus (*In Alc.* 328, 29; compare *Elem. theol.*, prop. 206).

5. But in this same passage of Plotinus there is at least the suggestion that the soul is somewhat to be blamed for its "excessive zeal," and in *Enn.* V, 1, 1 we are given a still clearer account of its "audacity" (*tolma*) and joy at its own independence that causes it to flee God. The prenatal sin theory, though hardly consonant with the rest of Plotinus' thought, was held by other thinkers. According to Iamblichus (Stobaeus, *Ecl.* I, p. 375), Albinus is among this number in making the fall a result of free choice, but this may refer to the common Pythagorean motif of the soul's choice of life before *palingenesia* (*Rep.* 617e: "the chooser is responsible; God is blameless"). Macrobius (1, 11, 11) speaks of a "longing for the body" (*appetentia corporis*). But the best-known adherents of the doctrine were undoubtedly the Gnostics who thought the material world an essentially evil place and for whom the fall of the soul was a commonplace (see Plotinus, *Enn.* II, 9, 10).

kathólou: universal

1. *Katholou* is an Aristotelian technical term, though there is evidence for its evolution in Plato (cf. *Meno* 27a, *Rep.* 392d–e). Aristotle defines the universal in *De interp.* 17a as "that which by its nature is capable of being predicated of several subjects," e.g. "man" is a universal, Callias is a singular. It is frequently identified with genus (see *genos; Meta.* 1049b, 1038b–1039). Aristotle specifically rejects the claim of the universal to be substance, and yet in the *Anal. post.* and elsewhere he is insistent that only the universal can be defined (*Meta.* 1036a), and is the true object of science (*episteme; Anal. post.* I, 87b–88a, *De an.* II, 417b). Aristotle severely criticized Plato for hypos-

tatizing the universals (*Meta.* 1086a–1087a): Socrates, however, did not make this mistake (*ibid.* 1078b).

For the perception of the universal in Epicurus, see *prolepsis;* for the possibility of a "concrete universal," *gnorimon.*

keísthai: *position,* situs

One of the ten *kategoriai* in Aristotle, *Cat.* 1b–2a; in other places, e.g. *Anal. post.* I, 83b, both *keisthai* and *echein* (state) are omitted from the list. In the list in *Cat.* 1b Aristotle's own examples of *keisthai* are "lying," "sitting"; it is a relative term, *ibid.* 6b (see *pros ti*).

kenón: *void,* vacuum

A void is admitted by the Pythagoreans as a separating element between natures, and, particularly, numbers (Aristotle, *Phys.* IV, 213b). It is attacked by Parmenides (Diels, fr. 8, lines 6–11), and denied by Melissus as sheer nonbeing (Diels, fr. 7). For both Empedocles and Anaxagoras air is corporeal, and hence to be distinguished from the void, which is denied as nonbeing (Aristotle, *Phys.* IV, 213a, *De coelo* IV, 309a). The Atomists embrace the Parmenidean paradox and assert the existence of the nonbeing void, which, together with "the full," they make the new principles of the universe (Aristotle, *De gen. et corr.* I, 325a, *Meta.* 985b). It is discussed, defined ("place [*topos*] with nothing in it"), and denied by Aristotle (*Phys.* IV, 213a–217b). *Kenon* is affirmed by Epicurus as a good Atomist (D.L. x, 38–41), but denied by the Stoics (D.L. VII, 140); see *topos.*

kénōsis: *emptying, depletion*
See *hedone.*

kínēsis: *motion, movement, change*

1. Motion presents no problem for the Milesian philosophers; it is an unquestioned part of their pervasive vitalism (see *zoe*), and it is in this spirit that both Anaximander (Diels 12A11) and Anaximenes (Diels 12A9, 13A6) posit an eternal motion. It is noteworthy too that when Xenophanes wishes to temper the contemporary anthropomorphism he denies his God *kinesis* (Diels 21A25, 26). *Kinesis* is present in all reality in Heraclitus, as illustrated in the famous river image (see Plato, *Crat.* 402a, *rhoe,* and *episteme*).

2. Suddenly all of this is changed with Parmenides' attack on all forms of change (see *genesis, on*), and particularly motion (see fr. 8, line 26), undoubtedly as a result of his denial of the void (*kenon*) on the grounds of nonbeing, thus depriving body of a place into which to move (see Plato, *Theaet.* 180e). Zeno's four arguments contrived to

support the position of Parmenides and deny the possibility of motion (see Aristotle, *Phys.* VI, 239b; answered, *ibid.* 263a–b) are, of course, polemical and derived *ex hypothesi* against the Pythagorean reluctance to relinquish the *void* (see *megethos*).

3. *Genesis* (q.v.), at least on the secondary level, recovered from Parmenides' assault, and his successors tended to substitute some derivative of *kinesis*, e.g. mixture or association, for the ground previously held by *genesis* properly so called. But what was now markedly different was that *kinesis* was no longer natural or inherent in things, as with the Milesians, but required some type of agent (*kinoun*, q.v.) operating from outside the system. An external force to explain *kinesis* appears in Empedocles and is identified as Love and Strife (fr. 17), and in Anaxagoras' *nous* (frs. 12–14); all of these forces are still, however, material.

4. At this point the only serious proponents of an inherent, natural motion in bodies are the Atomists. Democritus held such an eternal motion for the *atoma* that moved in all directions (Aristotle, *De coelo* III, 300b; D.L. IX, 44), a movement that he called "vibration" (*palmos;* Aetius I, 23, 3) and that occurs by necessity (Aristotle, *Phys.* II, 196a; D.L. IX, 45). It is from the resultant collisions that aggregates are formed (see *genesis*) that in turn move into a vortex or whirl (*dine*), gradually finding their places in the *kosmos* (Diels 67A14).

5. Epicurus' explanation is somewhat different. For him the *atoma* have, in addition to size and shape, weight (*baros*) as one of their primary characteristics (D.L. X, 54). Thus their eternal downward motion would seem to be derived rather than an inherent property (D.L. X, 61; Lucretius II, 83, 217). Their collision and consequent aggregation into bodies is brought about by a swerve (*parenklisis*) in their parallel motions (Aetius I, 12, 5; Lucretius II, 216–293; Cicero, *De fin.* I, 6, 19; compare *genesis*).

6. At *Soph.* 248c–249a Plato departs from his Parmenidean viewpoint. Where earlier there was a firm insistence on the unchangeable nature of the *eide* (see *Phaedo* 78d), now *kinesis* too has its place in the world of reality. The soul, for instance, which is akin to the *eide* (*Phaedo* 78b–79b), is self-moving (and hence immortal) and the source of movement in others (*Phaedrus* 245c–246a; for the Platonic causal category of "self-mover," see *Laws* X, 894c), including the heavenly bodies (see *ouranioi*). Indeed, in *Soph.* 254d Plato maintains that *kinesis* is one of the most important *eide*, and it seems to serve for him the same function that *metabole* (q.v.) does for Aristotle: a generic term for change that has as its species at least locomotion (*phora*) and qualitative change (*alloiosis;* see *Theaet.* 181c) and that is expanded, in *Laws* X, 894b–c, to embrace ten distinct species, including, as the Aristotelian *metabole* does not, both *genesis* and *phthora*

(qq.v.). None of these is, of course, the *eidos* of *kinesis* mentioned in the *Sophist*, but the tenth (really, as Plato points out, the *arche* of all the others) self-moved motion is the soul, which mediates between the other nine and the *eidos* (see *psyche*).

7. Aristotle attacks the Platonic position in *Phys.* III, 200b where he declares that there is no *kinesis* apart from things. He then offers his own definition (*ibid.* III, 201a) of *kinesis* as "the actualization [*entelecheia*] of a potentiality [*dynamis*] *qua* potentiality." It occurs only as a *metabole*, i.e., a change in the category of quality, quantity, or place (*ibid.* V, 226a). The latter *kinesis*, i.e., locomotion (*phora*), is primary (*ibid.* VIII, 265b–266a), taking precedence even over *genesis* (q.v.).

8. Aristotle follows Plato back along the road to the inherent Milesian motion by describing *physis* (q.v.) as the principle and cause of *kinesis* (*Phys.* II, 192b); this does not, of course, free him from the necessity of the external, self-moving cause; see *kinoun*. *Kinesis* is, together with nutrition, sensation, and thought, one of the four main functions of the *psyche* (*De an.* 413a–b), and is resolved into the operation of desire (*orexis*) in conjunction with what is perceived as a real or apparent good (*ibid.* III, 432a–433b).

For Aristotle's theory of "natural motion," see *stoicheion, aither;* for the application of *kinesis* to perception, *aisthesis;* on the possibility of *actio in distans, sympatheia.*

kinoún: *mover, agent, efficient cause*

1. The problem of an external agent or *arche* for movement is not a problem for the early *physikoi* since in their vitalistic view *kinesis* was inherent in things (see *kinesis* 1). But once Parmenides had denied that *kinesis* was an attribute of true being, the obvious phenomenon of motion in the physical world had to be explained by recourse to an external mover that would give at least the initial impetus to *kinesis*.

2. The first such attempt is the "Love" and "Strife" of Empedocles (fr. 17, lines 19–20; compare Diels 31A28), drawn from an analogy with the motive forces operative in man (*ibid.*, lines 22–24; compare Aristotle, *Meta.* 985a, who stresses the moral aspect of these forces and sees them as a manifestation of moral dualism; see *kakon* 3). Shortly thereafter there is an epoch-making shift away from the moral to the intellectual sphere: Anaxagoras' source of motion is intelligence (*nous*), which is not only the initiator of motion but a guiding force as well (see *nous* 3; *noesis* 4). The lineaments of Aristotle's God are already present: *noesis, kinesis, telos.*

3. Plato's earlier preoccupation with the immutable *eide* apparently excluded any serious consideration of *kinesis*. But in the later

dialogues, particularly in the *Sophist, Philebus, Timaeus,* and *Laws,* there is a full-blown theory of *kinesis* (q.v. 6) with two related points of focus: the attribution of the principle of self-motion to the soul (see *psyche* 19) and the admission of *kinesis,* by reason of its being a function of soul, to the realm of the "completely real" (*pantelos on; Soph.* 248e–249b). There is, moreover, an *eidos* of *kinesis* (*ibid.* 254e) and, indeed, it is one of the *megista gene* (see *eidos* 13).

4. Motion, then, occurs on three levels in Plato: as the transcendental *eidos* of motion; as the self-motion of soul, which holds an intermediary position between the *eide* and sensible particulars and which is the *arche* of motion described in the *Laws* x 895b; and, finally, as the various types of secondary motions in the *kosmos* described in *Laws* x, 893b–894c.

5. In terms of this analysis Plato's *proton kinoun* or First Mover is the noetic part of the semitranscendent or World Soul (see *psyche tou pantos*). There seem to be, moreover, grounds for identifying the *nous* of the *Philebus* and *Timaeus* with this same World Soul, even though it is mythically described as creating the World Soul (see *nous* 6). We have, then, not merely a *kinoun* but a final and exemplary cause as well. The *demiourgos* (q.v.) is good and makes the world to be as similar to himself as possible (*Tim.* 29e–30a) and, we are told, the human soul is made of the same "stuff" as the World Soul (*ibid.* 41d). But not only is the *kosmos* related to the *kinoun* as *eikon* to *paradeigma,* the movement known as "procession" (*proödos,* q.v.) in later Platonism; there is, as well, a "return" (*epistrophe,* q.v.). The immediate result of the self-moving motion of the World Soul is the perfect circular motion of its own body, the visible universe (*ibid.* 34a, 36e, 40a–b). This regular visible and eternal motion of the heavens provides, in turn, a model by which men should regulate the *harmonia* (q.v.) in their own souls (*ibid.* 47b–c; astronomy is, of course, only preliminary to the higher thrusts of the "return" effected by *eros* and *dialektike:* see *ouranos* 2).

6. The same passages in the *Timaeus* introduce another consideration: the heavenly bodies are also "a race of Gods." Each is endowed with intelligence and it is this intelligence that explains the axial rotation of the stars, rotary because "each always thinks the same thoughts about the same things" (*ibid.* 39e–40a; on this rotary motion compare *Rep.* 436b and *Laws* x, 898a). Plato seems to be in some doubt about the mode of connection between these heavenly bodies and their guiding intelligences. Some suggestions are made in *Laws* x, 898e, but Plato is uncertain whether their soul is an immanent motor, like our soul, or an extrinsic force that may be either corporeal (possibly the theory of Eudoxus that the stars are carried around by the corporeal sphere in which they are imbedded, a theory adopted by

Aristotle; see 7, 11 *infra*) or incorporeal (the Aristotelian "object of love"?). But whatever the exact relationship, the Platonic tradition maintained its belief in these planetary movers to the end (see *ouranioi*).

7. Among the various causes involved in *genesis* Aristotle specifies the *kinoun* or agent that initiates change (*Phys.* II, 194b). What is coming into question here are Aristotle's revised notions of *physis* (q.v. 3). *Physis* has dislodged *psyche* from much of the ground held by the Platonic soul, most notably from its position as the source of purpose (*telos; Phys.* II, 194a) and movement (*ibid.* VIII, 250b–253a) and, given the existence of things in motion, there must be a single cause of motion, a "first mover" (*proton kinoun*) that is itself unmoved (*ibid.* 256a–258b): everything that is moved is moved by something and there cannot be an infinite regress of such movers (*ibid.* 256a and VII, 242a–243a). Thus there is an eternal First Mover and an eternal first moved, the latter the sphere in which are embedded the fixed stars (VIII, 260a–266a), moving in an eternal, circular locomotion (locomotion is prior to all other forms of change, even *genesis; ibid.* 260a–b and see *genesis* 15).

8. But Aristotle apparently did not always hold this view. The line of reasoning cited above from the *Physics* is essentially an argument from *energeia/dynamis* (qq.v.) that rests on the premiss that the passage from potency to act demands the prior presence of an agent already in act that leads, via the denial of infinite regress, to an eternal *energeia* that cannot be other. But there is also "Platonic motion" whereby the soul is the source of motion. In this way Plato explained the axial rotation of the stars, and it was the same explanation that Aristotle himself relied upon in attributing souls to the stars in his early Platonizing dialogue *On Philosophy* (fr. 24 = Cicero, *De nat. deor.* II, 44; here the motion is called "voluntary"). But cannot the heavenly bodies also be moved by their *physis*, which Aristotle has substituted for the *psyche* as an internal source of motion? This seems to be the theory held in the *De coelo* where the motion of the "first body," i.e., the sphere of the fixed stars, is the "natural" eternal, circular motion of the fifth element, *aither* (q.v.; *De coelo* I, 268a–270b; see *stoicheion* 17). The fixed stars themselves move because they are embedded in this sphere (*ibid.* II, 298b–290b). But even though he is capable of giving this explanation of the motion of the stars in terms of the *physis* of the sphere, he is somewhat embarrassed as to what to do with his Platonic legacy of the star souls (compare *ibid.* II, 291 and 292a).

9. This would seem to be a view different from that of the transcendent mover of the *Physics* (although there are a number of dubious and/or obscure references to just such a transcendent mover in

De coelo, e.g. 279a–b). But it is, nonetheless, the *kinoun* of *Physics* VIII
that is taken up and elaborated in the *Metaphysics*. At the end of the
former work it is stated that the *proton kinoun* is without magnitude
(*megethos*, q.v.). This leads to an immediate difficulty since, in the
Aristotelian system, all *kinesis* is effected by contact (*haphe;* see *sympatheia* 7). To answer the difficulty Aristotle resorts to a principle
borrowed from nature. The perception of the good gives rise to appetite
(*orexis*, q.v.) for that good, in rational beings the object of rational
desire (*boulesis;* see *De an.* III, 433a and *proairesis*), and in irrational
nature by its imitation of the movement of the heavenly bodies expressed by the constant passage of the elements from one into the other
(see *Meta.* 1050b; *De gen. et corr.* II, 337a; and *genesis* 15). In this
way the *proton kinoun* is the good of the entire universe "as an object
loved" (*Meta.* 1072b), and the *kosmos* and all its parts "move toward
it" by their *mimesis* of its *energeia* translated into physical terms: the
heavenly bodies by their perfect circular revolutions and corruptible
bodies by their cyclic *genesis-phthora*. Man's *mimesis* is somewhat
more direct; he is capable of the same kind of *energeia* as the *proton
kinoun*, i.e., *noesis*, but he performs it only intermittently because it
involves a passage from potency to act and so is wearisome (*Meta.*
1050b, 1072b; see *noesis* 21, *nous* 10).

10. Within the categories of act and potency the Prime Mover
must be an immaterial substance eternally actualized (*Meta.* 1071b).
What is this *energeia?* It is at this point that the whole Platonic world
of the *eide* is swept away. Aristotle no longer needs the *eide* to explain
universal predication (see *katholou*), and their static qualities ill accord with his own search for an *arche* of movement (particularly if he
thinks of the *eide* as numbers; see *Meta.* 992a and *arithmos* 3). What is
left, in effect, is Plato's World Soul of the *Sophist-Philebus-Timaeus:* a
transcendent substance, a living *nous* that imparts motion to the *kosmos*. And it is precisely in these terms that the Aristotelian *proton
kinoun* is described: *ousia aidios, nous, zoe* (*Meta.* 1072b–1073a; for
the subsequent career of this illustrious trio, see *trias*). There are, of
course, corrections. The Platonic World Soul has a World Body, the
kosmos aisthetos; this would be *dynamis* and limitation in the Aristotelian system. Plato's *psyche* had involved *kinesis;* Aristotle's *nous* en-
joys the odd "activity of immobility" (*energeia akinesias; Eth. Nich.*
VII, 1154b): its *energeia* is *noesis* (see *nous* 9).

11. But Chapter VIII of Book Lambda of the *Metaphysics* introduces a new difficulty into the kinetics of the system. One unmoved
mover had been posited earlier to explain the eternal circular motion of
the sphere of the fixed stars. But there are other eternal circular
motions in the *kosmos* and so there should be as many unmoved movers
as is necessary to explain the complicated motions of the spheres, the

exact number to be calculated by the astronomers (*Meta.* 1073a–b; the numbers offered by Aristotle in the following passages are forty-seven and fifty-five). They too must be intellectual substances that move the spheres as final cause (see *Meta.* 1074a).

12. What is the relationship of these unmoved movers to the spheres and to the *proton kinoun* of the rest of the argument? Aristotle nowhere explains. To make them the souls of the spheres would be to return to the "Platonic motion" of *On Philosophy* and make it impossible to explain how they are always in act; to make them immaterial forces external to the body of the sphere (would, in that event, the sphere have an immanent soul in addition?) is to raise the question of their individuation. If they are not united to a body how do they differ one from another since matter is the principle of individuation (see *hyle* 2 and compare *diaphora* 4 where the genus is said to supply an "intelligible matter" for the species)? It has generally been assumed that they are somehow subordinated to the *proton kinoun* described as ruling the entire universe (*Meta.* 1070b, 1072b, 1076a and see 9 *supra*), and this despite the fact that they are unmoved. In fact, the argument on the basis of which they are posited in the first place necessitates that they too be intellectual *ousiai* perfectly actualized, a consideration that would seem to eliminate their having any desire (*orexis*), and consequently a lack of fulfillment, toward the *proton kinoun*.

13. Aristotle, then, admits a variety of movers. There is the immanent principle of natural motion of things, *physis* (q.v.). There is also, as an immanent principle, *psyche*, not the Platonic model that Aristotle himself had once held, but the immanent *eidos* that moves the substance in which it inheres "by thought or choice" (see *psyche* 20). It is present in all animate things but it does not meet (nor does *physis*) the general requirement of the theory of *energeia/dynamis* that demands an external, prior cause of motion. Thus there must be at least one transcendent mover that is a complete intellectual substance (on the "separateness" of intellect, see *nous*). As to the question of whether there are more than one such, at least at some point in his career, in Lambda VIII of the *Metaphysics* (which was not necessarily written at the same time as VII and IX) Aristotle held that there was more than one, a position that continued to exercise the Peripatetic tradition and provoked a refutation from Plotinus (*Enn.* v, 1, 9).

14. After Aristotle the question of a transcendental cause of motion recedes into the background. The noetic function of the cosmic cause is retained, as is the plurality of intermediary intelligences (see *nous, daimon*), but its causal activity is seen as making rather than moving. The reasons are twofold. There is, in the first place, the radically different Stoic concept of God who becomes immanent and operative in matter, much in the manner of Aristotle's *physis* (see

physis 3, *logos* 4, and *pneuma* 4). Secondly, there is the general revival of Platonism and, with it, the restoration of the *demiourgos* image. It was undoubtedly under the influence of this image that the object of divine thought, simply *noesis* in Aristotle, becomes the *noeta* as exemplary causes of things (see *noeton* 2).

koinōnía: *combination, communion*
See *diairesis, eidos.*

kósmos (scil. aisthētós): *ornament, order, the physical, visible universe* (see kosmos noetos)

1. There is a tradition (Aetius II, 1, 1 and D.L. VIII, 48) that the first one to describe the universe as a *kosmos* was Pythagoras; but the notion of the universe as an order turns up in the fragments of his predecessors (Anaximander, Diels, fr. 12A10; Anaximenes, Diels, fr. 13B2), and in any event it is difficult to trace its exact evolution through the stages: order, order of this universe, the universe as order. It had certainly reached this final connotation by the time of Empedocles (fr. 134), while the related notion of man as the microcosm of the universe appears with Democritus (fr. 34). Whatever the origins of the original insight, the Pythagoreans did have a theory of *kosmos;* the universe was a *kosmos* because it could be reduced to mathematical proportions (*harmonia*), since the *arche* of all things was number (*arithmos*) (Aristotle, *Meta.* 985b), with its ethical corollary of attempting to restore this cosmic harmony in the soul (see *katharsis*). The same basic idea had been expressed by the Milesians, not in the mathematically oriented formulae of Pythagoras, but in a series of figures borrowed from the ethical sphere (see Anaximander, Diels, fr. 12A9, B1, and *dike;* Empedocles, fr. 30) to explain cosmic process, replacing the sexual metaphors of earlier myths.

2. Heraclitus is the first we know of to take the further step and identify this cosmic order with "law" (*nomos*) (fr. 114), thereby setting in motion a train of thought leading to the notion of Natural Law (see *nomos*). Heraclitus called the law that ensured this order "divine" (*theios*), but this is only one of several strands leading to a belief in the divinity of the *kosmos;* the others are the vitalism of the Milesians (see *zoe, pyr*) and a belief in the divinity of the heavenly bodies (see *ouranioi*). There is some late evidence (D.L. VIII, 25) that the Pythagoreans held the divinity of the *kosmos*, as may have Xenophanes as well (Diels, fr. 21A36; Aristotle, *Meta.* 986b). Plato calls the *kosmos* a "visible God" (*horatos theos*) in *Tim.* 92c, not on vitalist grounds but because of the ethical role it plays in his *harmonia-*

katharsis theory (see *ouranos*). His mimetic point of view led him to posit another *kosmos* not apprehensible by the senses, as ours is, but only by the intelligence (see *kosmos noetos*).

3. In his early *De philosophia*, fr. 18, Aristotle reaffirms the divinity of the *kosmos*, echoing the Platonic formula "visible God"; but by the time of the later treatises most of the Platonic theology has disappeared in the wake of a revised theory of *physis* (q.v.). In the fully developed Aristotelian system there are only two divinities (see *theos*) and one of them, the First Mover, is outside the *kosmos* (*De coelo* I, 279a–b). The other is the outer sphere of the *kosmos*, the sphere of the fixed stars and the domain of *aither* (q.v.); this is divine because of its eternal circular motion (*ibid.* II, 286a).

4. Stoic pantheism restores the divinity of the *kosmos* (*SVF* II, 1027) and, following upon the theories of fire (see *pyr*) and *pneuma*, considered it a living, ensouled, and intelligent being (D.L. VII, 138–139). The Sceptics denied both of these positions (Cicero, *De nat. deor.* III, 9, 22–24). The organic nature of the *kosmos* was defended by Poseidonius and was the point of departure for his theory of *sympatheia* (q.v.). As against the Gnostics, who viewed it as the product of evil and ignorance (see Irenaeus, *Adv. haer.* I, 4, 1–2; I, 5, 3), both Philo and Plotinus defended the sensible universe, both calling it a "son of God" (*Quod Deus*, 6, 31; *Enn.* V, 8, 12) in its function as an image (*eikon*) of its ultimate transcendent source (see *Enn.* II, 3, 18).

kósmos noētós: *intelligible universe*

1. One of the problems arising from Plato's theory of Forms is the question of their location. Plato is emphatic that the *eide* do not exist in any place (*Symp.* 211a; compare Aristotle, *Phys.* III, 203a). There are, however, other passages that indicate that they do have a "location" in a wider sense of the word (*Rep.* 508c, 507b; *Phaedrus*, 247c–e). The figurative language of the *Timaeus* forces him to be more explicit; his theory of *mimesis* (q.v.) suggests a model of which the visible universe (*kosmos aisthetos*) is an image (*eikon*), *Tim.* 30c–d. This is the intelligible universe that "contains" the main families of *eide* (*loc. cit.;* see *zoön*). "Contains" is a difficult word; it is not at all clear how Plato saw the higher groupings of the *eide* (see the chief parallel text, *Soph.* 253d; but here the context is dialectical).

2. The intelligible *kosmos* reappears in Philo, but with two major differences; Plato's *eide* were eternal, Philo's are created (*De opif.* 4, 16), and they are embraced, as a total *kosmos noetos*, within the divine mind, *ibid.* 4, 17–20 (see *eidos*), and this is one of the meanings of Philo's *Logos* (q.v.). Philo's *Logos* becomes Plotinus' *nous* that em-

braces within it all the *noeta* (*Enn.* VI, 2, 21) as the objects of its thought.

krásis: blending, mixture
See *genesis.*

1

logismós: reasoning, discursive thought
See *noesis.*

logistikón: rational faculty
See *psyche, nous, pathos, oneiros.*

lógoi spermatikoí: seminal reasons, rationes seminales

The Stoic *logoi spermatikoi*, which are designed to explain both plurality and teleology in a monistic system, appear to be patterned after the Aristotelian *eidos* (q.v.) in its role as *physis*. The *logos* (q.v.) considered as a unified entity contains within itself, on the analogy of animal sperm, the growth powers of exemplars of all the individuals (*SVF* II, 1027; D.L. VII, 135). These individual *logoi* are imperishable (*SVF* II, 717), i.e., they survive the cyclical conflagration (*ekpyrosis*) that consumes the *kosmos* and are the seedlings of the next *kosmos* (*ibid.* I, 497). Despite their paradigmatic character they are more Aristotelian than Platonic in that they are immanent in matter (*ibid.* II, 1074). They also play a major role in Plotinus: they reside in the *psyche* (*Enn.* II, 3, 14; IV, 3, 10) where they are the cause of its movement (*ibid.* IV, 3, 15); the *logoi* contain all the details of the being (*ibid.* III, 2, 1) and are the reasons why individuals differ (*ibid.* IV, 4, 12); unextended themselves, they are individualized only by the matter in which they inhere (*ibid.* IV, 9, 5).

For their development into the occult powers, see *dynamis.*

lógos: speech, account, reason, definition, rational faculty, proportion

1. A major difficulty in the interpretation of *logos* is determining when this common and amorphous Greek word is being used in a technical, specialized sense. Thus Heraclitus, in whom it first plays a

major role, frequently employs it in its common usage, but he also has a peculiar doctrine that centers around *logos* in a more technical sense: for him *logos* is an underlying organizational principle of the universe, related to the common meaning of *logos* as proportion (frs. 1, 50), the rule of change so frequently associated with Heraclitus' thought (e.g. frs. 60, 111). And this harmony, which is really a tension of opposites, is not to be understood in the sense of a cyclic return, but as a stable state (frs. 10, 51). This *logos* principle, though it is hidden and perceptible only to the intelligence (frs. 54, 114; see *noesis* 1), is still material, as can be seen from the identification of the Heraclitan *logos* with cosmic fire (compare frs. 41, 64; see *pyr*), and his description of the process of thinking (Diels, fr. 22A16; see *noesis*); on the theory of tension, see *tonos*.

2. Plato also used the term *logos* in a variety of ways, including the opposition between *mythos* and *logos* (see *mythos*), where the latter signifies a true, analytical account. This is common usage, but it leads off into an epistemological theory. In *Phaedo* 76b Plato marks as a characteristic of true knowledge (*episteme*) the ability to give an account (*logos*) of what one knows. In *Theaet.* 201c–d this aspect of *logos* is incorporated into the definition of *episteme:* true opinion (*doxa*) accompanied by an account. Socrates discusses what *logos* would mean in this context (*ibid.* 206c–210b), and from his analysis emerges a description of *logos* as the statement of a distinguishing characteristic of a thing (*ibid.* 208c). The validity of this is denied on the ground of its being of no value in the case of sensible, individual beings (compare Aristotle, *Meta.* 1039b).

3. But when this conception of *logos* is moved higher up the Platonic scale of being it obviously does have a role to play; in *Rep.* 534b Plato describes the dialectician (see *dialektike*) as one who can give an account (*logos*) of the true being (or essence, *ousia*) of something, i.e., the term of the process of division (*diairesis*) described in the *Sophist*, the Aristotelian definition (see *horos*) by genera and species; indeed, Aristotle frequently uses *logos* as a synonym for *horos, horismos*. Another typical Aristotelian use is *logos* as reason, rationality, particularly in an ethical context, e.g., *Pol.* 1332a, *Eth. Nich.* v, 1134a, and frequently in the combination "right reason" (*orthos logos*, the Stoic *recta ratio*), *Eth. Nich.* II, 1103b; VI, 1144b. He also understands *logos* as mathematical proportion, ratio (*Meta.* 991b), a usage probably going back to the Pythagoreans, even though it is unattested in their fragments (see *apeiron, peras, harmonia;* for the application of *logos* as proportion to the question of mixtures, see *holon;* to sensation and the sense organ, *aisthesis;* and, in general, *meson*).

4. The Stoic point of departure on *logos* is Heraclitus' doctrine of

an all-pervasive formula of organization, which the Stoics considered divine (see *nomos*). *Logos* is the active (*poioun*) force in the universe (D.L. VII, 134), creative in the fashion of sperm (*SVF* I, 87; D.L. VII, 135; see *logoi spermatikoi*). As in Heraclitus it is material and identified with fire (see *pyr*), Cicero, *Acad. post.* I, 11, 39; *SVF* II, 1027. It is also identical with nature (*physis*, q.v.) and Zeus (see Cleanthes, *Hymn to Zeus; SVF* I, 537). This pervasive presence in the universe develops in several directions: since it is a unity it grounds the theory of cosmic sympathy (see *sympatheia*) and of natural law and the ethical imperative "to live according to nature" (see *nomos*). Stoic linguistic theory further distinguished interior *logos* (= thought) and exterior *logos* (= speech) (*SVF* II, 135; Sextus Empiricus, *Adv. Math.* VIII, 275; see *onoma*), a distinction that clearly influenced Philo's notoriously difficult vision of *logos*.

5. Philo knew the distinction between interior and exterior *logos* and could apply it in an orthodox Stoic fashion (*De vita Mos.* II, 137), and it was perhaps this distinction, together with the Jewish scriptural tradition about the "Word of God," that led to his new treatment of *logos*. In the first instance *logos* is the Divine Reason that embraces the archetypal complex of *eide* that will serve as the models of creation (*De opif.* 5, 20). Next, this *logos* that is God's mind is externalized in the form of the *kosmos noetos* (q.v.), the universe apprehensible only to the intelligence (*ibid.* 7, 29). It is transcendent (*Leg. all.* III, 175–177), and it is God, although not *the* God (*De somn.* I, 227–229), but rather the "elder Son of God" (*Quod Deus* 6, 31). With the creation of the visible world (*kosmos aisthetos*) the *logos* begins to play an immanent role as the "seal" of creation (*De fuga* 2, 12), the Stoic "bond of the universe" (*De plant.* 2, 8–9) and *heimarmene* (q.v.; *De mut.* 23, 135). Philo differs from the Stoics in denying that this immanent *logos* is God (*De migre. Abr.* 32, 179–181); for the providential role of Philo's *logos*, see *pronoia*. Philo gives his *logos* a distinct role in creation: it is the instrumental cause (*De cher.* 35, 126–127); it is also an archetypal light (*ibid.* 28, 97), this latter image reappearing in Plotinus, *Enn.* III, 2, 16. But there is a difference between the two thinkers; what was in Philo both *logos* and *nous* is divided in Plotinus who uses the *logos* concept in a fashion akin to the Stoic *logoi spermatikoi* (q.v.); see *Enn.* III, 2, 16 where *nous* and *logos* are distinguished.

m

mantikḗ: *divination*

1. Although the terminology remained fluid one may, with Cicero, *De div.* I, 11, distinguish two distinct types of communication, frequently of future events, vouchsafed by the gods to men: one, the direct communication through a human "medium," the *prophetes*, possessed by a god, typically Apollo, and hence a spokesman for that god. A variant of this was the apparition of a god to an individual in a dream (*oneiros*, q.v.). The second method, which was less idiosyncratic since it could be learned instead of appearing as a more or less fortuitous divine favor, was the "reading" of various natural phenomena such as the habits of birds (augury), the entrails of various sacrificial animals (haruspicy; for the physiological theory see *oneiros*), the physiognomy of the palm (chiromancy), or the use of lots (cleromancy) or arbitrarily chosen passages of a favored author (compare the medieval *sortes Vergilianae* and *sortes Biblicae*).

2. Plato associates the method of direct communication through a medium with a divinely inspired madness (*mania*). The examples he cites are those of the priestesses and prophets at Dodona and Delphi and the Sibyl (*Phaedrus* 244b–c). He then proceeds to link this "divine madness" with that of the inspired poet who is also, in a sense, "possessed by a god," *entheos* (*ibid.* 245a), an analogy that makes its first appearance in literature with Democritus (frs. 17, 18; see *Apol.* 22b: the notion may be Socratic).

3. The concept of possession (*enthousiasmos*) that provides the theoretical ground for the inspired utterances of the prophet is not susceptible of exact definition. The ancients themselves were aware that it was an arational state (see Plato, *Apol.* 22b–c; *Ion* 536c), and a later more psychologically sophisticated and curious age was well informed on the various psychic phenomena attendant upon *enthousiasmos* (see Iamblichus, *De myst.* 3, 4–7, 110–112), as well as the possibilities of a homoeopathic "cure" (see *katharsis*).

4. The distance between Plato and Iamblichus is marked by another significant change: the decline of the institutionalized oracular sites like Delphi and Dodona with their organized mediumship, and the rise of individual *prophetai* who trafficked in a great variety of psychic phenomena and who frequently claimed miraculous powers. Such types, e.g., Apollonius of Tyana and the Alexander of Lucian's satire,

belong properly to the history of religion. But they share with the contemporary Neoplatonic school of Iamblichus a penchant for the miraculous and the wonderful. It need hardly be noted that in Neoplatonism the various species of wonder-working were accompanied by a fairly elaborate philosophical theory based at least in part on the Stoic notion of universal sympathy or *sympatheia* (q.v.).

5. This Neoplatonic *theourgia* or "working upon god" consisted chiefly in the manipulation of certain objects to produce a divine presence in either a statue or a human medium (see Proclus, *In Tim.* III, 155, 18; Iamblichus, *De myst.* III, 4–7). Indeed, such binding of divine powers has an oracular end and the ancient world's most famous collection of oracular responses, the *Chaldaean Oracles*, is cited continuously in the Neoplatonic tradition from Porphyry to Proclus, the latter writing an extensive commentary on them.

The philosophical ground of divination is discussed under *sympatheia;* that of *theourgia*, under *dynamis* 10–11.

mathēmatiká: *mathematical numbers and entities; the objects of the mathematical sciences*

1. A reading of the *Metaphysics* yields a variety of views on the ontological status of the mathematical numbers (*arithmoi mathematikoi*) or *mathematika*. According to Aristotle's account the Pythagoreans maintained that mathematical number is *in* sensible things as their *arche* (*Meta.* 987b, 1090a; see *arithmos*), while for Plato, who also held the existence of another class of Ideal Number (see *arithmos eidetikos*), they constituted a class between the *eide* and the *aistheta*, the so-called "intermediaries" (*metaxu*) (*Meta.* 997b–998a). Finally, there is an unidentified group who made the *mathematika* immanent but not constitutive of or identical with the *aistheta* (*Meta.* 998a, 1076a).

2. Aristotle is critical of all these views, particularly the Platonic one. Does this latter appear in the dialogues? The evidence rests primarily on an interpretation of a section of the Diagram of the Line in *Rep.* v, 510b–e where the intelligibles (*noeta*) are divided into the objects of *noesis* (q.v.) and *dianoia*. The latter is described first by its methodology, which uses images in its reasoning process, and then (510d), by its subject matter, e.g., "the Square itself" and "the Diagonal itself," phrases that in their formulation and singularity could refer with equal appropriateness to the *eide* and to the intermediary class of *mathematika* that, as Aristotle says (see *metaxu*), are characterized by their plurality. But *noesis* clearly has the *eide* as its object (511b–c), and so it may be legitimate to infer that the objects of *dianoia* belong to another class, i.e., the *metaxu*.

3. Aristotle's own theory of mathematical number is found in

Meta. 1076a–1078b; he rejects all three previously cited positions. Certain qualities of the *aistheta* are abstracted and studied *as if* they were separate from matter (for the "matter" of *mathematika*, see *aphairesis, hyle*). The abstractive process (*aphairesis*, q.v.) actualizes what was present only potentially in sensible things. But for all that the *mathematika* have no separate (*choriston*) substantial existence.

4. Plato's successor Speusippus replaced the entire structure of the *eide* with *mathematika*, generating first the *arithmoi mathematikoi* and then the geometrical magnitudes from the One and the Infinite Dyad (*Meta.* 1028b, 1080b, 1086a; see *dyas*). Another early Academic, Xenocrates, identified the *mathematika* and the *eide* (*Meta.* 1028b, 1069a, 1076a). For Plotinus mathematical number is an image (*eidolon*) of the Ideal Numbers (*Enn.* VI, 6, 9; see *arithmos*).

mégethos: *greatness, magnitude*

1. According to Aristotle (*Meta.* 1020a) magnitude is a measurable quantity (*poson*, q.v.) that is potentially divisible into continuous (*syneches*) parts in one, two, or three dimensions, i.e., lines, planes, and solids. These latter are the subject matter of geometry, a science whose generic subject is magnitude (*Eth. Nich.* VI, 1143a); but magnitude is not, however, an attribute of the units (*monades*) that constitute number, as the Pythagoreans assert (*Meta.* 1080b). Aristotle also attacks what seems to be a later species of Pythagoreanism that was moving toward Atomism and that defined its units as "indivisible magnitudes": mathematical units are indivisible units and hence cannot have magnitude (*ibid.* 1083b); see *arithmos, monas.*

2. The question of an indivisible magnitude (*adiaireton* or *atomon megethos*) raises for Aristotle the whole question of primary bodies, i.e., bodies that cannot be reduced to others and so are the subject of *genesis* and change. The monist tradition (for Empedocles and the pluralists, see *stoicheion*) stemming from Parmenides is represented by the Pythagoreans, Plato, and the Atomists.

3. The Pythagorean position that reduced bodies, through number, to units is, in effect, demolished as soon as the distinction between the mathematical unit (*monas*), the geometrical point (*stigme*), and a body with extension (*megethos*) is established, as Aristotle seeks to do in various places (see *Meta.* 1080b, 1083b, 1090b; *De an.* 409a). Thus the ambiguities of an only partially mathematicized Pythagoreanism are resolved into a physical Atomism. Since magnitude is extended in three dimensions it is conceivable that the primary body might be either line, plane, or solid. The latter is, of course, Leucippus' *atomon* (q.v.) that has magnitude but cannot be divided because it is so small (Diels 58B4). We also know that Plato reduced his primary solids to triangles, accompanied by an enigmatic hint that further reduction was

perhaps possible (*Tim.* 53c–d). Finally, the ancient tradition asserts that the Academician Xenocrates maintained the theory of indivisible lines (so Simplicius and Philoponus commenting on Aristotle's *Phys.* I, 187a; according to Simplicius' account, p. 142, Xenocrates admitted that they were theoretically divisible but because of their smallness effectively indivisible).

4. Aristotle opposes the theories of indivisible magnitudes in whatever dimension (*De gen. et corr.* I, 315b–317a; *De lineis insecabilibus*, which is an Aristotelian pseudepigraph, deals with the problem in 968a–b). He realized that it was Zeno and his paradoxes that had driven philosophers to this position (*Phys.* I, 187a). Aristotle's solution dismisses Leucippus' and Xenocrates' contentions about size. He is not discussing actual physical division but conceptual division, and the argument here hinges on the notion of a continuum (*syneches; Phys.* VI, 231a–b) that, by eliminating the view that a line is a row of contiguous or successive points, both undermines the Pythagorean void (*kenon,* q.v.) between units and at the same time sets the stage for a solution of Zeno's paradoxes, since the same arguments pertain to both time and movement that are *per accidens* magnitudes (*Meta.* 1027a).

On the problem of irrational numbers or, better, incommensurable magnitudes, see *asymmetron;* for the relation of magnitude to matter, see *hyle.*

mē on: *nonbeing*
See *on.*

méson, mesótēs: *mean*
The Pythagoreans looked upon existent things as a "just balance" (*isomoira*) between opposites (*enantia*), see D.L. VIII, 26. Plato begins to move this "mean" position into the area of ethics in *Phil.* 23c–26d (where the extremes are called "unlimited" [*apeiron*] and the quantified, mixed, "limit" [*peras*]). The mathematical overtones are apparent in this text and the medical ones appear in both *Phaedo* 86b–c (see *harmonia, hedone*) and in Aristotle's early *Eudemus,* fr. 7. Aristotle's classic identification of virtue (*arete*) with the *meson* of emotions (*pathe*) and acts (*praxeis*) is to be found in *Eth. Nich.* 1106a–1109b, where he makes specific reference to limit (*peras*) as good; see *dike.*

For the application of *meson* to perception, see *aisthesis;* as a factor in deriving the elements, *stoicheion;* in the derivation of the *hypostases, trias.*

metabolē: *change*
Aristotle's most generic term for passage from one state into another, whether on the level of substance where the *metabole* is called

genesis, or in one of the three categories of quality (see *pathos, genesis*), quantity, or place, where the *metabole* is called *kinesis;* see *Phys.* v, 224a–225b, and *kinesis;* for the matter implied by the various changes, see *hyle*.

metaxú: *intermediaries*

1. In the Platonic view of reality there are a class of "intermediaries" that come between the Forms (*eide*) and the sensible, particular things (*aistheta*). Like the *eide* they are eternal and unchanging, but unlike the Forms they are plural (Aristotle, *Meta.* 987b). This class, which represents the objects of the sciences of mathematics and geometry, embraces both mathematical numbers and geometrical magnitudes (*ibid.* 991b, 997b; see *mathematika*). Thus Aristotle. The only support for the existence of the general class of the *metaxu* in the Platonic dialogues themselves is the mention of plural forms in *Phaedo* 74c and *Parm.* 129b. The existence of the mathematical numbers is, however, somewhat more strongly attested (see *mathematika*).

2. The real "intermediary" in the Platonic system is Plato's later doctrine of the *psyche;* see the important admission of life, soul, and *nous* into the world of quasi-being in *Soph.* 248e–249d, and the striking description of *psyche* (*Tim.* 90a–d) that "lifts us from earth to heaven"; this, of course, Aristotle accepts (for its evolution, see *psyche* 29, 35).

On the question of a medium (*metaxu*) for sensation, see *aisthesis, sympatheia*.

metempsýchōsis: *transmigration of souls*
See *palingenesia*.

méthexis: *participation*

Methexis is the term used by Plato to describe the relationship between the *eide* and sensible particulars; see *Phaedo* 100d, and *Parm.* 130c–131a (where participation is criticized as implying division). Aristotle sees nothing but a verbal difference between *methexis* and the other Platonic term, "imitation" (*mimesis*), *Meta.* 987b. Plotinus prefers to use other metaphors, but *methexis* becomes important again in the systematization of Proclus: prop. 65 of the *Elem. theol.* discusses the metaphysical implications of *methexis*, while props. 163–165 lay out the series of projections consequent upon *methexis*.

For the more general context, see *eidos;* some of the difficulties arising from *methexis* are touched upon in *diairesis;* for its use in Proclus, see *trias*.

mímēsis: *mimicry, imitation, art (i.e., fine art; for the*
applied sciences, see techne)

1. *Mimesis*, in all its shades of meanings, is of central importance
in Plato. We read in *Sophist* 265b that the productive arts (*poetikai
technai;* see *techne*) are divided into divine craftsmanship and human
craftsmanship (called in *Rep.* 597d–e *phytourgia* and *demiourgia*),
and that there is, in addition, another type of productivity shared by
both God and man that does not produce "originals" but merely copies
(*eikones*). This is *mimesis*, the art of the poet, the painter, the sculptor, or that of the actor who, unlike the others named, does not use tools
but creates the image in his own person (*Soph.* 267a; Plato uses
mimesis for the craft of the actor as well, but for purposes of distinction "mimicry" is probably closer to what the context demands).

2. The craftsman (*demiourgos*), then, whether human or divine,
produces on two levels: "originals" or real objects, and imitations or
images that can only more or less approximate the reality of their
models. Plato is not always consistent in his application of this theory.
In *Rep.* 596b the divine craftsman creates the original, i.e., the *eidos* of
the bed, the carpenter produces the physical bed that is only an *eikon*
vis-à-vis the *eidos* but is the "original" for the bed of the painter. In
Soph. 265c–d the originals made by the divine craftsman are not the
eide but the natural objects of this world, while the products of his
mimetic activity are the shadows and mirages in this world. Finally, in
the *Timaeus* the divine *demiourgos* does not create the preexistent *eide*
and this world seems to be the product of his mimetic activity (*Tim.*
30c–31b).

3. The confusion doubtless arises from the differing contexts and
clearly one should not rest too heavily on the Form of Bed or the divine
demiourgos as its creator; most of what Plato wrote suggests the
exclusion of *eide* for manufactured objects and of any maker for the
eide (see *eidos*). But one point is clear: the activity known as *mimesis*
has as its product an entity whose ontological status is inferior relative
to that of its model. Thus, on the cosmic level this principle sets the
relationship between this world and the world of *eide*, it grounds
Plato's theory of knowledge, and in the moral sphere it is the point of
departure for his attack on "art."

4. *Mimesis* is one of the explanations (see also *methexis*) or,
better, one of the images offered by Plato to express the relationship of
the *eide* to sensible particulars. It finds a fairly elaborate expression in
Parm. 132c–133a, and again in *Tim.* 30c–d where the *demiourgos*
(q.v.) takes as his model (*paradeigma*) the intelligible living creature
(*zoön noeton*) that embraces all the Forms and thus creates the *kosmos*. The same principle is evident even earlier in *Crat.* 298a–c, and by

implication in the theory put forth in *Phaedo* 74a–75a Aristotle (*Meta.* 987b) states that the explanation derives from the Pythagoreans who held that things "imitate" numbers and he subjects it (*ibid.* 991a) to a harsh criticism. Although *mimesis* as applied to sensible particulars falls into disuse, the concept that the intelligible world (*kosmos noetos*, q.v.) is the *paradeigma* for the sensible world remains current in later Platonism; see Philo, *De opif.* 6, 25; Plotinus, *Enn.* v, 8, 12.

5. The distinction between a "true" reality and a mimetic reality will have obvious epistemological implications and these are rendered explicit in the schema of the Line in *Rep.* 509d–511e. True knowledge (*episteme*, q.v.) will be of the "originals," while opinion (*doxa*, q.v.) is the best one can hope to attain in confronting imitative being. But even here there are distinctions: sensible particulars (see *aistheton*), though imitations of the *eide*, are in some sense "original" when compared to certain physical phenomena that are images of other phenomena, e.g. the shadows and mirages that are God's "joke" (see *Soph.* 234b, 266b–c) on the physical world. This knowledge of images (*eikasia;* see *eikon*) is the lowest segment of the Line (*Rep.* 509e), but at this point in the *Republic* Plato says nothing about man's "joke" on the world, i.e., art (more fully, *techne poietike mimetike;* for the genus and differentia, see *techne*).

6. The subject of man's mimetic activity is explored in *Rep.* 595a–608b. Plato distinguished craft (*demiourgia*) and art (*mimesis*) in the *Sophist* in the context of a search, via division (*diairesis*, q.v.), for the *infima species* that is the sophist. In the *Republic* passages the context is strongly ethical and the emphases somewhat different. The poets were the traditional teachers of wisdom, but in the *Republic* Plato had replaced them with the philosophers; he vindicates his own position by attacking the poets' qualifications to teach wisdom.

7. Plato's objection to the fine arts is twofold: they are untrue and they are injurious. They are untrue in the ontological sense that has already been discussed: their claim to reality is tenuous since they are imitations of imitations (*Rep.* 597e). But in addition they are guilty of the falsity of discourse: they lie. Plato consistently judges art by its own contemporary claim of realism and he finds the poets' portraits of gods and heroes to be inexact in that they portray as evil what is essentially good (*Rep.* 377d–e). Furthermore, art has a distinctly moral end (*ibid.* 401b), and even though there are obviously evil men whom the arts might realistically portray, by choosing to portray such they create harmful moral effects in the viewer and even, if it is a question of dramatic art, in the performer himself (*ibid.* 392c–398b, 606c–608b).

For the mimetic origins of language, see *onoma;* for its application to time, *chronos;* for a mimetic element in Aristotle, *energeia*.

míxis: *mixture*
See *genesis, holon.*

monás: *unit, the one*
The unit is either *the* primary *arche* of the Pythagoreans (D.L.
VIII, 25) or, together with the *Dyas*, one of the primary co-principles
(Aristotle, *Meta.* 986a), ethically associated with the good (*agathon*),
and considered a god (*theos*) (Aetius I, 7, 18), even though the
position of limit (*peras*) and *apeiron* at the head of the list would
suggest that they were more primary. Aristotle is quite explicit that
number (*arithmos*) has its own more basic elements (*stoicheia*), i.e.,
"Even" and "Odd" (*Meta.* 986a). According to Aristotle all philosophers agree in making the *monas* the *arche* of number (*arithmos*), yet
the Pythagoreans are peculiar in that their units have spatial magnitude (*ibid.* 1080b) that is indivisible (*ibid.* 1083b), a confusion between the arithmetical unit and the geometric point, which was cleared
up later (Nichomachus, *Arith. intro.* II, 6 and 7). Aristotle's own
definition of the *monas* is "substance without position," clearly distinct
from the "point" (*stigme*) that is "substance with position," *Anal.
post.* I, 87a; see *arithmos, megethos.*

mousikế: *the Muses' art, music*
See *katharsis.*

mýthos: *myth*
1. The traditional attitude of philosophy toward myth is expressed in the contrast *mythos-logos,* where the latter is intended to
signify a rational, analytic, and true account (see Plato, *Phaedo* 61b,
Tim. 26e, etc.). It runs parallel to the distinction *theologos-physikos*
(see *theologia*), but the relationship of the former pair is somewhat
more complex. It is clear that both Socrates and Plato had strenuous
moral objections to the traditional myths (*Euth.* 6a–c, *Phaedrus*
229c–230a, *Rep.* 376e–380c), a type of criticism that went back at least
as far as Xenophanes (see fr. 11). One attempt to meet this type of
attack was the belief that there was an underlying sense (*hyponoia*) to
the old myths. This was apparently popular in fifth-century philosophical circles; see Prodicus (Diels, fr. B5), Anaxagoras (D.L. II, 11), and
Antisthenes (Dio Chrysostom, *Orat.* 53, 4–5; compare Xenophon,
Symp. III, 6). Plato will have none of *hyponoia* (*Rep.* 378d), but in the
subsequent literature the use of an allegorical interpretation (*allegoria*), either moral, physical, or cosmogonical, to extract the hidden
sense became a potent method of reconciling philosophy and the traditional material in the poets. The Stoics were particularly active in

allegoria (see Cicero, *De nat. deor.* II, 24, 25, 64, 65, and *passim;* the Stoic facility in etymologizing names was of considerable help here; see *onoma*), and with Philo *allegoria* passed into the service of accommodating philosophy and scripture (cf. *Leg. all., passim*).

2. But *mythos* was not quite so easily dismissed: Aristotle felt that there was a point in the early cosmogonies where *logos* and *mythos* overlapped (*Meta.* 982b, 1074b; see *aporia, endoxon*), but the presentation of the latter was childlike (*Meta.* 1000a; compare Plato, *Soph.* 243a), and Plato, for one, was sceptical of the results (see the heavy irony of *Tim.* 40d–41a). Yet the dialogues are filled with myths that play a central part in the development of the argument, as for instance, in the *Phaedo* and *Republic* (eschatological; see *athanatos*), *Phaedrus* (psychological), and *Timaeus* (physical). Nor is the technique new with Plato; it can be seen in Protagoras (if the myth in *Protagoras* 320c–323a is his own and not Plato's), in the proem to Parmenides' poem (fr. 1) and the half-disguised abstractions of Pherecydes' myths (D.L. I, 119; compare Aristotle, *Meta.* 1091b); see *theos*.

n

nóēsis: the operation of nous (q.v.), thinking (as opposed to sensation), intuition (as opposed to discursive reasoning)

1. Subtle differences between the mere perception of an object or objects, i.e., sensation (*aisthesis*, q.v.) and another kind of psychic awareness that goes beyond the sense data and perceives less tangible things, like resemblances and differences between objects, is already present in Homer and is identified with the organ called *nous*. With the philosophers the difference becomes a problem. Heraclitus suspects the unreliability of sensation for the perception of the *true* nature of things. He is tireless in his assertion that "nature loves to hide" (see fr. 123 and *logos* 1), and this hidden reality is clearly beyond the reach of men who trust too implicitly in their senses (fr. 107). How the other faculty that is capable of discerning the hidden *logos* of things might operate is not immediately apparent; though we are told (Sextus Empiricus, *Adv. Math.* VII, 129) that the *nous* that is within us is activated by its contact, via the channels of sensation (*aisthetikoi poroi*), with the divine *logos* in the universe, a contact that is maintained in an atten-

uated fashion during sleep by breathing (see *pneuma*). The senses, then, are obviously some sort of condition for *noesis*, though not, as is clear from fr. 107 and its congeners, identical with it.

2. Aristotle remarks (*De an.* III, 427a; *Meta.* 1009b) that the pre-Socratics generally made no distinction between *noesis* and *aisthesis*. It is easy to understand why he thought so since they all attempted to explain the operations of the *psyche* in purely physical terms, a procedure that, according to Aristotle (*loc. cit.*), cannot account for error (*pseudos*) since like must know like (see *homoios*, *aisthesis*). From one point of view this is true; but it is likewise true that since Parmenides' assault on sense perception in terms of the instability of its object (see *on* 1, *episteme* 2) it became an epistemological necessity to distinguish between the obvious perils of *aisthesis* and a "true knowledge" more or less independent of the senses.

3. These attempts can be seen in Empedocles' doubts about the reliability of our sense perception and the need of divine assistance (Sextus Empiricus, *Adv. Math.* VII, 122–124). But the limitations of sensation here seem to be due to our misuse of them rather than to any inherent weakness of their own (fr. 3, lines 9–13). When he comes to explain the possibility of error (called ignorance and opposed to *phronesis;* Theophrastus, *De sens.* 9), Empedocles resorts to a mechanistic explanation of how the effluences (*aporrhoai;* see *aisthesis* 7) of one sense object are symmetrical only with the pores of its proper sense organ, and so cannot be judged by the others (Theophrastus, *op. cit.* 7). If thought is anything to Empedocles it is a special type of sensation that occurs in the blood by reason of its being a perfect mixture of all the *stoicheia* (*ibid.* 9).

4. It is somewhat more perplexing to find Anaxagoras, the eminent proponent of *nous*, in Aristotle's catalogue of those who failed to distinguish sensation and thought. In the fragments we do find the usual statements casting doubts on sensation (e.g. fr. 21), but there is no explanation of *noesis*. Indeed *nous* does not seem to be a cognitive principle at all but rather a cosmological one. It initiates motion (and in this it has obvious affinities to soul; see *psyche* 1, 7, and *passim*) and it guides and rules all (fr. 12). What Anaxagoras is obviously offering is the presence of some intelligent and hence purposeful principle in the universe. But it appears the *nous* is an immanent principle as well and we are told that it is not present in everything (fr. 11). Alcmaeon of Crotona, who had already sharply distinguished *phronesis* from *aisthesis*, maintained that the former was characteristic of men only (Theophrastus, *De sens.* 25), but we have no idea of the extension of the immanent *nous* in Anaxagoras. Presumably it would cover the same territory as *psyche*, i.e., the entire animate world.

5. For Diogenes of Apollonia, who also addressed himself to the

problem, *aer* (q.v.), the intelligent and divine *arche*, is continuous and present in all things that are (fr. 5), but it is present in varying degrees. The degree is based on the dryness and warmth of the air, distinctions of texture that explain progressively higher cognitive acts (Theophrastus, *op. cit.* 40–43). In this way are explained the complete absence of cognitive activities in plants and the relatively higher degree of *phronesis* in man as compared to the other animals (*ibid.* 44).

6. The Atomists' theories of sensible qualities (see *aisthesis* 11, *pathos* 4) demanded refinements in the cognitive faculties. Many so-called qualities are merely subjective impressions and the true nature of the *atomon* is not visible to sight. Hence Democritus draws the distinction (fr. 11) between a genuine and a bastard knowledge; the latter is sensation and the former, presumably (the text breaks off), reason, the operation of the *logikon* that is located in the breast (Aetius IV, 4, 6; see *kardia* 2 and *psyche* 7). But even though *phronesis* and *aisthesis* have different objects and different seats, the mechanics of their operation are the same (Aetius IV, 8, 5; IV, 8, 10).

7. To resume the pre-Socratic attitude: there were solid epistemological grounds for making a distinction *in kind* between thought (*noesis, phronesis;* in the epistemological context, *episteme*) and sensation (*aisthesis;* in the epistemological context, *doxa*), and, indeed, the differentiation could be specified when it came to giving them different locations in the body (*aisthesis* tied to the sense organs; the higher faculty in a central location, though not always distinguished from the more generic notion of *psyche;* see *kardia*). But the operations of this higher faculty could be distinguished from those of sensation only *in degree*, e.g. finer or warmer in composition.

8. Plato, while adhering firmly to the Parmenidean epistemology (see *episteme* 2), has, in addition, a new spiritualized conception of soul that, though originally posited on religious grounds (see *psyche* 13), is incorporated in Plato's theory of knowledge (*ibid.* 14). It is this pure unitary soul of the *Phaedo* that becomes the epistemological correlative of the *eide* and, being absolutely different *in kind* from the body, can perform all the cognitive activities that the post-Parmenidean philosophers associated with *nous* but were unable to explain on the level of substance. But the problem is considerably more complex than this. Even in the *Phaedo* the soul is the *arche* of *all* cognitive activity: sensation is perception *by* the soul *through* the body; *phronesis* is an operation of the soul alone (*Phaedo* 79d; see *aisthesis* 15–16).

9. In the *Phaedo* the distinction between the two operations is largely in terms of the objects known; in the *Republic* it reappears, in a much more complex form, based as well upon the internal operations of the soul. This latter is now divided into three parts (see *psyche* 15) and the upper part, the *logistikon* (*ibid.* 16), is responsible for noetic

activity. But the psychology is far more sophisticated here, and in the Diagram of the Line in *Rep.* VI the noetic activity is explained in some detail. The distinction drawn previously (*Rep.* IV, 476a–480a) between *episteme* and *doxa* is maintained here, but we discover that there is more than one type of *episteme*. The upper part of the Line that represented knowledge of the *noeta* (*ibid.* 509e) is further subdivided into what Plato calls *noesis* and *dianoia* (*ibid.* 511d).

10. These two operations of the *logistikon* have been much debated; one school of thought sees *dianoia* as that activity of the mind which has as its object the "mathematicals," while the objects of *noesis* are the *eide* (see *mathematika* 2); the other school sees *dianoia* as discursive reasoning in general and *noesis* as immediate intellectual intuition, in much the same way as Aristotle (see *Anal. post.* II, 100b; *epagoge* 3) and Plotinus (see 18–19 *infra*) distinguished between *logismos* and *nous*. What is clear, however, is that the method of *noesis* is that known to Plato as *dialektike;* q.v.; *ibid.* 511b) and the way of life based upon it is *philosophia* (q.v., and compare *phronesis, theoria*).

11. There are certain passages in Plato, echoed by Aristotle, that give somewhat more of a purely psychological insight into the workings of the intellective process. Both men seek to derive *episteme* from the Greek word to "stand" or "come to a halt" (*ephistamai*) and so explain intellection as a "coming to a halt" in the midst of a series of sense impressions, the "fixing" of an intuitive concept (*Crat.* 437a; *Phaedo* 96b; *Anal. post.* II, 100a; *Phys.* VII, 247b). But this psychological approach is overwhelmed by a flood of "physical" considerations. *Noesis* is an activity and so must be located within the general categories of change and *kinesis*. Plato speaks of revolutions in the World Soul (*Tim.* 37a) and in the immortal part of the individual soul (*ibid.* 43a). This owes nothing, of course, to introspection, but is based upon considerations of the revolutions of the body of the *kosmos* that reveal the motion of its own soul (*ibid.* 34b) and provide a visible moral paradigm for the motions of our own soul (*ibid.* 47b, and see *ouranos* 2–3; for sensation as motion, see *ibid.* 43c; and for the larger question of motion in the soul, *psyche* 19).

For the operation of cosmic *nous* in Plato, see *nous* 5–6; *kinoun* 5.

12. Aristotle's treatment of *noesis*, like his explanation of *aisthesis*, is conducted within the categories of potency (*dynamis*) and act (*energeia*, q.v.). The *nous* before it knows is actually nothing but potentially all the things it can know; the *eide* are present in it but only potentially (*De an.* III, 429a). When the *nous* begins to operate it passes from a passive to an activated state by reason of its becoming identical with its object, the intelligible form (*ibid.* III, 431a). There is in *noesis* a parallel with *aisthesis:* just as *aisthesis* extracts the sensible

forms (*eide*) of sensible objects (see *aisthesis* 19), so *noesis* thinks the
intelligible forms in sensible images (*phantasiai*), and *noesis* never
occurs without these latter (*ibid.* III, 431a–b). *Noesis* can be directly of
essences (for the intuitive role of *nous*, see *epagoge* 3–4 and compare
Meta. 1036a), or it can operate through judgments (*hypolepseis*), i.e.,
by the combination (*synthesis*) or separation (*diairesis*) of concepts,
and it is only in this latter operation that error (*pseudos*) is possible
(*ibid.* 430a–b; for the Platonic theory of judgment, see *doxa* 4).

For the operation of cosmic *nous* in Aristotle, cf. *nous, kinoun.*

13. The Atomists considered the soul, which was distributed
throughout the body (Aristotle, *De an.* I, 409a; Lucretius III, 370), to
be the seat of all sensation (for the mechanics of this, see *aisthesis*
22–23). But given that soul (*psyche*) and mind (*nous*) are substantially the same (*De an.* I, 404a), it would seem to follow that sensation
and thought are identical, and so Aristotle concluded (*Meta.* 1009b; see
Aetius IV, 8, 5; IV, 8, 10). As for its operation, since *nous* is nothing
more than a kind of aggregation (see *holon* 10) of soul-atoms in the
breast, it is reasonable to suppose that some of the *eidola* penetrate
beyond the surface sense organs, reach the interior of the breast, and
so cause this higher type of perception (see Lucretius IV, 722–731).

14. But we have already seen that the earlier Atomists had attempted to distinguish, by the purity of its constitution and its location,
mind from soul. The Epicureans preserved and refined the distinction
and it is specifically present in Lucretius' consistent use of *anima* for
psyche and *animus* for *nous* or *dianoia* (*mens* is somewhat too narrow
in connotation for the latter since the *animus* is the seat of volitional as
well as intellectual activity; III, 145). He clearly separates the two at
III, 396–416 where he argues that part of the *anima* may be lost (e.g.,
in the loss of a limb) and a man still survive, but the loss of the *animus*
means the instantaneous end of the organism.

15. For the Epicurean *nous* operates somewhat in the fashion of
the senses. It too may directly perceive the *eidola* given off by bodies
but that are not, in this case, grasped by the senses. Such are, for
example, the accidental mixtures of *eidola* that give rise to the imagin-
ing of centaurs and chimeras (Lucretius IV, 129), visions seen in
dreams (IV, 749–776), and the *eidola* of the gods (V, 148–149; Cicero,
De nat. deor. I, 49). These operations are akin to Aristole's *nous*
thinking of indivisible concepts (*De an.* III, 430a); there is, as well,
intellection *componendo et dividendo*, i.e., evaluating and passing
judgment on the data of sensation. The images (*phantasiai*) in which
the *eidola* are grouped are passed along to the *dianoia* or *nous* where
they accumulate into general "preconceptions" (*prolepseis*, q.v.).
These in turn serve as a standard of comparison for judgments (*hypolepseis*) about individual sensible things (D.L. X, 33). This is the area

of opinion into which error enters (see *doxa* 7; the Epicurean criterion of truth and error is discussed under *enargeia*). Finally, the mind is also capable of entering the realm of the imperceptibles (*adela*), i.e., to perform a discursive reasoning process (*logismos*, the *ratio* of Lucretius) dealing with entities not immediately perceptible to the senses, a class that would, of course, include the *atoma* themselves (see D.L. x, 32).

16. The Stoic version of *noesis*, the operation of the *hegemonikon* (q.v.), is properly *katalepsis* or apprehension. The process begins with an impression (*typosis*) on the senses that results in a sensible image (*phantasia;* see *aisthesis* 24–25). These are borne, via the *pneuma* (q.v.), to the *hegemonikon* where it is first assented to (*synkatathesis, adsensio*) and is thus apprehended (*katalepsis*, q.v.; Cicero, *Acad. post.* I, 40–42). In this way what was a sensible image (*phantasia*) becomes an intelligible image or concept (*ennoia*, q.v.). In the earliest years this is almost an unconscious process and the child builds up various "preconceptions" (*prolepseis*, q.v.) under whose influence the *hegemonikon* matures to the point where it is capable of creating its own conscious *ennoiai* (*SVF* II, 83; according to this same text, the full operation of the *hegemonikon* begins at the age of seven, or at least between seven and fourteen, a judgment not based on the observation of rational behavior in adolescents but on the onset of puberty and the first production of sperm; see *SVF* II, 764, 785). As in Epicureanism, *noesis* is not only of the *aistheta* but ranges freely over a wide area of thought, creating its own *ennoiai* by recourse to the principles of similarity, analogy, privation, opposition, etc. (*SVF* II, 87).

On the Stoics' primary *prolepsis* of good and evil, see *oikeiosis*.

17. This theory did not remain completely intact. Chrysippus made some important revisions that had as their effect the reunification of the *psyche* under the aegis of the *hegemonikon* so that even the *pathe* became intellectual judgments (*kriseis; SVF* III, 461) and, in direct opposition to Plato's vision of the tripartite soul, volitional activity was subsumed under the intellectual (*SVF* II, 823; see *aisthesis* 25, *pathos* 12). This is followed by a strong Platonizing reaction under Poseidonius who opposed Chrysippus on the intellectual nature of the *pathe* and restored the Platonic partition of the soul (Galen, *Placita Hipp. et Plat.* 448, 460). There follows from this a sharper distinction between *psyche* and *nous* (particularly apparent in Marcus Aurelius III, 16; XII, 3) with emphasis on the divine and immortal nature of *nous* as opposed to the other parts of the soul (see *sympatheia* 5), and, by reason of the presence of this *daimon* in it (so Galen, *op. cit.* 448; Plutarch, *De genio Socr.* 591c–f; Platonic inspiration in *Tim.* 90a and see *daimon*), a new interest in the medial position of the soul (see *psyche* 29).

18. Middle Platonism concentrated its attention on the cosmic aspects of *nous* (q.v.) and it is not until Plotinus that we have any significant contribution to the workings of the immanent *nous*. As did Plato and Aristotle, Plotinus distinguishes two types of intellectual activity, one intuitive and one discursive. The former, *noesis*, is, in the first instance, the life and *energeia* of the cosmic hypostatized *nous*. It is not, however, an activity of the One since for Plotinus even so self-integrated an act as *noesis* bespeaks duality and so is anathema to the One (*Enn.* VI, 6, 3, with passing reference to Plato's remarks in *Soph.* 254d and *Parmenides* 146a on the role of "the Other" [*heteron*] in being and therefore in intellection). What need, Plotinus asks (VI, 7, 4), would the eye have to see something if it were itself the light?

19. *Noesis*, then, in its genuine form is a unity of subject and object that, though they differ only logically, constitute a plurality (*plethos*). It is characteristically internalized: the *noeta* that are the objects of *noesis* are in the *nous* that knows them (VI, 2, 21). *Noesis*, which is the life of *nous*, casts forth its image (*eikon*) in the form of an *energeia* in the lower *hypostasis* of the soul. This is *logismos* or discursive reasoning, an operation that, unlike the immediate and internalized *noesis*, comprehends the *phantasmata* of objects outside itself offered to it by sensation, and makes judgments (*kriseis*) concerning them by invoking rules (*kanones*) transmitted from *nous* (V, 3, 4), or, as he puts it elsewhere, by composition and division (*synagoge, diairesis:* V, 3, 2; see the Platonic antecedents of these terms under *dialektike*). What he refers to here is a knowledge of the *eide* supplied by the *nous* that contains them and that make possible our comparative judgments (cf. V, 1, 11; V, 3, 3; and compare *Phaedo* 74a ff.).

20. The soul is capable of two activities: when "turned upward" it gives itself over to *noesis/logismos;* when "downward," to *aisthesis* and the operation of the other faculties (VI, 2, 22; see *aisthesis* 26). Sensation uses a medium, an image (*phantasma*), separated from its model and yet different from the thing in which it resides; *noesis* is immediate: knower and known confront each other directly and become identified (V, 3, 8). But we do not have *noesis* in its purity. *Noesis* is a vision of unity; our image of it, *logismos*, deals with plurality, and the more one frees oneself from the composing and dividing that is our imitation of *noesis* and turns instead to a contemplation of self, the more one will be assimilating oneself to the true operation of *nous* (V, 3, 6). Why the soul is forced to endure this *logismos* is part of the general condition of its descent into a body (see *kathodos*). It is, like its external manifestation, language, a weakness, a sign of the soul's preoccupation with areas not akin to itself (IV, 3, 18).

21. In this passage (IV, 3, 18) Plotinus makes use of the principle of attention (*phrontis*) to explain the degeneration of *noesis* into *logis-*

mos (compare the elaborate metaphor in IV, 3, 17 where the soul's preoccupation with the material is compared to that of a ship's captain toward his ship and its cargo; for the further degeneration of thought into activity, see *physis* 5) and he resorts to a similar type of explanation in confronting another problem. If *nous* is a faculty in the soul, how is one to explain the intermittent nature of *noesis* in man as compared to its continuous exercise in the higher principle? Aristotle had already faced the question and had suggested that while the objects of *noesis* are always *in* the mind, they are not always present *to* the mind; in short, man must choose to think (*De an.* II, 417b). Further, this activity can last for only brief periods in man since it involves a passage from potency to act and so fatigues the thinker (*Meta.* 1050b, 1072b; *Eth. Nich.* 1175a). For Plotinus it is a question of awareness. The immanent *nous* is always in operation but we, because our attention is turned elsewhere, are not always aware of it (IV, 8, 8). This view, based as it is on a desire to keep the human soul perpetually linked, via the *nous*, to the *kosmos noetos*, Proclus finds a novelty in the Platonic tradition (*In Tim.* III, 333–334) and therefore returns to the position of an intermittent functioning of *noesis* in the "descended" soul (*Elem. theol.*, prop. 211; see *kathodos* and *psyche* 35).

noētón: *capable of being grasped by the intellect; the object of the intellect, the intelligible (opposite of aistheton)*

1. The *noeton* is the object of the operation of the faculty of *nous*. Among the pre-Socratics, where the distinction of *nous* from the general cognitive principle of the *psyche* was a very gradual one (see *noesis* 7), the objects of the former faculty were not very closely considered. They do, of course, constitute "true knowledge" (*episteme*, q.v.), for Heraclitus the knowledge of "the nature that loves to hide," for Parmenides the knowledge of "true being." With Plato the distinctions become sharper. The *noeta* are the objects of the faculty of the soul called *logistikon* (see *psyche* 15–18); they are, in short, the transcendent *eide*. But for Aristotle the *eide* are immanent (see *eidos* 15) and so further distinctions are in order. The *eidos* in things can be considered from two points of view. With respect to the substance in which it inheres, it is the formal cause of that substance; with respect to the *nous* of another, it is potentially intelligible (*noeton*) by that *nous*. But before it becomes actually *noeton* it must be carried to and presented to that *nous*. This is the function of the *phantasma* that is like a visual image except that it is without matter: the *nous* thinks the *noeta* in the *phantasmata* (*De an.* III, 431b–432a). In the final analysis, then, the *noeta qua noeta* are in the *nous*, first potentially, then actually. This transition from potency to act occurs in the *nous pathetikos*

(see *nous* 11). But in terms of Aristotelian act-potency theory, the *noeta* should all be present in act in the *nous poetikos* (see *nous* 12). But Aristotle never says this, resorting to a comparison of the operation of the agent intellect to that of a light source: the active intellect illumines the passive intellect (*ibid.* III, 430a).

2. During the period of Middle Platonism a number of revisions were made in the *eidos*-theory, part of what was very probably an extensive syncretizing of Platonism and Peripateticism (baldly put in Cicero, *Acad. post.* I, 17–18) in such a fashion as to include both the Platonic transcendent *eidos* and the Aristotelian immanent *eidos* within the causality schema (its progressive development can be traced in Seneca, *Ep.* 65, 8 and Basil the Great, *De spiritu sancto* 76a). Authors of the period began to draw a distinction between the *eidos* that is immanent in things as their formal cause and the *idea* that is the exemplary cause of natural things (Seneca, *Ep.* 58, 19; Albinus, *Epit.* IX, 2; compare Aristotle, *Meta.* 1070a). They appealed to such Platonic proof-texts as *Tim.* 48e and 50c–d (see Chalcidius, *In Tim.* 304, 9 where *idea = species intelligibilis* and *eidos = natura corporis;* on the general question of the immanence of the Platonic *eide*, see *genesis* 10–11), and the constant invocation of the example of the artisan, with its overtones of the Platonic *demiourgos*, seems finally to have led to the explicit description of the *ideai* as "the thoughts of God" (Philo, *De opif.* 17–20; D.L. III, 12–13; Seneca, *Ep.* 65, 7; Albinus, *Epit.* IX, 1: *noeseis theou*). This was not, of course, a completely novel concept. It does seem alien to Plato for whom the *nous-demiourgos*, for all its being a God, was markedly subordinate to the transcendent *eide* (see *nous* 6). But Aristotle speaks (*De an.* III, 429a) as if someone in the Academy were holding that the *nous* was "the place of the Forms" (*topos eidon*) and, as we have already seen, the direction of Aristotle's own theorizing would seem to suggest that the *noeta* are actually present in the *nous poietikos* and, possibly, in the cosmic *nous* as well (see *nous* 9).

3. Two points are to be noted in the subsequent history of the transcendent *noeta*, the *ideai* of Albinus, which serve as the exemplary cause of things. First, since Albinus' first principle is a *nous* and a *demiourgos* (see *nous* 15), there is nothing to militate against the *noeta* being the thoughts (*noeseis*) of God. But between Albinus and Plotinus the transcendence of the One has displaced *nous* from the first place in the hierarchy of hypostases, and the question immediately arises as to whether the *noeta* are the thoughts of the One and, indeed, whether there is any noetic activity at all in the One. Secondly, granting that the *noeta* are in the cosmic *nous*, what exactly is their ontological status?

4. The question of the noetic activity of the One was almost

certainly raised by Aristotle's description of the *energeia* of the First Mover as *noesis* (see *nous* 9). Such a position is irreconcilable with Plotinus' view of the One and he devotes an entire essay (*Enn.* v, 6) to a refutation of Aristotle's view. The arguments are drawn from a variety of sources (they are, in fact, so schematic as to suggest a Platonic repertoire on the subject) but they hinge essentially on the necessary plurality in any type of *noesis* and on the ontological status of the *noeta* that, in Plotinus' view, are not thoughts at all. Proclus, however, returns to a more Aristotelian position. There is a cognitive activity in God that is undivided, necessary, and perfectly determined, even though its objects are not; this is possible because God's knowledge (*gnosis*) is not of particulars in themselves, but in himself as in their cause (*Elem. theol.*, prop. 124); see *trias*, *nous* 9.

5. The second point, the ontological status of the *noeta*, is taken up by Plotinus in *Enn.* v, 9, 7. The possibility that the *eide* were mere ideas or concepts (*noemata*) had already been raised and denied in *Parm.* 132a–c. But the Academy went through a sceptical period under Arcesilaus and Carneades during which the transcendent *ideai* fell into disfavor (see Cicero, *Acad. post.* I, 17; for the restoration of the *ideai* by Antiochus of Ascalon, *ibid.* I, 30–33) and it was evidently still very much of a problem for Plotinus. He denies their purely conceptual reality. The *noeta* are not properly described as the thoughts (*noeseis*) of the cosmic *nous* because, unlike thoughts, their existence does not depend upon being thought: here thinking and thought are identical; *nous* eternally energized is the *noeta* (see v, 9, 5). Further, if they were thoughts, there would have to exist objects of thought (*nooumena*) prior to them. The *noeta* exist of themselves, not because *nous* thinks them (v, 9, 7). They are present in the cosmic *nous* as a unity in the way that a genus contains all its species (v, 9, 6) or a science contains all its theorems; it is we who separate them in our discursive mode of thought (v, 9, 8; see *noesis* 19–20).

6. For Plotinus there are two grades of *noeta*: the *ideai* that exist in a state of unity in the cosmic *nous*, and those that have a plural existence in our immanent, human *nous* and that are given to us by the transcendent *nous* that is the *dator formarum* (see *nous* 21). In v, 9, 8 he says that these latter are "close to reality [*aletheia*]," but in general he does not much insist on a difference between the two, and we are told that each of us is a *kosmos noetos* (q.v.), i.e., we have within our souls all the *noeta* (III, 4, 3). The emphases are somewhat changed in Proclus. The two men disagreed on the question of the degree of contact between the transcendent and immanent *nous* (see their different explanations of the intermittent nature of human intellection under *noesis* 21), and this disagreement is reflected in their views of the *noeta* in our souls. According to Proclus (*Elem. theol.*, props. 194–195) the

soul possesses the *eide* of sensible things (i.e., the *logoi spermatikoi*) in an exemplary manner (*paradeigmatikos*), without matter and without extension (see *physis*). It possesses the intelligible forms, the *noeta* in a reflected manner (*eikonikos*); it does not embrace the genuine articles but mere radiations (*emphaseis*) of them.

For *hyle noete*, see *aphairesis;* for the relativity of intelligibility, *gnorimon*. The faculty that grasps the *noeta*, whether on a cosmic or human level, is treated under *nous* and *psyche* and its operation under *noesis*. The earlier history of the *noeta qua* Forms is discussed under *eidos*.

nomos: *custom, convention, constitutional or arbitrary law*

1. The intrusion of *nomos* into philosophical discourse in the fifth century followed upon the shift of the notion of nature (*physis*) from the physical to the ethical realm. This may have been a result of medical influence ("On the Nature [*physis*] of Man" appears as a title in the Hippocratic *corpus*), but can be seen as well in the ethical coloring of the concept of *kosmos* (q.v.). From the other side there was an increasing understanding of the purely arbitrary and relative nature of *nomos* (see the two anecdotes in Herodotus III, 38). The first explicitly to embrace the position that justice and injustice are a question of *nomos* and not *physis* was Archelaus (D.L. II, 16), though it already seems to be implied in Heraclitus (fr. 102). The view became a common one among the Sophists, and their relativist views, whether in morality (Protagoras in *Protagoras*), politics (Thrasymachus in *Rep.* II), or epistemology (Protagoras at 152a), are frequently cited by Plato. Plato's own ethical and epistemological absolutism is not, of course, based on any defense of the old-fashioned notion of *physis*, but on the unchanging *eide*, and, as he grows older, on the existence of God. In *Laws* 716c Protagoras' *homo. mensura* theory is finally corrected: *God* is the measure of all things (*theios nomos*).

2. The idea of a divine law had already been advanced by Heraclitus, fr. 114 (see *kosmos*), and there were subsequent appeals to "unwritten law" (*agraphos nomos*), which, far from being mere convention, has a divine sanction (so Xenophon, *Mem.* IV, 4, 5–25; Sophocles, *Oed. Tyr.* 863–871, *Ant.* 449–460; Aristotle, *Rhet.* 1368b, 1373a–b). But none of them rests on a philosophical conception of a *physis* that grounds *nomos;* this appears in Stoicism with its doctrine of *physis* as an immanent *logos* (Seneca, *De benef.* IV, 7–8), and its definition of virtue as "living according to nature" (D.L. VII, 86–87) where "nature" is to be understood in both its cosmic and individual sense (*idem* VII, 89). It is this "nature," the *divina ratio* (see *logos*) that is immanent, eternal, and immutable (Cicero, *De leg.* II, 4, 8; *De*

republica III, 33) that founds human laws. Its operation is most eminently visible in man's first "instinctive" (*physikos*) impulse toward self-preservation that gradually extends to embrace all of mankind (see *oikeiosis*).

3. This is what may be called the immanent tradition in natural law; the transcendent tradition, based on the *nous* of a "separated God" can be seen in Plato, *Laws* 713e–714a and Philo, *De migre. Abr.* 32, 179–181; see *thesis, dike.*

nomothétēs: *law-given*
See *onoma.*

nous: *intelligence, intellect, mind*

1. A search for order or an ordering principle is implicit in both Greek mythology and philosophy from their beginnings, in the myths by the application of a genealogical arrangement back to an original source or "father" to the welter of gods drawn from a variety of sources, and among the Milesian philosophers by their search for an *arche* (q.v.). This latter quest for a "father" of things received its initial check with the discovery of a "father" who consumed all his "sons," i.e., the *on* (q.v.) of Parmenides. But regress to a source is only one type of order, and thinkers with a very different cast of mind were investigating the problem in other directions. There is, Heraclitus insists, an order hidden under the appearances of things, an order that he describes as *logos* (q.v. 1). The Pythagoreans went further still: they discovered that this order could be expressed in mathematical terms (see *harmonia*) and, made explicit, that it could be applied to the universe as a whole (see *kosmos*).

2. The kinetic conditions imposed by Parmenides had led his successors to posit some sort of external mover to explain change in the sensible world (see *kinesis* 2, *kinoun* 1). To do so Empedocles had reached into the moral sphere for hypostatizations of the human motive forces of "Love" and "Strife" (see *kinoun* 2), but for his choice of a mover Anaxagoras turned to another tradition. What Parmenides had done in ontology had already been accomplished in theology by Xenophanes. Part of Xenophanes' struggle against anthropomorphism (see *mythos* 1, *theos* 1) was his insistence that God must be completely immobile (fr. 26; the argument here is based on "what is fitting," *prepon*, a recurring aesthetic, moral, and theological motif) and one who accomplishes his ends by the power of his mind (*nous*) alone (fr. 25). These sentiments are pregnant with future developments. Apart from establishing, here at the onset of theological discourse, the intellectual nature of God, Xenophanes' view confronts the question of his activity in the world and draws the conclusion that this must take place

without any change in God himself (see Aeschylus, *Suppl.* 96–103).
How this difficult feat was to be accomplished was left to others to
determine (see *kinoun* 9, *pronoia* 2, *proödos* 2).

3. Anaxagoras turns to Xenophanes' notion of God as *nous* in
positing a motive force that causes the original "mixture" to rotate and
separate off into the various elements (see *genesis* 7). For Empedocles'
moral hypostases has been substituted an intellectual principle, *nous*,
that is separate from the mass upon which it works (fr. 12; but it is
also curiously immanent; see *noesis* 4). Its operation is described as
"ordering" (*diakosmesis*), and it knows all things, past, present, and
future (fr. 12 cont.). Here, then, the Heraclitan and Pythagorean order in the universe, governed, according to Heraclitus (fr. 64), by
the all-pervasive fire, is put under the tutelage of a purposeful intellectual force whose knowledge embraces not only the past and present but
future events as well.

4. The *aer* of Diogenes of Apollonia, which in its warmed state
is nous (see *noesis* 5), is more a Milesian *arche* than a post-
Parmenidean *kinoun* (see *noesis* 4), but has an even more strongly
developed sense of purpose (*telos*, q.v.). Both Socrates (*Phaedo* 97b)
and Aristotle (*Meta.* 984b) had criticized Anaxagoras for his mechanistic use of *nous*, but Diogenes is somewhat more careful in his
handling of the problem. The operation of *aer-nous* is witnessed by the
fact that all things operate according to a principle of measure (*metron*) and in the best way possible (fr. 3; his own example is the
regular succession of the seasons).

For the subsequent history of these teleological motifs, see *telos*.

5. In addition to the *nous* immanent in human souls (the *logistikon;* see *psyche* 15, 18) whose operation is to know the *eide* and rule
the other parts of the soul (see *noesis* 8–9), there is, in Plato, a cosmic
nous. This cosmic reason emerges in *Phil.* 26e–27c where it is called
"the maker" (*demiourgoun, poioun*), the "cause of the mixture" that
is the world of *genesis*. Almost the same terms are applied to the
demiourgos (q.v.) of the *Timaeus* where the *kosmos noetos* is called
the work of *nous* (47e). Now *nous* is an essential property of the gods
shared by only a few men (*ibid.* 51e) and it seems more than likely
that this cosmic *nous* is divine (see *Phil.* 30d, *Tim.* 30b). It rules
everything (*Laws* 875c–d), has ordered the universe (*ibid.* 966e), and
its revolution, reflected in the motion of the heavens, is a moral paradigm for man (*ibid.* 897d–898a; see *noesis* 10).

6. But any attempt to locate this divine *nous*, the cosmic cause
of the universe, within the framework of Plato's general metaphysics is
greeted with frustration, and not least by reason of the "mythical"
nature of the account in the *Timaeus*. On a number of occasions we are
informed that *nous* must exist in a soul (see *Soph.* 249a, *Phil.* 30c,

Tim. 30b), and there are no grounds for thinking that this refers only to human intellects. If this is true it locates *nous,* cosmic or otherwise, beneath the *eide.* The intermediary status of the soul in the Platonic system is well attested (immortal and immaterial like the *eide;* plural and subject to *pathe* like the *aistheta;* see *psyche* 14 and, for the later tradition, 29), and we are told quite specifically that *nous* has a dependent relationship on the *eide* that are the cause of *nous'* being in the soul: *nous* is the ability of the soul to perceive the *eide* (*Rep.* 508e). Thus are frustrated any attempts at finding a transcendent God or gods in Plato (in the *Phaedrus* Plato says the gods owe their divinity to their nearness to the *eide*), or even to identify it or them with the Good that is "beyond being" in *Rep.* 509b. Another school of thought, however, sees the cosmic *nous* as the *nous* of the World Soul (*psyche tou pantos*), dismissing as myth the fact that in the *Timaeus* the World Soul is created by the *demiourgos* (34c).

7. In this fashion, then, Plato fulfills the desideratum of Socrates' complaint against Anaxagoras' *nous:* first, it is stated in terms already formulated by Diogenes that the *kosmos* is as it is because it is the work of an intelligent cause, framed to be "as good as possible" (*Tim.* 30a–b), and then, in a peculiarly Platonic formulation, that it is an image (*eikon,* q.v.) of the intelligible, a visible god (*ibid.* 92c; on the general theory, see *mimesis*).

8. Aristotle's transcendent principle is first and foremost a "mover," developed out of a series of arguments that derive from the nature of *kinesis* and *genesis* (see *kinoun* 7–10) and that Aristotle, like Anaxagoras, chooses to identify with an intelligent principle, *nous.* But unlike Anaxagoras, he is now confronted with a "separation" between the material and the immaterial and so must resort, even in the case of this efficient cause, to the motive force of final causality (see *kinoun* 7, *sympatheia* 7). He has, as well, a more highly developed explanation of intellection (*noesis*) based upon his theory of *energeia/dynamis* and that he must also apply to his *proton kinoun.*

9. In the *De anima* Aristotle had described knowledge, in all its manifestations, as becoming another, but only with respect to its form, not its matter (III, 425b, 431b–432a). To speak more specifically of *noesis* (q.v. 12), it is a passage from potency to act (*energeia*) in becoming the intelligible form of another, and this is effected by knowing this intelligible in its sensible image (III, 431b). Now the *proton kinoun* is described as *nous* and its *energeia* as *noesis* (*Meta.* 1072b), but it is clear that this must somehow differ from the operations described in the *De anima.* In the first instance, cosmic *nous* is not activated by something else since this would be to say that it is in potency to something else and thus not an unmoved mover. The cosmic *nous,* then, does not *become* its object; it *is* its object, and this eternally

since its object is always present (*loc. cit.*). God thinks himself; he is thought about thought (*noesis noeseos; ibid.* 1074b), or perhaps thought about himself thinking. This activity is explicitly contrasted to all other forms of thought, *episteme, aisthesis, doxa, dianoia,* the first object of whose operation is "another" (*allon*) and then themselves thinking, but this latter only incidentally (*parergon; loc. cit.;* for the corollary of this, developed by Proclus, that God knows himself directly and the plural *noeta* only incidentally, see *noeton* 4).

10. In a number of places Aristotle compares human and divine *noesis.* Since man is a composite (*syntheton*) comprising body and a noetic soul, his *noesis* is intermittent and wearisome because it involves a passage from potency to act (*Meta.* 1050b, 1072b; *Eth. Nich.* x, 1175a). But *noesis,* for all the wearisome nature of its operation in us, is, nevertheless, the proper function (*ergon,* q.v.) of both God and man. And when we practice contemplation (*theoria*) we most approach the life of God and most contribute to our own happiness (*Eth. Nich.* x, 1177b–1178a, 1178b). But human *noesis* differs from its divine counterpart by more than its intermittency. The former is not only mediate (i.e., it knows the *noeta* in visible images), it is also discursive; it judges by combining and separating concepts (see *noesis* 12). Aristotle does have an intuitive form of human knowledge, which he calls *nous,* but it seems to be posited on epistemological grounds and never appears in a "mystical" context (see *epagoge* 3, *gnorimon* 2).

11. The functioning of the Aristotelian faculty of *nous* is clear in its general outlines, but the strict application of the principles of act and potency lead to a number of obscurities. There seems to be a distinction of faculty within the soul. The intellect must be potentially anything that it will know actually. But any passage from potency to act demands a principle already in act (the same argument that leads to the First Mover) and so Aristotle posits another intellect that "makes all things." These are distinctions (*diaphorai*) that occur *in the soul* and the two intellects stand to each other as matter to form (*De an.* III, 430a). One, the passive intellect (*pathetikos nous*), later called "hylic" (*hylikos*), is perishable. The other, described as "a kind of state [*hexis*] like the sun," is separable (*choristos*), unaffected (*apathes*), unmixed (*amiges*), and essentially an *energeia.* When it is separated (*choristheis*), it alone is immortal and everlasting (*aidion*).

12. All of this occurs in one brief passage in the *De anima* (III, 5), and it, together with a parallel passage in the *De gen. anim.* II, 736b that states that the *nous,* which alone is divine and has no commerce with any physical *energeia,* comes "from outside" (*thyrathen*), has provoked more comment than any other text in Aristotle. It appears clearly enough that we know because the *nous pathetikos* is energized, i.e., it becomes the intelligible form of the object known by reason of

the operation of another "part" of *nous* that is already in act (see
Meta. 1049b). But the origin and precise nature of the operation of this
latter *nous poietikos* or agent intellect, as it came to be known, was
fiercely debated.

13. Most of the later complexities stem from a series of essays on
the subject by the Peripatetic Alexander of Aphrodisias who distinguished another phase between the *nous pathetikos* and *poietikos*. This
is the intellect *in habitu* that results from the purely passive intellect
(also later identified with the imagination) becoming potentially intelligible by being illuminated by the *nous poietikos* and thus acquiring a
"state" (*hexis, habitus*) of intelligibility (*De intellectu*, p. 107). He
further measures the *nous poietikos* as it is described in the *De anima*
against that of the First Mover in the *Metaphysics* and concludes that
the agent intellect is, indeed, the first cause (*proton aition; De anima*,
p. 89), an identification that was later to be accommodated to the Neoplatonic belief in a series of intermediary intelligences, where the last
emanation, Aristotle's *nous poietikos*, becomes the bestower of forms,
i.e., the intelligible forms are not extracted from the material *phantasiai*, as in Aristotle, but are given to the human intellect by a higher
intelligence (see 20 *infra* and *noeton* 6).

14. The Epicureans recognized *nous* (Lucretius: *animus*) as a
cognitive faculty distinct from *aisthesis* (see *noesis* 14), but in a
materialist system devoid of providence (*pronoia*) it is given no important cosmic role. In Stoicism, however, the human *nous* or *hegemonikon* (see *noesis* 15) is a manifestation of the cosmic *nous* or *logos* that .
pervades, directs, and governs all (D.L. VII, 135, 138). To call the
logos both *nous* (in its providential aspect) and *physis* (in its creative
aspect) is to blur the distinction that Aristotle had drawn between the
two, but the more Aristotelian (and Platonic) view once more begins
to prevail in the tradition from the time of Poseidonius when *nous*
reappears as a characteristic of men alone, immortal, a product of the
superlunary world (see *noesis* 17, *sympatheia* 5). The Platonists of the
period, on the other hand, could assert the transcendence of *nous*
without the immanentist restrictions imposed by the Stoic tradition.

15. Since the revival of the *eidos*-theory with Antiochus of Ascalon (see Cicero, *Acad. post.* I, 30–33 where Varro gives the philosophical point of view of Antiochus) there was a new interest in the problems of causality in the *kosmos noetos*. To resolve some of the problems
Platonic scholars of the period did not hesitate to have recourse to
Aristotle. Thus the purely Platonic elements grow out of a synthesis of
the Good beyond being of the *Republic*, the One of the *Parmenides*, the
nous of the *Philebus*, and the *demiourgos* of the *Timaeus*: the first
cause is *nous*, the source of all good in the universe, beyond qualification and description (Albinus, *Epit.* X, 1–4; on the "unspeakable"

cause, see *agnostos*). This *protos nous* of the *Philebus* is also the *demiourgos* of the *Timaeus* who looks to the *eide* in his creation of the *kosmos*, save that the *eide* are now located in the mind of the *demiourgos* (*ibid.* XII, 1 and *noeton* 2).

16. But there is an Aristotelian side to this as well. The first *nous* thinks himself, and, though he is himself unmoved (*akinetos*), he moves others as an object of desire (*orekton; loc. cit.*). Aristotle had further designated the *proton kinoun* as God and his later commentators identified both with the *nous poietikos* of the *De anima*. Albinus, while he describes the *protos nous* as thinking himself in the prescribed Aristotelian fashion (*Epit.* x, 3), has a further subordinate principle, a second transcendent *nous* that is always energized and that is "the *nous* of the whole heaven," a description that at least suggests the *proton kinoun* of the *Metaphysics*. What seems likely is that Albinus has distinguished the final and efficient causality that Aristotle had united, and assigned the first to the *protos nous* that moves "as an object of desire" (x, 2) and the second to the subordinate *nous*. There is, finally, a third transcendent *nous*, a faculty of the World Soul (x, 3). Visible here are all the motifs of Neoplatonism: three transcendent hypostatized principles that may be denominated, in terms of their emphases, the Good, *nous*, *psyche*, all the causality proceeding from the first, even here described as "like the sun" or "Father."

17. Present too is another trait that is characteristic not only of later Platonism but of the entire philosophical tradition after Aristotle. Plato had considered the stars as intelligent living beings (see *ouranioi* 6) and Aristotle had given to each an intelligent mover (see *kinoun* 11–12; *ouranioi* 3). Middle Platonists incorporated this too into their systems. The planets are intellectual living beings dwelling in the *aither* (Albinus, *Epit.* XIV, 7) and beneath them are the *daimones* of the *aer*, also gods, children of the "Father," more perfect than men and responsible for omens and prodigies (*ibid.* xv, 2; Maximus of Tyre XI, 12; Apuleius, *De deo Socr.* 6; see *daimon* 3–4, *psyche* 35).

18. As has already been indicated (see 6 *supra*), the *nous-demiourgos* in Plato seems to be subordinated to the *eide*, and thus to the Good of the *Republic* as well. Albinus' first *nous* embraces all of these entities, but thereafter new emphases are to be seen. The *protos nous* begins to yield to the *hen-agathon* of the *Parmenides* and *Republic*, and the *nous-demiourgos* function to center on the second hypostasis. These are the views of Numenius (see Eusebius, *Praep. Evang.* XI, 356d–358b), as they will be of Plotinus, stolen, as some said, from Numenius (see Porphyry, *Vita Plot.* XVII, 1). But there are differences as well. The second hypostasis of Numenius is twofold; its primary function, which is *noesis*, degenerating into discursive *dianoia* by reason of its involvement with matter (Eusebius, *op. cit.* XI, 537;

Proclus, *In Tim.* III, 103). In Plotinus, who also avails himself of the concept of "attention" (*phrontis;* see *noesis* 21), the polarity is transferred to the third hypostasis; it is the cosmic soul that has an "upper" and "lower" side (see *psyche tou pantos, physis*).

19. Plotinus follows the general Platonic tradition in making *nous* the second of the three *hypostases* (q.v.). It is the *demiourgos* in that it supplies the *psyche* with the *logoi* that are the forms of sensible things (*Enn.* V, 9, 3), but in general the creative function belongs more properly to *physis*, the lower part of the *psyche*, whose contemplation lapses into activity (*praxis;* III, 8, 4). Proclus puts more stress on *nous* as the *arche* of this sensible world, but he agrees with Plotinus that creation (see also *proödos*) is a consequence of *theoria* or *noesis* (*Elem. theol.*, prop. 174).

20. The first principle, the One, is perfectly self-sufficient and needs nothing; the cosmic *nous*, on the other hand, has a need of itself, a need of thinking itself, and so its operation of *noesis* is, in a sense, a return to itself (*Enn* V, 3, 13). *Nous* is the *energeia* and *logos* of the One (V, 1, 6; compare Philo's view under *logos* 5) and a type of pluralistic externalization of the absolute unity of the One, just as our discursive reasoning is an *eikon* of the relatively unified operation of the cosmic *nous* (see *noesis* 18). The proper activity of *nous* is a direct intuitive grasp of the *noeta* as a unity, not in the sense that the *nous* "thinks" the *noeta*, but rather it *is* the *noeta* (see *noeton* 5).

21. The cosmic *nous*, a Platonic heritage, is linked with the reasoning power immanent in man by a species of Aristotelian bridge. The Aristotelian distinction of dissolution of *nous* into an active *energeia* and a passive *dynamis* is taken up and modified by Plotinus. In *Enn.* V, 9, 3 Plotinus asks himself, in his usual aporematic fashion, if there is a *nous choristos*, and then proceeds to answer by distinguishing between a *nous* that is in the soul as an *eidos* in matter and a *nous* that "gives the form to the soul as the maker [*poiotes*] gives form to the statue." Thus the Aristotelian *nous poietikos* is transformed into the *dator formarum.* The same passage goes on to draw a distinction between the *eide* themselves. The *eide* that the *nous* gives to the soul are "close to reality," those received by matter are "images and imitations" (*eidola, mimemata;* see *noeton* 6).

22. There are, then, three degrees of reality among the Plotinian *eide*. The lowest, the *eide aistheta* in material things, are *eikones* of the true Forms. They serve both a cognitive and paradigmatic end. As existing in others they form the basis of sensation on the Aristotelian model (see *aisthesis* 26); as existing in oneself they are the causal paradigms of the production of other beings (see *logoi spermatikoi, physis*). There are, too, the *eide noeta* or, as they are called from Middle Platonism on, the *ideai*, which exist primarily in the cosmic

nous where they constitute the *kosmos noetos* (q.v.) or, after bestowal, in the immanent human *nous* where, as "traces of *nous*," they provide the grounds for certain of our judgments (see *noesis* 19 and, for a more comprehensive treatment of the *ideai, noeton*).

O

óchēma: *vehicle, chariot, astral body*

1. As appears from the history of the *psyche* (q.v.), a number of apparently irreconcilable strains were present in its development almost from the beginning: the materialist view that sees the *psyche* as a refined form of one or other of the elements, and eventually, as the *pneuma*, a kind of fifth element akin to *aither* (q.v.); the spiritualist view flowing from the Pythagorean doctrine of the soul as a divine substance different in kind from the body; and, finally, the Aristotelian *entelecheia* (q.v.) theory that attempts to explain the *psyche* in terms of the function (see *ergon, energeia*) of some body.

2. Later Platonism was, in effect, forced to come to terms with the *entelecheia* view by reason of Plato's interest in function in the *Timaeus*. This they attempted to do by means of a theory that, in its most general terms, states that the soul has another quasi-physical body or *ochema*, usually acquired during the prenatal "descent" through the heavens (*kathodos*, q.v.; see Plotinus, *Enn.* IV, 3, 15; Macrobius, *In Somn. Scip.* I, 12). This becomes progressively heavier and more visible as it descends through the moist *aer* (Porphyry, *De antro nymph.* 11). With their usual textual piety the Neoplatonists professed to discover the origin of this doctrine in Plato, and particularly in *Tim.* 41d–e where the *demiourgos* sows each soul in a star, "as in a chariot" (*ochema;* compare *Phaedrus* 247b), preliminary to embodying some of them on earth and "storing" others in the planets (*ibid.* 42d). But when it comes to explaining the nature of these "vehicles," resort is made to Aristotle.

3. Aristotle had described *pneuma* (q.v.) as the seat of the nutritive (*threptike*) and sensitive (*aisthetike*) soul and analogous in composition to *aither* that is the material element of the stars (*De gen. anim.* 736b–737a). Thus the "vehicle" of the soul is described by the Neoplatonists as an aetherial (*aitherodes*) and light-like (*augoeides*)

body (Iamblichus, *De myst.* III, 14; the *sidereum* and *luminosum corpus* of Macrobius, *In Somn. Scip.* I, 12 and II, 13).

4. The theory is set out, with a considerable number of refinements, in Proclus, *Elem. theol.*, props. 205–209. Each human soul is initially under the influence of the divine soul (see *psyche, ouranioi*) in one or other of the planets (prop. 204; see *Tim.* 42d and Proclus, *In Tim.* III, 280). The astrological implications of this are obvious, but there was a general Neoplatonic consensus that the *theiai psychai* of the planets were not responsible for evil (Plotinus, *Enn.* II, 3, 10; Iamblichus, *De myst.* I, 18; Proclus, *In Tim.* III, 313). The astral body of the individual soul is consequently related to the body of the planetary soul (prop. 204; compare *Enn.* IV, 4, 31 and see *sympatheia*). But this is the immortal, immaterial body perpetually attached to the soul (props. 206–207); there is another perishable body that the soul acquires during its descent, composed of increasingly material "mantles" (*chitones;* prop. 209; see *In Tim.* III, 297). This is mortal and, though it survives death (just long enough, it would seem, to endure the corporeal punishments of the type described by Plato in *Phaedo* 114a), is eventually dissipated. The human individual soul, then, according to the revisionist version of Proclus, has three bodies: the immortal, immaterial "starry" (*astroeides*) or luminous body associated with the immortal part of the soul; the "spiritual" (*pneumatikon*) possessed by the mortal parts of the soul and the various *daimones* of the universe; and, finally, the fleshly body of the soul's sojourn on earth (*In Tim.* III, 236, 298; *Theol. Plat.* III, 125).

oikeíōsis: *self-appropriation, self-acceptance, self-love*

1. The Epicurean exaltation of pleasure (*hedone*, q.v.) followed a tradition going back as far as the Cyrenaics in taking as its starting point an analysis of man's instinctive, untutored impulses. The Stoics used the same point of departure in ethics but their inspection suggested to them that it was not pleasure that was primary, but rather what they termed *oikeiosis*, the acceptance of one's own being and the means of preserving it, the instinctive impulse (*horme*, q.v.) toward self-preservation (D.L. VII, 85; Cicero, *De fin.* III, 5, 16; its opposite is *allotriosis*, self-alienation). The *oikeion* is not completely absent from Epicureanism where it is the "appropriateness" of the object perceived that produces the pleasure or pain (see *pathos*); it is merely a shift of emphasis from the cause of pleasure to the process itself.

2. *Oikeiosis* has ever-widening circles of application: it operates, in the first instance, toward oneself, then toward one's offspring and family, and, finally, culminates in "love of the whole human race" (*caritas generis humani;* Cicero, *De fin.* III, 19, 62–63; V, 23, 65), thus

providing the ground for the Stoic emphasis on a social ethic based on nature rather than convention. See *nomos, physis.*

on, ónta (pl.): *being, beings*

1. The question of the nature of being first arose in the context of Parmenides' series of logical dichotomies between being and nonbeing (*me on*): that which is, cannot not be; that which is not, cannot be, i.e., a denial of passage from being to nonbeing or *genesis* (q.v.; fr. 2), and its corollary, a denial of change and motion (fr. 8, lines 26–33, 42–50; for the theological correlatives of this, see *nous* 2). Secondly, being is one and not many (fr. 8, lines 22–25). And finally, the epistemological premiss: only being can be known or named; nonbeing cannot (fr. 3; fr. 8, line 34); see *doxa.* Being, in short, is a sphere (fr. 8, lines 42–49). Most of the later pre-Socratics denied this latter premiss (cf. *stoicheion* and *atomon*), as did Plato for whom the really real (*to ontos on*) were the plural *eide*, and who directed the latter half of the *Parmenides* (137b–166c) against it.

2. The solution to the nonbeing dilemma (for its epistemological solution, see *doxa* and *heteron*) and the key to the analysis of *genesis* began with Plato's positing of space (see *hypodoche*) in which *genesis* takes place, and which stands midway between true being and nonbeing (*Tim.* 52a–c). For Plato, as for Parmenides, absolute nonbeing is nonsense (*Soph.* 238c), but there is a relative grade illustrated not only by the Receptacle cited above, but by sensible things (*aistheta*) as well (*Soph.* 240b; *Tim.* 35a, 52c). Among the Platonic hierarchy of Forms, there is an *eidos* of being; indeed it is one of the most important Forms that pervade all the rest (*Soph.* 254b–d; compare this with the peculiar nature of *on* in Aristotle, *Meta.* 1003a). Further, Plato distinguishes real beings (*ontos onta*) from those that have *genesis*, and in *Timaeus* 28a he works out an epistemological-ontological correlation: *onta* are known by thought (*noesis*) accompanied by a rational account (*logos*); generated beings are grasped by opinion (or judgment, see *doxa*) based on sensation (*aisthesis*).

3. Since being is the object of the science of metaphysics (*Meta.* 1031a) Aristotle's treatment of *on* is much more elaborate. The first distinction is between "being *qua* being" (*to on he on*), which is the object of metaphysics, and individual beings (*onta*), which are the objects of the other sciences. This is the view in *Meta.* 1003a, but Aristotle is not consistent on the point: elsewhere (see *Meta.* 1026a; *Phys.* 192a, 194b; *De an.* 403b) he states that metaphysics studies being that is separate and unmoving (see *theologia*). Again, "being" is peculiar in that it is defined not univocally or generically, but analogously through all the categories (*Meta.* 1003a), and in this it is

like "one" (*hen*) (*Meta.* 1053b) and "good" (*agathon*) (*ibid. Eth. Nich.* I, 1096b); see *katholou*. There follows a basic distinction (*ibid.* 1017a–b): something "is" either accidentally, or essentially, or epistemologically, or in the dichotomy act (*energeia*)/potency (*dynamis*). The epistemological "being" (see *doxa*) is dealt with elsewhere (see *Meta.* 1027b–1028a, 1051a–1152a), as is potency/act (see *Meta. Theta passim*), so Aristotle here concentrates his attention on what "is" essentially. It is something that falls within the ten *kategoriai* (*Meta.* 1017a) and is, primarily, substance (*ousia; ibid.* 1028a–b). A somewhat different point of view emerges from Aristotle's breakdown of the various senses of nonbeing (*me on*) in *Meta.* 1069b and 1089a: something is not either as a negative proposition, i.e., a denial of one of the predicates, or as a false proposition, or finally, *kata dynamin*, i.e., by being something else only potentially but not actually. It is from this latter that *genesis* comes about (see also *dynamis, energeia, steresis*).

4. In the Plotinian universe the One (*hen*) is beyond being (*Enn.* v, 9, 3; compare Plato's description of the Good beyond Being in *Rep.* 509b and see *hyperousia*). The realm of being begins on the level of *nous* since both being and *nous* are contained in *nous* (*ibid.* v, 5, 2; v, 9, 7). Nonbeing is treated in much the Platonic and Aristotelian fashion: matter (*hyle*) that is only a replica (*eikon*) of being is only quasi-being (*Enn.* I, 8, 3). Philo, with his strongly developed feeling of divine transcendence (see *hyperousia*), restricts true being to God alone (*Quod deter.* 44, 160), and introduces into the discussion the metaphysical interpretation of the famous phrase in *Exod.* 3, 14: "I am who am"; see *hypodoche, hyle, genesis*.

óneiros: *dream*
1. The common Greek attitudes toward dreams may be illustrated from Homer where they are considered as both objective realities, not very different in quality from waking experience, and as manifestations of an inner experience, some aspects of which shade off into symbolism (see *Il.* XXII, 199 ff.; *Od.* XIX, 541 ff.). But of more speculative consequence was the distinction found in Homer (*Od.* XIX, 560 ff.) between dreams that issue from the "gate of ivory" and that are nothing more than "glimmering illusion, fantasy," and those from the "gate of horn" that are portents of things to come, if only mortals know how to interpret them. That the Greeks made just such an effort from an early date is clear from the presence of a "dream interpreter" in *Il.* v, 148.
2. Macrobius, in his commentary on the *Somnium Scipionis* (1, 3, 2), divided portentous dreams into the symbolic, the visionary, and the oracular, to which others added direct converse with a god or a *daimon* (q.v.), e.g. Socrates in *Crito* 44b, *Phaedo* 60e, or the admoni-

tions that frequently led, on the testimony of Plato (*Laws* 909e–910a, *Epinomis* 985c), to religious dedications and foundations. Attempts to induce such dreams were most frequently associated with incubation or sleeping in a sacred place, a practice also designed to provoke medical cures.

3. The dream enters philosophy with Heraclitus who treats it as a subjective turning-inward (fr. 89), while Xenophanes begins a long rationalist tradition by complete denial of divination (Diels 21A32; see *mantike*) including, presumably, dreams. There is an attempt at theory in Democritus who accounted for dreams by the entry into the senses of various *eidola* (q.v.) or images, some of which foretold the future, and from which men derived their notions of the gods, or better, of the *daimones* since some of these visitations were baleful (fr. 166). These same visions were for Epicurus proofs for the existence of the gods (Lucretius, *De rerum nat.* v, 1169–1182; Aetius 1, 7, 34), presumably because of their clarity and universal occurrence. The sentiment is echoed almost exactly by the Christian Tertullian, *De anima* 47, 2; see *enargeia, prolepsis.*

4. Plato believes in the prophetic (and divinely inspired) nature of dreams, and in *Tim.* 71a–72b offers a curious physiological explanation of how they work. They have their origin in the liver, which is the instrument or medium by which the rational part (*logistikon*) of the soul communicates its thoughts, transformed now into visual images, the appetitive faculty (*epithymetikon*). It is the presence of these images in the liver that gives rise to dreams and at the same time explains the practice of divination (*mantike*) by the inspection of animals' livers.

5. Aristotle's earliest view on dreams is close to that of Epicurus and Democritus: in the *De philosophia* (fr. 10), though by now he is working his way clear of Plato's *eidos*-theory, Aristotle still accepts the notion of the separability of the *psyche* from the body, a phenomenon that may be experienced in dreams, as had earlier been pointed out by Pindar (see *psyche*). For Aristotle it is exactly this experience of the soul in dreams that leads to man's conviction as to the existence of the gods. But by the time he had come to write the treatises *De insomniis* and *De divinatione per somnum* he had worked out a completely physiological explanation of dreams, and explicitly denies (*De div.* 462b) their divine origin, though still allowing their occasionally prophetic nature.

6. Aristotle's attempt to place dreams in a purely psychophysiological context was foredoomed to failure. The increasingly religious and ethical interests of post-Aristotelian philosophy led to a reassertion of the divine origin of at least some dreams, while false dreams could be written off to the convenient physiological causes, so Cicero, *De div.*

62, 127–128. Typical of their intrusion into later philosophy is Iamblichus' preoccupation with dream phenomena in his *Life of Pythagoras*, where the now legendary older philosopher is made to counsel his disciples to induce prophetic dreams by nightly "mood-music" (65), and the proper diet (106–107; compare D.L. VIII, 24, where the well-known Pythagorean taboo on beans is explained in this way). On a more popular level the testimonies range from the famous "dream book," the *Sacred Discourses* of Aelius Aristides to the still extant *Oneirocriticon* of Artemidorus of Ephesus, a systematic treatise on the interpretation of dreams.

ónoma: *name*

1. The philosophical problems attendant upon language are introduced by Heraclitus' insistence on the fact of change and the ambiguity of both phenomena and our ways of naming them (see frs. 67, 32). But they appear in a more rigidly conceptualized formula with the Sophists' distinction between nature (*physis*) and convention (*nomos*, q.v.). Gorgias, for one, denies all connection between the word and the object described (Sextus Empiricus, *Adv. Math.* VII, 84), thereby raising the question of the "correctness" of names. Prodicus gave expensive lectures on the subject (Plato, *Crat.* 384b), and we know from Xenophon, *Mem.* III, 14, 2 that it was a frequently discussed topic at Athens.

2. Plato takes up the question in detail in his *Cratylus* where the position that names have a natural connection with the things named is maintained by the Heraclitan Cratylus (383a; see *rhoe*), and the theory of the conventional origin of language by Hermogenes (384d). Socrates' position is that things have a permanent quality of their own (the *eidos*-theory is presumed throughout; for medical investigation along these lines, see *eidos*), and that the function of language is a social one: the name is an instrument to teach us about the *ousia* of a thing and to enable us to distinguish it from other things (388b–c). It follows then that there must have been a wise legislator (*nomothetes*) who has imposed names on things using a kind of ideal name as his model (389a–390e).

3. There follows (423a–b) a theory as to the mimetic origin of language: the name is a phonetic *mimesis* (q.v.) of the object, a gesture in sound. But for all the etymological mockery in the *Cratylus* it is clear from a number of passages in Plato that he takes seriously the philosophical content of names: they are a constituent of every statement (*logos; Soph.* 261c–262e) and part of the process leading toward *episteme* (q.v.; *Ep.* VII, 342a ff.).

4. Aristotle agrees with Plato on the mimetic character of language (*Rhet.* 1404a20), but sounds only become names when they take

on a meaning established by convention (*De interp.* 16a), i.e., when they become symbolic. Again, like Plato, Aristotle is much indebted to linguistic analysis as a philosophical tool: the *kategoriai* are, in the first instance, modes of *predication*.

5. Epicurus was concerned with a solid epistemological basis for philosophical discourse and was at some pains to insist on an intimate connection between the concept (*ennoia*, q.v. and see *prolepsis*) and its name, i.e., on the world of thought (already tied to the world of objects by his sensualist theory of *aisthesis;* see *aistheton* and *eidolon*) and that of language (D.L. x, 37–38). The name, therefore, must be clear and immediate evidence of the concept (*ibid.* x, 33; compare *enargeia*). He then proceeds (*ibid.* x, 75–76) to offer his theory of the origins of language.

6. Speech flows from man's natural desire to express his own feelings (*pathe*). Lucretius considerably expands this stage of development (*De rerum nat.* v, 1028–1090), tracing the evolution of language from gesture (following Plato, but rejecting, in the same passage, both the Platonic and Stoic *nomothetes*), through animal sounds, to the babbling of children. On this point the Epicureans and Stoics parted company in a radical fashion: for the latter speech is a function of *logos* and hence only men have true speech; animals and children emit mere sounds that are "like speech" (Varro, *De ling. lat.* vi, 56; Seneca, *De ira* i, 3). After this original natural-mimetic stage Epicurus allows for the use of a conventionalized standardization (*loc. cit.*).

7. Between Aristotle and the Stoics occurred great advances in linguistic research connected with the Alexandrine elucidation of the text of Homer. The results may be witnessed in the not always happy etymologizing (*etymos*, an adjective meaning "true" in Homer, is substantivized into *etymon*, the true sense of a word) in post-Aristotelian philosophy and particularly in the developed and sophisticated theories of Stoic philosophical linguistics. The linchpin of Stoic theory is the close relationship between interior *logos* (thought) and exterior *logos* (speech; see *logos*). Thus the *onoma* signifies the thing because the connection is by nature (*physis*) and not, as Aristotle said, by convention (*SVF* ii, 146). But the Stoic explanation of "nature" is much closer to the Socratic exposition already cited from the *Cratylus*. The Stoics too believed that the connection between names and the true nature of things springs from the wisdom of a primitive lawgiver who "imposed" names upon things (see Ammonius, *In de interp.* 35, 16; 36, 23; compare *SVF* ii, 1066, 1070), just as Adam is described as doing by Philo in *Leg. all.* ii, 14–15. In this fashion exterior *logos* reveals the inner essence of things, and the Stoics consequently paid a great deal of attention to etymologies, which in turn led them into complex discussions of whether names were related to things through the etymological

principle of analogy (*analogia*) or its converse, anomaly (*anomalia;*
Varro, *De ling. lat.* ix, 1, citing Chrysippus; see the notorious derivation of *lucus* from *non lucendo* in Quintilian 1, 6, 23). Stoic etymologizing becomes pervasive in all subsequent philosophical literature.

órexis: *appetite*

The appetitive (*orektikon*) is that faculty of the soul which
pursues (Aristotle, *De an.* 431a). It embraces the three functions of
desire (*epithymia*), spirit, and wish (*ibid.* 414b), and is, in conjunction with sensation (*aisthesis*) or intellection (*noesis*), the ultimate
cause of motion in the soul (*De an.* iii, 433a–b; see *kinoun* 9). Aristotle's general treatment of *orexis* is in *De motu anim.* chaps. 6–8; for
its role in Platonism, see *epistrophe;* in Stoicism, *horme.*

órganon: *instrument, organ,* Organon
See *aisthesis, dialektike, holon.*

ouránioi: *heavenly bodies*

1. The belief in the divinity of the heavenly bodies is an old one
among the Greeks. In *Apol.* 26d Socrates says that everyone believed in
them, all, perhaps, except Anaxagoras who was tried on a charge of
impiety, part of which involved the divinity of the *ouranioi* (D.L. ii,
12). Indeed, the belief was so ancient that both Plato (*Crat.* 397c–d,
Laws 885e; compare *Laws* 966d where the emphasis is somewhat
different) and Aristotle (*De phil.*, fr. 10) trace back the beginnings of
man's belief in God to a contemplation of the heavens. The motives are
various: the identification of air-*psyche*-life (see *aer*), coupled with the
apparent eternity of their motion, and the discovery of the order (*kosmos*) in their movements; the argument from everlasting motion is
specifically attributed to the Pythagorean Alcmaeon by Aristotle (*De
an.* i, 405a; compare Cicero, *De nat. deor.* i, 27).

2. Plato accepted their divinity (*Rep.* 508a) and gave them an
important place in his cosmology (*Tim.* 38c–39e); they were, in fact,
the only material things made by the *demiourgos*. In both the *Laws*
(898d–899b) and the *Epinomis* (981e) they are said to possess souls,
and to move by the most perfect deliberation (*Epinomis* 982c). The
exact connection between the bodies and souls of the *ouranioi* is not
specified, but three possibilities are outlined in the *Laws* (see *kinoun*
3).

3. When he wrote his early dialogue *On Philosophy* Aristotle
still believed in the Platonic star souls and gave them a role in his
theory of the causality of motion (fr. 24; see *kinoun* 8). But when he
came to write the *De coelo* he was somewhat ambivalent on the subject.
They are still present (ii, 292a) but they seem to have no role in the

motion of the stars, which is now explained in terms of the *physis* of the material composing the sphere in which they are imbedded, i.e., *aither* (q.v.). In the *Metaphysics* they are nowhere to be seen and when Aristotle comes to explain the motions of the heavenly bodies he resorts instead to a theory of multiple prime movers that can be and have been construed as the souls of the various planets but are much more likely separated intelligences (see *kinoun* 11–12).

4. This is not to say, however, that Aristotle ceased believing in the divinity of the heavenly bodies; he merely discarded them as philosophical causes. For him, as for Plato (see *Tim.* 39e) they were "visible Gods" (see *Meta.* 1028a) and more divine than men (see *Phys.* II, 196a and *Eth. Nich.* VI, 1141a). And again the reason is the apparent lack of any change in their activities, a fact confirmed by millennia of astronomical records (see *De coelo* I, 270b). In the same passage Aristotle averts to another type of historical argument. All men believe in gods and they have invariably located them in the heavens, linking, he argues, the conceptually immortal to the visibly incorruptible. Again, in *Meta.* 1074b he resorts to a confirmatory proof from the popular religious belief in the divinity of the. planets, a tradition passed down in the form of a myth. Aristotle may here be referring to the fairly recent custom of associating the planets with the gods of Greek mythology. The first such reference in Greek literature is in *Tim.* 38d where Plato speaks of the "holy star of Hermes," and the first full list occurs in *Epinomis* 987b–d where the origin of the custom is described as Syrian.

5. In succeeding periods the belief in the heavenly bodies was encouraged by the growing importance of astrology and so it frequently turned out that their influence on human affairs was debated more vehemently than their existence. There is a long polemic against the astral gods in Lucretius v, 110–145 (compare Epicurus in D.L. x, 77), probably directed against the Stoics since it contains arguments against the divinity of the earth and sea as well. Stoic pantheism did tend to move in that direction (see *SVF* II, 1027), and the specific doctrine of the divinity of the heavenly bodies could be connected, as Aristotle had done in the *De coelo*, with the nature of the *aither* (so the Stoic in Cicero, *De nat. deor.* II, 39–43), and precisely because of its fiery substance and rapid movement, infallible indications of life and intelligence. But these positions were strongly criticized by the Sceptics (*ibid.* III, 23–24, 51) who were opposed to all sorts of divination (*mantike*, q.v.).

6. The argument that the rapidity and fiery quality of the *aither* is an indication of its intellectual nature goes back ultimately to perception theories like those of Diogenes of Apollonia (see *aisthesis* 12, *noesis* 5) but has more immediate origins in the young Aristotle. Plato

had maintained that the stars were composed of a fiery stuff and were intelligent living beings (*Tim.* 40a–b), and that human souls first came into existence in the stars before being incorporated on earth (*ibid.* 41d–e). And it is for this reason, according to Plato, that the divine intellect in us is located in the head (see *kardia* 4) so that it may be closest to its "heavenly congener" (*ibid.* 90a). These suggestions were taken up by Aristotle and incorporated into his doctrine of the "fifth element" (*quinta essentia;* see *aither*) that is the substance from which both the heavenly bodies and our *nous* is made (*De philosophia*, fr. 27 = Cicero, *Acad. post.* I, 26; this is, of course, incompatible with his later theory of *nous* as a spiritual *energeia;* see *nous* 11). We are further told (Cicero, *Tusc.* I, 22) that he coined a new term to describe its perpetual and uninterrupted motion, *endelecheia* (compare the similar approach to *aither* in *De coelo* I, 270b). Also Aristotelian may be the corollary mentioned by Cicero (*De nat. deor.* II, 42–43) that the stars feed upon the *aither.*

7. The theory continued to thrive in all its ramifications. It reappears in the revival of Pythagoreanism at the turn of the Christian era (D.L. VIII, 26–27) and plays a part in Poseidonius' theories of soul (see Cicero, *Tusc.* I, 42–43 and compare *sympatheia* 5). For Philo the heavenly bodies are "intellectual animals" (*zoa noera*) or, better, each is an intelligence (*nous*) remote from evil (*De opif.* 73). The cult of these heavenly gods, encouraged by the consuming interest in astrology and demonology (cf. Macrobius, *In Somn. Scip.* I, 12, 14; Plutarch, *De defec. orac.* 416d–f), must have appeared at times on the brink of overwhelming the patiently constructed rationalist position. This seems to be the mood of the defensive struggle put up by Plotinus. As a good Platonist and as a somewhat reluctant heir to the Peripatetic tradition, he accepted the doctrine of celestial intelligences and the stars as living beings (*Enn.* V, 1, 2) that lead a life of goodness and happiness (IV, 8, 2). But he is firm in his detailed resistance to the contemporary astrology (IV, 4, 30–45; see *sympatheia* 8).

For celestial immortality, see *aer, aphthartos;* for the question of astral bodies, *ochema;* on the movement of the heavenly bodies, *kinoun;* and on their intelligences, *nous.*

ouranós: *heaven*

1. Heaven is a generative principle in the ancient cosmogonies (see Plato, *Tim.* 40d–e; Aristotle, *Meta.* 1091b). It first appears in a strictly philosophical context in a difficult passage of Anaximenes (Diels 12A17) where he is represented as positing "innumerable *ouranoi* that are gods." Henceforth the Greek view of heaven as a single entity is at least partially replaced by that of a multiplicity of heavenly spheres that envelop the earth and carry the sun, moon, and planets,

while the final outermost sphere carries the fixed stars (see Aristotle, *De coelo* I, 278b). In this same passage in the *De coelo* Aristotle points out that *ouranos* is also used in the sense of the entire universe, and indeed Plato had still used the terms *ouranos* and *kosmos* interchangeably (*Phaedrus* 247b, *Pol.* 269d, *Tim.* 28b); see also *kosmos*.

2. In addition to the belief in the divinity of the heavenly bodies (*ouranioi*), the heaven had another connection with religion: tied to the increasing astronomical sophistication and the consequent identification of the heaven as an extraordinary "order" (see *kosmos*) was the belief that the role of the philosopher was the contemplation of the eternal verities on high. Best known in this regard are the series of anecdotes about Anaxagoras (see D.L. II, 2 and 7; Iamblichus, *Protrept.* 51, 6–15; perhaps Aristotle's remark about Xenophanes in *Meta.* 986b should be understood in the same sense). The same motif is present in Philo, *De opif.* 17, 53–54, now combined with a providential creation; God created the heavens so that man, in contemplating their *harmonia*, might be drawn further upward to the study of philosophy.

3. For Plato too the spectacle of the heavens has a distinct educational effect: in *Rep.* 528e–530c astronomy serves as an introduction to *dialektike* (compare *Laws* 820a–822d, 967a–968a); a vision of the order of the heavens is a feature of the myth of the soul's destiny in both the *Phaedrus* 246d–247c and the *Rep.* 616c–617d. The nuance is slightly different in *Tim.* 47a–c; here the contemplation of the heavens is directed toward a restoration in the *harmonia* (q.v.; see *kinoun* 5) in the soul. By the time of the late Academic *Epinomis* 980a–988e these considerations have been incorporated into (and overwhelmed by) the prevalent astral theology (see *ouranioi* 7). Heaven then becomes the dwelling place of these heavenly gods, Olympus (so *Epinomis* 977b; see *Tim.* 30e–40b and the remarkable fragment of Critias preserved in Sextus Empiricus, *Adv. Math.* IX, 54).

ousía: *substance, existence*

1. From the fact that Socrates cites Dorian dialectical variants of *ousia* in *Crat.* 401c it has been conjectured that the philosophical origins of the term are Pythagorean. The word has, however, in accordance with Plato's usual technique of variable terminology, a number of different meanings in the dialogues. Thus, it sometimes means existence as opposed to nonexistence (*Theaet.* 185c, 219b); it is applied to the existence of sensible things in *Theaet.* 186b, and probably the phrase "coming into being" (*genesis eis ousian*) in *Phil.* 26d is a similar usage. But in other places it is explicitly contrasted to *genesis* and the world of becoming (*Soph.* 232c, *Tim.* 29c) as the mode of being of the "really real" (*ontos on;* see *Rep.* 509b, where the Good is beyond even *ousia*, and compare *hyperousia*). *Ousia* even approaches

the Aristotelian usage as "essence" in *Phaedo* 65d, 92d, and *Phaedrus* 245e where it is equivalent to "definition."

2. Aristotle's search for substance begins in the *Categories* where it is described as that which is not said of a subject or not present in a subject, e.g. the particular man or the particular horse. This individual (*tode ti*) is substance in the primary sense, but "substance" may also be used to describe the genus (*genos*) and the species (*eidos*), and of these *eidos* has more of a claim to be substance since it is nearer to the individual primary substance: to call an individual tree "an oak" is more revelatory of what it is than to call it "a plant" (*Cat.* 2a–b). Aristotle is further convinced that the problem posed by metaphysics, and indeed by all of philosophy, i.e., "what is being [*on*]"? really comes down to "what is *ousia*"? since being is, first and foremost, substance (*Meta.* 1028b).

3. In *Meta.* 1069a Aristotle distinguishes three types of *ousiai:* 1) sensible (*aisthetos*) and everlasting (*aidios*), i.e., the heavenly bodies that, because the natural motion of their element, *aither*, is circular, are also everlasting (see *aphthartos*); 2) the sensible and perishable, i.e., what everybody recognizes as substances, plants, animals, etc.; and 3) the unchangeable (*akinetos*). All the substances in classes 1) and 2) are composites, and Aristotle sets about determining which of their components have the best claim to be called substance (*Meta.* 1028b–1041b). The choice is narrowed down to four: the substratum (*hypokeimenon*), genus (*genos*), the universal (*katholou*), and the essence (*ti esti*). The results are the same as those reached in the *Categories:* it is the essence or *eidos* that has the best claim to be substance (*ibid.* 1041a–b), not now as a predicational entity, i.e., "species," but as the immanent formal cause in compound beings (see *eidos*). It fulfills the two prerequisites of substance: it is separable (see *choriston*) and, as embodied in matter, individual (*tode ti*) (*ibid.* 1029a). Aristotle deals with the first two classes in the *De coelo* and the *Physics* and then takes up the question of unchangeable substances in a later book of the *Metaphysics* (1071b–1076a). Their existence is necessary because both motion (*kinesis*) and time (*chronos*) are everlasting (1071b). To account for this perpetual movement there must be an unmoved substance, i.e., something that moves as final cause: this is the First Mover (*ibid.* 1072a–1073a; see *kinoun* 7–10). There are a number of such movers, and their exact number must be determined by astronomical calculations (47 or 55?) (1073a–1074a; see *kinoun* 11–12).

4. The Aristotelian category of substance as *hypokeimenon* becomes, for the Stoics, matter (*SVF* I, 87; II, 369). Ontologically it is used in the same sense, see Marcus Aurelius, *Med.* VI, 1; XII, 30. Plotinus criticizes and rejects the Aristotelian analysis of substance

(*Enn.* VI, 3, 3–5); the only thing that matter, form, and the composite have in common is being, and even this is different in the three cases (*ibid.* VI, 3, 6–7). What sensible *ousía* is, then, is nothing more than a conglomeration of qualities and matter (*ibid.* VI, 3, 8).

P

palingenesía: *rebirth, transmigration of souls*
(metempsychosis *is a very late word*)
That Pythagoras held such a doctrine is attested by his contemporary Xenophanes (fr. 7), and there is the later, more dubious testimony (D.L. VIII, 4–5) that he remembered four of his own previous reincarnations. That the quality of the reincarnations is tied to an ethical scale is clear from Orphism and from Empedocles (frs. 115, 117, 127, 146, 147). Plato has heard of this doctrine (*Meno* 81a) and in *Phaedo* 70c–72e he incorporates it into his proofs for the immortality of the soul, and, in a more Orphic context, in *Phaedrus* 249a and *Tim.* 42b–c, where the successive rebirths are tied to moral purity. Its most elaborate presentation is in the "Myth of Er" in *Rep.* 614b–621b. For Herodotus' mistaken notion as to its origins see *Hist.* II, 123.

The philosophical presuppositions of *palingenesia* are closely linked with the nature and separability of the soul, see *psyche;* its epistemological use may be seen in *anamnesis* (q.v.), and some of its religious aspects in *kathodos.*

parádeigma: *model*
See *mimesis.*

parénklisis: *swerve (of the atoms)*
See *kinesis.*

páschein: *to suffer, be affected, passion*
1. Passion (*paschein*), the general state of which *pathos* (q.v.) is the formalized affect, is, together with its correlative, action (*poiein*), a function of the ancient notion of "power" (*dynamis,* q.v.). But their isolation and conceptualization seems to have been the doing of Plato (but see *Gorg.* 476a–e where their facile manipulation suggests an earlier usage) who divides change (*kinesis,* q.v.) into active

and passive aspects (*Theaet.* 156a; compare *Laws* x, 894c) that he later calls hallmarks of the world of becoming (*genesis; Soph.* 248c).

2. The association of action and passion with *genesis* remains constant, not in the sense of qualitative change or locomotion as Plato suggests (*Theaet.* 156c), but in the technical sense of the Aristotelian *genesis* (q.v.), i.e., substantial change, and particularly the passage of one element (*stoicheion*) into another. The key to action and passion is contrariety (*enantion*, q.v.); identical things cannot act upon each other (Plato, *Tim.* 57a; Aristotle, *De gen. et corr.* i, 323b). Thus the powers or qualities involved in *genesis* must be generically the same but specifically different, and *genesis* can be defined as "passage to the contrary" (Aristotle, *op. cit.* i, 324a).

3. But mere contrariety is not enough: the contrary powers must have the capacity for action and passion. It is significant that when Aristotle is attempting to discern which powers are present in the *genesis* of the elements he rules out "the light" and "the heavy" precisely on the ground that though they are contraries, they do not have *poiein* and *paschein* (*ibid.* ii, 329b).

4. In Aristotle *paschein* is one of the ten *kategoriai* (q.v.; *Cat.* 1b–2a), and his examples are "is cut," "is burnt." Like *poiein* it admits of both contrariety and degree (*ibid.* 11b). In Stoicism the "patient" (*paschon*) is identified with matter (*hyle*), the agent (*poioun*) with *logos* (q.v.; D.L. vii, 134). Both Aristotle and the Stoics distinguish between the active and passive elements or, better, the qualities in them (*Meteor.* iv, 378b; *SVF* ii, 418; see *genesis*).

For the active and passive *archai* of movement, see, respectively, *kinoun* and *physis;* for their metaphysical import, *energeia* and *hyle;* for their role in perception, *aisthesis;* for *actio in distans* and the question of contact, *sympatheia* 7.

páthos: *event, experience, suffering, emotion, attribute*

1. The history of the word *pathos* is beclouded by a multiplicity of connotations. In its most general acceptance it means "something that happens," either in reference to the event itself (so Herodotus v, 4; Sophocles, *O.T.*, 732) or the person affected (so Plato, *Phaedo* 96a: "my experiences"), the latter type of use considerably enlarged into ethical directions, as for example, in the "instructive suffering" of the tragedians (see Aeschylus, *Aga.* 177). Philosophical speculation goes off into two different directions from this point, investigating *pathos* as both "what happens to bodies" and "what happens to souls," the first under the general rubric of qualities, the second under that of emotions. The bridge is provided by the materialist theories of sensation that reduce sense knowledge to a *pathos* of the senses that, in turn, is

capable of triggering the *pathe* of the soul.

2. But to discuss the *pathe* as "what happens to bodies" is to set the terms in a way they were not understood until the time of Plato. He was certainly capable of distinguishing between a body (or subject) and what happens to it (see *Tim.* 49a–50a), but there is little evidence that the pre-Socratics were capable of such distinctions and the implied isolation of a "quality"; the pre-Socratic ancestor of quality, *dynamis* (q.v.), was looked upon as a "thing." This is perfectly clear in Anaxagoras' treatment of the "seeds" (see *stoicheion* 11–12). At first there is only a mixture (*meigma*) that contains "all things [*chremata*] together" (fr. 1), and these latter turn out to be not only the conventional Empedoclean *stoicheia* but the *pathe/dynameis* as well: the moist and the dry, the hot and the cold, the bright and the dark (fr. 4). None of these is perceptible, because they are fused in the *meigma*.

3. By the instigation of a rotary motion by *nous* various "seeds" are separated off (*apokrisis*) and they too contain a portion of everything but are qualitatively distinct (see fr. 4, *init.*), presumably due to the predominance of one or other of the *pathe*. Why are they not therefore perceptible? They are not perceived because of their minute size and it is only when they associate (*synkrisis*) into large composites that these latter become perceptible and sensibly different because of the predominance of one type of constituent (Aristotle, *Phys.* I, 187a).

4. In Atomism the *pathe* have a more restricted role. In this view there exist only atoms (*atoma*, q.v.) and the void (*kenon*), and the former have only two qualities, size and shape (Diels 68A37; perhaps also weight, see Aristotle, *De gen. et corr.* I, 326a, though this seems a later addition to Atomism; see *kinesis*). This leads to the position that all perception and, indeed, all sensible knowledge may be reduced to contact or touch (*haphe;* Aristotle, *De sensu* 442a; on the question of intellectual knowledge, see *noesis* 6). We are aware of other types of sense experiences, of course, but they are merely subjective and conventional (*nomos*), passive impressions (*pathe*) of the senses to which we accord some type of reality (Theophrastus, *De sens.* 61, 63).

5. What is clearly at stake here is the distinction betweeen the active powers (*dynameis*) inherent in things and that have the capacity to act (*poiein*) and passive activations (*pathe*) of the body acted upon (*paschein*, q.v.). Democritus had severely delimited the active qualities (*poion*, q.v.) by rejecting the entire pre-Socratic mechanism of "the opposites" (*enantia*, q.v.) and reducing all "activity" to touch. Thus his stress on the subjective quality of sense knowledge would appear to be the result of purely theoretical considerations, though it agreed with the more ethical strains of relativism (which had epistemological corollaries) being promulgated by the Sophists (see *nomos*).

6. In Plato the ethical *pathe* appear, at least in places, as a function of materiality: they appear in the moral, corporeal parts of the soul and are present there as a result of the soul's conjunction with the body (*Tim.* 42a–b, 69c). He follows the Atomist position both in making the *pathe* a species of perception and in attempting to reduce sensation (*aisthesis*) to contact (*ibid.* 61c–63e). Where he departs from it is in noting that when the contacts are excessive there results pleasure and pain (*ibid.* 64a–65b). This rather materialistic explanation is not Plato's only or final word on the subject (see *hedone* 2–3), but it is interesting in that it provides the link between *pathos* as a physical quality and *pathos* as an ethical phenomenon.

7. The ethical side of the *pathe* is revealed by other considerations. Plato holds, again, in places, the tripartition of the soul (see *psyche* 15). Are the *pathe* characteristics of all parts of the soul or only of the two lower and corporeal parts? Plato is not at all clear on this. In the *Timaeus* (*loc. cit.* and 69c–d) they seem to be excluded from the *logistikon*, while in the *Laws* (897a) and *Phaedrus* (245c) this is not so. Indeed, the whole doctrine of the tripartite soul seems to be based on the recognition of the existence of conflicting *pathe*, and we are told quite clearly in the *Republic* (580d, 581a) that *each* part of the soul has its own appropriate *pathe*. To all appearances Plato never quite reconciled the incorporeal, separate, and somewhat remote *logistikon*, perhaps derived from Pythagoreanism and necessary to his theory of *palingenesia* and a knowledge of the *eide*, with the more "engaged" soul of his ethical analyses of conduct.

8. In *Meta.* 1022b Aristotle succinctly resumes his predecessors' use of *pathe* as experiences of a body. Since he has already distinguished *dynamis* (q.v.) into its two meanings of power and potentiality, *pathos* may be used in both these senses or, to locate it within the category of substance and accident, it is a capacity for change in a subject (*hypokeimenon*) or else the actual change itself, and particularly qualitative change. Thus change in the category of quality (*alloiosis*, alteration) is defined as "change [*metabole*] with respect to *pathos*" (*Meta.* 1069b; for its difference from *genesis*, change with respect to *ousia*, see *stoicheion* 15).

9. In the *Ethics* Aristotle gives his full attention to the *pathe* of the soul. In the *Phaedrus* (245c) Plato had already described the soul as the subject of experiences (*pathe*) and the source of activities (*erga*), and Aristotle makes these the subject matter of morality (*Eth. Nich.* 11, 1106b; see *praxis;* the third state of the soul, *hexis*, q.v., is merely our disposition toward the other two). Virtue consists in a man's achieving a mean position (*meson*, q.v.) with respect to them; see *arete.*

10. The truly psychic nature of the *pathe* is illustrated by the fact

that they are accompanied by pleasure or pain (*ibid.* II, 1105b). But this is not to be construed as indicating that they are completely immaterial even though they are the affects of the incorporeal soul. The *pathe* are always accompanied by certain purely physical changes and it is for this reason that the *psyche* cannot be considered a separate substance but rather the *entelecheia* of a body (*De an.* I, 403a). And when the same criterion is applied to the *nous*, its very lack of *pathe* suggests that it is immortal (*ibid.* I, 408b); see *nous*.

11. By the time Atomism appears in its Epicurean version, the Platonic and Aristotelian refinements on *pathe* can be marked. The subjective element, prominent in Democritus, has been tempered (see *holon*), and while the *pathe* are still essentially tactile sensations, they are now distinguished by the concomitant presence of pleasure or pain. It is these latter that now become the center of attention in that they reflect the appropriateness (*oikeion*) or nonappropriateness (*allotrion*) of the object perceived and thus provide criteria for the choice of good and evil (D.L. x, 34, 129; see *hedone*. For the newly expanded role of "appropriateness" in Stoicism, see *oikeiosis*).

12. Apparently Zeno held that all the *pathe*, which were defined as "excessive impulses" (*hormai*, q.v.; essentially the same idea is expressed in *Tim.* 42a–b), were irrational movements of the soul (D.L. VII, 110), while Chrysippus preferred the more intellectualist position of looking upon them as a state of the rational faculty (*hegemonikon; SVF* III, 459, II, 823; see *aisthesis* 5, *noesis* 17). For the Stoic the virtuous life consists not in finding a mean for the *pathe*, as in Aristotle, but in extirpating them entirely. The wise man, then, is one who has reached the stage of *apatheia* (q.v.). The four main *pathe* are pain, fear, desire, and pleasure (D.L. VII, 110; they are defined *SVF* III, 391; compare the Platonic and Aristotelian lists in *Tim.* 42a–b and *Eth. Nich.* II, 1105b; see also *noesis* 17).

For the *pathe* of matter, see *paschein, dynamis, poion, onoma;* for the cure of the ethical *pathe* on the homoeopathic principle, *katharsis;* for their extirpation, *apatheia;* for their connection with perception, *aisthesis.*

péras: limit

Though the notion of limit is obviously an ingredient in Anaximander's *apeiron* (absence of internal determination?), it begins to play a formal role among the Pythagoreans for whom, on Aristotle's testimony, it was, together with the unlimited, an ultimate principle of reality, standing behind even number (*Meta.* 986a). Limit stands at the head of one of the Pythagorean tables of opposites cited in *Meta.* 986a, and in *Eth. Nich.* 1106b is explicitly connected with the Good. The Pythagorean *peras* may be related to their discovery of numerical proportions in musical harmony (see Aristotle, *De coelo* 290b12). Such seems to be the intent of Plato's use of *peras* in *Phil.* 23c–26d; for its ethical implications, see *meson, agathon, harmonia.*

For limit as a factor in the definition of number, see *poson;* for a possible Plotinian adaptation, *aisthesis.*

phantasía: *imagination, impression*

Plato uses the term *phantasia* as a blend of judgment and perception (*Theaet.* 195d). For Aristotle imagination (*phantasia*) is an intermediary between perceiving (*aisthesis*) and thinking (*noesis*), *De an.* III, 427b–429a (compare the analogous position of *phantasia* in Plotinus, *Enn.* IV, 4, 12). It is a motion of the soul caused by sensation, a process that presents an image which may persist even after the perception process disappears. *Phantasia* is defined by Zeno as "an impression in the soul" (Sextus Empiricus, *Adv. Math.* VII, 236), an "impulse from the outside" capable of being grasped (*katalepsis*) by the soul and assented to (Cicero, *Acad. post.* I, 11, 40–42). Its sensual nature was changed from "impression" to "alteration" by Chrysippus (Sextus Empiricus, *Adv. Math.* VII, 228–231, 233) who also maintained that it and not the *katalepsis* was the criterion of truth (D.L. VII, 54; see *katalepsis*).

For the role of "fantasizing" in the creation of "false pleasures," see *hedone;* for further remarks on its role in intellection, *noesis.*

philosophía: *love of wisdom, philosophy*

1. By the traditional Greek account Pythagoras was the first to use the term *philosophia* (see D.L. I, 12; Cicero, *Tusc.* V, 3, 8), and endowed the word with a strongly religious and ethical sense (contrast the neutral "Ionian" usage in Herodotus I, 30), which can best be seen in the view of the philosopher put forth by Socrates in *Phaedo* 62c–69e. In Aristotle it has lost these Pythagorean overtones (the same process is visible in Plato, see *phronesis*): *philosophia* has now become a synonym for *episteme* (q.v.) in the sense of an intellectual discipline seeking out causes (*Meta.* 1026a). In the same passage Aristotle mentions "first philosophy" (*prote philosophia*) or "theology" (see *theologia;* "metaphysics" is a later word) that has as its object not mutable things as does physics (also called "second philosophy," *ibid.* 1037a), or those connected with matter, as does mathematics, but being (*on*) that is eternal, immutable, and separated from matter. This is the same science called *sophia* in *Meta.* 980a–983a.

2. The division of philosophy into physical, ethical, and logical probably goes back to Stoicism (D.L. VII, 39; Cicero, *Acad. post.* 5, 19), and it was also the Stoics who broadened *philosophia* to once again embrace the practical as well as the theoretical: see Cicero's definition,

De fin. III, 2, 4 as *ars vitae;* see *sophia, ouranos.*

For the methodology of philosophy, see *aporia, dialektike, endoxon.*

phorá: locomotion

According to Aristotle all locomotion can be reduced to 1) circular motion around a center, or 2) rectilinear motion toward or away from a center (*De coelo* 268b). Circular motion is primary (*De coelo* 269a; *Phys.* VIII, 265a–266a) and is the natural motion of *aither*, the fifth element from which the heavenly bodies are made (*De coelo* 269b–270b), while the rectilinear motions are natural to the other four elements; see *kinesis, stoicheion.*

phrónēsis: wisdom, practical wisdom, prudence

1. There was always believed to be some sort of intellectual control in virtue, witness the remark of the Cynic Antisthenes (D.L. VI, 13) and Plato, *Rep.* VI, 505b where the Cynics are probably referred to as identifying the good with *phronesis.* For Socrates this intellectual insight into the transcendental ethical values becomes synonymous with virtue (*arete*), see Xenophon, *Mem.* III, 9, 4; Plato, *Gorg.* 460b; *Meno* 88a–89a (but compare *Phaedo* 69a–b, where it is only one ingredient of true *arete*); Aristotle, *Eth. Nich.* 1144b.

2. With Plato's more metaphysical concerns *phronesis* begins to lose its practical and ethical coloring until it means the intellectual contemplation of the *eide* (see *Rep.* 505a ff.), and in the *Philebus* it is commonly used as a synonym for *nous* as the highest type of knowledge (22a, 22d, 66b; see *hedone*), a usage common enough among the pre-Socratics in their discussions of the similarities and differences between sense knowledge and thought (see *aisthesis, noesis*). In the early *Protrepticus* (fr. 52) Aristotle still holds the Platonic position, but in *Eth. Nich.* VI, 1140a–b *phronesis* is once again restricted to the moral sphere, while the *theoria* side of the Platonic *phronesis* is separated as (theoretical) wisdom (*sophia*), see *ibid.* 1143b–1145a. Despite his hedonism *phronesis* still plays a central role in Epicurus (D.L. X, 131), as well as in Stoicism (Plutarch, *De vit. mor.* 2; *SVF* III, 256), and Plotinus (*Enn.* I, 2, 7; I, 6, 6).

On the seat of *phronesis,* see *kardia.*

phthorá: *passing away, corruption*

Phthora, as the term of the process known as *kinesis*, is a correlative of *genesis*, the beginning of the process, and must be seen in that context (so Anaximander, Diels 12B1). Thus, beings that are without *kinesis*, like the *on* of Parmenides (fr. 8, line 26) and the *eide* of Plato (*Phaedo* 78a), lack both *genesis* and "passing away" (see Parmenides, fr. 8, line 27 where the corollary is specified). Within the world of the sensibles (*aistheta*) Plato had a highly developed analysis of change (see *metabole*) in which *genesis-phthora* occur in the category of what is for Aristotle "substantial change." In one of these passages (*Laws* 894a) there is a quasi-definition of *phthora* as "change into another constitiution [*hexis*]." In Aristotle *genesis* is perpetual because each *phthora* is, in effect, a new *genesis* (*De gen. et corr.* I, 318a); see *genesis*.

The question of the corruption of the *kosmos* is discussed under *aphthartos*, and that of the soul under *athanatos*.

physikós: *student of physis* (q.v.)*, natural philosopher*
See *theologia, aphairesis, ergon.*

phýsis: *nature*

1. Although the word itself is not strongly attested until the time of Heraclitus (it does appear earlier in the titles of works by Anaximander and Xenophanes), it is clear that the inquiry which uses the methodological approach known as *logos* and later known by Pythagoras as *philosophia* (q.v.), had, as its general subject matter, *physis*. Such was the understanding of both Plato (see *Phaedo* 96a) and Aristotle (*Meta.* 1005a) who calls the early philosophers *physikoi*, i.e., those concerned with *physis*. It meant these different but connected things: 1) the growth process or *genesis* (so Empedocles, frs. 8, 63; Plato, *Laws* 892c; Aristotle, *Phys.* 193b); 2) the physical stuff out of which things were made, the *arche* (q.v.) in the sense of *Urstoff* (so Plato, *Laws* 891c; Aristotle, *Phys.* 189b, 193a); and 3) a kind of internal organizational principle, the structure of things (so Heraclitus, fr. 123; Democritus, fr. 242).

2. Meanings 1) and 2) must be seen in the context of the theism of the pre-Socratics: this "stuff" was alive, hence, divine, hence immortal and indestructible (see Aristotle, *De an.* I, 411a, *Phys.* III, 203a–b; Plato, *Laws* 967a; compare *Epinomis* 991d). Thus the *physis* of the earliest philosophers had movement and life, but with Parmenides' emphatic removal of *kinesis* from the realm of being (see *on*), the notion of *physis* was in effect destroyed, the initiation of movement passing to outside agents, e.g. the "Love and Strife" of Empedocles

(see Diels, fr. 31A28) and the *nous* (q.v.) of Anaxagoras, or, and in the eyes of Plato this is the more religiously pernicious doctrine (*Laws* 889c), movement was random and necessary, probably a reference to the Atomists (see *tyche*). What Plato finds faulty in contemporary views of *physis* is its materiality (*Laws* 892b) and the absence of design (*techne;* see *Soph.* 265c). It was to correct these two misconceptions that Plato substituted *psyche* (q.v.) as a source of movement.

3. With Aristotle there is a general rehabilitation of *physis* that takes over many of the functions of the Platonic *psyche:* it is defined (*Phys.* II, 192b) as "the principle [*arche*] and cause [*aitia*] of motion and rest for the things in which it is immediately present." Like *psyche*, it is spiritual because it is primarily form (*Phys.* II, 193a), and it works toward an end (*telos; Phys.* II, 194a). Two difficulties arise: in replacing *psyche* with *physis* Aristotle has severed the connection between movement and life, and, on the other hand, between purpose (*telos*) and intelligence (*nous*). The first is solved by extending *physis* down into the realm of the inanimate elements and positing the doctrine of "natural movement" for each (see *stoicheion, kinoun* 8), but in *Phys.* VIII he reverts to a more Platonic position: "ensouled," i.e., living, things, have within them both the principle of movement and the initiator of movement, and they thus differ from inanimate things that have within them the passive (*paschein*) principle of movement, but not the active (*poiein*), which consequently must operate from outside (*Phys.* VIII, 255b–256a): thus all motion, in effect, requires an efficient cause (*kinoun*). On the second question, the connection between *telos* and *nous*, he is likewise ambivalent; juxtaposed in *Phys.* II, 199a are two arguments for the teleology of *physis*, one of which suggests the presence of *nous* while the other denies it.

4. Stoic monism led to the identification of God-nature-fire (*SVF* II, 1027; Cicero, *De nat. deor.* II, 22, 57). In its immanent, active role *physis* is *logos* (Seneca, *De benef.* IV, 7) and, on the level of the individual existent, the *logoi spermatikoi* (q.v.). It is a moral principle, in that the purpose of man was to live "harmoniously with nature" (for the Stoic "natural" morality and the theory of the interconnection of nature, see *nomos* and *sympatheia* respectively).

5. Plotinus' doctrine of nature is bound up with his view of soul; both the soul of the universe (see *psyche tou pantos*) and the individual, immanent souls of men have two different aspects: an upper, contemplative side, soul proper (though in *Enn.* IV, 4, 13 it is called *phronesis*), and a lower side, *physis*, that is forever turned away from *nous* and whose resultant weakening of its contemplative power causes it to lapse from *theoria* into activity (*praxis*); it produces not mechanically but as a weakened form of contemplation (*Enn.* III, 8, 2–5). Within the individual *physis* is the vegetative faculty that operates

without thought and without imagination (*Enn.* IV, 4, 13); see *psyche,* *telos.*

pístis: 1] faith, belief (subjective state) ; 2] something that instills belief, proof

1) The term occurs both in Parmenides (fr. 1, line 30; fr. 8, line 50) and in Empedocles (frs. 3, 4, 114), but it is doubtful whether it is being used in any technical sense. In Plato's "divided line" the mental states that are not true knowledge (*episteme*) but have to do rather with "opinion" are divided into two classes: one has to do with images (*eikones*) of sensible things, while the other, described as *pistis,* is the perception of sensible things (*Rep.* 509e–511e). *Pistis* does not play an important role in Aristotle's epistemology; rather, he was concerned with it in the context of the relationship between proof and conviction; 2) *pistis* (subjective conviction) is the object of the art of rhetoric (*Rhet.* I, 1355b), and the various means of persuasion are outlined in *Rhet.* I, 1356a.

pléthos: plurality

According to Aristotle (*Meta.* 1020a) a plurality is that which is potentially divisible into noncontinuous (*me syneches*) parts. Thus one possible definition of number (*arithmos,* q.v.) is "a *plethos* with limit" (*peras*) (*loc. cit.*). This discrete, numerable quantity (*poson*) that is *plethos* is thus contrasted with the continuous, measurable quantity that is magnitude (*megethos,* q.v.).

For the final Platonic solution to the problem of the One (*hen*) and the many (*plethos*), see *trias* 5.

pneúma: air, breath, spirit, spiritus

1. *Pneuma,* which means air or breath (the cognate Greek verb is used in both senses in Homer), is used in the former sense when it first appears in Anaximenes. *Pneuma* or *aer,* he says, binds the *kosmos* together just as our *psyche,* which is also *aer,* binds together our body (fr. 2; the language of the fragment has impressed many as being somewhat too "modern" for the genuine sentiments of Anaximenes). The identification of air and breath, implicit in the analogy of Anaximenes, is made explicit by the Pythagoreans when they maintain that *pneuma* and void are inhaled by the universe (Aristotle, *Phys.* IV, 213b).

2. But the connection of respiration and the vital principle leaps, as it does in the concept of *psyche* itself, to a further connection with cognition in the speculation of some fifth-century writers. According to Diogenes of Apollonia, *aer* (q.v.) is the *arche* of all things and the warm air within us is soul (fr. 5; the same passage points out that the air within us is warmer than the surrounding air but considerably

cooler than the air around the sun; compare Cleanthes, 4 *infra* and see *nous*). We are then told (Theophrastus, *De sens.* 39, 44) that it is the source of cognition, both sensation (*aisthesis*, q.v.) and thought (*phronesis*). The internal air must be dry and hot (compare Heraclitus' fiery soul) and circulates through the body with the blood (see *kardia*). A similar theory appears among the medical writers (see *De morbo sacro* 16).

3. Aristotle continues to make use of *pneuma* in its ordinary senses of air, breath, and wind, but he introduces, in addition, something called innate (*symphyton*) *pneuma* that is some type of hot, foamy substance analogous in composition to the element of which the stars are made (for the growth of this suggestion into the astral body of the Neoplatonists, see *ochema*). It starts from the heart and its function is to provide the sensitive and kinetic link between the physical organs and the *psyche* (see *De gen. anim.* II, 736a–737a). This *pneuma* is present in the sperm and transmits the nutritive and sensitive soul from progenitor to offspring (*ibid.* 735a).

4. Aristotle's philosophical interest in *pneuma* was not considerable, but it is given a central position by the Stoics. *Pneuma* is a composite of air and fire (*SVF* II, 442) and it is a heated version of this that is soul (*ibid.* I, 135). This *pneuma*, which is innate (*symphyton*), is circulated with the blood throughout the body (*ibid.* II, 885; see *psyche* 28) in the same way that God, who is also called *pneuma*, is spread throughout the *kosmos* (*ibid.;* see Poseidonius' view, *ibid.* II, 1009), varying only by its degrees of tension (*tonos*, q.v.). Each pneumatic system has its *hegemonikon* (q.v.) or ruling part: that of man in the heart (*kardia*, q.v.); that of the *kosmos* in either the *aither* (q.v.; so Zeno and Chrysippus, *ibid.* II, 642–644) or in the sun (so Cleanthes, *ibid.* I, 499).

5. Such a materialistic view of the soul found little sympathy among either the Aristotelian functionalists or the Platonic adherents of a divine, immaterial soul. Plotinus suggests (*Enn.* IV, 7, 4) that the Stoics themselves, *ab ipsa veritate coacti*, saw the inadequacy of their views and so were constrained to add to the hylic *pneuma* some sort of qualitative or formal notation, calling it "intelligent [*ennoun*] *pneuma*" or "intellectual [*noeron*] fire."

6. But even before the time of Plotinus other currents were transforming the Stoic concept. Some Stoics were themselves disengaging the *hegemonikon* from the corporeality of *pneuma* (see *nous*), a position strongly suggested by the Stoic ethic that drew a sharp distinction, moral and intellectual, between man and the other animals (see Cicero, *De leg.* I, 7, 22; Seneca, *Ep.* 121, 14). There was, moreover, the Judaeo-Christian religious tradition that made the same distinction and, though it continued to use the expression *pneuma* or *spiritus*, employed it in a spiritualized, nonmaterial sense. Thus Philo describes

man as created of an earthly substance and a divine spirit (*theion pneuma*), but goes on to point out, commenting *Gen.* II, 7, that the latter is a part (or as he calls it, "a colony") of the divine nature, and this is *nous* (*De opif.* 135).

poieín: *to act, action*

Action is one of the ten Aristotelian *kategoriai* listed in *Cat.* 1b–2a; his examples are "cuts," "burns." Both action and passion (*paschein*) admit of contraries and degrees (*ibid.* 11b). But in an ethical context Aristotle distinguishes (*Eth. Nich.* VI, 1140a) between *poiein*, in the sense of "to produce" (hence *poietike episteme*, productive science) from *prattein* (to act), (hence *praktike episteme*, practical science); see *paschein, poietike, praxis, episteme, ergon.*

poiētikē (scil. episteme): 1] *productive science, art;* 2] *poetics*

1) The proper term used by Aristotle for the productive or applied science is *techne* (q.v.); 2) the *poietike techne* par excellence is poetics, to which Aristotle devoted an entire treatise, which is only partially preserved.

poión, poiótēs: *what kind, quality*

Democritus distinguished between primary qualities based on the shape and characteristics of the *atomon*, and secondary or derived qualities, like sweet, bitter, warm, cold, etc., which are conventional (Sextus Empiricus, *Adv. Math.* VII, 135) and essentially subjective and passive (see *pathe*). Some of Plato's *eide* are, of course, hypostatized qualities, e.g., the ethical qualities in *Parm.* 130b; and yet Plato, who was the first to use the abstract *poiotes* (*Theaet.* 182a), was well aware of the difference between quality and substance (see *Tim.* 49a–50a; for Plato's theory of sensible qualities, see *aisthesis*). *Poios* is one of the ten Aristotelian *kategoriai* listed in *Cat.* 1b–2a and discussed *ibid.* 8b–11a (compare *pathos*). In Epicurus the primary qualities of the *atoma* are shape, size, and weight (the latter an addition to Democritus), D.L. X, 54. Stoic materialism demanded that even the qualities of the *psyche* be bodies, *SVF* II, 797; see *enantia, dynamis, symbebekos, genesis.*

pónos: *pain*

See *aisthesis, apatheia, hedone.*

posón, posótēs: *how much, quantity*

One of the ten Aristotelian *kategoriai* listed in *Cat.* 1b–2a and discussed *ibid.* 4b–6a. Time is a continuous quantity, as is space, *ibid.*

5a. In the Epicurean ethic quantity and not quality is the criterion for the choice of pleasure, Eusebius, *Praep. Evang.* xiv, 21, 3; see *megethos*, *hedone*.

poté: *when, time*
One of the ten Aristotelian *kategoriai* listed in *Cat.* 1b–2a; his own examples are "yesterday," "next year"; see *chronos*.

pou: *where, place*
One of the ten Aristotelian *kategoriai* listed in *Cat.* 1b–2a; see *topos*.

praktiké (scil. episteme): *science of action*
See *praxis*.

práxis: *action, activity*
According to Aristotle, when actions follow upon a deliberate choice (*proairesis*) they may be judged moral or immoral (*Eth. Nich.* I, 13b), and hence fall within the scope of the "practical" sciences (*episteme praktikai*), i.e., ethics and politics, which have as their object the good that is aimed at by action, *ibid.* 1094a–b; see *ergon*.

proaíresis: *deliberate choice*
Though there must have been some previous discussion of moral choice (see Aristotle, *Eth. Nich.* III, 1111b), the first preserved treatment is that of Aristotle (*ibid.* 1111b–1115a) who defines it (1113a) as "an appetite, guided by deliberation [*bouleusis*], for things within our power." Choice is always of means; it is only wish (*boulesis*) that is directed toward the end (*ibid.* 1111b; see *kinoun* 9). Two things are to be noted about choice: it is precisely this that brings human actions (*praxeis*) within the realm of morality; secondly, by positing this voluntary act (it is not pure voluntarism; *proairesis* is preceded and based upon the intellectual act of *bouleusis;* see *ibid.* 1140a), Aristotle moved discussions of morality out of the area of intellection (the Socratic position; see *arete*, *kakon*) into that of will. The early Stoa embraced the intellectualist position (*arete = episteme;* see *SVF* III, 256), but with Epictetus *proairesis* once again becomes central; it is the condition of man's liberty (*Diss.* I, 29). Yet, even here there is a strong intellectualist strain. *Proairesis* is preceded by *diairesis*, the distinction between what is in one's power and what is not (*Diss.* II, 6, 24; I, 1–3), and *proairesis* itself seems more like judgment than choice (*ibid.* III, 9, 1–2).

prólēpsis: *prior grasp, anticipation, preconception*
In the Epicurean epistemology there was one ultimate criterion of truth, sensation (*aisthesis;* see also *aletheia*); but there were, as well, the subsidiary criteria of the emotions (*pathe;* see *hedone*) and a mental apprehension described by Epicurus as *prolepsis* (D.L. x, 31), and by Lucretius as *notitia* (*De rerum nat.* IV, 476). *Prolepsis* operates in much the same way as the Stoic *katalepsis* (q.v.), except that the *prolepsis* is the result of a repeated apprehension of the same type of object, e.g. men, and hence is a universal concept, a kind of residual, composite "Man" based on many sensations of "men." It provides a kind of standard against which the truth of subsequent apprehensions can be judged. The Stoics used *prolepsis* in much the same manner (thus for both Epicurus and the Stoa we have a *prolepsis* of the gods; compare Cicero, *De nat. deor.* I, 43–44 and *SVF* II, 1009 and *noesis* 15), but under the title of "common concepts" (see *ennoia*) developed it to a considerably greater extent.

prónoia: *forethought, providence*
1. The earlier history of the concept of providence is to be seen in the emergence, from Diogenes to Aristotle, of a notion of an intelligent purpose (*telos,* q.v.) operating in the universe. In all of these thinkers it is clearly associated with the intelligent God whose features begin to appear in the later Plato (see *Laws* 899 where the denial of *pronoia* is reckoned blasphemy) and in Aristotle. For the Stoics the immanent *Logos* governs all by *nous and pronoia* (D.L. VII, 138; *SVF* I, 176). It is given a new turn in the direction of anthropocentrism by Chrysippus (see Porphyry, *De abstinentia* III, 20) where the rest of the *kosmos* is subjected to the good of man. Stoic *pronoia,* identified as it was with *physis,* was essentially immanent.

2. Later Platonism, like the newly appeared Semitic tradition, was transcendent and believed in a series of intermediate deities (see *daimon*), with the result that *pronoia* began to be distributed through the entire range of deities (Plutarch, *De fato* 572f–273b; Apuleius, *De Platone* I, 12). As the supreme principle grows more remote, its direct involvement in *pronoia* becomes markedly less. So in Philo, *De fuga* 101, the *Logos* exercises providence through the immanent *dynameis,* just as in Plotinus (*Enn.* IV, 8, 2) the World Soul has a general providence and the individual souls a particular providence for the bodies they inhabit; the One, of course, is beyond providence (*Enn.* VI, 8, 17). Implicit in this distinction between general and particular providence, i.e., between command and execution, is the reconciliation of the necessary transcendence of God and the necessary immanence of providential activity; compare Proclus, *Elem. theol.,* prop. 122.

For the problems arising from the existence of evil in a providential system, see *kakon;* on *pronoia* without contact, *sympatheia;* on God's knowledge of particulars, *noeton* 4.

próödos: *going forth, procession*

1. In its most general terms "procession" is later Platonism's attempt to solve the Parmenidean difficulties of unity and plurality. If the One (*hen*) *is,* and is transcendent (see *hyperousia*), whence the subsequent plurality of the *kosmos?* Plotinus, who faces the question on various levels (e.g. the unity and plurality of the soul in *Enn.* IV, 3, 2–6; see *psyche*), frequently resorts to metaphorical explanations, and particularly to the figure of the sun and its rays (see *eklampsis*). But the metaphysical basis of the solution to the question "if one, why many?" rests on the nature of the One, and particularly its perfection (*telos; Enn.* v, 4), and the identification of the efficient and final cause (see *Tim.* 29e and compare *Enn.* IV, 8, 6; v, 4, 1; hence the later *bonum est diffusivum sui*).

2. This provides the ingredients for Proclus' more systematic derivation of the *hypostases* (q.v.). He begins (*Elem. theol.,* prop. 21) by citing a mathematical parallel of the series generated from the *monas* (q.v.). For Proclus this is a better figure than *eklampsis* since it allows transit in both directions in the series, thus permitting the important ethical correlative of procession, "return" (*epistrophe,* q.v.).

3. There follows (props. 25–30) a description of proödos itself. Every complete or perfect being (*teleion*) generates (props. 25, 27; compare *Enn.* v, 1, 6), but the cause remains undiminished and immobile (*menon;* prop. 26), as, indeed, had already been understood by Plato (*Tim.* 42e). This principle, designed to safeguard the integrity and transcendence of the *arche,* is a commonplace in Plotinus (see *Enn.* v, 1, 6; v, 2, 1) and comes particularly to the fore with the introduction of a Creator-God into the systems (see Augustine, *Conf.* I, 3). The effect is similar (*homoios*) to the cause (prop. 29) and so the effect is both present in the cause and proceeds from it (prop. 30; see *Enn.* v, 5, 9). Thus there is a triad of three "moments": every effect (*aitiaton*) remains (*menon*) in its cause, proceeds (*proödos*) from it, and returns to it (*epistrophe;* prop. 35) *qua* good (see Proclus, *Theol. Plat.* II, 95).

4. The applications of these principles are immense. The similarity principle, here expressed in the outgoing procession, will be applied in the counter *epistrophe* (prop. 32) and so will provide a means for both the moral ascent of the soul to its source (for an ethical view of its "fall," see *kathodos*) and the epistemological grounds for the cognitive approach to God (see *Enn.* I, 8, 1 and *agnostos;* for the similarity principle in the wider context of cognition, see *homoios, aisthesis*). It

gives, moreover, a view of the entire *kosmos*, in both its sensible and intelligible aspects, as a magnificent organism (*holon*, q.v.) with its parts linked in a relationship of compatibility (*sympatheia*, q.v.) and descending, in an unbroken chain of analogous beings, from a common *arche*.

For the position of *proödos* in a more general ontological context, see *trias*.

prophḗtēs: *spokesman, medium, prophet*
See *mantike*.

pros ti: *relation*
In Plato there are *eide* of relatives that are immanent within things, see *Phaedo* 74a–77a, *Rep.* 479b, *Parm.* 133c–8, and *Soph.* 255d–3 where the relative character of the Form "Different" is clearly acknowledged (and denied by Aristotle in *Meta.* 990b). In Aristotle relation is one of the list of the ten *kategoriai* in *Cat.* 1b–2a. It is further described *ibid.* 6a–8b. *Hyle* is a correlative of *eidos* and so falls in this category (*Phys.* II, 194b), as does at least one aspect (the "useful") of Plato's notion of the Good (*Eth. Nich.* 1096a). *Pros ti* is one of the four Stoic *kategoriai* (*SVF* II, 369).

For the relativity of intelligibility, see *gnorimon*.

pseúdos: *error, falsity*
See *doxa, noesis*.

psychḗ: *breath of life, ghost, vital principle, soul,* anima
1. One of Aristotle's most detailed excursions into the history of philosophy (see *endoxon* for the method and principle involved) occurs in Book I of the *De anima* where he reviews and criticizes his predecessors' opinions on the nature of *psyche*. As he sees it, earlier speculation came to the soul from two angles that tended to coalesce: the soul as the principle of movement (*kinesis*) and of perception (*aisthesis*). This seems to be correct, though, of course, a great deal of the evidence on the subject consists only in what Aristotle chooses to cite. But there are two additional facets in the history of *psyche* that Aristotle largely ignores: the prephilosophical use of the term and *psyche* as a religious phenomenon.

2. The connection between life and movement on the one hand and consciousness on the other is not at all obvious in Homer who designates two separate entities to explain life and consciousness. For Homer *psyche* is the "breath of life" (and also, in what may be a completely different stratum of belief, an individualized "ghost" that lives on in an attenuated fashion after death) that escapes, normally,

from the mouth of the dying hero (this connection with the head may be the suggestive beginning of the later theory that located the seat of the soul in the brain; see *kardia* and compare *pneuma*). In contrast there is the *thymos*, the spirit, located in the midriff (*phrenes*) whereby a man thinks and feels (see *kardia*).

3. The Homeric *psyche* was closely associated with motion in that its departure turned the aggregate of churning limbs that was the hero's "body" into a *soma* or motionless corpse. The *thymos* too is connected with motion in a sense later explored by Aristotle; it is the promptings of *thymos* that impel the hero to activity.

4. The philosopher, unlike the poet, concludes rather than describes. We can see this habit of mind at work in Thales. Since, he maintains (Aristotle, *De an.* 1, 405a), the power to cause *kinesis* is an indication of the presence of soul, should not one conclude that even something as seemingly inanimate as a stone is ensouled since the Magnesian stone (magnet) is capable of moving other things? The thought here is especially bold since it bypasses completely the presence of air or breath. But the more archaic attitude reappears with Anaximenes who does, however, betray a certain boldness of his own in extending the soul-principle to the universe at large (fr. 2; see *pneuma*).

5. The connection between *psyche* and breath is intermittent among the pre-Socratics. Anaximander said the soul was "airy" (Aetius IV, 3, 2), as did Anaxagoras (*ibid.*). Heraclitus makes breathing part of the cognitive process (Diels 22A16; see *aisthesis*), but only during sleep when the other senses are sealed off from the cosmic *logos*. Diogenes of Apollonia, on the other hand, strongly maintains the connection between the *psyche* and *aer* (q.v.; see *pneuma*) because life depends on it (frs. 4, 5).

6. This link with the Homeric past becomes more and more tenuous as the Homeric psychology itself is revised. By the sixth century the *psyche* had absorbed the functions of the Homeric *thymos* and was then the term used to describe the psychic totality of man, while at the same time the physical aggregate of limbs and bodily parts was yielding to *soma*, not now as a corpse, but as the physical unity that has *psyche* as its psychic correlative.

7. Thus released from its immediate pneumatic associations, *psyche* finds its place, as Aristotle suggests, within the larger cadres of motion and perception. Typical in this regard are the views of the Atomists and Empedocles. The former had reduced reality to *atoma* and the void (*kenon*) and were evidently concerned with the soul as the source of motion when they described it as an aggregate (*synkrisis*; see *genesis*) of atoms that are spherical and fire-like on the grounds that these atoms are the most mobile and most competent to cause motion in others (Aristotle, *De an.* 1, 405a). There are, of course,

difficulties here, largely arising from the relationship between soul and body and that between soul and mind or spirit (*nous*). Where is this aggregate that, by reason of the movement of its own *atoma*, is capable of moving the body (see *ibid.* I, 406b)? The answer is preserved by Lucretius who tells us (III, 370–395) that Democritus held that soul and body *atoma* were juxtaposed (*appositio, parathesis;* see Diels 68A64), an arrangement Lucretius found indefensible (see *noesis* 6).

8. A higher, more reliable type of perception had been distinguished from mere sensation from the time of Heraclitus and Parmenides (see *aisthesis, episteme, doxa, noesis*), and, despite Aristotle's conviction that they thought the two were the same, the Atomists did make a serious attempt, even within the confines of their materialistic system, to distinguish *psyche* and *nous* both in terms of function (see *noesis*) and location (see *kardia*).

9. Although the Atomists were keenly interested in sensation (for their theories, see *aisthesis*), the sensation approach to soul is even more apparent in Empedocles. Aristotle sees behind the reduction of soul to one or other of the elements (*stoicheia*) of physical bodies the assumption that "like knows like" with the consequence that, if the soul knows, it must be composed of the same material as the thing known (*De an.* I, 409b). He cites Empedocles as the chief witness to this view (fr. 109). But it is clear enough that Empedocles, who may have said that this similarity (*homoiotes*, q.v.) was the reason why sensation occurs, did not mean to suggest that each of his four elements *was* the soul. Rather, it seems more likely that it is blood that is a perfect blend of the elements (frs. 105, 98; this also links the theory with considerations of natural heat; see *kardia*). There is a third possibility and Aristotle considers (and rejects) this as well. Perhaps, as in the case of blood, the Empedoclean soul is not the mixture but the proportion (*logos*) itself (*ibid.* I, 408a; see *holon*).

10. Aristotle cites this latter possibility as one instance of a more general school of thought that attempted to define *psyche* as a *harmonia* (q.v.; *ibid.* I, 407b and compare *Pol.* 1340b). Plato too knows the *harmonia* theory; it was advanced by Simmias in the *Phaedo* (85e–86d) and subsequently refuted by Socrates (91c–95e). The origins of the theory have been much debated. The word *harmonia* is Pythagorean and there are Pythagorean affinities in the *Phaedo* (Echecrates holds the theory [88d] and he was a Pythagorean [D.L. VIII, 46]; Simmias had studied with the Pythagorean Philolaus [61d]; see the late evidence for him in Diels 44B22, 23). But nowhere does either Plato or Aristotle identify it as Pythagorean and the theory, at least as it appears in the *Phaedo*, has to do with the *harmonia* of physical opposites (*enantia*, q.v.).

11. But the theory of a balance or equilibrium of opposite powers

(*dynameis*) of a body is not the same thing as the numerical proportion as worked out by the Pythagoreans. And, though it may have Pythagorean affinities, it seems to stem from medical circles that used it to explain health as an equilibrium (*isonomia*) of opposite qualities in the human body and where it is associated with Alcmaeon of Crotona (Aetius v, 30, 17; it appears too in the speech of the physician Eryximachus in *Symp.* 188a). But there is no evidence that Alcmaeon applied it to the soul (see *De an.* i, 405a).

12. What, then, was the Pythagorean doctrine of soul? There was, in fact, more than one, and this strange ambivalence is equally apparent in Empedocles. The Pythagoreans reduced all things to the *arche* of number (*arithmos*, q.v.) and so it comes as no surprise to discover that they considered soul and *nous* as "properties [*pathe*] of numbers" (Aristotle, *Meta.* 985b). This may be a version of a mathematical *harmonia* theory, but the same cannot be true of the view, dismissed in *De an.* i, 407b as a Pythagorean *mythos*, which suggests that the soul is completely distinct from the body and that it is possible for "any chance soul to enter any chance body." And turning to Empedocles, while the theory that the soul is blood makes perfect sense within the framework of his mechanistic explanations of the elements and their mixtures, what is to be said of the view, put forth in his *Purifications*, that the soul is a *daimon* (q.v.) that committed an "original sin" (see *kathodos*) and undergoes a series of reincarnations (fr. 115)?

13. What has appeared here, at the center of the Pythagorean tradition in philosophy, is another view of *psyche* that seems to owe little or nothing to the pan-vitalism or pan-deism (see *theion*) that is the legacy of the Milesians. All the implications of this new belief that the divine nature of the soul is radically different from all other things may be seen in the famous passage from Pindar (fr. 131), one of its first appearances: the soul that is of divine origin survives the death of the body; its operation can best be observed in dreams where it is active while the body slumbers. The origins of this new belief in the special divinity and immortality of the soul and its basic difference from and antagonism to the body are somewhat obscure; one suggestion is that it came to the Greeks through contact with Scythian shamanism. But whatever its origins the belief appears, with all its ramifications, in Pythagoras, Empedocles, and the Orphic literature, and its most notorious forms are the doctrine of bilocation and reincarnation (*palingenesia*, q.v.) and its associated theory of recollection (*anamnesis*), the antagonism between body and soul that becomes so familiar from Plato's metaphor of body/prison (*soma/sema*; see *Crat.* 400c, *Phaedo* 62b) and a series of eschatological myths that also appear in Plato (see *athanatos*).

14. Plato's debt to the Orphic-Pythagorean view of the soul is

clearly marked in the earlier dialogues. In *Charm.* 156d–157a all the traditional motifs of this "ancient account" (*palaios logos: Phaedo* 70c; see *Meno* 81a, *Ep.* VII, 335a) are present: the *psyche* is a unity, immortal (*athanatos*, q.v.), subject to a cyclic rebirth into a body that is the source of all its ills. The end of life, and the definition of *philosophia* (q.v.), is a purification (*katharsis*, q.v.) that is a preparation for death and the return of the soul to its natural habitat. Associated with this complex of ideas is the theory of recollection (*anamnesis*, q.v.; according to a later authority in D.L. VIII, 4 Pythagoras remembered his previous incarnations; for Empedocles, see *ibid.* VIII, 77) and it is this that leads Plato to more novel considerations. In the *Phaedo, anamnesis* suddenly shifts to the level of *episteme* (q.v.) and what is recollected is not the details of some other life but a knowledge of the Forms (*eide*). The *psyche* is the faculty whereby we know the *eide* (65a–67b) and this because the soul is most akin to the *eide* (78b–79b), like them immortal, immaterial, and invisible.

15. Gradually the more radical aspects of the difference between body and soul are modified in Plato. In many respects this represents a return to the more traditional categories by acknowledging that various somatic functions also belong to the soul, which in the *Phaedo* strives to operate only in the noetic sphere and apart from the senses. This accommodation is accomplished by the tripartition of the soul (*Rep.* IV, 435e–444e). The *psyche*, like the *politeia* itself, is divided into three parts: the rational (*logistikon*), the "spirited" (*thymoeides*), and the appetitive (*epithymetikon*), with virtues and *pathe* (q.v.) appropriate to each. The division appears again in *Rep.* IX, 580d–581a, in *Phaedrus* 246a–b, 253c–255b, and again in *Tim.* 69d–72d where the parts are assigned their appropriate bodily seats, linked together by the spinal marrow (73b–d; the connection of the brain (*enkephalos*) with the spinal column was well known, though denied by Aristotle, *De part. anim.* II, 652a; see also *kardia*).

16. As the functions of the soul are expanded from the *Republic* on, the upper part or *logistikon* begins to take on the characteristics of the unitary *psyche* of the *Phaedo*. It is divine, created by the *demiourgos* (*Tim.* 41c–d), lodged in the head (*ibid.* 44d; see *kardia*), vouchsafed a prenatal vision of the *eide* (*Phaedrus* 247b–248b, *Tim.* 41e–42a), and subject to cyclic *palingenesia* (*Phaedrus* 248c–249d, *Tim.* 42b–d). It is, moreover, immortal, as contrasted to the two other parts of the soul that are mortal and created by lesser gods (*Tim.* 69c–d; see *Rep.* X, 611b–612a, *Pol.* 309a–c).

17. One of the difficulties arising from Plato's treatment of the soul is the fact that he clearly has posited the tripartition of the soul on ethical grounds, while the unitive soul of the *Phaedo* is suggested by epistemological considerations. Since the *psyche* of the *Phaedo* is

clearly enough the *logistikon* of the later dialogues, we may integrate their functions and see it as the cognitive *arche* of a nonsensory *dianoia* (*Phaedo* 79a, *Soph.* 248a) and the ethical ruler of the two lower parts of the soul (*Rep.* IV, 441e; *Phaedrus* 253c–254e). But it is less clear what the cognitive powers of the lower parts of the soul are, if any. That sensation (*aisthesis*, q.v.) involves the soul as well as the body is mentioned more than once; pleasure, we are also told, extends from the body to the soul (*Rep.* IX, 584c) and, in *Phil.* 33d–34a, this ethical *pathos* (q.v.) is extended to include the cognitive *pathos* of sensation as well (compare the parallel passage in *Tim.* 64b). But the temptation to locate sensation in the *thymoeides*, somewhat in the fashion of an Aristotelian *psyche aisthetike*, must be resisted. The *Timaeus* lodges the *logistikon* in the head and at the same time makes the brain (*enkephalos*) the seat of sensation (44d, 73b). The *logistikon*, it would appear, is the only cognitive part of the *psyche*. Its normal and natural function is *dianoia* or *logismos*, but because of its connection with the alien body at birth it is assailed by various *pathe* of that body and when these reach the soul sensation results (*Tim.* 42e–44a; for the mechanics of these bodily *pathe*, see *aisthesis*, 15–17). The function of the *thymoeides*, located in the breast, is, on this view, to receive communications from the *logistikon* and act upon them (*ibid.* 69d–70b). The *epithymetikon*, located in the abdominal cavity, receives no message from the *logistikon*, but its headlong pursuit of physical pleasures is occasionally tempered by the presence of the liver, which is the seat of dreams (*oneiros*, q.v.) and the basis of divination (*mantike*, q.v.; for a later ground for divination, see *sympatheia* 8).

18. The *logistikon* then can hardly be called the *arche* of sensation as that might be understood by the pre-Socratics. It is rather a cross between a shamanistic Pythagorean "other self" and the faculty of "true knowledge" in the Parmenidean sense. It is capable of *episteme* because of its similarity to the things known, the *eide* (*Phaedo* 79b; in *Soph.* 248e–249b, with its changed perspectives, it is granted a share of the "really real"), and is capable of sensation *faute de mieux*.

19. In *Tim.* 43a–d and *Laws* x, 896e–897b Plato makes a distinction between primary motions that are proper to the soul and secondary motions that originate in the body and come into the soul, and in *Phil.* 33d he describes sensation as a kind of shaking (*seismon*) that is peculiar to the body and to the soul and at the same time common to both. Thus Plato is led to approach the *psyche* in another fashion that is more akin to the other pre-Socratic motif of *kinesis*. One of Plato's major proofs for the immortality of the soul, i.e., the *logistikon*, is the fact that it is always in motion (*aeikineton*) and hence must be self-moved (*autokineton*), otherwise *genesis* would fail (*Phaedrus* 245c–e). The argument is not entirely new; it was used by Alcmaeon

who did not, however, argue from self-motion but from the fact that the soul was *aeikineton* (Aristotle, *De an.* I, 405a). Plato's, on the other hand, derives from self-motion, the self-motion of *nous* that has a share in reality (*Soph.* 249a–b) and is related to the *eidos* of kinesis (*ibid.* 254d where it is one of the *megista gene;* see *eidos* 13 and *kinesis* 6). This then is not one of the many types of secondary causality detailed in *Laws* x, 893b–894c, but the primary motion with which the catalogue ends, "real" motion that moves itself and that is the *arche* of *kinesis* (*Laws* x, 895b; compare *Phaedrus* 245d). He is prepared to go even further. Self-motion is the essence (*ousia*) and definition of the soul (*Phaedrus* 245e).

20. Aristotle takes up this theory in *De an.* I, 406b–407b and objects to it on a number of scores, but chiefly because he thinks that thereby Plato has reduced the soul to a magnitude (*megethos*, q.v.). To his way of thinking the *kinesis* would have to be circular locomotion (see *noesis*) so that Plato, like Democritus, has the soul move a body by being in motion itself, instead of seeing that the soul moves things by being their final cause and thus may be said to originate movement by thought (*noesis*) or choice (*proairesis; ibid.* I, 406b). For Aristotle's other approaches to the question of the soul as the *arche* of *kinesis*, see *kinoun* 8 and *physis* 3.

21. He next deals with the view that the soul is self-moved number, the theory of another member of the Academy, Xenocrates (*ibid.* I, 408b–409b; see Plutarch, *De procr. an.* 1012d). Now number is an aggregate of units (*plethos monadon;* see *Meta.* 1053a), and, apart from the absurdities of applying the now popular fluxion theory of moving points into lines, etc. (see *arithmos*), the theory of Xenocrates appears open to the same type of mechanistic charges made against Democritus.

22. Aristotle cuts into the heart of the pre-Socratic theories. The soul, it is true, is a moving principle, not in the mechanistic sense of Democritus or as he understood Plato and Xenocrates to say, but as the final cause: it moves by thought and desire (*De an.* III, 433a–b; *Meta.* 1072a–b; for some of the difficulties involved in this, see *sympatheia* 7). But it is not self-moved except accidentally (*ibid.* I, 405b–406b), since what moves others does not necessarily have to be in motion itself (*Phys.* VIII, 256a–258b).

23. His own treatment, however, deserts the category of *kinesis* (which he shifts over to *physis*, q.v.) and moves in another direction. Earlier on, during his more Platonic period, Aristotle had treated the soul as if it were a complete substance (*Eudemus*, frs. 45, 46) that had little need of the body (*ibid.*, fr. 41). But in the *De anima* it is quite otherwise. A complete substance is an individual being, a *tode ti* (q.v.), and one such is the "living or ensouled body" (*soma empsy-*

chon) composed of a material (*hyle*) and a formal (*eidos*) principle. The latter is the soul and if it is approached from the direction of function (*ergon;* see *energeia*) it may be defined (*ibid.* II, 412b) as the first (i.e. not necessarily operating) *entelecheia* (q.v.) of an organic body (see *holon*).

24. Plato frequently gives the impression that he is more interested in soul than in the soul. The proof of immortality already cited from the *Phaedrus* is set out to cover "all soul." In the detailed passages in the *Timaeus*, moreover, where Plato describes the composition of the soul from its elements (35b–36b), it is the World Soul (*psyche tou pantos*, q.v.) to which he refers; the individual souls are second- or third-rate versions of it (*ibid.* 41d). For Aristotle, however, it is the individual living being that is the paradigm and the method of approach is to investigate its various activities. In this way he proceeds to an investigation of the faculties (*dynameis*) of the soul of a living organism.

25. Plato had divided the soul into parts (*mere;* see 15) and at times his language suggests that the parts of the soul are really individual souls within the same being (see *Tim.* 69d–e and the open question in *Laws* IX, 863b). Aristotle also calls them parts, but he treats them as faculties (see *De an.* III, 433b), i.e., *dynameis* in the word's primary sense of the power to effect change in another or in itself *qua* other (*Meta.* 1046a and see *dynamis* 3). There are a great variety of these *dynameis*, but they are the most appropriate way to study the nature of the soul (*De an.* II, 415a). Aristotle proposes to work his way from the most fundamental, the nutritive *threptike* (*ibid.* II, 414a–415a), through the ascending series (each higher *dynamis* presupposes the existence of the lower), to the sensitive (*aisthetike;* see *aisthesis*), and finally to the distinctive faculty of man, the *noetike* (see *nous, noesis*).

26. Aristotle is clear on the subject of personal immortality. Since the soul is the formal and final cause of an organically qualified body it cannot survive the dissolution of the union with that body, except, perhaps, as part of the species (*ibid.* II, 415b). But there is nothing to prevent a faculty of the soul from being separable (*choriston; ibid.* I, 408b) and this is actually so in the case of the *nous* (q.v.; *ibid.* III, 430a).

27. For Epicurus and Lucretius soul is a composite body made up of various atoms (D.L. X, 63). But this is a far cry from the mere aggregation of fiery atoms proposed by Democritus. First, the notion of body has been refined to that of an organic compound (*concilium;* see *holon* 10). Secondly, the relationship of the soul and the body is now specified as the *atoma* of the soul being spread throughout and contained within the sheath (*stegazon*) of the body (D.L. X, 43, 64). The *atoma* that go into the composition of the soul are no longer merely

"fiery" but include breath (*pneuma*) and air (see Lucretius III, 231–236). There is a more startling addition, the atoms of an "unnamed element" that are not like any of the others but are subtler, smoother, and more mobile than any other kind of atom (D.L. x, 63; Aetius IV, 3, 11; the *quarta natura* of Lucretius III, 241–257). It is this latter that begins the movements that are sensation (see *aisthesis* 23 and *holon* 10) and transmits them to the rest of the body (*ibid.* III, 262, 281).

28. The Stoic theory of soul illustrates the curiously qualified materialism of their positions. In a definition reminiscent of Heraclitus the soul is material fire or heated *pneuma* (Cicero, *De fin.* IV, 12; D.L. VII, 157 and compare Plotinus' critique in *Enn.* IV, 7, 4; further details on the Stoic view under *pneuma* 4–5). It has eight faculties: the *hegemonikon* (q.v.), the five senses, and the speaking and generative faculty (*SVF* I, 143; see *noesis* 16), each represented by a stream of *pneuma* stretched out to the appropriate organ and reaching back to the *hegemonikon* (*SVF* II, 836) and relaying to it the various sense impressions (*phantasiai*), impulses (*hormai*), and affections (*pathe*) to which the senses are prone (for the revisions in Stoic psychology, see *noesis* 17).

29. The later Platonic tradition, with its highly developed theory of *sympatheia*, expanded Plato's suggestion of the similarity of the *psyche* to the *eide* (see 18 *supra* and compare *metaxu* 2) to give it a strongly emphasized medial position between the *noeta* and the *aistheta* (see Simplicius, *In De an.* I, 2, p. 30, citing Xenocrates; Plutarch, *De procr. an.* 1023b, citing Poseidonius; on the efforts to fill the gaps in the *scala naturae*, see *sympatheia* 3). Plotinus strongly affirms this (*Enn.* IV, 8, 7), but he also perceives the paradox in the Platonic view: how to reconcile the heaven-sent, immortal soul of the *Phaedo* and the *Phaedrus*, whose sojourn in the body is compared by Plato to an incarceration, with the immanent and directive soul of the *Timaeus*, which has a distinctly benign function *vis-à-vis* the organism (*Enn.* IV, 8, 1)? The former attitude raises the entire problem of the descent of the soul into matter (see *kathodos*); the latter, the vitalistic function of soul seen as nature (*physis*).

30. Soul, taken as a single entity, is a *hypostasis* (q.v.), a production of *nous* and its image (*eikon; Enn.* V, 1, 2), and in turning toward *nous* it becomes itself fertilized and produces, in the opposite direction, various activities that are a reflection of itself and the terms of which are sensation (*aisthesis*) and growth (V, 2, 1). Soul, then, by the very nature of things has a double orientation: it is turned toward its source, the intelligible, and it is turned toward the world, which it vitalizes (see *noesis* 20).

31. But the soul is more than a unitary *hypostasis;* its turning

downward away from the One (*hen*) has caused it to become multiple, and Plotinus is constrained to explain at some length the relationship of the various souls that vitalize bodies to the unitary *hypostasis* of which they are parts (IV, 3, 1–8). They are not, of course, material parts of a material whole. They are unified in that they have a common origin and a natural operation; they are divergent because they operate in and over different bodies (IV, 3, 4). This gives rise not only to a plurality of souls but also grades of souls (IV, 3, 6), ranging from the World Soul (*psyche tou pantos*), which is still close to the intelligible source and whose activities are consequently closer to that of *nous*, down to the souls of plants, the furthest extension of the soul principle away from *nous*. The distinction is a useful one: the unitive nature of soul enables Plotinus to affirm the systematic structure of the plural souls in terms of cosmic *sympatheia* (q.v.; see *Enn.* IV, 3, 8), and the distinction of grades provides a basis for a continued belief in reincarnation (*palingenesia; Enn.* III, 4, 5).

32. The function of soul, then, is to vitalize and govern matter (see *Enn.* IV, 8, 3). How this is accomplished is explained in a series of metaphors: the soul illuminates matter like a light that, though remaining at its point of origin (on this motif, see *proödos* 3), sends forth its rays into a gradually deepening darkness. Or it vitalizes matter in the same way that a net, inert out of water, spreads out and seems to come alive when cast into the sea, without at the same time affecting the sea (IV, 3, 9). It is in this fashion that the soul of the universe affects its body, the sensible *kosmos*.

33. As for the individual souls, the question here is considerably more complex due to the obvious diversity of functions. Aristotle's view of the soul as an *entelecheia* of the body seems to suggest too close a functional connection between the soul of the body and Plotinus rejects it (*Enn.* IV, 7, 8). Instead he turns to the microcosmic principle: each human soul has, like the World Soul, a "part" that remains turned toward the intelligible and is unaffected by the descent into the body (IV, 3, 12). But the fact that it has gone forth to a body, from the heavenly bodies (*ouranioi*) down to the plants, leads to a diminution of the natural power of the soul. Thus its normal nondiscursive intellectual activity (see *noesis*) degenerates to lower forms of activity: *theoria* becomes *dianoia* and, eventually, *praxis* (IV, 3, 18; see *physis* 5, *noesis* 20).

34. The individual soul, once "in" the body (the localization is not, of course, spatial; the soul is "in" the body in the same sense that light is "in" the air; IV, 3, 22; see *kardia*), sends out a series of reflections of itself, the first of which is *aisthesis*, followed by the other faculties (I, 1, 8). These enable the material body to act without in any way affecting the soul (I, 1, 6–7; see *aisthesis* 26–27).

35. Proclus begins his treatment of the soul by applying to it his familiar doctrine of the mean (see *trias*). There are three types of soul: the divine (including the souls of the planets; see *ouranioi* and, for their influence, *ochema* 4), those capable of passing from intellection to ignorance (see *noesis* 21), and an intermediate grade that is always in act but inferior to the divine souls (*Elem. theol.*, prop. 184). This mediating grade, in addition to being demanded by Proclus' triadic principle, had a previous history in the tradition. These are the *daimones* already defined by Plato as intermediaries (*Symp.* 202d), integrated by his pupil Xenocrates into the various grades of intelligence (*logos;* see Plutarch, *De defec. orac.* 416c; and divided by Proclus into *angeloi, daimones,* and *heroes* (*In Tim.* III, 165, 11).

36. Plato's view of soul as substance is still in evidence in Proclus where it is described (*Elem. theol.*, prop. 188) as both life (*zoe*) and a living thing (*zoön*). Its intermediate position is affirmed (prop. 190), and, having such, participates in both eternity (*aion,* q.v.) by reason of its *ousia* and in time by reason of its *energeia* (prop. 191; see Plotinus, *Enn.* IV, 4, 15). *Palingenesia* is still maintained (prop. 206), but Proclus denies that the soul can be reborn into animals (*In Remp.* II, 312–313).

On the faculties of the soul, see *aisthesis, noesis, nous, orexis;* its immortality, *athanatos;* descent into the world, *kathodos;* periodic rebirth, *palingenesia;* its astral body, *ochema;* for the interrelation of soul and body in Stoicism and Epicureanism, *genesis;* for attempts at distinguishing *psyche* from *nous, noesis;* on the World Soul, *psyche tou pantos.*

psyché tou pántos: World Soul

1. The existence of a soul for the entire world seems to be another example of Plato's use of analogous reasoning (see *kosmos noetos*): if the *kosmos* is thought to be a living organic unity (see *zoön*), it follows that it, like the other animals, must have a soul. This line of reasoning appears in *Pol.* 269d–273b (though here the *psyche* is not yet a source of continuing motion), in *Phil.* 30a, and, finally, in a completely integrated fashion in *Tim.* 34a–37c. It is composed by the *demiourgos* from intermediary types (i.e., mixtures that combine elements appropriate to the intelligible world of being and the sensible world of becoming) of Existence (*ousia*), the Same, and the Other, three of the five most important *eide* mentioned in *Soph.* 254d. Aristotle's explanation of why these mixtures were chosen is based on the epistemological principle of "like knows like" (*De an.* I, 404b; see *homoios, aisthesis*). These ingredients are arranged in bands in certain harmonic intervals (*Tim.* 35b–36b), and thus the World Soul becomes, in true Pythagorean fashion, a paradigm not only for the

harmonious movement for the heavenly bodies, but for ethical restoration of *harmonia* in the individual human soul (*ibid*. 90c–d; see *katharsis*).

For the existence of an evil World Soul in the Platonic system, see *kakon*.

2. Aristotle no longer needs *psyche* to explain motion (see *physis*), and so the World Soul is quietly dropped. It reappears, however, in the late Platonic tradition (see *Philo, De migre. Abr.* 32, 179–180; Albinus, *Epit.* x, 3) and becomes one of Plotinus' *hypostases* (q.v.); *Enn.* v, 2, 1. The viewpoint is now much more complex: the World Soul has an upper and lower part, the former engaged in contemplation (*theoria*), the latter corrupted into activity (*praxis*) and called *physis* (q.v.); it is divisible, yet indivisible (*Enn.* IV, 3, 4); unlike the World Soul of Plato, however, it produces the sensible world, *Enn.* v, 2, 1; see *proödos*.

pyr: fire

Though fire is present in the systems of both Anaximander (Diels, fr. 12A10) and Anaximenes (13A7), it is, for both of them, a product, while for Heraclitus, the universe (*kosmos*) is a fire (Diels 22B30), not as an *arche* but rather as "archetypal matter," probably because of its connection with *psyche* and life (fr. 36) and, hence, with *aither* (q.v.). Among the Pythagoreans fire held the central position in the universe (with the earth as a planet!), Aristotle, *De coelo* II, 293b. It was given its place as one of the four elements by Empedocles (see *stoicheion*). Fire plays a fundamental role in Stoic physics as the element with the most active *dynamis*, the hot (see *dynamis*). Of prime importance here is the connection between fire and life (*SVF* II, 23) and, through the intermediacy of the *psyche*, with the *pneuma*, the medically derived principle of vital heat, which the Stoics understood as a combination of fire and air (*SVF* II, 787) and as an all-pervasive force in the *kosmos* (*ibid*. II, 473); see *ekpyrosis, logos*.

r

rhoḗ: *flowing, stream, flux*

From the time of Plato on, the position of Heraclitus and his followers, one of whom, Cratylus, apparently exercised some influence on Plato (see Aristotle, *Meta.* 987a), was described in terms of the metaphor of "flowing" or "streaming" (so for Heraclitus, Plato, *Crat.* 402a; for his followers, *Crat.* 440c–d and *Theaet.* 179d–181b; the celebrated expression "everything is in a state of flux" [*panta rhei*] does not occur until Simplicius, *Phys.* 1313, 11). Whether Heraclitus himself used the expression or whether, indeed, it is an exact description of his view of change may be debated, but what is notable is that this popular tag (the Heraclitans contemporary with Plato were actually called "flowers": *Theaet.* 181a) was never conceptualized. Plato rejects the implications of the metaphor, chiefly because it renders knowledge impossible (*Crat.* 440a–b, and see *episteme*), but when he comes to treat of it as a philosophical problem it appears under the rubric of "becoming" (*genesis*, q.v.; *Theaet.* 152e–153a is a good example of Plato's passing over the metaphor in preference for the more fully conceptualized *genesis*) or, as in Aristotle, as part of the problem of "change" (see *metabole, kinesis*). As far as the technical language of philosophy was concerned, *rhoe* was never more than a striking image.

S

schḗma: *appearance, shape*
See *aisthesis, stoicheion.*

sophía: *wisdom, theoretical wisdom*
The original meaning of the word connects it with craftsmanship, see Homer, *Il.* xv, 412; Hesiod, *Works*, 651 (compare Aristotle, *Eth. Nich.* vi, 1141a). By the time of Herodotus it also embraced a more theoretical type of preeminence, *Hist.* i, 29 (Seven "Sages"), iv, 95 (Pythagoras as a *sophistes*). Heraclitus (Diels, fr. 129) says that this *sophia* of Pythagoras is nothing but polymathy and malpractice. For Plato there is an implied distinction between true *sophia* that is the object of *philosophia* (see *Phaedrus* 278d) and that, like *phronesis*, is to be identified with true knowledge (*episteme*) (*Theaet.* 145e), i.e., a knowledge of the *eide*, and, on the other hand, the practitioner of false *sophia*, the *sophistes* of the dialogue of the same name. For Aristotle *sophia* is the highest intellectual virtue, distinguished from *phronesis* or practical wisdom, (*Eth. Nich.* 1141a–b, 1143b–1144a), and also identified with metaphysics, the *prote philosophia* in *Meta.* 980a–983a. The "sage" (*sophos*) becomes the Stoic ideal of virtue, see *SVF* i, 216; iii, 548; D.L. vii, 121–122, and the critical portrait in D.L. vii, 123 and Cicero, *Pro Mur.* 29–31; see also, *philosophia, phronesis, episteme, endoxon.*

sōphrosýnē: *self-control, moderation*
1. *Sophrosyne* is the subject of one of Socrates' ethical enquiries, as described in the *Charmides*, where no solid definition is reached. Its etymological meaning as "moral sanity" is discussed in *Crat.* 411e, but the true Platonic position of *sophrosyne* is rooted in the Pythagorean notion of *harmonia* (q.v.). The two concepts are brought together in *Rep.* 430e–432a, and later, 442c, it is closely linked with Plato's tripartite division of the soul (see *psyche*): *sophrosyne* is the harmonious subjection of the two lower parts to the ruling, the rational part (compare *Phaedrus* 237e–238a where the *harmonia* embraces only two elements).
2. For Aristotle *sophrosyne* is the mean (*meson*) between the extremes of pleasures and pains (*Eth. Nich.* ii, 1107b); its area is

restricted to body pleasures (*ibid.* III, 1118a) and particularly those of touch and taste. Zeno (Plutarch, *Stoic repugn.* 1034c), like Plato (*Rep.* 435b), makes *sophrosyne* one of the four chief virtues (*Eth. Nich.* I, 1103a). The more intellectualizing Stoa denied this distinction (see *arete*), and defined *sophrosyne* as the "knowledge of the good to be chosen and the evil to be avoided" (*SVF* III, 256, 262). Plotinus has a similar definition (*Enn.* I, 6, 6), but relates it to a purification preparatory to the "return" (*epistrophe*); see *katharsis*.

spérma: *seed*
See *stoicheion, pneuma, noesis* 16.

spoudaíos: *serious man*
See *ergon*.

stérēsis: *privation*
Steresis, which Aristotle defines (*Meta.* 1011b) as "the negation of something within a defined class," is one of the three essential elements in Aristotle's analysis of *genesis* in *Phys.* I: the permanent substratum (*hypokeimenon*) and the passage of one form to its opposite (*enantion*) demands the existence of a lack of that second form in the substratum (*Phys.* I, 191a–191b). Thus *steresis* both permits *genesis* and solves the Parmenidean problem of nonbeing (see *on*). For Plotinus evil is not a substance but rather a *steresis* of good (*Enn.* I, 8, 11).

stigmế: *spot, point, geometrical point*
See *megethos, monos*.

stoicheíon: *letter of the alphabet, primary body,*
           element
1. The comparison of the basic bodies of the physical world to the letters of the alphabet, and so, by implication, the introduction of the term *stoicheion* into the language of philosophy, probably goes back to the Atomists. In this context the comparison is an apt one since the letters, like the *atoma*, have no significance of their own, but by manipulating their order (*taxis*) and position (*thesis*) one can construct them into aggregates with different meanings (Aristotle, *Meta.* 985b; *De gen. et corr.* I, 315b; see *genesis*). But the earliest attested use of the term *stoicheion* is in Plato, *Theaet.* 201e where it is obvious that Plato still feels the original connotation of "letter of the alphabet." By the time of Aristotle the original meaning is largely ignored and *stoicheion* means the basic ingredient of a composite (see *Meta.* 1014a).

2. The reality behind the term is, of course, far more venerable. It is the object of the Milesian quest for the primary something or *Urstoff* of which the physical reality of the world is made, an attempt to trace the undeniable fact of change back to its starting point. The candidates for this *arche* are well known: the most important substances in man's experience, and generally those with mythological credentials as well (see *arche*).

3. There is an important development with Anaximander. The search for a single *arche* had suggested a kind of linear *genesis* whereby the other bodies were derived from this single starting point. But when Anaximander thrust the *arche* back beyond the perceptible material substances (see *apeiron*), he effectively made *all* perceptible bodies secondary and so led the search for a starting point off into new nonsensible directions, but he intruded into the problem the possibility of a cyclic *genesis* whereby the perceptible substances pass into each other in a continuous cycle. Such a mutual transformation of the basic bodies becomes a commonplace in much of Greek philosophy (see Plato, *Phaedo* 72b, *Tim.* 49b–c; Aristotle, *De gen. et corr.* II, 337a), leading, after Parmenides, to the belief in an external agent, itself unmoved, to keep the cycle in operation (mediated, in Aristotle, by the eternal movement of the sun along the elliptic; see *genesis, kinesis, kinoun*), and even the *stoicheia* of Empedocles seem to undergo such cyclic change (frs. 17, 26).

4. The quest for the *arche* came to term in Parmenides who, reversing Anaximander's perfectly undefined *apeiron*, posited his own perfectly defined *on* (q.v.). But perfect definition provides not only an *arche* but a *telos* as well, and so Parmenides was led to deny sensibly perceived change (see *genesis, kinesis*) and, indeed, the validity of sensation itself (see *episteme*). The Parmenidean *on* is the absolute radical *stoicheion*.

5. Empedocles and the Atomists, by restoring plurality and the void (*kenon*), reopened the possibilities of secondary *genesis* and rehabilitated sense knowledge. The Milesian search for basic ingredients was resumed and Empedocles himself took the lead and selected, as the four basic bodies (or "roots" as he called them) of this material world, earth, air, fire, and water, the canonical four elements (fr. 6; see Aristotle, *Meta.* 985a). "Selected" is the appropriate word in the circumstances since these were by no means the only candidates; there were at hand a great number of substantivized "powers" (*dynameis*), e.g. "the hot," "the cold," "the light," "the heavy," etc., that had been isolated up to this point.

6. To all appearances Empedocles was both the first and the last to hold that these four were the irreducible primary bodies and the efforts of his successors were bent toward reducing these "so-called

elements" (the phrase is Aristotle's; see *Meta.* 1066b) to something more basic, as well as to how they came to pass into more complex bodies.

7. One group, taking its lead from both Anaximander and Parmenides, held that the *archai* of physical bodies were themselves not perceptible to sense and thus were to be sought in entities that had no other characteristics than mass and position. Such was the *atomon* of Leucippus and Democritus and the mathematical atom of the Pythagoreans, the *monas* (q.v.; see *arithmos*). These are the real "elements" that could, in turn, be constructed into more complex bodies, the *atoma* by the process of association (*synkrisis*), the monads by the geometrical construction of points into lines, thus to surfaces and bodies; see *genesis.*

8. But since both groups had so denuded their basic particle of characteristics they were somewhat hard pressed to explain how such "nothings" could issue in the strongly characterized "something" that was the Empedoclean body. What of the undeniable presence of the sense-perceived qualities (*pathemata aisthetika;* see *Tim.* 61d) of these latter? In both cases there is a marked inclination to reduce all sensation to touch or contact (*haphe;* see Aristotle, *De sensu* 442a), with the strong suggestion, at least on the part of Democritus, that all other sense experiences are subjective conventions (fr. 9; see *aisthesis, nomos*).

9. We are not quite so well informed on the Pythagorean answer to the same question posed to them by Aristotle (*Meta.* 1092b): how do you possibly explain white and sweet and hot in terms of number? A suggestion of an answer appears in Plato. The *Timaeus* includes two approaches to the question of the elements. One is a description of the state of things before the universe came into being (*Tim.* 52d) and relies on a dynamic, nongeometrical analysis of *genesis* (q.v. and see *infra*). But the later (*ibid.* 53c ff.) postcosmic account is markedly geometrical and, if not purely Pythagorean, has strong affiliations in that direction.

10. This Platonic account follows Atomism in reducing the Empedoclean *stoicheia* to aggregates of more basic bodies, the latter characterized chiefly by their position and shape (*schema*). But while the Atomists were apparently chary of pushing the notion of shape (on the testimony of Aristotle, *De coelo* IV, 303a, they did say that the *atoma* of fire were spherical), Plato has an elaborately worked out system whereby each of the elements is associated with one of the regular geometrical solids capable of being inscribed in a sphere (the so-called "Platonic bodies"): the cube (earth), the pyramid (fire), the octahedron (air), and the icosahedron (water) (*Tim.* 553–56c);

the remaining figure, the dodecahedron, is reserved for the sphere of the heaven (*ibid.* 55c; see *aither, megethos*). Up to this point the account could pass as a somewhat suspicious version of Atomism. But where it betrays its Pythagorean forebears is in the fact that these geometrical solids have their own *archai:* they are constructed out of planes, with at least the suggestion that the reduction could go further (*ibid.* 53c–d). The Atomist *atoma*, on the other hand, are indivisible bodies (see Aristotle, *De gen. et corr.* I, 325b for a comparison of the two systems). And here too sensation is reduced to contact with various combinations of these bodies, which in turn give rise to sensible experiences (*Tim.* 61c ff; see *aisthesis*).

11. Though Pythagorean monadism antedated Atomism, it was not its immediate antecedent. The Atomist tradition rather saw the line of descent come down from Empedocles through Anaxagoras to themselves (see Lucretius I, 830–920). Anaxagoras rejected Empedocles' contention that there were four irreducible bodies (passage from one to the other would still be the taboo *genesis*, q.v.), but held instead that there are an infinite number of infinitely divisible bodies, known as *homoiomereiai*, "things with like parts," as Aristotle called them, or "seeds," the term employed by Anaxagoras himself (fr. 4). These are Anaxagoras' *stoicheia* (Aristotle, *De coelo* III, 302a), originally submerged in a precosmic mixture, then separated off by *nous*, the initiator of movement in the system (frs. 9, 13), and which by their aggregation form perceptible bodies (see *genesis, holon*).

12. These *homoiomereiai* are obviously different from the *atoma* in that they are infinitely divisible (see fr. 3 and *megethos*; Lucretius objects to this aspect of the theory in I, 844–846); but there is, in addition, the suggestion that the "seeds" carry within them their own *archai*, viz., all the things that are (or will be) are "in" these basic particles (see fr. 12). What is this "everything" that is "in everything," i.e., in each "seed"? It embraces not only the Empedoclean *stoicheia* (see Lucretius I, 840–841, 853) and natural bodies such as hair, flesh, and bone (fr. 10), but the sensible *pathe* and opposed "powers" as well (fr. 4; see Aristotle, *Phys.* I, 187a). The reappearance of these powers (*dynameis*, q.v.) was to have important consequences.

13. Aristotelian physics chose a path other than that which led back to one or more *archai* that transcended sense perception. In Aristotle's mind the attempt to differentiate the *stoicheia* by shape is senseless; the real solution is in the study of the functions and powers of things (*De coelo* III, 307b). It was, in effect, a return to the sensible *dynameis* of Milesian philosophy that had never lost their vogue in medical circles and that Anaxagoras had recently reemphasized. But

this was more than the substitution of other "bodies" for the four of the Empedoclean canon; it rested on the important distinction between a body and its qualities (see *poion*).

14. The formulation of this distinction was certainly not originally Aristotle's. Plato was well aware of it and explicitly states it, by way of preface to his account of precosmic *genesis*, in *Tim.* 49a–50a: the Empedoclean *stoicheia* are not really things at all but, rather, qualities (*poiotetes*) in a subject. Such a statement was, of course, impossible for someone who viewed the hot, the dry, etc. as things (*chremata*), as it is likely Anaxagoras did.

15. Here, then, already in Plato, was a clear resolution of the question of the *stoicheia;* they had their own *archai:* a substratum and immanent qualities capable of passing in and out of that subject. Thus was opened the possibility of the transformation of the elements into each other (see *genesis*). And this is, in general, the same tack as that taken by Aristotle. The Platonic substratum is refined into *hyle* (q.v.), which is the common subject for all four of the *stoicheia* (it should be noted that this *hyle*, the substratum for the elements, is imperceptible; thus *genesis*, or substantial change, differs from *alloiosis*, or qualitative change, in that the latter has a perceptible matter; see *De gen. et corr.* I, 319b). Finally, Aristotle adds the notion of privation (*steresis*) to facilitate the passage of the qualities/powers.

16. But there are other marked changes as well. For Plato the source and cause of movement is *psyche* (q.v.; see *Laws* x, 896a, 897a), while physical bodies have of themselves only a kind of random motion, agitation rather than movement (*Tim.* 52d–53a); and in the later postcosmic or Pythagorean-type account of the formation of the *stoicheia* Plato has, as might be expected, even less to say about motion: *kinesis* is notoriously absent from geometrical bodies. It is otherwise in Aristotle. All natural bodies have their own principle of movement that is *physis* (q.v.; *Phys.* II, 192b), a radical departure from the entire Parmenidean strain of speculation in which *inherent* motion was anathema (see *kinesis, kinoun*).

17. Thus for Aristotle the simple bodies that are the *stoicheia* have their own simple natural motion (*De coelo* I, 269a). Their operation is governed by the principle already set down (*Phys.* III, 201a) that *kinesis* is the actualization of a potency. In this case, however, the privation (*steresis*) is that the element is not in its "natural place," since motion and place are correlative concepts (*De coelo* I, 276a–277a). Thus lightness is the capacity for linear motion away from a center, a motion that will cease when the subject has reached its natural place; and heaviness is the contrary (*ibid.* IV, 310a–311a). In this fashion Aristotle derives fire from absolute lightness and earth from absolute heaviness (*ibid.* IV, 311a–b), and then, in a more curious

fashion, air from relative lightness and water from relative heaviness (*ibid.* IV, 312a; compare Plato's parallel derivation of air and water as the mean terms in a geometric proportion in *Tim.* 31b–32b). And by relying on the same argument, from simple motions Aristotle derives the existence of the fifth element that has as its motion the other kind of simple *kinesis*, perfect circular motion (see *aither;* for the difficulties this involves in the theory of the First Mover, see *kinoun* 8; for its movement, *endelecheia*, see *ouranioi* 6).

For the transformation of the elements and for the Stoic attitude toward them, see *genesis;* for the *stoicheia* of the soul in Platonism, see *psyche tou pantos.*

symbebēkós: accompaniment, accident (logical), accidental event (see tyche)

1. The early history of the ontological reality behind the notion of *symbebekos* was fought out on the fields of quality (*poion*, q.v.; see also *dynamis*). The radical in this history was Democritus who was inclined to deny any objective existence to qualities (D.L. IX, 72; Sextus Empiricus, *Adv. Math.* VII, 135), while Plato was enunciating an archaic point of view when he hypostatized them (the suprasensible *mode* of hypostatization represented by the *eide* was, of course, quite alien to his predecessors). Plato was, nonetheless, well enough aware of the difference between things and the qualities of things and goes out of his way to correct the general pre-Socratic reification of qualities (*Tim.* 49a–50a; see *genesis, pathos*).

2. Plato's remarks occur in a treatise on this sensible world of material things; Aristotle's analysis of the same phenomenon is in his logical works, and so the emphases are quite different. The distinction between a thing and its quality is broadened to embrace that between a thing or subject (*hypokeimenon*) and its attribute or accompaniment (*symbebekos*). The latter is defined as something that "belongs to a thing, not of necessity or for the most part, . . . but here and now" (*Meta.* 1025a). Unlike the *genos* or the definition, it does not express the essence (*ti esti*) of a thing, nor, like the property (*idion*), is it necessarily linked with that subject (*Top.* I, 102b). Since there is no necessity (they can be otherwise) in such accidental beings, it follows that there can be no demonstration (*apodeixis*) and hence no scientific knowledge (*episteme*) based on them (*Anal. post.* I, 75a–b; *Meta.* 1026b). *Symbebekos* is one of the "predicables" (see *idion*).

3. One would have thought that Epicurus would adhere to Democritus' Atomistic point of view and restrict all reality to the atoms and the void (*kenon*). But since he has accepted sensation (*aisthesis*, q.v.) as an infallible criterion of truth, he cannot fall back upon convention (*nomos*) as the origin of sensible qualities. And so Epicurus has a fully

developed theory of accidents (see D.L. x, 68–69). These perceptible and hence corporeal qualities that adhere to bodies may be divided, as in Aristotle, into those that are necessarily connected with the nature of bodies and so always present in a body, and those that happen to a body from time to time. The first category, Aristotle's *idion*, Epicurus calls *symbebekos*, precisely reversing the Aristotelian nomenclature. For the second type of qualities he devises the new term "accident" (*symptoma*). Examples of *symptomata* are the sensible qualities of composite bodies (Plutarch, *Adv. Col.* 1110) and sensation that is a *symptoma* of the "unnamed element" present in the soul (D.L. x, 64; see *holon*, *psyche*). There are even more complicated entities, such as time, that can be described as nothing else but "accidents of accidents" (see *chronos*).

4. The Stoics kept the Aristotelian doctrine of subject and accidents but in an altered form. The distinction between a subject and its attributes is preserved (*SVF* II, 369), but the attributes are reduced to three: quality, state, and relation, the latter presumably attributes of the primary active principle of the universe, *logos* (D.L. VII, 134; see *logos*, *paschein*).

symmetría: symmetry
See *aisthesis* 6, 8 and compare *asymmetron*.

sympátheia: affected with, cosmic sympathy
1. The theory of cosmic sympathy, associated by modern scholars with the philosopher Poseidonius, rests upon a series of premisses present in Greek philosophy almost from the beginning. The Milesians had seen the world as alive and the Pythagoreans as an ordered whole (see *kosmos*). And though Plato's interests had earlier lain in other directions, he devotes a full-scale treatment to the order and operation of the sensible world in the *Timaeus*, undoubtedly his single most widely studied work in the later tradition. Here he describes the *kosmos* as a visible living creature (*zoön*), having within it all things that are naturally akin (*kata physin syngene; Tim.* 30d).

2. Stoic pantheism led in the same direction. God as *logos* pervades the universe as our soul pervades our bodies (D.L. VII, 138; see *pneuma*) and as *physis* he vitalizes the whole (Seneca, *De benef.* IV, 7; see *logoi spermatikoi*). Thus the *kosmos* is a unity (D.L. VII, 140), an organism (*holon*, q.v.) rather than a totality (*pan; SVF* II, 522–524), a rational living being (*zoön logikon; SVF* I, 111–114).

3. Refinements appear in the era of Poseidonius, many of which are attributed directly to him. First, the earth itself is a living being, pervaded throughout by a vital force (*zotike dynamis, vis vitalis;* Cicero, *De nat. deor.* II, 33, 83) and so, it is argued by Plotinus

somewhat later, also endowed with sensation (*Enn.* IV, 4, 26). Things cohere by a unifying force within, a force that seems to be different tensions (*tonos*, q.v.) of the *pneuma*: in inorganic matter it is called *hexis;* for plants, *physis;* for animals, *psyche;* and for men, *nous* (Sextus Empiricus, *Adv. Math.* IX, 81–85; Philo, *Quod Deus* 35). That these are not radically distinct orders of reality is clear from certain natural phenomena, like growth of rocks for as long as they are in contact with the *vis vitalis* of the earth (Plotinus, *Enn.* IV, 4, 27), and the presence in nature of zoophtyes (Nemesius, *De nat. hom.* I, 509a–b), all calculated to fill the gaps of the *scala naturae* (a common theory since Aristotle's classic description in *Hist. anim.* 588b–589a; for its application to the spiritual world, see *trias* 4).

4. From the insight into the natural interrelationship (*symphyia;* Sextus Empiricus, *Adv. Math.* VII, 129) of both organic and inorganic things proceeds the doctrine of *sympatheia* or their mutual interaction, illustrated by a great variety of natural phenomena and particularly by the complex of effects exercised by the sun and the moon over life on earth (Sextus Empiricus, *op. cit.* IX, 78–80; Cicero, *De nat. deor.* II, 7, 19), and prominent later in Marcus Aurelius, Philo, and Plotinus.

5. Poseidonius was apparently very interested in the sun and the moon. Cleanthes had already located the *hegemonikon* of the universe in the sun (see *pneuma*; it is frequently referred to as the "heart of the *kosmos*" as well, based on an analogy with the location of the seat of the soul; see *kardia*) and Poseidonius makes it the source of all physical life (D.L. VII, 144). He may have been the author of the belief in its spiritual powers as well, and specifically of the view that the *nous* or *mens* comes from and returns to the sun, the *psyche* from and to the moon, and that the body begins and ends as earth (see Cicero, *Tusc.* I, 18–19; Plutarch, *De facie* 28–30; and compare *noesis* 17, *ouranioi* 7). But even at this point purely religious considerations must have been at work as well, even though the full impact of solar theology is not visible until somewhat later (see *Corpus Hermeticum* XVI and Julian's *Hymn to the Sun*).

6. Plotinus, whose entire emanation theory is grounded on a solar image (see *eklampsis, proödos*), adopts both the affective role of the sun (*Enn.* IV, 4, 31; compare the role of the sun in Aristotle's theory of generation; see *genesis*) and the doctrine of cosmic sympathy. The *kosmos* is a living organism (*zoön*) all of whose parts are suffused by the universal soul (*psyche tou pantos*, q.v.). The parts interact not by reason of their being in contact but because of their similarity (*homoiotes; Enn.* IV, 4, 32).

7. This latter consideration raises for Plotinus the important questions of contact (*haphe*) as a necessary condition of action and passion and the presence of a medium (*metaxu*) in perception. Aris-

totle had answered the first affirmatively, maintaining that all movement (*kinesis*) necessarily demands contact (*Phys.* VII, 242b; VIII,
528a), though this clearly cannot be maintained in the case of the
Prime Mover (see *kinoun* 9) that is immaterial and moves things "as
something loved" (*Meta.* 1072b). There is a possible escape in *De gen.
et corr.* I, 323a where Aristotle appeals to someone being "touched
by grief," but the *proton kinoun* does seem to pose an unassailable
example of *actio in distans*. On the second point too Aristotle holds that
there must be a medium between the object perceived and the operative
sense organ (*De an.* II, 419a). Plotinus, however, consistent with his
views on *sympatheia*, denies the necessity of a medium of sensation
(*Enn.* IV, 5).

   8. *Sympatheia*, conceived of in these terms, enables Plotinus to
settle some related problems, that of providence (*pronoia*), astrology,
divination (*mantike*), and magic. The transcendence of God is preserved in this theory since his providence may be exercised indirectly
through the interrelation of things (*Enn.* IV, 8, 2) and neither the
World Soul nor the star souls need direct contact with the things they
affect (so, earlier, Philo, *De migre. Abr.* 179–181); deliberation (*proairesis*) is also excluded (*Enn.* IV, 4, 31). The planets by their various
movements have a variety of effects on things; they can both produce
(*poiesis*) and portend (*semasia; Enn.* IV, 4, 34–35; compare *Enn.* II, 3,
7, which admits astrological divination within the context of a general
attack on astrology; for the relation of individual men to individual
planets, see *ochema, ouranioi* 7). In this way is established a theoretical base for divination (*mantike,* q.v.) that consists in the reading of
just such portents, an approach long current in Stoic circles (see
Cicero, *De div.* II, 14, 33). But Plotinus extends the argument a step
further and maintains the possibility of the manipulation and use of the
sympathetic powers of things; these magical activities are not, however, of a preternatural nature; they are merely another example of
sympatheia and the wise man who resorts instead to contemplation is
well above them (*Enn.* IV, 4, 40–44).

   The successors of Plotinus had a somewhat different attitude
toward these powers; see *dynamis* 6.

synagōgé: collection

The Platonic type of "induction" (for the more normal type of
induction, i.e., a collection of individual instances leading to a universal, see *epagoge*) that must precede a division (*diairesis*) and that is a
survey of specific forms (*eide*) that might constitute a genus (*Phaedrus* 265d, *Soph.* 253d). An example is *Soph.* 226a, and the process is
also suggested in *Rep.* 533c–d, and *Laws* 626d; see *diairesis.*

synaítion: *accessory cause*
See *aition* 1.

synécheia: *continuity*
For the continuity of physical bodies and the problem of the *continuum*, see *megethos;* for the continuity of the physical world, *sympatheia* 3; for that of the spiritual world, *trias* 4.

sýnkrisis: aggregation, association
See *genesis* 6–8, 14; *holon* 8–9; *pathos* 3; *stoicheion* 7.

sýntheton: *something composed, composite body*
1. The problem of the *syntheton* or composite body is closely related to that of the *archai* and *stoicheia* on the one hand, and to that of *genesis* on the other. It depends for its solution on the judgment as to what exactly are the basic bodies or units out of which more complex natural entities come into being. Thus the enquiry would logically proceed from the ultimate *archai* to the primary perceptible bodies, i.e., the *stoicheia*, the grouping of these into *syntheta*, to the question of the composition of the most all-embracing *syntheton*, the *kosmos* itself (see *agenetos*).

2. The *syntheta* then may be considered on three different levels: the traditional *stoicheia* themselves as composite bodies, natural bodies as *syntheta*, and the *kosmos* as a *syntheton*, and in each case the appropriate questions are "how did they come to be," "what is their genesis," and "what constitutes their unity?"

See, in ascending order, *arche, stoicheion, genesis*, and for their unity, *hen, hexis, holon, tonos*.

t

táxis: order, arrangement
See *stoicheion* 10.

téchnē: *craft, skill, art, applied science*

1. Generally speaking Plato has no theory of *techne*. As frequently happens, a word that ends in Aristotle as a carefully defined and delimited technical term is still employed by Plato in a nontechnical and popular way. The contemporary usage of *techne* was to describe any skill in doing and, more specifically, a kind of professional competence as opposed to instinctive ability (*physis*) or mere chance (*tyche*). And it is precisely in these senses that Plato uses the term (*Rep.* 381c; *Prot.* 312b, 317c); nowhere does he trouble himself to give an exact or technical definition for this word whose common acceptance suited him perfectly well.

2. Where *techne* does enter technical philosophical discourse is in the *Sophist* and the *Politicus*. Here Plato is concerned with coming to an understanding of the sophist and the statesman by means of the dialectical method (*dialektike*, q.v.) that consists of the processes of collection (*synagoge*, q.v.) and division (*diairesis*, q.v.). There is scant evidence of any collection here, but the divisions are elaborate and, to a certain extent, overlap. In both instances they begin with *techne* and, even though in *Pol.* 258b he calls the genus to be subdivided "knowledge" (*episteme*), it is clear from the context that it does not refer to the technical use of that term as it appears, for instance, in the Analogy of the Line (see *episteme*), but rather to what he had previously called *techne*.

3. By collating the two dialogues it appears that Plato divides the "arts" into acquisitive (*Soph.* 219c–d), separative (of which Socrates' cathartic art is an example; *ibid.* 226a–231b), and productive (*poetike*). The "acquisitive arts" include the acquisition of knowledge that may in turn be used for either practical (*praktike*, e.g., building; in general the applied sciences correspond to the Aristotelian *techne: Pol* 258d–e; contrast the Aristotelian usage of *praktike*, q.v.) or theoretical (*gnostike; Pol.*, *loc. cit.;* see the Aristotelian *theoria*) ends. Here Plato further distinguishes the "theoretical arts" into the "directive" (*epitaktike*, e.g., statesmanship) and "critical" (*kritike, Pol.* 260b). His sole example of the latter is "reckoning" (*logistike; Pol.* 259e), but

presumably this is the division that would embrace the study of philosophy or, as Plato would prefer to call it, dialectic.

4. The "practical arts" of the *Politicus* probably overlap the "productive arts" (*poietike;* defined *Soph.* 219b, 265b). These may be divided into the products of divine craftsmanship (some wish to say they are produced by nature, *physis,* but Plato prefers the theistic explanation since intelligence is a concomitant of all *techne; Soph.* 265d) and of human craftsmanship (*ibid.* 265e). The former produces natural objects, e.g., the elements and the more complex bodies that come from them; the latter, manufactured objects (the *praktike episteme* of the *Politicus*).

5. But there is a further extremely important distinction to be made here (*Soph.* 266a–d). Both human and divine productivity are capable of creating both originals and images (*eikones*), and it is the epistemological correlative of this image-producing that appears as the lowest segment of the Line in *Rep.* 509e. Plato's generic name for image-productivity is imitation (*mimesis*), and while its divine manifestation, e.g. shadows, dreams, mirages, is of little or no interest in this context, human *mimesis* is the basis of the entire Platonic aesthetic. See *mimesis.*

6. As defined by Aristotle (*Eth. Nich.* vi, 1140a) *techne* is a characteristic (*hexis*) geared toward production (*poietike*) rather than action (*praktike*). It arises from experience (*empeiria*) of individual instances and passes from experience to *techne* when the individual experiences are generalized (see *katholou*) into a knowledge of causes: the experienced man knows how but not why (*Meta.* 981a). Thus it is a type of knowledge and can be taught (*ibid.* 981b). It also operated rationally, with *logos* (*Eth. Nich., loc. cit.*), and its goal is *genesis,* which distinguishes it from purely theoretical knowledge (*theoria,* q.v.) that has to do with being (*on*) and not becoming. Its rational element further distinguishes it from *tyche* or chance, another possible factor in *genesis.* Again, it is an external not an internal principle of *genesis,* which sets it off from *physis* (q.v.; *Phys.* ii, 199a). Finally, since it is productive rather than practical it differs from *phronesis* (q.v.; *Eth. Nich.* vi, 1140b); see also, in this same context, *ergon.*

télos: *completion, end, purpose*

1. Although it had obvious antecedents in Heraclitus' notion of the celestial fire governing all (fr. 64) and in Anaxagoras' use of mind (*nous,* q.v. 3), a clearly defined sense of purpose in the operations of the *kosmos* does not appear in Greek speculative thought until Diogenes of Apollonia. In his view the *arche* of all things is *aer* (fr. 4), which is both soul (when warmed) and intelligence (*nous;* fr. 5; cf. *nous* 4), and which is divine and governs all things for the best (fr. 3),

the latter attribute apparently suggested by the periodic renewals in nature.

2. Socrates was extremely interested in the teleological motif; he had examined Anaxagoras' theory of *nous* from this point of view (*Phaedo* 97d) but found it disappointing: it was the same old mechanistic explanation of things (*ibid.* 99a), what Plato would call a confusion of *synaitia* for *aitia* (q.v.), and Aristotle (*Meta.* 985a) concurs in this evaluation of Anaxagoras' teleology. But there are grounds for thinking that Socrates found somewhat greater satisfaction in Diogenes (see Xenophon, *Mem.* I, 4, 5–8). Plato's own approach is the same, particularly in his concern with the visible world in the later dialogues. In the *Timaeus* (47e) there is a general contrast between the works produced by *nous* and those that came about by necessity (*ananke*), and in the *Laws* (888e) we find that the latter are identified with the blind workings of nature (*physis*, q.v.) and that the former are by design (*techne*). *Psyche* initiates movement, but it is its association with *nous* that guarantees the purposeful outcome of this movement (*Laws* 897b).

3. There is a radical change in Aristotle: for Plato *nous* was the dominating factor in the teleological scheme; for Aristotle *nous* operates only in the human sphere of *techne*, purposeful design, and, indeed, all the artisan is doing is attempting to imitate *physis*, which has its own purpose (*telos*) as well as being a source of movement (*Phys.* II, 198a, 199b); it is, in short, the "final cause" described *ibid.* II, 194b. The doctrine of teleology is basic in Aristotle: it appears in his earliest works (see *Protrepticus*, fr. 11) and it finds its completion in the *Metaphysics*. It is explained in various places that the *telos* is the Good (*Phys.* II, 195a; *Meta.* 1013b), and in *Meta.* 1072b the ultimate Good, and hence the final cause of the entire *kosmos* is the First Mover, the *noesis noeseos* of 1074b (see *kinoun, nous*).

4. Aristotle's student Theophrastus apparently had some difficulties with teleology (Theophrastus, *Metaphysics* IV, 14–15, 27), but it never lost its place in philosophy, particularly with the ever-increasing theism of the later Schools; in this context it becomes divine providence (*pronoia*, q.v.).

For the role of *telos* in Aristotle's analysis of change, see *ergon, energeia, entelecheia;* in Neoplatonic emanation theories, *proödos*.

theíon: divine

1. The ascription of divinity to the ultimate *arche* is a commonplace in pre-Socratic philosophy. The motivation seems to be twofold: the legacy of a primitive animism, most obvious, perhaps, in Thales' movement toward a pan-vitalism (Aristotle, *De an.* I, 405a) and the further statement that "all things are full of gods" (*ibid.* I, 411a; see

Plato, *Laws* 899b and *physis*). Closely connected with this is the identification of life through the presence of motion; the only exception to this seems to be Xenophanes, whose critique of anthropomorphism led him to deny motion to his God (Diels, fr. 21A25), and places him well outside the tradition.

2. The equation *kinesis-theion* focuses gradually onto motion that is regular and/or circular (see *aither, aphthartos, ouranioi*). The second motive appears explicitly in a fragment of Anaximander (Aristotle, *Phys.* III, 203b) where the philosopher's "Unlimited" (*apeiron,* q.v.) is called *theion* "because it is immortal [*athanatos*] and indestructible." Here is a direct association of the chief property of the Homeric gods, their immortality, with a material *arche* (see Diels, fr. 12A11 where the epic strain in the language is even more pronounced). Aristotle goes on to say (*Phys., loc. cit.*) that most of the "physical speculators" called their originative *arche* divine. This seems to be true and the process of de-divinization to have begun with Parmenides' strokes against the vitalism of being (see *on*); if *genesis* and *kinesis* no longer pertain to being, they must be produced from an outside source, the "mover" (*kinoun*) evident from Empedocles on. And, with the attribution of intelligence (*nous*) and purpose (*telos,* q.v.) to this mover, the stage is set for the disappearance of *theion* and the arrival of *theos* in philosophical speculation; see *theos*.

theología, theologikḗ: 1] accounts about the gods, myth, 2] "first philosophy," metaphysics

1. *Theologia* first appears in Plato, and the term is used both by him (*Rep.* 379a) and by Aristotle (*Meta.* 1000a, 1071b) to designate the activity of the poets who gave cosmogonical accounts. Aristotle particularly uses it in contrast with the philosophical speculations of the *physikoi* (e.g. *Meta.* 1075b); in effect, it is parallel to the distinction between *mythos* and *logos* (qq.v.).

2. In *Meta.* 1026a a sharply distinct meaning emerges. Aristotle had divided the theoretical sciences into three classes, of which the third deals with substances that are "separate" (for the sense, see *choriston*) and without *kinesis;* this is the "first philosophy" or *theologike,* so called because such substances are the realm of divinity (for another view of the subject matter of *theologike,* see *on*).

3. Theology later expanded to once again embrace all discourse about the gods, and this new understanding of its scope may be seen in the division of theology into "mythical, physical, and political," a division originating in the Middle Stoa (see Augustine, *De civ. Dei* VI, 5, citing Varro; compare, *ibid.* IV, 27 and Eusebius, *Praep. Evang.* IV, 1).

theōría: *viewing, speculation, contemplation, the
contemplative life*
According to some, the contemplative life as an ideal is a tradition
going back to Pythagoras (see Cicero, *Tusc.* v, 3, 8–9 and D.L. VIII,
8), but the authority is a later Academic and so the ideal may be no
older than Plato who gives a digressive sketch of such a life in *Theaet.*
173c–175d, and identifies the highest type of human activity with the
contemplation of the Good (*Rep.* 540a–c) and the Beautiful (*Symp.*
210b–212a). The theme appears early in Aristotle (*Protrepticus*, fr.
6), and reaches its fullest development in his discussion of the contemplative life in *Eth. Nich.* x, 1177a–1179a. It is the chief activity of the
Prime Mover in Aristotle (*Meta.* 1072b; see *nous* 10), and of the soul
in Plotinus (*Enn.* vi, 9, 8), but in a much more extended fashion than
Aristotle had ever envisioned (see *Enn.* iii, 8, 2–7). For Plotinus
activity (*praxis*) is a debased form of contemplation (see *physis*), but
the later Neoplatonic tradition, probably beginning with Iamblichus
(see *De myst.* ii, 11) tended to rank *theourgia* (see *mantike* 4–5)
above *theoria*.

theós: God
1. As a philosophical term "the divine" (*theion*, q.v.) is much
older than the notion of a personalized God. Indeed, there is among the
philosophers a strong strain of scepticism about such anthropomorphized figures present in Greek mythology (see *mythos*, the well-
known emphatic critique by Xenophanes [frs. 11, 15], and Plato's
ironic remarks in *Tim.* 40d–e). Even where the old mythological
apparatus is used by the philosophers, as in Empedocles (see fr. 6), it
is only to reduce the Olympians to natural forces. The earliest trace of
a personal God in philosophical analysis is probably to be seen in the
identification, by Anaxagoras and Diogenes, of intelligence (*nous*, q.v.
3) as a motive and purposeful factor in cosmology. *Nous* was, of
course, divine (*theion*), and with its Milesian legacy of *psyche* it could
scarcely be otherwise; where it fell short of being God was in its
obvious lack of transcendence (see Anaxagoras, fr. 14; Diogenes,
fr. 5).
2. Plato's sharp distinction between the sensible (*aistheton*) and
the intelligible (*noeton*) provided the grounds for transcendence, but in
the earlier dialogues he is still in the grip of the Parmenidean denial of
kinesis to true being (see *on*), and so there is no place for a dynamic
God in the static landscape of the *eide*. The great theological break-
through occurs in the *Sophist* and the *Philebus*; in the former
(248e–249b) when soul and intelligence are granted a place in the
realm of the truly existent, and in the latter (26e–30d) when cosmic

nous is described as the efficient cause of the universe and identified with Zeus. This is undoubtedly the *demiourgos* (q.v.) of the *Timaeus* who when stripped of his metaphorical trappings is cosmic *nous* and whose transcendence is considerably limited by its subordination to the *eide* (see *nous*).

3. Beyond the *Timaeus*, however, lies another theoligical motif: the belief in the divinity of the heavenly bodies (see *ouranioi*). Aristotle is still under their influence in his dialogues, but the treatises display only two gods, or better, one God and one divine substance: the First Mover as it is described in *Meta.* 1072a–1073a, and the *aither* (q.v.; see *aphthartos*) of *De coelo* I, 268b–270a. The existence of both are deduced from *kinesis: aither* is divine because its movement is eternal (*De coelo* I, 286a), and the First Mover is God because its movement is unmoved (*Meta., loc. cit.;* see *nous*).

4. The Epicureans are not atheists; they admit the existence of gods, but deny their creation of the world or provident rule over it (D.L. x, 123–124, 139; Lucretius, *De rerum nat.* II, 646–651, V, 165–174, 1183–1197; for the role of the dream in the Epicurean proof for the existence of the gods, see *oneiros*). Stoic materialism tended to thrust God back to the level of a Milesian *theion* (see *SVF* I, 87), but their monism was not absolute and their distinction between active and passive principles (see *paschein*) allows them to identify God as some sort of a creative, immanent element and hence his, or rather, its definition as "creative fire" (*pyr technikon*), *SVF* II, 1027; D.L. VII, 156. Nor were other, more spiritualized implications absent: God is also *logos* (q.v.) and *nous* (D.L. VII, 135; *SVF* I, 146). The Cynics were probably the first philosophical school to make a systematic use of allegorical exegesis (*allegoria*) to reconcile a philosophically derived monotheism against popular polytheism (see Antisthenes under *mythos*), and in this, as in much else, they were followed by the Stoics. But it is clear that the monistic principle led to pantheism, just as the parallel movement on the level of popular religion was leading to henotheism and not to genuine monotheism (see Seneca, *De benef.* IV, 7–8). Seneca at least must be excluded from Stoic pantheism (*Ep.* 65, 12–14), and possibly Cleanthes whose *Hymn to Zeus* (= *SVF* I, 537) does not read like a pantheistic tract.

5. A variety of factors led away from a unified Godhead; Stoic monistic materialism was rejected and Platonic transcendence reasserted, now with the notion of a hierarchy of transcendent principles (see *hyperousia, hypostasis*). Difficulties with providence (*pronoia*) also led to a distinction between command and execution and the consequent attribution of both the creative (see *demiourgos*) and providential activities of God to a secondary principle. The "second God" is already visible in Philo, *De somn.* I, 227–229, *De cher.*, 126–127, and

particularly in Numenius (cf. Eusebius, *Praep. Evang.* XI, 17, 18, 22), finally ending in Plotinus' conception of *nous*, *Enn.* V, 5, 3.

For the "third God," see *psyche tou pantos;* for another treatment of the various versions of Cosmic Reason, *nous*.

theourgía: wonder-working
See *mantike* 4–5; *dynamis* 10–11.

thésis: position, positing, convention
(as opposed to nature, physis)
In the Stoic discussions of morality the term *thesis* generally replaces the *nomos* (q.v.) employed by the Sophists in drawing the distinction between a morality based on convention and the operation of a physical universe controlled by an unalterable nature (*physis*, q.v.). Another aspect of this same polarity, and one particularly discussed by the Stoics, was the question of the philosophical status of language, and specifically the relationship between things (*onta*) and their names (*onomata*); see *onoma*.

The problem of position and place is discussed under *topos;* for *thesis* as an element in Atomistic change, see *genesis;* in sensation, *aisthesis*.

thymós: spirit, animus
See *nous, psyche, kardia*.

ti ésti: what is it? the what-it-is, essence
That which responds to the question of "what is it?" by revealing the essence (*ousia*) of the thing, i.e., by definition (*horos*) through *genos* and *diaphora* (Aristotle, *Top.* VIII, 153a); see *ousia*.

tóde ti: this something, individual
For Aristotle the concrete individual existent; the singular as opposed to the universal (*katholou*), *Meta.* 1003a; it is substance (*ousia*) in the fullest and primary sense, *Cat.* 2a.

See *ousia*, and, for the principle of individuation, *hyle*.

tónos: tension
Taking as their point of departure a celebrated aphorism of Heraclitus that describes the *logos* of the world as "a tension, as in a bow or a lyre" (fr. 51; see *logos* 1), the Stoics attempted to explain the constitution of the *kosmos* and of the things in it in terms of the tension of the *pneuma* (q.v.) or soul principle within them (see *SVF* I, 514 where the cosmic *tonos* is symbolically identified with Heracles). The states of tension in the *pneuma* are distinguished on various levels.

Present in organic things there is *hexis*, characterized by a "tonic motion" (see *ibid*. II, 496) of a feeble type that does no more than circulate within the being and give it unity (*ibid*. II, 458; see *hexis*). The next higher stage is *physis*, the *tonos* of plants whose stronger movements manifest themselves primarily in the capacity for growth (*auxesis;* see *ibid*. II, 708–712). Next there is *psyche*, the grade that belongs to *zoa* characterized by movement in terms of reaction to outside cognitive and desiderative stimuli. Finally, there is *logos*, the strongest and purest *tonos* of the *pneuma*, signaled by the capacity for self-induced motion (see, in general, for the grades, *ibid*. II, 458–462 and, for the types of motion, II, 989). This doctrine, present even in the early Stoa, found its most general application in Poseidonius' theory of cosmic sympathy (see *sympatheia* 3).

tópos: *place*
The pre-Socratics up to the Atomists associated being with spatial extension so that even the Pythagorean *arithmos* has magnitude (see Aristotle, *Meta*. 7080b, 1083b), and the supposition forms the hypothesis of one of Zeno's arguments quoted in *Phys*. IV, 209a: "if all that exists has a place. . . ." Plato's interest in the question is rather in the area (*chora*) *in which genesis* takes place (*Tim*. 52a–c), a role analogous to that played by *hyle* in Aristotle, hence Aristotle's charge that Plato identified *chora* and *hyle* (*Phys*. IV, 209b). Aristotle's own approach is from the point of view of *kinesis*, which underlies the entire discussion of *topos* in *Phys*. IV, 208a–213a, and he defines *topos* (*ibid*. 212a) as the "fixed boundary of the containing body"; since objects can change place, the latter is obviously different from the objects in it (*ibid*. 208b).

For Aristotle's theory of "natural place," see *stoicheion;* on the question of the "place of the Forms" (*topos eidon*), *eidos* 17 and *noeton*.

triás: *triad, triadic structure*
1. One of the more characteristic features of later Platonism is the presence of a triadic structure in its *hypostases* (q.v.). Its employment is rather modest in Plotinus whose great hypostatic triad of *Hen, Nous, Psyche tou pantos* (qq.v.) seems based on historical considerations of syncretism rather than any *a priori* triadic principle. *Enn*. v, 1, 7, for instance, is quite unschematized, and II, 9, 1 only slightly more so.

2. The same is true of Plotinus' other great triad: Being (*on*), Life (*zoe*), and Intellect (*nous*). This has its ground in the Platonic tradition's exegesis of a celebrated text in *Soph*. 248e where Plato admits into the realm of the "completely real" (*pantelos on*) change

(*kinesis*), life, soul, and thought (*phronesis*). Whatever the exact motives and import of Plato's introducing this radical shift in position (see *kinesis* 6), it had an undeniable effect on his successors. It is prominently used by Plotinus to refute the materialism of the Stoics: being is not a corpse; it is possessed of life and intelligence (*Enn.* IV, 7, 2; V, 4, 2).

3. But his most frequent use of this set is in connection with the structure and operation of the transcendent *nous*, and here there is probably the converging influence of another potent text, this time of Aristotle where he describes the life of God as the *energeia* (q.v.) of *nous* (*Meta.* 1072b; on the denial of this to the Plotinian One, see *noeton* 4). For Plotinus being, life, and intelligence are all characteristics of *nous* on the cosmic level; it has an interior *energeia* that is life and that brings together being and thought (VI, 7, 13). It also seems to be related to another triad, which comes to full term in Proclus. Life is a thrust outward, an undefined (*aoristos*) movement away from a source. It receives its definition by turning back to that source; and this turning back is *nous* (see *Enn.* II, 4, 5 and compare *apeiron* 3).

4. The landscape is quite different in Proclus. *On, zoe, nous* are still prominent, more prominent, in fact, than in Plotinus (see *Elem. theol.*, props. 101–103), but here they are dominated by a triadic principle with the force of ontological law: every cause (*aition*) proceeds to its effect (*aitiaton*) by a "mean term" (*meson*). This arithmetical principle is, in turn, an operational mode of a still broader view that sees the spiritual world as the same type of uninterrupted *continuum* as was concurrently being propagated for the physical world (on the absence of interruptions in the *scala naturae*, see *sympatheia* 3). These principles find explicit statement in Proclus (*op. cit.*, prop. 28) and probably go back to Iamblichus (see Proclus, In *Tim.* II, 313: Sallustius XXVIII, 31; on the continuity of the spiritual world in Plotinus, see *Enn.* II, 9, 3).

5. Proclus' applications of the principle of triadic structure are manifold. In addition to being-life-intellect there is cause-power-effect (for the middle term of this, see *dynamis*), definite-indefinite-mixture (the "*Philebus* triad"; see *peras*, *apeiron*), remaining-procession-return (see *proödos*, *epistrophe*), and the particularly characteristic one of unparticipated (*amethekton*)-participated (*metechomenon*)-participant (*metechon*). This latter triad codifies and canonizes later Platonism's final answer to the Parmenidean hypothetical dilemma: if One, how Many? the One is unparticipated, but it produces something that is capable of being participated (*metechomenon;* for the reasons for this production, see *proödos* 3), capable because it *is* participated by a plurality of participants (*metechonta*) (*Elem. theol.*, prop. 23).

The second term, the mean in the progression, is superior to its participants since they depend upon it for their completion (prop. 24). The same proposition states the principle in summary: the unparticipated is unity-before-plurality, the participated is unity-in-plurality, i.e., one and nonone, while the participants are not-one, yet one in their source (see a similar schema under *holon* 11).

týchē: chance

As a metaphysical term *tyche* falls under the general heading of accidental cause (*symbebekos*), i.e., a cause having an unintended effect. Aristotle distinguishes such accidental causes (which are efficient causes, *Phys.* II, 198a) into those where there is no deliberation, *automaton* (spontaneity), and those where there is some degree of rational choice (*proairesis*), in which case it is *tyche* (*Phys.* II, 197a–198a). The role of *tyche* as a causal principle finds its strongest appeal to the Atomists (see D.L. IX, 45; Aristotle, *Phys.* II, 196A24) where chance is equated with a kind of blind physical necessity (*ananke*) operating without purpose. The identification of chance and physical necessity is made quite specific by Plato in his castigation of current physical theories (*Laws* X, 889c). Aristotle's final view on *tyche* is to separate it from material *ananke* and to render it inferior to both *nous* and *physis*, the two causes that operate with purpose (*telos*), *Phys.* II, 198a.

týpōsis: imprinting, impression
See *aisthesis, noesis*.

Z

zōē: life

1. For the Milesians life was a coordinate of soul (*psyche*, q.v.) and movement (*kinesis*, q.v.), a prephilosophical attitude that required no proof, and the prevailing vitalism can clearly be seen in Thales (see Aristotle, *Meta.* 983b), and in Anaximenes (Aetius I, 3, 4) and the later Diogenes of Apollonia (frs. 4, 5), both of whom stress the priority of air as an *arche*. Conversely, its absence after Parmenides' denial of change to being (*on*, q.v.) is attested to by the Atomists'

particles that have mass and movement but no life (see *kinesis* 4) and by the necessity for the other post-Parmenidean philosophers to supply an external source of movement (see *kinoun* 1–2).

2. But even though life ceased to be something innate in things, its connection with soul remained constant and Plato's proof of the immortality of the soul hinges on that very point (*Phaedo* 105b–107a). Plato's positing of an *eidos* of life is not improbable in the light of the connection between the *eide* and predication (see *eidos* 11), and he does seem to mention such at *Phaedo* 106d (though the remark here could refer to something immanent). But what is far more revolutionary is his admission, in *Soph.* 248e, of all the Parmenidean undesirables, life, soul, intellect, change, into the realm of the really real (see *psyche* 18, *kinesis* 6), and his consequent interest in the "intelligible living being" (see *zoön*).

3. For Aristotle life is immanent not transcendent and his approach is functional (see *ergon* 3, *psyche* 25). He defines *zoe* as the capacity for self-sustenance, growth, and decay (*De an.* II, 412a) and gives (413a) more elaborate criteria for determining the existence of life: the presence of mind (*nous*), sensation (*aisthesis*), movement and rest in space, nutrition, decay, and growth. Its seat is in the heart (*De part. anim.* III, 665a; see *kardia* and compare *pneuma* 3).

For time treated in terms of life, see *chronos*; for the Neoplatonic triad of Being, Life, Intellect, *trias*.

zóön: living being, animal

1. Although Anaximander has something that looks like a theory of spontaneous generation (Diels 12A10, 11, 30: fish generated from the operation of the sun upon the moist slime; men born of fish; on the primacy of fish, compare Philo, *De opif.* 65–66), Empedocles has the most complete zoogony of the pre-Socratics (summary passage in Aetius V, 19, 5; frs. 57–62). Plato's zoogony is to be found in the *Timaeus* where the lower animals evolve in a fashion consonant with his earlier theory of *palingenesia* (q.v.; *Tim.* 91d–92c). What are sketches and remarks in earlier thinkers becomes, in Aristotle, a science, elaborated in a whole series of treatises, and particularly the *De generatione animalium*.

2. A feature of the Aristotelian treatment is the famous *scala naturae*, a graduated linking of all the forms of life found in the *Hist. anim.* 588b–589a (see *sympatheia* 3). At the top of the series stands man whom both Plato (*Tim.* 90a–c) and Aristotle (*Pol.* 1253a, 1332b) tended to separate off from the rest of animated beings by reasons of his possession of a rational faculty (*nous*) that was nonmaterial. The earlier Stoic materialism tended to blur this distinction, but a later Platonizing movement within the school reseparated *nous* from *psyche*

(see *noesis* 17) and the results of this can be seen in the sharp distinctions made between animal instincts and human reason (Seneca, *Ep.* 121, 19–23) and the consequent absence of morality toward or in the animal kingdom (Cicero, *De fin.* III, 67; Philo, *De opif.* 73).

3. But if there was a difference between the material and the spiritual that effectively separated men from the beasts, there was also a connection between the two realms. In terms of the Platonic theory of *mimesis* (q.v.) the sensible world was a reflection (*eikon*) of the spiritual. But the sensible world was not merely a collection of random animated parts; it was seen, from the very beginnings of Greek philosophy, as some kind of ordered whole, a *kosmos* endowed with movement and so with life. This was the primitive view of Anaximenes (Aetius I, 3, 4) and the early Pythagoreans (see Aristotle, *Phys.* IV, 213b), and this is still the view of Plato who calls the visible *kosmos* that embraces all living creatures an animal (*zoön; Tim.* 30b) with a soul (see *psyche tou pantos*). This in turn has a model, an "intelligible living being" (*zoön noeton*) that embraces within itself all the intelligible creatures (*ibid.* 30c–d). When he comes to describe the parallel classes of *zoa* contained within the sensible and intelligible animal he mentions only four: the heavenly race of gods, winged things, aquatic animals, and those that dwell on dry land (*ibid.* 39e–40a; with the introduction of *aither* [q.v.] this becomes five in the *Epinomis* 984b–c). In the later Platonic tradition these intelligible animals grow and multiply. Philo, for example, confronted with two accounts of creation in *Genesis*, can explain them as the creation of the sensible and the intelligible world, and is not a whit embarrassed at the prospect of having "intelligible grass" and "sensible grass" (*De opif.* 129–130; *Leg. all.* I, 24). Plotinus too traces out in detail the congruence between the intelligible and the sensible *zoa* (*Enn.* VI, 7, 8–12).

On the intelligible world, see *kosmos noetos;* and for its contents, *noeton;* further on the *kosmos* as a living organism under *sympatheia, holon.*

English–Greek Index

*The numbers cited refer not to page numbers but to
paragraphs under each specific heading in the text.*

abstraction/*aphairesis*: conceptual separation of matter in the study of the
objects of mathematics, *aphairesis;* as basis of the *via negativa,
agnostos* 2

accessory cause, *synaition* distinguished from true cause by Plato, *aition* 1

accident, *symbebekos, symptoma* Aristotelian theory of, *symbebekos* 2; Epicurean, 3; Stoic, 4; change in the category of accident, *genesis* 2, 15,
kinesis 7; distinguished from property, *idion, symbebekos* 2

account, *logos* connection with true judgment, *episteme* 2; ability to give an
account as hallmark of true knowledge in Plato, *logos* 2; contrasted
to myth, *mythos* 1

act, *energeia* Aristotelian theory emerges from analysis of change, *energeia*
1; compared to *kinesis* 3; derived from function 4, *ergon* 2; the
ultimate *energeia* 6; application to the theory of perception, *aisthesis*
19; contrasted to potentiality, *dynamis* 4; immanent form as, *eidos*
15; pleasure the completion of, *hedone* 7; unifying factor, *holon* 8; of
First Mover, *kinoun* 9, *nous* 9; the "activity of immobility," *ibid.* 10;
applied to intellection, *noesis* 12, *noeton* 1

action, *poiein, praxis, ergon* distinction of acting and making, *ergon* 1–2,
poiein; active powers associated with *logos* by Stoics, *genesis* 16; as a
"material" principle, *hyle* 7; virtue as a mean of, *meson;* in Plotinus a
degeneration of contemplation, *nous* 19, *physis* 5; activity and experience in Aristotle, *pathos* 9; as subject matter of morality, *praxis,
proairesis*

actuality, *energeia, entelecheia* for the former, see act; for the latter, entelechy

affection, *pathos* Platonic theory, *pathos* 6–7, *psyche* 15–17; in Aristotle,
9–10; in Stoicism, 12; irrational, violent, unnatural in Stoicism,
apatheia 3; the four major affections, *epithymia;* contrasted to action,
ergon 3; pleasure and pain in, *hedone* 8; reduced to judgments by
Chrysippus, *noesis* 17; properties of organism in Epicureanism,
holon 9; Epicurean criterion of truth, *prolepsis;* virtue as a mean of,
meson

age of reason⁻ in Stoicism, *noesis* 16

agent intellect, *nous poietikos* in Aristotle, *nous* 11–12; in Alexander of
Aphrodisias, 13; in Plotinus as a *dator formarum,* 21

aggregate, *synkrisis* see association

agnosticism see unknowable

air, *aer, pneuma* origins as an *arche* and later contrast with *aither, aer;*
cognitive principle in Diogenes, *aisthesis* 12, *noesis* 5, *pneuma* 2; and
purposeful, *nous* 4; modes of change in Anaximenes, *genesis* 3;
habitation of the *daimones, nous* 17; for *pneuma,* see breath

alienation, *allotriosis* correlative of Stoic doctrine of self-acceptance, *oikeiosis*

allegory, *allegoria* and the fall of the soul, *kathodos* 3; in the interpretation
of myths, *mythos* 1; in the reconciliation of monotheism and polytheism, *theos* 4

alteration, *alloiosis, heteroiosis* pre-Socratic reduction of all change to, *genesis* 13; in Plato, *kinesis* 6; defined by Aristotle, *pathos* 8; in Aristotelian theory of sensation, *aithesis* 20; in Stoic theory, *ibid.* 25, *phantasia;* substantial and qualitative change, *stoicheion* 15

analogy, *analogia* matter known by, *hyle* 1; a principle in Stoic theory of
intellection, *noesis* 16; and in their etymologizing, *onoma* 7

angel, *angelos* identified with the *daimones* of Greek philosophy, *daimon* 4;
with the "powers," *dynamis* 6; angelic souls in Proclus, *psyche* 35

anima, *psyche* distinguished from mind in Lucretius, *noesis* 14; see also soul

animal, *zoön* heavenly bodies as intellectual animals in Philo and Plotinus,
ouranioi 7; sensible and intelligible animals in the Platonic tradition,
zoön 3; distinguished from men, *pneuma* 6, *zoön* 2; universe as,
sympatheia 1, *zoön* 3; ancient theories of zoogony, *zoön* 1

animus, *nous* distinguished from soul in Lucretius, *noesis* 14; see also mind

anomaly, *anomalia* principle in Stoic etymologizing, *onoma* 7

apathy, *apatheia* Stoic doctrine of, *pathos* 12, *apatheia, passim;* origins in
Cynicism, *apatheia* 4; connection with immortality of soul and intellect, *pathos* 10

appetite, *orexis, horme* its operation in Aristotle, *epithymia;* embraces desire,
spirit, wish, *orexis;* role in Empedocles' theory of pleasure, *hedone* 1;
the problem in Stoicism, *horme;* the Neoplatonic return as a function
of, *epistrophe;* leads to motion, *kinesis* 8, *kinoun* 9; the First Mover
as an object of, *kinoun* 9, *nous* 16; for the appetitive soul in Plato,
see desire

applied science, *poietike, techne* in Plato, *techne* 3–4; in Aristotle, *ibid.* 6,
episteme 4

apprehension, *katalepsis* Stoic theory of, *katalepsis, noesis* 16; relation to
concepts, *ennoia;* grasp of the sensible image, *phantasia*

appropriate, *oikeion* object of love, *eros* 4; reflected by pleasure, *pathos* 11

area, *chora* designation of Platonic receptacle, *hyle* 6; corrected by Plotinus, *ibid.* 9

arrangement, *taxis* in the composition of bodies in Atomism, *stoicheion* 1

art, *poietike, techne, mimesis* generalized meaning in Plato, *techne* 1; technical term in a division, *ibid.* 2–3; practical and productive, 4; produces both "originals" and images, 5; in Aristotle, 6; contrasted with necessity, *telos* 2; no design in Atomists' concept of nature, *physis* 2

assent, *synkatathesis* in Stoic theory of intellection, *noesis* 16

assimilation, *homoiosis* present in Pythagorean-Platonic tradition, *homoiosis;* purification a prerequisite of, *katharsis* 4

association, *synkrisis* as an explanation of exchange in Anaxagoras, *genesis* 6–7, *pathos* 3; in Atomism, *ibid.* 8, *kinesis* 4; rejected by Plato, *genesis* 11; and by Aristotle, *ibid.* 14; the soul an aggregate in Atomism, *psyche* 7

astral body, *ochema* the theory in Plato and the later Platonic tradition, *ochema*

astral immortality connected with the nature of air or *aither*, *aer* 2; maintained by Poseidonius, *athanatos* 2

astral theology growth in later antiquity, *ouranioi* 7, *ouranos* 3

astrology in later antiquity, *ouranioi* 7

astronomy in Plato's educational theory, *ouranos* 3

atom, *atomon* monist solution to Parmenidean problematic, *atomon* 1; operations of, *ibid.* 2; formation into aggregates, *genesis* 8; pleasure and pain are atomic dislocations, *hedone* 8; inherent natural motion, *kinesis* 4; derivative in Epicurus, *ibid.* 5; indivisibility of, *megethos* 3; object of discursive reason, *noesis* 15; qualities of, *pathos* 4; soul-atoms, *psyche* 27; atoms as elements, *stoicheion* 7, 10

attention, *phrontis* as a principle in Plotinus, *noesis* 21, *nous* 18, *hen* 13

beauty, *kallos* in Plato, *eros* 5–7; in Stoa and Plotinus, *ibid.* 10

becoming, *genesis* contrasted to being by Parmenides, *genesis* 4; by Plato, *ibid.* 9; object of productive activity, *techne* 6

befitting acts, *kathekonta* in the Stoic moral system, *adiaphoron* 2, 3

begetting, *genesis* in Platonic theory of love, *eros* 5

being, *on* the Parmenidean antinomies on, *on* 1; being *qua* being the object of metaphysics, 3; in Plotinus begins at the level of *nous* 4; characterized by oneness, *hen* 3–4; transcendence of, *hyperousia, on* 3; denied motion by Parmenides, *kinesis* 2; the One beyond being, *hen* 11–12; the Good beyond being, *agathon;* as substance, *ousia* 2; as the object of contemplation, *techne* 6; endowed with life and intelligence, *trias* 2

belief, *pistis* subdivision of opinion in Plato, *doxa* 2, *pistis*

blood most perfect blend of elements in Empedocles, *aisthesis* 8, *psyche* 9; connection with perception, *kardia* 2, *noesis* 3, *pneuma* 2; in Stoicism, *pneuma* 4

body, *soma* reduction of quality to body in Stoicism, *genesis* 18, *poion;* geometrical solids in Platonic theory of change, *genesis* 12, *megethos* 3; extended body distinguished from unit and point, *megethos* 3; role of body in sensation, *noesis* 8; the quasi-physical astral body, *ochema* 2; in Homer and after, *psyche* 3, 6; body and soul in Atomism, *psyche* 7; in Epicureanism, *ibid.* 27; as a prison of the soul, *psyche* 13–14; involved in psychic functions in Plato, *ibid.* 17; the "Platonic bodies," *stoicheion* 10; types of human body in Proclus, *ochema* 4

brain, *enkephalos* as seat of perception, *kardia* 3–6; in Plato and Aristotle, *psyche* 15, 17

breath, *pneuma* in early views on the living universe, *pneuma* 1, *zoön* 1; and cognition, *pneuma* 2; as generative factor in Aristotle, *ibid.* 3; Stoic theory of, 4; Plotinian corrections, 5; as nonmaterial "spirit," 6; soul as breath of life, *psyche* 2–7; Stoic *pneuma* as soul, *ibid.* 28; various states and tensions of, *sympatheia* 3, *tonos*

Capacity, *dynamis* see potentiality

categories, *kategoriai* Platonic, *eidos* 13; Aristotelian and Plotinian, *genos;* matter not included in, *hyle* 1; Aristotelian listings, *kategoriai;* being, one, and good defined analogously through all the categories, *on* 3

catharsis, *katharsis* see purgation, purification

cause, *aition* causality in Plato, *aition* 1; Aristotelian doctrine of four causes, *ibid.* 2; necessity as a quasi-cause in Plato, *ananke* 2; subject of true knowledge, *episteme* 3; revision of causality schema, *noeton* 2; in the Neoplatonic derivation of the hypostases, *proödos* 3, *trias* 4

chance, *tyche* religiously pernicious to Plato, *physis* 2; Aristotelian theory of, *tyche*

change, *genesis, metabole, alloiosis, kinesis* pre-Socratic interest in, *genesis* 2; denial by Parmenides, *ibid.* 4, *stoicheion* 4; restoration of secondary change, *ibid.* 5; Anaxagoras on, 6–7; Atomists on, 8; Platonic theory of precosmic change, 10–11; postcosmic, 12; Aristotelian analysis, 13–14; various types of, 15, *metabole;* Stoics, 16–18; in the intellectual faculty, *hegemonikon;* varieties of change in Plato, *kinesis* 6; in terms of action and passion, *paschein* 1–3; substantial change in Plato, *phthora;* and privation in Aristotle, *steresis;* cyclic change, *stoicheion* 3; substantial and qualitative change, *ibid.* 15

character, *ethos, hexis* various views of its role, *ethos*

choice, *proairesis* soul's choice of life, *kathodos* 5; man must choose to think, *noesis* 21; and morality, *praxis;* in Aristotle and Epictetus, *proairesis;* soul moves by, *psyche* 20; differentiates chance and spontaneity, *tyche*

clarity, *enargeia* see self-evident

collection, *synagoge* the Platonic version of induction, *synagoge, diairesis* 2; in *Sophist* and *Politicus, techne* 2

combination, *koinonia* tentative use to describe relationship of *eide* and sensibles yields to that of interrelationship of *eide, diairesis* 3, *eidos* 12

common sense, *aisthesis koine, endoxon* for the former, see *sensus communis;* for the latter, *communis opinio*

communis opinio, *endoxon* majority view as an ingredient in dialectical reasoning, *dialektike* 4; quantitative and qualitative aspects of, *endoxon* 4–5; Aristotelian use of predecessors, *ibid.* 8–9; on the soul, *psyche* 1

completion, *telos, entelecheia* creation of men to complete the universe, *kathodos* 4; for *entelecheia*, see entelechy

composite, *syntheton* questions related to, *syntheton;* as substance, *ousia* 9; components of, *ibid.*

composition, *synthesis* judgment operates by composing and dividing concepts, in Aristotle, *noesis* 12; in Epicurus, *ibid.* 15; in Plotinus, *ibid.* 19

concept, *ennoia* Forms as thoughts or concepts of God, *eidos* 17, *noeton* 2; or as thoughts of man, *noeton* 5; the concept in Stoic epistemology, *ennoia, noesis* 16; concepts and names in Epicureanism, *onoma* 5

conflagration, *ekpyrosis* possible Heraclitan origins and Stoic theory, *ekpyrosis;* survived by seminal reasons, *logoi spermatikoi*

contact, *haphe* Atomists reduce all sensation to, *aisthesis* 9, *dynamis* 1, *pathos* 4; in the formation of aggregates, *genesis* 8; as basis of sensation in Plato, *pathos* 6; all motion caused by, *kinoun* 9; cosmic sympathy based on contact and similarity, *sympatheia* 6; problem in Aristotle and Plotinus, *ibid.* 7

demon, *daimon* in Greek popular religion and thence applied to the soul, *daimon* 1; as an intermediary god, 2; in the oriental tradition, 4; and character, *ethos;* and original sin, *kathodos* 2; dwells in the air, *nous* 17; converse with in dreams, *oneiros*, 2–3; *eros* as, *eros* 1, 5; soul as, *psyche* 12; demonic soul in later Platonism, *ibid.* 35

demonstration, *apodeixis* Aristotelian technical usage defined, *apodeixis;* first principles of, *arche* 7; rests upon true and primary premisses, *doxa* 6; in true knowledge, *episteme* 3; begins from definition, *horos*

depletion, *kenosis* role in Empedocles' theory of pleasure, *hedone* 1; in Plato and Aristotle, *ibid.* 2; accepted by Epicurus, *ibid.* 9

descent (of the soul), *kathodos* religious origins of belief, *kathodos* 1; connection with Pythagorean view of the soul, 2; in later Platonic tradition, 3–5; and the acquisition of an astral body, *ochema* 2

desire, *epithymia, eros* position and function in Plato, *psyche* 15, 17; reduced in scope by later philosophers, *epithymia;* reason communicates with it in dreams, *oneiros* 4; directed toward First Mover, *kinoun* 9; see appetite and, for *eros*, love

dialectic, *dialektike* Eleatic and Socratic origins, *dialektike* 1; synoptic and diacritic in Plato, 2–3; Aristotelian view, 4; Stoic, 5; Plotinian, 6; Zenonian dialectic, *hen* 4; as a means of knowing the Forms, *eidos* 8

difference, *diaphora* see specific difference

difficulty, *aporia* see problem

directive faculty, *hegemonikon* see intellect

discursive reasoning, *dianoia, logismos* the problem in Plato, *mathematika* 2, *noesis* 10; normal function of the rational soul, *psyche* 17; use as a generic term in Aristotle, *dianoia;* role in Epicureanism, *noesis* 15; in Numenius, *nous* 18; in Plotinus, *noesis* 19; a degenerate and imitative form of true intellection, *ibid.* 20, *psyche* 33

disposition, *diathesis* contrasted with more permanent state of soul, *hexis*

distinction, *diairesis, diaphora* as an element in moral choice, *proairesis;* see also division, specific difference

divination, *mantike* and philosophy, *mantike, passim;* denied by Xenophanes, *oneiros* 3; and by Sceptics, *ouranioi* 5; origins as explained by Plato, *oneiros* 4, *psyche* 17; theoretical basis in Plotinus, *sympatheia* 8

divine, *theion* divinity of Milesian *Urstoff, physis* 2, *theion* 1; linked with motion and immortality, *theion* 2; divinity of the universe, *kosmos* 2, 4; denied by Aristotle, *ibid.* 3; of the heavenly bodies, *ouranioi, passim;* divine souls in Proclus, *psyche* 35 division, *diairesis* use in Platonic dialectic, *diairesis* 1–3; Aristotelian, *ibid.* 4; use of differences in Platonic version, *diaphora* 1–2; exhaustion method in Speusippus, *ibid.* 2; Aristotelian choice of *differentiae,* *ibid.* 3; division and definition, *logos* 3; division of concepts in judgment, *noesis* 12, 15, 19; divisibility of genera and intelligible matter in Plotinus, *hyle* 8; and discrete quantity, *plethos;* in *Sophist* and *Politicus, techne* 2–3

division of the sciences Platonic, *techne* 3–5; Aristotelian, *episteme* 4; Stoic, *philosophia* 2

dream, *oneiros* and philosophy in antiquity, *oneiros, passim;* for Plato they originate in the liver, *psyche* 17

dualism possible moral dualism in Empedocles, *kinoun* 2; in early Pythagoreanism, *hen* 2; in the later Plato, *kakon* 3, 5; in the Gnostics' view of the Creator, *demiourgos* 2

dyad, *dyas* either derived from or coexisting with monad, *dyas;* Platonic theory, *ibid.;* One and Dyad in Speusippus, *mathematika* 4; and the One, *hen* 9–10

efficient cause, *kinoun* see mover

effluences, *aporrhoai* in Empedoclean theory of perception, *aisthesis* 7

element, *stoicheion* origin in the opposites, *enantion* 1; origins of the term, *stoicheion* 1; the Empedoclean elements, *ibid.* 5; and simple bodies in Plato, 10; in Aristotle, 17; role in change, *genesis, passim;* elements and principles in Pythagoreanism, *hen* 2; the "unnamed element" in Epicureanism, *psyche* 27

emanation, *eklampsis* Plotinian metaphor of creation, *eklampsis, proödos* 1; Proclus' preference for a mathematical analogy, *proödos* 2

emotion, *pathos* see affection

end, *telos* the ends of making and acting, *ergon* 1; in Stoicism happiness not an end, *eudaimonia;* see also purpose

endelechy, *endelecheia* eternal motion of ether, *ouranioi* 6

entelechy, *entelecheia* Aristotelian theory, *entelecheia;* compared to act, *energeia* 4; related to function and end, *ergon* 2; related to organs, *holon* 8; Aristotelian soul as entelechy, *psyche* 23; rejected by Plotinus, *ibid.* 33

enthusiasm, *enthousiasmos* possession by God of the poet and prophet, *mantike* 2–3; homoeopathic cure of, *katharsis* 3

equilibrium, *ataraxia, isomoiria, isonomia* distinction of Epicurean doctrine from Stoic apathy, *apatheia* 2–3; application to theory of pleasure, *hedone* 1; physical and psychic in Epicurus, *ibid.* 9; and medical theory of health, *psyche* 11

equity, *epieikeia* defined in connection with justice, *dike* 6

eristic Plato's attitude toward, *dialektike* 1

error, *pseudos* unaccountable in early perception theories, *noesis* 2; in Empedócles, *ibid.* 3; no error in the senses, *aisthesis* 24, *doxa* 7; arises in the judgment, *doxa* 4, *noesis* 12, 15

essence, *ti esti, ousia, eidos* in Plato, *ousia* 1; Aristotelian search for, *ibid.* 2–3; the subject of definition, *ti esti;* and the object of intellection, *noesis* 12; revealed by name, *onoma* 2

eternity, *aion* transcendent mode of existence, *aion;* incorporated into Platonic theory of time, *chronos* 5; and into Plotinian, *ibid.* 9; soul participates in time and eternity, *psyche* 36

ether, *aither* introduced as fifth element by Aristotle, *aither, ouranioi* 6; in Stoicism, *ouranioi* 5; motion of, *kinoun* 8, *stoicheion* 17; divinity of, *kosmos* 3; its motion gives motion to stars, *ouranioi* 3; habitation of intelligible planets, *nous* 17; as the *hegemonikon* of the universe, *pneuma* 4; and *pneuma, ochema* 3

etymology, *etymon* in the exegesis of myth, *mythos* 1; philosophical tool in Stoicism, *onoma* 7; in the identification of the traditional gods with the "powers," *dynamis* 10

everlasting, *aidios* everlasting perduration in time, *aidios;* heavenly bodies, *ousia* 3

evil, *kakon* Socratic attitude toward, *kakon* 2; Form of in Plato, 3; violation of mean in Aristotle, 4; Epicurean and Stoic theories, 5; and matter, 6–8; in Proclus, 9; sensible universe evil in Gnosticism, *kosmos* 4; as a privation of good in Plotinus, *steresis*

exegesis, *allegoria* of myths by philosophers, *mythos* 1

exemplars, *paradeigmata* distinction of formal and exemplary cause, *noeton* 2; possession of sensible forms as exemplars, *ibid.* 6; and the seminal reasons, *logoi spermatikoi;* the intelligible world as exemplar of the sensible world, *mimesis* 4

existence, *ousia, on* in Plato, *ousia* 1; see also being

experience, *pathos, empeiria* and activity as subject matter of morality, *pathos* 9; generalized into art, *techne* 6

exoteric writings, *exoterikoi logoi* and the problem of the Aristotelian dialogues, *exoterikoi logoi* faculty, *dynamis* of the soul in Aristotle, *psyche* 25; matched with an organ, *holon* 8; in the Stoa, *psyche* 28

fall, *kathodos* see descent

falsity, *pseudos* in the fine arts, *mimesis* 7; see also error

fate, *heimarmene* Stoic identification with *logos* and providence, *heimarmene;* in Philo, *logos* 5

filling up, *anaplerosis* in Empedocles' theory of pleasure, *hedone* 1; in Plato and Aristotle, 2; accepted by Epicurus, 9

final cause, *telos* soul as mover through final causality, *psyche* 20, 22; First Mover as, *kinoun* 9, *telos* 3; incorporated into Platonic tradition, *nous* 16; efficient and final causes identified in Platonism, *proödos* 1, *hen* 14; One as final cause in Proclus, *hen* 14

fine art, *mimesis* Plato's theory of, *mimesis* 6–7

fire, *pyr* in Heraclitus, *logos* 1, *pyr;* Stoic principle, *genesis* 17, *logos* 4; and spirit in Stoa, *pneuma* 4–5, *psyche* 28, *pyr;* God as creative fire, *theos* 4

First Mover, *proton kinoun* love as, *eros* 1; Aristotelian theory, *kinoun* 7, 9–10; its activity, *nous* 9; identified with agent intellect by Alexander of Aphrodisias, *nous* 13

first philosophy, *prote philosophia* in Aristotle, *philosophia* 1, *sophia*, *theologia* 2

flux, *rhoe* as an image rather than a concept, *rhoe;* leads to denigration of sensation, *episteme* 1

fluxion method of generating solids from points, *arithmos* 1, *psyche* 21

form, *eidos* pre-Platonic meaning, *eidos* 1–2; "friends of the Forms," 3; possible Pythagorean origins, 4–5; Socratic influence, 6; Platonic theory of transcendent Forms, 7–11; their interrelationship, 12–13; Aristotelian immanent form, 15–16; Aristotle's attack on Plato's separation of Forms, *choriston;* transcendent Forms in later Platonic tradition, *eidos* 17; ground of true knowledge, *episteme* 2; men drawn to by love, *eros* 6–8; question of immanence in Plato, *genesis* 10, *eidos* 10; and the Other, *heteron;* Form of individuals in Plotinus, *hyle* 10; Form of motion, *kinesis* 6; location of Forms, *kosmos noetos* 1; creation of Forms in Philo, *ibid.* 2; in the mind of God, *logos* 5; identified with mathematicals by Xenocrates, *mathematika* 4; and participation, *methexis;* and imitation, *mimesis* 4–5; role of Aristotelian form in cognition, *noesis* 12; in Plotinus supplied by *nous* for purposes of judgment, *ibid.* 19; as immanent and intelligible in Aristotle, *noeton* 1; *eidos* and *idea*, *ibid.* 2; as unified concepts in the cosmic intellect, *ibid.* 5; in Proclus, 6; varieties in Plotinus, *nous* 21–22; bestowed by *nous* on the soul, *ibid.* 19

formal cause, *eidos* Aristotelian, *eidos* 15; One as formal cause, *hen* 2; and intelligible form, *noeton* 1; and exemplary cause, *ibid.* 2

friendship *philia* in Plato, *eros* 4; in Aristotle, *ibid.* 9

function, *ergon* Aristotelian theory of, *ergon* 3; role in ethics, 4; function of man, 5, *nous* 10; leads into notion of act, *energeia* 4; and, eventually, to that of perfection, *entelecheia* 1

functioning, *energeia* develops from notion of function, *energeia* 4; see also act

genus, *genos* genera in Plato, Aristotle, Plotinus, *genos;* stands to difference as matter to form, *diaphora* 4; presence in an interpretative crux in Plato, *eidos* 13; divisibility of and intelligible matter in Plotinus, *hyle* 8; identified with universal, *katholou;* as substance, *ousia* 2

god, *theos* denial and acceptance of personal God by philosophers, *theos* 1; appearance of a dynamic God in Plato, 2; demonstration of existence from movement in Aristotle, 3; Epicurean and Stoic view, 4; the second and third God, 5; denied motion by Xenophanes, *kinesis* 1, *nous* 2, *theion* 1; communications from and possession by, *mantike, passim, oneiros* 2; God in Plato, *nous* 6; in Aristotle, *ibid.* 8–10, *kinoun* 9; Stoic view of, *pneuma* 4; and Philo, *logos* 5, *on* 4; existence of gods known through dreams in Epicureanism, *oneiros* 3; and in Aristotle, *ibid.* 5; the heavenly bodies and a belief in, *ouranioi* 1; gods of mythology identified with planets, *ibid.* 4; first and second God, *hen* 9, 11

good, *agathon* in Plato, Aristotle, and Plotinus, *agathon* 1–3; identified with unhypothetized first principle, *dialektike* 2, *epistrophe;* the anticipated, *epithymia;* the good for man, *ergon* 5; object of love in Plotinus, *eros* 10; happiness as the good for man, *eudaimonia;* and pleasure, *hedone, passim;* identified with the One, *hen* 1; perceived good leads to motion, *kinesis* 8, *kinoun* 9; defined analogously through all the categories, *on* 3; the Good and the One, *hen* 3, 8–9; identified with limit, *peras;* as an object of ethics and politics. *praxis;* as final cause, *telos* 3

habit, *hexis* character as result of, *ethos;* contrasted to more transient state, *hexis*

happiness, *eudaimonia* its definition by various philosophers, *eudaimonia;* pleasure calculated over a lifetime, *hedone* 6; in Epicurus, *ibid.* 9

harmony, *harmonia* applications of the original theory, *harmonia;* as a purification of the soul, *katharsis* 1; restored to soul by contemplation of motion of the heavens, *kinoun* 5, *ouranos* 2–3; in the universe, *kosmos* 1; the Stoic "harmony with nature," *nomos* 2, *eudaimonia;* the soul as harmony, *psyche* 10–11; in the World Soul, *psyche tou pantos* 1; and moderation, *sophrosyne*

heart, *kardia* as seat of perception, *kardia, passim;* and generation, *pneuma* 3

heaven, *ouranos* paradigmatic purpose of its motion, *kinoun* 5, *ouranos* 2–3; descent of the soul through, *kathodos* 3

heavenly bodies, *ouranioi* belief in divinity of, *ouranioi* 1; Plato's attitude, 2; Aristotle's varying views, 3–4; growing importance in later antiquity, 5–7; their material, *hyle* 4; nature and movement in Plato, *kinoun* 6; movement imitated by *genesis, ibid.* 9; as substances, *ousia* 3; both produce and portend, *sympatheia* 8

henad, *henas* in Plato, *hen* 6; in Proclus, *henas*

hidden meaning, *hyponoia* in the allegorical interpretation of myths, *mythos* 1

homoeomeries, *homoiomeres* in Anaxagoras' theory of the elements, *stoicheion* 11–12

homoeopathy in medical theories of purgation, *katharsis* 3

homo mensura in the theory of Protagoras, *nomos* 1

hypostasis, *hypostasis* the supreme principles of being in later Platonism, *hypostasis;* separability of, *choriston;* Aristotle accuses Plato of hypostatizing universals, *katholou;* the three transcendent hypostases in Middle Platonism, *nous* 16, 18, *hen* 11–12, 14; the derivation of, *proödos* 2–3; triadic structure of, *trias, passim*

hypothesis, *hypothesis* role in earlier Platonic dialectic, *dialektike* 2, *hypothesis;* in Zeno and Plato's *Parmenides, hen* 4; primary hypotheses in Aristotle, *hypothesis*

ideal number, *arithmos eidetikos* Forms of numbers in Plato, *arithmos eidetikos;* in Plotinus, *mathematika* 4

image, *eidolon, eikon, phantasia* in Atomists' theory of perception, *aisthesis* 9, *noesis* 13, 15; Platonic distinction of images, *eidolon;* knowledge of them constitutes lowest form of opinion, *doxa* 2, *mimesis* 5; the product of art, *mimesis* 1–2, *techne* 5; qualified existence, *eikon;* in Aristotle, *noesis* 12, *noeton* 1; in Stoicism, *noesis* 16; in Epicureanism, *aisthesis* 22; sensible universe an image of the intelligible, *kosmos* 4, *kosmos noetos* 1; time an image of eternity, *chronos* 5; the role of the sensible image in perception, *phantasia, psyche* 28; in Plotinian number theory, *mathematika* 4; in Proclus soul possesses intelligible forms in the manner of an image, *noeton* 6; so too in Plotinus, *nous* 21 imagination, *phantasia* in Plato, Aristotle, and the Stoa, *phantasia*

imitation, *mimesis* in Platonic theory of art, *mimesis* 1–3, *techne* 5; applied to Forms, *mimesis* 4–5; in Platonic theory of time, *chronos* 5; according to Aristotle only verbally different from participation, *methexis;* of Aristotelian First Mover, *kinoun* 9; language as, *onoma* 3–4

immortal, *athanatos* the gods, *theion* 2; individual immortality connected with new view of the soul, *athanatos, psyche* 13–14; Platonic views on, *palingenesia, psyche* 16; in Aristotle, *psyche* 26; and the intellect, *athanatos* 2, *pathos* 10

impassibility, *apatheia* of soul in Aristotle, *apatheia* 1; of intellect, *pathos* 10; of soul in Plotinus, *aisthesis* 26

impression, *phantasia, typosis* essence of sensation in Zeno, *aisthesis* 24–25, *noesis* 16; in general Stoic theory, *phantasia;* role in Plotinus, *aisthesis* 27

impulse, *horme* and affections in Stoa, *pathos* 12, *psyche* 28

incommensurable, *asymmetron* Pythagorean discovery, *asymmetron* 1; philosophical implications, *ibid.* 2

incorruptible, *aphthartos* the Milesian *Urstoff, physis* 2; the heavenly bodies, *ouranioi* 4, *ousia* 3; the universe, *aphthartos*

indefinite *apeiron* see indeterminate, unlimited

indestructible, *aphthartos* see incorruptible

indeterminate, *apeiron* Anaximander's choice as a principle, *arche* 2; indeterminate and determinate motion, *trias* 3; see also unlimited

indifferent, *adiaphoron* see neutral

individual, *tode ti* no definition of, *horos;* substance in a primary sense, *ousia* 2, *tode ti*

individuation matter as the principle of in Aristotle, *hyle* 2; form in Plotinus, *ibid.* 10; of celestial intelligences, *kinoun* 12

indivisibility of form, *hyle* 2; indivisible magnitudes, *megethos* 2–4

induction, *epagoge, synagoge* Socratic and Platonic antecedents, *epagoge* 1–2; foundation of all scientific knowledge, 3; grasps universal, 4; complete, 6; for *synagoge* or Platonic induction, see collection

infima species, *atomon eidos* term of Platonic division, *diairesis* 2; contrast in Plato and Aristotle, *dialektike* 3; in Aristotle, *eidos* 16; all specific differences resumed in, *diaphora* 4

infinite, *apeiron* see indeterminate, unlimited

instinct, *horme* instinctive pursuit of pleasure, *hedone* 6, 8; natural instinct in Stoicism, *nomos* 2; instinct toward self-preservation, *oikeiosis*

instrument, *organon* see organ

instrumental cause in Philo, *aition* 2, *logos* 5

intellect, *nous, logistikon, hegemonikon* as the God of Xenophanes, *nous* 2; in Anaxagoras, *ibid.* 3, *noesis* 4; cosmic intellect in Plato, *nous* 5–7; and in Aristotle, *ibid.* 8–9; the Platonic *logistikon, psyche* 16–19; Aristotelian theory of human intellect, *nous* 10–12; as seen by his commentators, 13; the hypostatized intellect of Middle Platonism, 15–16; Numenius, 18; cosmic intellect in Plotinus, 19–20; his theory of the human intellect, 21; Stoic theory, *hegemonikon;* its involvement in sensation, *aisthesis* 24–25; as a tension of the *pneuma, sympatheia* 3; divine intellect in Philo, *logos* 5; human intellect as divine spirit in Philo, *pneuma* 6; Platonic transcendent intellect and the World Soul, *kinoun* 5, *nous* 6; located in the heart or brain, *kardia, passim;* composed of ether, *ouranioi* 6; originates in and returns to the sun, *sympatheia* 5; present in the stars, *kinoun* 6, 11–12, *nous* 17, *ouranioi* 7; as "the place of the Forms," *noeton* 2; the *hegemonikon* of the universe, *pneuma* 4; intellect and emotions in Plato, *pathos* 7; immortality of, *ibid.* 10; being, life, and intelligence, *trias* 2–3

intellect in habitu in cognitive theory of Alexander of Aphrodisias, *nous* 13

intellection, *noesis, phronesis* pre-Socratic theories of, *noesis* 1–7; Platonic, 8–11; Aristotelian, 12; Atomist and Epicurean, 13–15; Stoic, 16–17; later Platonic, 18–21; in Diogenes dependent upon purity of air, *aer, aisthesis* 12; in heavenly bodies, *kinoun* 6, *ouranioi* 5–6; recognition of pleasure attendant upon intellection, *hedone* 2; incorporated by Plato into the good life, *ibid.* 3; in the Aristotelian First Mover, *nous* 9; human and divine compared, *ibid.* 10

intelligence, *nous* see intellect

intelligibility distinguished by Aristotle into *per se* and *quoad nos, gnorimon* 1; based on Platonic precedent, 4; function of immateriality, *ibid.*

intelligible, *noeton* objects of intellection in pre-Socratic philosophy, *noeton* 1; connected with "powers," *dynamis* 7; continuous with the sensible, *ibid.* 8

intelligible form, *eidos, noeton* role in Aristotelian theory of cognition, *noesis* 12, *noeton* 1; in Plotinus, *nous* 22; in Proclus, *noeton* 6; see further, form

intelligible matter, *hyle noete* role in mathematical abstraction, *aphairesis* 2; genus a type of intelligible matter, *diaphora* 4; Plotinus' different theory, *hyle* 8; generated from the One as "Otherness," *kakon* 8

intelligible universe, *kosmos noetos* in Plato, Philo, and Plotinus, *kosmos noetos;* as an externalization of the Divine Reason in Philo; *logos* 5

intermediaries, *metaxu* the mathematicals as intermediaries in Plato, *mathematika* 2–3, *metaxu* 1; the soul as an intermediary between the sensible and the intelligible, *psyche* 29, 36

interrogation, *elenchos* at root of dialectic, *dialektike* 1; relation to induction, *epagoge* 2; as cathartic of the soul, *katharsis* 2; growth into aporematic method of Aristotle, *aporia* 1

intuition, *nous* connection with problem of the first principles of demonstration, *arche* 7; in Plotinus, *noesis* 18

irrational number connected with discovery of incommensurability of magnitudes, *asymmetron* 1–2

Judgment, *doxa, krisis, hypolepsis* Platonic theory, *doxa* 4; true judgment with an account, *episteme* 2; Aristotelian theory, *noesis* 12; contingent in Aristotle, *doxa* 5; Epicurean view, *noesis* 15; reduction of all affections to judgments by Chrysippus, *ibid.* 17; Plotinian, *ibid.* 19

justice, *dike* prephilosophical use, *dike* 1; in cosmic process, 2; in the *nomosphysis* controversy, 3; Plato's view, 4; Aristotle's, 6; Stoic, 7; and happiness in Plato, *eudaimonia*

Kind, *genos, eidos* see genus

knowability, *gnorimon* see intelligibility

knowledge, *gnosis, episteme, noesis* types in Atomism, *noesis* 6; exaltation of *episteme* at expense of sensation, *episteme* 1–2; in Plato connected with Forms, *ibid.* 2; for Aristotle a knowledge of causes, *ibid.* 3; proceeds from necessary premisses, *doxa* 5; rests upon induction, *epagoge* 3; grasps the universal, *gnorimon* 2

lack, *endeia* in Platonic theory of love, *eros* 4–5; in theories of pleasure, *hedone* 1, 9

language Platonic theory of origins, *onoma* 3; Epicurean, *ibid.* 6; Stoic linguistic theory, *logos* 4; a weakness necessarily flowing from soul's preoccupation with matter, *noesis* 20

law, *nomos* cosmic order as law in Heraclitus, *kosmos* 2; arbitrary nature of man-made law, *nomos* 1; divine law, *ibid.* 2

lawgiver, *nomothetes* as bestower of names in Plato, *onoma* 2; rejected by Epicurus, *ibid.* 6; in Stoa and Philo, *ibid.* 7

life, *zoe* pre-Socratic view, *zoe* 1; in Plato, 2; and Aristotle, 3; time and eternity in terms of, *chronos* 9; of heavenly bodies, *ouranioi* 5; distinguished from consciousness in Homer, *psyche* 2; identified with consciousness, *ibid.* 6; linked with motion, *psyche* 4; being, life, and intelligence, *trias* 2–3

life-span, *aion* and the notion of eternity, *aion*

like, *homoios* the "like knows like" theory of perception, *aisthesis* 6–12, *homoios, passim;* and particularly in Empedocles, *psyche* 9; role in Stoic theory of intellection, *noesis* 16; as an explanation of love, *eros* 4; as a principle in the construction of the World Soul, *psyche tou pantos* 1

limit, *peras* in Pythagoras and Plato, *peras;* in the explanation of time, *chronos* 4–5; and the Aristotelian mean, *meson;* as a good, *ibid.;* and the One, *hen* 2, 6; in the definition of number, *plethos*

locomotion, *phora* in Plato, *kinesis* 6; and Aristotle, *ibid.* 7, *phora;* and the first moved, *kinoun* 7

love, *eros* a force in mythology, *eros* 1; as mover in Empedocles, *ibid.,* *kinoun* 2; Socrates as lover, *eros* 3; Platonic theory of, 4–8; and passion, 9; in Plotinus, 10–11

Madness, *mania* in Plato, *mantike* 2; love as madness, *eros* 7

magic see theurgy

magnitude, *megethos* definition, *megethos* 1; indivisible magnitude, 2–4; geometrical magnitudes, *metaxu* 1; spatial magnitude attributed to units in Pythagoreanism, *monas;* difference between Aristotelian and Stoic view, *hyle* 7; absence in First Mover, *kinoun* 9; soul as, *psyche* 20; contrasted with discrete quantity, *plethos* 1

materia prima, *prote hyle* · see prime matter

material cause, *hyle* described by Aristotle, *hyle* 2; cf., further, matter, principle

mathematical number, *arithmos mathematikos* in Pythagoreanism it is "in" sensibles, *mathematika* 1; Aristotelian theory, 3; Speusippus, 4; Plotinus, *ibid.;* as product of abstraction, *aphairesis*

mathematicals, *mathematika* theories of, *mathematika* 1; Platonic version, 2, *metaxu* 1; Speusippus, *mathematika* 4

matter, *hyle* pre-Socratic search for material cause, *arche* 2–4; knowledge of, *hyle* 1; not subject to definition, *horos;* Aristotelian principle of individuation, *hyle* 2; quasi-substance, 3; types of, 4; distinguished from privation, 5; Stoic, 7; Plotinian, 8–10; Aristotle identifies material principle with dyad, *dyas*, *hyle* 6; for Plotinus the Platonic receptacle is "second matter," *hypodoche*; as an image of being, *eikon*; as evil, *kakon* 6–8; as "the Other," *ibid.* 8; as quasi-being, *on* 4; as a relative term, *pros ti*; perceptible and imperceptible matter, *stoicheion* 15

mean, *meson* origin of the theory, *meson*; virtue the mean of experiences and activities, *pathos* 9; moderation as a mean in Aristotle, *sophrosyne* 2; evil as a violation of the mean, *kakon* 4; air and water as mean terms in Plato, *stoicheion* 17; organ as a mean state in Aristotelian theory of perception, *aisthesis* 21; and in Plotinus, *ibid.* 27; as applied to justice, *dike* 6; as a good for Speusippus but rejected by Plato, *hedone* 4; in Proclus' triadic structure, *trias* 4

medium, *prophetes* as an instrument of divine communication, *mantike* 1–2, 4

medium of perception in Democritus' theory of vision, *aisthesis* 10; in Plotinus, *noesis* 20, *sympatheia* 7

metempsychosis, *metempsychosis* see reincarnation

microcosm man the microcosm in Democritus, *kosmos* 1

mind, *nous*, *logistikon*, *hegemonikon* see intellect

miracle wonder-working as a characteristic of later Platonism, *mantike* 4–5; see also theurgy

mixture, *krasis*, *mixis*, *meigma* used by Empedocles to explain change, *genesis* 5; primordial state in Anaxagoras, *ibid.* 6–7; elements in, *pathos* 2–3; rejected by Plato, *genesis* 11; in the World Soul, *psyche tou pantos* 1; Stoic theory of, *genesis* 18; the good life as a mixture in Plato, *hedone* 3; proportion in, *holon* 3–5

moderation, *sophrosyne* in Plato, *sophrosyne* 1; in Aristotle and the Stoa, 2

motion, *kinesis*, *phora* subsistent among Milesians, *kinesis* 1; denied to being by Parmenides, 2; inherent motion affirmed by Atomists, 4–5; in Plato, 6, *kinoun* 3, *psyche* 19; Aristotelian theory of, *kinesis* 7–8; essence of sensation in Atomism, *aisthesis* 23; rotary motion effects change in Anaxagoras, *genesis* 7; primary in all change, *ibid.* 15; in the Epicurean organism, *holon* 9; all motion effected by contact, *kinoun* 9; initiated by *nous* in Anaxagoras, *noesis* 4; the kinetics of intellection in Plato, *ibid.* 11; denied to God by Xenophanes, *kinesis* 1, *nous* 2; of heavenly bodies, *ouranioi*, *passim*; in Aristotle caused by nature, *physis* 3; as an indication of the presence of soul, *psyche* 4; as the essence of soul in Plato, *ibid.* 19; natural motion of the elements in Aristotle, *stoicheion* 17; "tonic motion," *tonos*; and place, *topos*; undefined and defined motion, *trias* 3

mover, *kinoun* origins of the notion, *kinoun* 2; soul as mover in Plato, 5–6; Aristotelian movers, 7–13; in Anaxagoras, *noesis* 3; love as, *eros* 1;

Aristotelian movers as substances, *ousia* 3; nature and efficient causality, *physis* 3

music, *mousike* as a means of restoring harmony to the soul, *katharsis* 1; as a homoeopathic purgative, *ibid.* 3

myth, *mythos* moral objections to, *mythos* 1; use in philosophy, 2; shares sense of wonder with philosophy, *aporia* 1; called "theology," *theologia*

Name, *onoma* relation to concept and object, *onoma, passim*

natural law in the Stoa based on a philosophical understanding of nature, *nomos* 2

natural philosopher, *physikos* objects of his study, *ergon* 3, *aphairesis* 1; how understood by Plato and Aristotle, *physis* 1

nature, *physis* pre-Socratic views, *physis* 1; Plato, 2; Aristotle, 3; Stoa, 4; Plotinus, 5; correlation with pleasure, *hedone* 8; principle of motion in Aristotle, *kinesis* 8, *kinoun* 7; and the seminal reasons, *logoi spermatikoi;* as opposed to convention, *nomos* 2–3; nature and reason in the Stoa, *nous* 14; and names, *onoma* 7; as a state of the *pneuma* in plants, *sympatheia* 3; contrasted to art, *techne* 6; Plato's identification of nature and necessity, *telos* 2

necessity, *ananke* operates without purpose, *ananke* 1; a quasi-cause in Plato, 2; a role in Aristotelian syllogistic reasoning, 3; necessary motion in Atomism, *kinesis* 4; identified with nature and contrasted to design, *telos* 2; and chance, *tyche*

neutral, *adiaphoron* Stoic distinction of moral content of human acts, *adiaphoron*

nonbeing, *me on* the problem as stated by Parmenides, *on* 1; the Platonic solution, *on* 2, *heteron;* the Aristotelian, *on* 3, *steresis;* connected with the problem of false judgments, *doxa* 4; renders change impossible, *genesis* 4; relative, *ibid.* 13; matter as, *hyle* 6

notio communis, *ennoia koine* Stoic theory of, *ennoia*

number, *arithmos* Pythagorean and Aristotelian theory, *arithmos* 1; as a plurality of units, 2; Platonic identification of Forms with number, 3; perceived by *sensus communis* 4; Greek view as integers and the problem of incommensurability, *asymmetron* 2; time reduced to, *chronos* 4–5; mathematical number in Aristotle, *mathematika* 3; and in Plotinus, *ibid.* 4; things imitate number, *mimesis* 4; the elements of number, *monas, hen* 2, 8–9; as plurality with limit, *plethos;* soul as a property of, *psyche* 12; soul as self-moved number in Xenocrates, *ibid.* 21

nutrition, *threptike* nutritive soul in Aristotle, *aisthesis* 22.

Occult power, *dynamis, symbolon* in later antiquity, *dynamis* 10–11

one, *hen, monas* as a principle or an element in early Pythagoreanism, *hen* 2; in Parmenides, 3; the hypotheses of the *Parmenides*, 4; Platonic theory, 6–7; Aristotelian, 8; Speusippus and Xenocrates, 9; in the Pythagorean revival, 10–11; Plotinus, 12–13; Proclus' derivation of, 14; identified with the Good, *epistrophe;* and the henad, *henas;* One and Dyad in Speusippus, *mathematika* 4; in Numenius, *nous* 18; the One and *nous* in Plotinus, *ibid.* 20; defined analogously through all the categories, *on* 3; denied intellection, *noeton* 4; and providence, *pronoia* 2; the one and the many in Neoplatonism, *proödos* 1, *trias* 5

opinion, *doxa* epistemological contrast with knowledge, *doxa* 1–2; in Epicureanism akin to but distinct from sensation, *ibid.* 7; is about the contingent, *episteme* 3; for commonly held opinions, see common sense

opposite, *enantion* the opposed powers in pre-Socratic philosophy, *enantion* 1; in the Platonic theory of becoming, 2, *genesis* 11; Aristotelian reduction to two sets, *enantion* 2; in the Aristotelian analysis of change, *genesis* 13; Heraclitan tension of opposites, *logos* 1; and the mean, *meson;* opposition a principle in Stoic theory of intellection, *noesis* 16; joined by love, *eros* 1; in terms of action and passion, *paschein, passim;* rejected by Atomists, *pathos* 5; soul as balance of opposites, *psyche* 10–11

order, *kosmos* the universe as, *kosmos;* search for order, *nous* 1; the ordering function of intellect in Anaxagoras, *ibid.* 3

organ, *organon* in Aristotle's theory of sensation, *aisthesis* 21; in Plotinus, *ibid.* 27; contrasted with part, *holon* 8; man as organ of the universe in Stoicism, *ibid.* 10; for Stoics logic no longer an instrument, as in Aristotle, but has wider scope, *dialektike* 5

organism, *holon* Aristotelian theory of, *holon* 8; and the soul in Epicureanism, *aisthesis* 23

original sin mythical and philosophical expression of, *kathodos* 1–2; Platonic "mischance," *ibid.* 4; Plotinian "audacity," *ibid.* 5

other, *heteron* in Plato and Plotinus, *heteron;* connection with error, *doxa* 4; in Aristotle the object of all knowledge except that of First Mover, *nous* 9; relative nature of, *pros ti;* matter generated from the One as "otherness," *kakon* 8; in the World Soul, *psyche tou pantos* 1

Pain, *algos, ponos* presence in Anaxagoras' theory of perception, *aisthesis* 14; due to loss of balance, *hedone* 1; as atomic dislocation, *ibid.* 8; mixed with pleasure, *ibid.* 9; as evil in Epicureanism, *kakon* 5

painlessness, *aponia* the Epicurean correlative of psychic equilibrium, *hedone* 9 pair, *dyas* see dyad

participation, *methexis* in Plato and Proclus, *methexis;* Proclus' adaptation to triadic structure, *trias* 5

passing away, *phthora* see corruption

passion, *paschein, pathos* first conceptualization of, *paschein* 1; and the opposed powers, 2; in Aristotle and the Stoa, 3–4; passive principle of motion, *physis* 3; cf., further, affection

passive intellect, *nous pathetikos* in Aristotle, *nous* 11–12; in Alexander of Aphrodisias, *ibid.* 13

perceptible, *aistheton* see sensible

perception, *aisthesis* see sensation

perduration, *aidios* see everlasting

perfection, *telos, entelecheia* for the former, see end, purpose; for the latter, entelechy

philosophy, *philosophia, sophia* origins of the term, *philosophia* 1; division of, 2; and myth, *mythos* 1–2; as the study of nature, *physis* 1; Pythagorean notion as a purification, *katharsis* 1, *psyche* 14; historical approach in Plato, *endoxon* 6; and in Aristotle, *ibid.* 7–9; the "first philosophy," *theologia* 2

physics, *physica* its subject matter described, *ergon* 3; studies separate substance, *aphairesis* 1; as "second philosophy," *philosophia* 1; the "new Physics" of later antiquity, *dynamis* 9, 11

place, *topos, pou* Aristotelian theory of, *topos;* as an Aristotelian category, *pou;* theory of "natural place," *stoicheion* 17; the place of the Forms, *eidos* 10

planets see heavenly bodies

pleasure, *hedone* Sophistic and medical theories, *hedone* 1; Platonic view of, *ibid.* 2–3, *psyche* 17; Speusippus, *hedone* 4; Eudoxus, 5; Aristippus, 6; Aristotle, 7; Epicurean theories, 8–9, *oikeiosis* 1; as excessive contact in Plato, *pathos* 6; accompanies experience, *ibid.* 10–11; indicates "the appropriate," *ibid.* 11, *oikeiosis* 1; chosen on the basis of quantity, *poson;* moderation, *sophrosyne* 2

plurality, *plethos* number as a plurality of units, *arithmos* 2; identified with dyad by Speusippus, *dyas;* approached dialectically, *hen* 2; connoted by wholeness, *holon* 2; characteristic of the mathematicals, *mathematika* 2; as that which is divisible, *plethos;* of souls, *psyche* 31; in the operation of intellect, *noesis* 18–19, *nous* 20; the problem of the one and the many, *hen* 6; in later Platonism, *proödos* 1, *trias* 5

poetics, *poietike* an Aristotelian productive science, *poietike* point, *stigme* geometrical point distinguished from mathematical unit, *megethos* 3; substance with position, *monas*

position, *keisthai, thesis* in Atomism, *stoicheion* 1; role in Plato's theory of perception, *aisthesis* 18; in the Aristotelian distinction between unit and point, *monas;* the Aristotelian category, *keisthai;* in Plato's distinction of whole and total, *holon* 6; in the Epicurean organism, *ibid.* 9

possession, *echein, enthousiasmos* as an Aristotelian category, *echein;* for divine possession, see enthusiasm

potentiality, *dynamis* Aristotelian theory of, *dynamis* 4; compared to actuality, *energeia* 5; matter as, *hyle* 1

power, *dynamis* pre-Socratic use, *dynamis* 1; Platonic, 2; Aristotelian, 3; Stoic, 5; as intermediary beings, 6, *nous* 17; as intelligibles, *dynamis* 7; related to cosmic sympathy and occult powers, *ibid.* 8–11; role in Platonic theory of perception, *aisthesis* 15–16; sensible powers reduced to touch by Aristotle, *arche* 5; matched with an organ, *holon* 8; its connection with action and passion, *paschein, passim;* and the principles, *arche* 6; and the elements, *stoicheion* 5, 13–15

practical science, *praktike* in Plato, *techne* 3–4; in Aristotelian division of the sciences, *poiein*

practical wisdom, *phronesis* see wisdom

preconception, *prolepsis* in Epicureanism and Stoicism, *prolepsis;* self-evidence a characteristic of, *enargeia;* naturally acquired concepts, *ennoia, noesis* 16

predicable Aristotelian doctrine of, *idion*

predicaments the ten Aristotelian categories, *kategoriai;* relationship with predicables, *idion*

predication, *kategoria* connection with the theory of Forms in Plato, *eidos* 11; in Aristotle, *ibid.* 16; and the substratum, *hypokeimenon;* the universal of predication, *katholou*

preferable acts, *proegmena* in the Stoic moral system, *adiaphoron* 1

presence, *parousia* One of Plotinus known by the presence of unity, *hen* 13

prime matter, *prote hyle* Aristotelian concept of, *hyle* 5; in Stoa, *ibid.* 7

prime mover, *proton kinoun* see first mover

principle, *arche, hypothesis* nature of the pre-Socratic "stuff," *physis* 2; Milesian search for material cause, *arche* 2–3; post-Parmenidean violations of the single-principle theory, *ibid.* 4; relation to the problem of change, 5–6; first principles of demonstration, 7, *hypothesis;* first principles of morality contained in Stoic "preconceptions," *ennoia; archai* of bodies in Plato, *genesis* 12; *archai* of number, *monas;* first principles of judgment transmitted by *nous* in Plotinus, *noesis* 19

privation, *steresis* in Aristotelian analysis of change, *genesis* 13, *steresis;* and matter, *hyle* 6, 10; a principle in Stoic theory of intellection, *noesis* 16; in Plotinus, *kakon* 8

problem, *aporia* origins in sense of wonder and related to Socratic interrogation, *aporia* 1; Aristotelian technical usage, *ibid.* 2; application of by Aristotle, *endoxon* 1–2; history as, *ibid.* 9

process, *genesis* pleasure is a process, *hedone* 4; cosmic processes described in ethical terms, *kosmos* 1

procession, *proödos* theory and mechanics of, *proödos*

product, *ergon* not necessarily an object, *ergon* 1

productive science, *poietike* distinguished from practical science, *ergon* 1–2, *poiesis;* in Plato, *mimesis* 1, *techne* 4

proof, *apodeixis, pistis* first principles of syllogistic proof, *arche* 7; proofs that convince, *pistis*

property, *idion* definition of and distinction from accident, *idion;* Epicurean terminology, *symbebekos* 3

prophet, *prophetes* see medium, divination

proportion, *logos, analogia* extension of the concept into various areas, *harmonia* 2; in Heraclitus' theory, *enantion* 1, *logos* 1; as a unifying factor in mixtures, *holon* 3–5; how perceived, *noesis* 1; mathematical proportion in universe, *kosmos* 1; justice as, *dike* 6; in Aristotle, *logos* 3; and limit, *peras;* proportion as soul, *psyche* 9–11; geometric proportion in derivation of elements in Plato, *stoicheion* 17

providence, *pronoia* immanent and transcendent, *pronoia* 1; distinction of command and execution, 2; God's providence indirect, *sympatheia* 8; exercised by lesser gods, *daimon* 3, *pronoia* 2, *theos* 5; identified with fate by Stoics, *heimarmene*

prudence, *phronesis* its counsels sometimes conflict with justice, *dike* 7

purgation, *katharsis* the medical aspect of the concept of catharsis, *katharsis* 2–3; homoeopathic purgation in tragedy, 3

purification, *katharsis* the religious aspect of the concept of catharsis, *katharsis* 1

purpose, *telos* first appearance in universe, *telos* 1, *nous* 3–4; Socratic and Platonic interest in, *telos* 2; nature as a source of purpose in Aristotle, *ibid.* 3, *physis* 3; distinguishes intellect and nature from necessity, *tyche*

Qualitative change, *alloiosis* see alteration

quality, *poion, pathos* identification of opposites as qualities by Plato, *enan-tion* 2; active and passive qualities, *paschein* 4; in the pre-Socratics, *pathos* 2; qualities of atoms, *ibid.* 4; primary and secondary, distinction from substance, *poion;* distinguished from elements, *stoicheion* 13–15; Aristotelian category, *poion*

quantity, *poson* as an Aristotelian category, *poson;* discrete and continuous, *plethos;* measure of pleasure, *hedone* 9

quintessence see ether

rationes seminales, *logoi spermatikoi* Stoic theory of, *logoi spermatikoi;* yield to more vitalistic view, *dynamis* 9; in Plotinus, *logos* 5

reason, *logos, nous, logistikon, hegemonikon* defines, for Aristotle, the proper function of man, *ergon* 5; problem of appetites in rational man, *horme;* the Stoic *recta ratio, logos* 3; identified with fire, *logos* 1, 4; grounds natural law, *nomos* 2; as nature, *physis* 4; see also intellect

reasonable defense, *eulogon, pithanon* the justification of moral choice in Stoicism and Scepticism, *adiaphoron* 1, 2

reasoning, *logismos* see discursive reasoning

rebirth, *palingenesia* see reincarnation

receptacle, *hypodoche* Platonic description of, *hypodoche;* powers present in before the operation of intellect, *dynamis* 2; role in change, *genesis* 11–12; identified by Aristotle with material cause, *hyle* 6; its ontological status, *on* 2

recollection, *anamnesis* Platonic theory and connection with Forms, *anamnesis;* origins of the belief, *psyche* 13–14; means of knowing the Forms, *eidos* 8; connected with love, *eros* 7

reflection, *eikon* see image

refutation, *elenchos* see interrogation

reincarnation, *palingenesia* in Pythagoras and Plato, *palingenesia, psyche* 13–14; in Empedocles, *psyche* 12; in Plotinus, *ibid.* 31; in Proclus, *ibid.* 36

relation, *pros ti* in Plato and Aristotle, *pros ti*

return, *epistrophe* Neoplatonic theory of, *epistrophe;* affects the entire scale of being, *dynamis* 8–9; intellection as a return to self, *nous* 20; in Proclus, *proödos* 2–4

Scala naturae Aristotelian formulation of, *sympatheia* 3, *zoön* 2

science, *episteme* the various sciences in Aristotle, *episteme* 4; cf., further, division of the sciences

scrutiny, *elenchos* see interrogation

seed, *sperma* in the primordial mixture of Anaxagoras, *genesis* 6, *pathos* 2–3; predominance of seeds in, *holon* 4; homogeneous composition, *stoicheion* 11–12

self-acceptance, *oikeiosis* Stoic theory of, *oikeiosis*

self-control, *sophrosyne* see moderation

self-evident, *enargeia* guarantee of validity of sensation in Epicureanism, *enargeia;* sensation true but not necessarily self-evident, *doxa* 7; name as self-evident testimony to concept, *onoma* 5

self-motion, *autokinesis* in Plato a function of soul, *kinesis* 6, *psyche* 19; soul as self-moved number, *ibid.* 21

self-presence eternity as total self-presence in Plotinus, *chronos* 9

self-preservation, *oikeiosis* see self-acceptance

self-sufficiency, *autarkeia* a characteristic of happiness and a hallmark of virtue in Aristotle, Stoa, and later Platonism, *autarkeia*

seminal reasons, *logoi spermatikoi* see *rationes seminales*

sensation, *aisthesis* the "like-knows-like" school, *aisthesis* 6–12; like-knows-unlike, 13–14; Platonic theory, 15–18, *psyche* 19; Aristotelian, *aisthesis* 19–21; Epicurean, 22–23; Stoic, 24–25; Plotinus, 26–27; relative nature of, *doxa* 2; denigration of, *episteme* 1, *noesis* 1–7; necessary antecedent to true knowledge in Aristotle, *episteme* 3; distinguished from intellection, *noesis, passim;* role of body in, *noesis* 8, *psyche* 17; as motion, *psyche* 27, *aisthesis* 23, *holon* 10; as an affection, *psyche* 17; earth endowed with, *sympatheia* 3

sensible, *aistheton* contrasted position in Platonic and Aristotelian epistemology, *aistheton, gnorimon* 4; object of opinion and not true knowledge, *doxa* 1–2; sensible substances, *ousia* 3

sensus communis, *aisthesis koine* the cognitive faculty and its objects, *aisthesis koine;* and the perception of number, *arithmos* 4 separation, *apokrisis* employed by Anaximander to explain change, *genesis* 2; and by Anaxagoras, *ibid.* 6–7

separate substance, *choriston* object of the science of physics, *aphairesis* 1; separability a characteristic of substance, *choriston;* Socratic definitions are not, *eidos* 6

serious man, *spoudaios* as the norm of ethical behavior, *ergon* 4

shape, *schema* factor in Plato's theory of sensation, *aisthesis* 18, *dynamis* 2; and in his theory of change, *stoicheion* 10; in Democritus, *dynamis* 1; in Epicurus, *aisthesis* 22

sheath, *stegazon* ensheathed soul in Epicureanism, *aisthesis* 23, *genesis* 8, *psyche* 27

similar, *homoios* similarity of cause and effect, *proödos* 3; cosmic sympathy based on both contact and similarity, *sympatheia* 6; see also like

situs, *keisthai* see position

solution, *lysis* correlative in the aporematic method, *aporia* 2

soul, *psyche* connection with life and movement in prephilosophical thought, *psyche* 2–3; and breath, 4–5; revision of Homeric psychology, 6; in Atomism, 7–8; Empedocles, 9; Pythagorean harmony, 10–11; shamanistic soul, 12–13; unitáry soul in Plato, 14; tripartite soul, 15–19; Aristotelian critique of Platonists, 20–22; Aristotelian view, 23; parts and faculties, 24–25; immortality of, 26; Epicurean, 27; Stoic, 28; medial position in later Platonism, 29; Neoplatonic hypostasis, 30; partition in Plotinus, 31–32; individual souls in Plotinus, 33–34; Proclus' theory, 35–36; doxographical approach to, *endoxon* 8; connection with the body in Stoicism, *genesis* 18; states of the soul in Aristotle, *hexis;* as a cause of evil in Plato, *kakon* 3; and Proclus, *ibid.* 9; fall of, *kathodos, passim;* purification and purgation of, *katharsis, passim;* functions of in Aristotle, *kinesis* 8; human soul and World Soul in Plato, *kinoun* 5; as a source of motion in Plato, *ibid.* 4–5; in Aristotle, *ibid.* 8; intermediary position, *metaxu* 2, *nous* 6; cognitive principle in Plato, *noesis* 8; soul and mind in Atomistic tradition, *kardia* 2, *noesis* 13–14; temporary intellectualization in Stoa under Chrysippus, *noesis* 17; demonic soul, *ibid.;* soul and intellect in Plato, *nous* 6; under influence of star souls, *ochema* 4; question of its immortality, *pathos* 10; nature as the underside of soul in Plotinus, *physis* 5; how transmitted, *pneuma* 3; Stoic soul, *ibid.* 4; criticized by Plotinus, *ibid.* 5; soul and providence, *pronoia* 2; as a tension of the *pneuma, sympatheia* 3; and the moon, *ibid.* 5

space, *chora* as continuous quantity, *poson;* for Platonic "space," see receptacle, area

species, *eidos* claim to be substance, *ousia* 2; species and essence, *ibid.* 3

species intelligibilis as exemplary form in later Platonism, *noeton* 2 specific difference, *diaphora* employed in Platonic division, *diaphora* 1; Speusippus attempts to include all differences, 2; in Aristotle's division, 3; all differences resumed in *infima species*, 4

speech, *logos* as externalization of thought in Stoa, *logos* 4; and Philo, 5; a function of reason, *onoma* 6

spirit, *pneuma*, *thymos* "spirited" faculty in Homer and beyond, *psyche* 2–3, 6; spirited soul in Plato, *ibid.* 15, 17; in Aristotle analogous in composition to the ether, *ochema* 3; immaterial spirit in later Stoicism, *pneuma* 6

spontaneity, *automaton* as a type of cause, *tyche*

stars, *ouranioi* see heavenly bodies

star souls in Plato, *kinoun* 6, *ouranioi* 2; in Aristotle, *kinoun* 8, *ouranioi* 3; effects on human souls, *ochema* 4

state, *hexis*, *pos echein* states of soul in Aristotle, *hexis*, *pathos* 9; in Peripatetic theory of intellection, *nous* 11–13; as a tension of the *pneuma* in inorganic matter, *sympatheia* 3; "to be in a certain state" as a Stoic category, *echein*

strife a mover in Empedocles, *kinoun* 2

substance, *ousia*, *hypostasis*, *tode ti* Aristotelian quest for, *ousia* 2; types in Aristotle, 3; Stoic and Plotinian reaction to Aristotle, 4; distinguished from quality by Plato, *poion*; in the primary sense, *tode ti*; change in substance as opposed to accidental change, *genesis* 2, 15; one is not a substance, *hen* 2; matter not substance for Aristotle, *hyle* 3; nor for Plotinus, *kakon* 8; as unit or point, *monas*; what "is" essentially is substance, *on* 3

substratum, *hypokeimenon* role in Aristotelian analysis of change, *hypokeimenon*; matter as, *hyle* 2, *stoicheion* 15; claim to be substance, *ousia* 3; in Stoa, *ibid.* 4; soul as, *psyche* 23; logical substratum and logical attribute, *symbebekos* 2

summa genera the Aristotelian categories as the *summa genera* of being, *kategoriai*, *genos*

summum bonum in Plato, *agathon* 1; in Aristotle, 2; in Plotinus, 3; of the universe, *telos* 3

sun, *helios* role in Aristotelian theory of change, *genesis* 15; as *hegemonikon* of the universe, *pneuma* 4; in Poseidonius, *sympatheia* 5; in Plotinus, *ibid.* 6

supernatural spirit, *daimon* see demon

suspension of judgment, *epoche* its place in Scepticism, *endoxon* 10 swerve, *parenklisis* in the Epicurean version of the formation of bodies, *kinesis* 5

symmetry, *symmetria* role in Empedoclean theory of perception, *aisthesis* 7, *noesis* 3; in Stoic theory of beauty, *eros* 10

sympathy, *sympatheia* see cosmic sympathy

system, *systema* Epicurean theory of organism, *holon* 9

tabula rasa Stoic image, *hegemonikon*

teleology in Anaxagoras and Diogenes, *nous* 4; in Plato, *ibid.* 7, *telos* 2; in Aristotle and his successors, *telos* 3–4; of parts in an organic whole, *holon* 6, 8

tension, *tonos* in Heraclitus, *logos* 1; Stoic doctrine of, *tonos*

theology, *theologia* technical and nontechnical usage, *theologia* 1–2; in Aristotle, *philosophia* 1; Stoic division of, *theologia* 3

theoretical science, *theoria, theoretike* Aristotelian usage, *episteme* 5; his distinction of theoretical and practical wisdom, *phronesis* 2, *sophia*

theurgy, *theourgia* theoretical basis of, *dynamis* 11; practice in later Platonism, *mantike* 5

thinking, *noesis, logismos, dianoia* see intellection, discursive reasoning

time, *chronos, pote* as a personified figure, *chronos* 1–2; reduced to number by Pythagoreans, 4; Platonic theory, 5–6; Aristotelian, 7; Epicurean and Stoic, 8; Plotinus, 9; *per accidens* extended, *megethos* 4; as a continuous quantity, *poson;* as an Aristotelian category, *pote;* as an accident of an accident, *symbebekos* 3; soul participates in time and eternity, *psyche* 36

token, *symbolon* occult powers in natural objects, *dynamis* 11

total, *pan* contrasted to whole by Plato, *holon* 6; by Aristotle, *ibid.* 7

touch, *haphe* sensible powers reduced to touch by Aristotle, *arche* 5; see also contact

transcendence, *hyperousia* in Parmenides and Plato, *hyperousia* 1; revival in the later tradition, *ibid.* 2, *theos, passim;* and the problem of cognition, *agnostos*

transmigration, *metempsychosis* see reincarnation

triad, *trias* theory of structure in later Platonism, *trias, passim;* applied to the question of souls, *psyche* 35 tripartite soul in Plato, *noesis* 9; *psyche* 15; restoration in the later Stoa, *noesis* 17; and the emotions in Plato, *pathos* 7

truth, *aletheia* arises in the judgment, *doxa* 4; in senses in Epicurus, *ibid.* 7; see also criterion

Unaffected, *apatheia* see apathy

uncreated, *agenetos* see ungenerated

understanding, *dianoia* type of cognition on the Platonic line, *dianoia;* difficulties in interpretation, *noesis* 9–10; generic term for discursive reasoning in Aristotle, *dianoia*

ungenerated, *agenetos* speculations on the origins of the universe, *agenetos*

unit, *monas* its characteristics in Pythagoreanism, *monas;* distinction of unit, point, and body, *megethos* 3; question of divisibility, *ibid.* 1, 3; possible source of dyad, *dyas, monas;* as a principle of ontological procession, *proödos* 2; number as a plurality of units, *arithmos* 2; identified with Good, *dyas;* the Platonic Form as monad, *hen* 6; the One of Plotinus is not a monad, *ibid.* 12

unity form as a cause of in Aristotle, *holon* 7; Stoic principles of, *hexis;* in terms of tension, *tonos;* see also whole

universal, *katholou* Aristotelian theory of, *katholou;* Epicurean theory, *prolepsis;* concrete universal grasped by sensation, *gnorimon* 2; as the term of induction, *epagoge* 1, 4

universe, *kosmos, holon* as order, *kosmos* 1; divinity of, 2–4; government of in Heraclitus and Anaxagoras, *nous* 3; Plato's views on, *kinoun* 5; pervaded by spirit, *pneuma* 4; Stoics' notion of cosmic organism leads to introduction of "universe," *holon* 10, *sympatheia* 2

unknowable, *agnostos* transcendence of God and modes of cognitive approach, *agnostos*

unlimited, *apeiron* various meanings of Anaximander's principle, *apeiron* 1; subsequent history in Pythagoreanism and as a function of the dyad, 2; as a material principle, 3; place in the concept of time, *chronos* 4–5; ranked with evil and identified with the dyad, *kakon* 4, 6, *dyas;* opposites separated from, *dynamis* 1; and the One, *hen* 2, 6, 10; connection with Aristotelian mean, *meson*

unmoved, *akinetos* First Mover, *kinoun* 7; the "activity of immobility," *ibid.* 10; the God of Xenophanes, *nous* 2

unwritten doctrines, *agrapha dogmata* the oral tradition in Plato and its relation to Aristotle's critique, *agrapha dogmata* unwritten law, *agraphos nomos* the divine sanction of, *nomos* 2

urstoff, *arche* see principle

Vacuum, *kenon* see void

vehicle, *ochema* see astral body

via eminentiae as a cognitive approach to God, *agnostos* 2

via negativa as a cognitive approach to God, *agnostos* 2

vibration, *palmos* the inherent motion of atoms, *kinesis* 4

virtue, *arete* Socratic identification with knowledge, *arete* 2, *phronesis;* as a mean for Aristotle, *arete* 3, *meson, pathos* 9; preparation for in Plotinus, *dialektike* 6; connected with definition by Socrates, *dike* 4; and with function by Aristotle, *ergon* 4; a habit for Aristotle but a disposition for the Stoics, *hexis;* virtue and purification in Plotinus, *katharsis* 4

vis vitalis, *dynamis zotike* see vital force

visual image, *emphasis* in Democritus' theories of vision, *aisthesis* 10; and in Plato, *ibid.* 17

vital force, *dynamis zotike* incorporation into world view of later antiquity, *sympatheia* 3, *dynamis* 9

void, *kenon* Pythagorean, Atomist, and Aristotelian position on, *kenon;* denied by Parmenides and Zeno, *kinesis* 2; denied by Aristotle in his retort to Zeno, *megethos* 4

vortex, *dine* role in atomic change, *kinesis* 4; in Anaxagoras, *genesis* 7, *pathos* 3

Weight, *baros* primary characteristic of atoms in Epicurus, *kinesis* 5

when, *pote* see time

where, *pou* see place

whole, *holon* denied of the One, *holon* 2; Empedoclean sphere, 3; true whole is homogeneous, 5; contrasted to total by Plato, 6; Aristotelian theory of, 7–8; in Proclus, 10

wisdom, *phronesis, sophia* doxographical approach to, *endoxon* 4, 7; in highest type of knowledge, *episteme* 3; as "first philosophy," *philosophia* 1; its ethical side, *phronesis* 1; predominance of intellectual coloring in Plato, *ibid.* 2; true and false in Plato, *sophia;* Stoic ideal, *ibid* wish, *boulesis* part of appetite, *orexis;* directed toward an end, *proairesis*

wonder, *thauma* initial motivation to philosophize, *aporia* 1

world soul, *psyche tou pantos* Platonic theory of, *psyche tou pantos* 1; in later Platonism, *ibid.* 2; as a mover in Plato, *kinoun* 5; analogue in Aristotle, *ibid.* 10; and cosmic intellect, *nous* 6; exercises general providence, *pronoia* 2; as transcendent source of evil, *kakon* 3

world, *kosmos* see universe

Yonder, *ekei* the intelligible world, *ekei*

Lightning Source UK Ltd.
Milton Keynes UK
UKHW040408100119
335321UK00002B/225/P